Ed McKean

Ed McKean
Slugging Shortstop of the Cleveland Spiders

RICH BLEVINS

McFarland & Company, Inc., Publishers
Jefferson, North Carolina

LIBRARY OF CONGRESS CATALOGUING-IN-PUBLICATION DATA

Blevins, Richard.
   Ed Mckean : slugging shortstop of the Cleveland Spiders / Rich Blevins.
      p.   cm.
   Includes bibliographical references and index.

    ISBN 978-0-7864-7334-2 (softcover : acid free paper) ∞
    ISBN 978-1-4766-1553-0 (ebook)

   1. Mckean, Ed, 1864–1919. 2. Baseball players—United States—Biography. 3. Shortstop (Baseball) 4. Cleveland Spiders (Baseball team)—History. I. Title.
GV865.M312345B54 2014
796.323092—dc23
[B]   2014020394

BRITISH LIBRARY CATALOGUING DATA ARE AVAILABLE

© 2014 Rich Blevins. All rights reserved

No part of this book may be reproduced or transmitted in any form or by any means, electronic or mechanical, including photocopying or recording, or by any information storage and retrieval system, without permission in writing from the publisher.

On the cover: Ed McKean, detail from the 1895 Cleveland champs' team photograph (National Baseball Hall of Fame, and Library, Cooperstown, New York)

Printed in the United States of America

McFarland & Company, Inc., Publishers
  Box 611, Jefferson, North Carolina 28640
  www.mcfarlandpub.com

Dedicated to
Tom, Alice, & Mary
("The McKean Gang"),
Doris Wildenheim,
& my Doris.

The hands are the instruments of man's intelligence.
—*Maria Montessori*

The Fame that follows death is nothing to us;
And what is Fame in life but half-disfame,
And counterchanged with darkness?
—*Alfred Tennyson*

Sometimes, in a tight game with runners on,
digging in at short, ready to break with the ball,
a peace I'd never felt before would paralyze the diamond.
For a moment of eternal stillness I felt as if I were cocked at the very heart of the Midwest.
—*Stuart Dybek*

Table of Contents

Acknowledgments	ix
Preface: Before Boudreau, or Why McKean Matters	1
Prelude: October 11, 1895, 187 Superior Avenue, Cleveland	7
ONE. The Fields of Ohio (1884)	19
TWO. The Best Shortstop in the International League (1885–1886)	38
1895 Temple Cup: October 1, Cleveland	56
THREE. The Invention of the Slugging Shortstop (1887–1888)	71
FOUR. Ed McKean and the Players' Revolt (1889–1890)	88
1895 Temple Cup: October 2, Game One	111
FIVE. The Spiders Make a "World's Series" (1891–1892)	119
SIX. Patsy's Hibernian Spiders (1893–1894)	144
1895 Temple Cup: October 3 and 5, Games Two and Three	166
SEVEN. Temple Cup Champs (1895–1896 seasons)	172
EIGHT. Home on the Road (1897–1899)	200
1895 Temple Cup: October 7, Game Four	232
NINE. The Hero of Rochester Revisited (seasons of 1902, 1905–1906)	238
TEN. A Pennant for Springfield (1907–1908 seasons)	265
1895 Temple Cup: October 8, Final Game	293

Appendix A: Ed McKean's Major League Career Batting Record	299
Appendix B: Ed McKean's Year-by-Year Offensive Rankings	300
Appendix C: Lines from a Poem Attributed by Elmer Bates to Ed McKean	305
Chapter Notes	307
Bibliography	325
Index	331

Acknowledgments

This book required a team effort. My debt to SABR is the most evident and extensive. I especially thank Peter Mancuso, chair of SABR's Nineteenth-Century Committee, Deb Jayne at the SABR home office, Jonathan Frankel, and Richard McBane. David Nemec's work is my adamantine resource and inspiration. The beginnings of this book, I realize, date from the day I found Nemec's *The Great Encyclopedia of 19th-Century Major League Baseball* in a Water Street bookstore in Kent, Ohio; as I wrote, his emails were unfailingly generous and useful.

I deeply appreciate the selfless contributions made by the librarians, archivists, and booksellers I met and corresponded with into extra innings: Robert Ault and Christine Adams, Youngstown State University Library; Mary McManman, Bay City Public Library; Chris Applin, Saginaw Public Library; Pat Duck, University of Pittsburgh at Greensburg; Dean Keller, Cara Gilgenbach, and Paul Bauer, in Kent, OH; Pamela Speis, Mahoning Valley Historical Society; Ron Bloomfield, Bay County Historical Society; Mark Moore, Cleveland Public Library; Joe Territo, Rochester Baseball Historical Society; Katie Papas, University of Rochester Library; Martin Hauserman, chief archivist for the City of Cleveland; Nick Sciarratta, Rochester Red Wings Baseball Club; Dennis Frank, archivist at St. Bonaventure University; Denise Michaud, Madison Historical Society, OH; Vicki Catozza, Western Reserve Historical Society; Rebecca Knab, at Loganberry Books, Shaker Heights, OH; Mark Stueve, proprietor of Old Erie Street Books, Cleveland; Andy Young, editor for the Lorain *Chronicle-Telegraph*; Patrice Hamitar, Cleveland Public Library; Freddy Berowski, Susan Kay, and John Horne, National Baseball Hall of Fame; and John Ransom and Gil Gonzalez at the Rutherford B. Hayes Presidential Center.

I feel the most fortunate of rookie biographers to have had the best guides to Ed McKean's hometown of Grafton, Ohio: the McKean family and Doris

Wildenheim. I grew up in the next county, but it took Ed's book for me to make their valued acquaintances. My friend Tom Kryss was my guide on pilgrimages to League Park, Cleveland's West Side, and Calvary Cemetery. Tom was subjected daily to the streaks and slumps of writing this book, and he carefully read the manuscript; throughout the extended season, he always answered the bullpen phone. On my various research trips to Ohio, Margaret Koehler and John Wright, Mark Blevins, and Mike Ferrell put me up for the night and put up with this project.

The errors that have persisted into the printing of this book, in spite of the scrutiny of many Gold Glovers, are entirely my own.

Every effort has been made to identify the sources of copyrighted photographs in this book. Unidentifiable images published prior to January 1, 1923, are in the public domain. I wish to recognize, in alphabetical order, Doug Allen/Legendary Auctions, Al Crisafulli/Love of the Game Auctions, Brian Drent/Mile High Card Company, Fiona Elias/Heritage Auction, Lyman Hardeman/*Old Cardboard* magazine, John Husman, Troy Kinunen/Mears Auctions, Tom Kryss, Rob Lifson/Robert Edward Auctions, sage Lew Lipset/Old Judge Auction, Richard Masson, Suzanne Morrissey, editor/*Holy Cross Magazine*, Doris Wildenheim, and Josh Wulkan/Huggins and Scott Auctions, for all their generous help in collecting the rare images from Ed McKean's world.

Preface

Before Boudreau, or Why McKean Matters

I undertook a line of questioning that became this book in order to confirm, or discredit, a basic fact in the playing record. Initially, I took it for a mistake, an egregious printer's error that had gone uncorrected for 125 years, or maybe the photographer's visual gag with his conspiring player. There he posed, in the tiny, faded image of my Old Judge card. Ed McKean was a left-handed batter? But every baseball reference and encyclopedia I'd consulted along the way listed McKean, without exception, among the great right-handed slugging shortstops of the nineteenth-century.[1]

Edward John McKean's legacy has been effectively effaced from baseball history. For a thought experiment, try to imagine that every book and online site for Lou Boudreau, the Hall of Fame shortstop we remember from Cleveland's celebrated championship team of 1948, *assures us mistakenly that he batted from the left side of the plate.* The original shortstop for a Cleveland championship team, Ed McKean died an early death in 1919, at the age of 50, having lived long enough to suffer the premature deaths of his career and fame. For a century now, his reputation has been blighted by McKean's tragic inability to become Honus Wagner. His career and the controversial success story of the Spiders' 1895 Temple Cup have ceased to be recounted by most fans in McKean's beloved city of Cleveland, and by all but the most devout experts of vintage baseball. After all, we can still talk to fans who saw Boudreau play, but no one alive witnessed the great McKean steal a base or drive a ball off the right-field fence in old League Park. This belated biography would have been a much different, and richer, book if it could have been written earlier. After his playing career, McKean, a practiced storyteller after the Irish tradition, could have been found tending bar at the Short Stop Inn in Cleveland. There could have been interviews with his three sons

Ed McKean was a left-handed batter, as seen in this Old Judge N172 tobacco card, from 1887 (Mile High Card Company).

(Robert D. McKean was senior cashier for the city of Cleveland) and grandchil-dren (among them, an assistant Cleveland safety director and a Cleveland Heights police officer), who outlived him by half a century and more.[2] One of McKean's Lorain County, Ohio, neighbors and minor league teammates, Pit Gilman, was 86 years old when he passed away, in Elyria, in 1950. Bobby Wallace, the last of McKean's teammates in the major leagues, was still playing in 1918. A total of 132 men wore the uniform of the Cleveland Spiders; the last living Spider, Lewis (Sport) McAllister, died on July 17, 1962.[3]

E.J. McKean was the iconic shortstop in Cleveland for a dozen seasons, shortly following Jack Glasscock's reign and the return of major league baseball to the city. He was so reliable and started for so many consecutive seasons that Cleveland sportswriters took to calling his position "McKean's garden." George Davis and Bobby Wallace embarked on what eventually became Hall of Fame careers as shortstops only after leaving McKean's Spiders. The immortal Ed Delahanty jumped to the Players' League in part to realize his own boyhood dream of playing shortstop in hometown Cleveland.

And yet, the man who exiled them all has never been able to crack the Cooperstown lineup. Until now, there has been no full-length biography. This book attemps to fill the gap, providing as full an account as possible of McKean's life and career. It follows a largely chronogical plan, but to highlight McKean's greatest triumph in baseball, the games of the 1895 Temple Cup are recounted in short chapters interspersed through the main narrative.

In recent years, McKean's reputation as a star player has been kept alive by a select few research specialists and admirers who do tend to be enthusiastic. Some of our best nineteenth-century baseball historians arrived independently at the same exalted opinion of Ed McKean. The late godfather of Cleveland Spiders research John Phillips asserted that McKean is no less than "the Lou Boudreau of last century."[4] "The debate in Cleveland now is whether Omar Vizquel has replaced Lou Boudreau as the greatest [shortstop] in Cleveland [major league] history, and those who favor Boudreau," counsels David Nemec, the distinguished baseball encyclopedist, "need to take a closer look at McKean. The two were eerily similar." Nemec's research indicates that "prior to the pitching-distance change of 1893 and the attendant increase in hitting, McKean was the most productive [shortstop] offensively in the game's history to that point, ahead of Frank Fennelly, Herman Long, and even Jack Glasscock, his three closest pursuers, in runs created per game with 7.23."[5] (Keep in mind that McKean put together his greatest seasons at the plate starting with 1894, *the following year*.) "He has the stats to rank as the finest all-around performer among shortstops who spent at least two seasons in the [American Association]," Nemec observes in another book.[6] Bill James lists Ed McKean among those all-time shortstops "who are not in but who meet the most Hall of Fame standards."[7] Statistician Frederick Taylor groups Ed McKean with Hugh Jennings, George Davis, and Sam Wise as the great hitting shortstops of their era, and he rates McKean seventh among the best-hitting shortstops of all time.[8] McKean is one of only nine shortstops to hit .300 lifetime between 1871 and 1941.[9] McKean didn't play in obscurity: he was a high-profile contributor to the three Spiders teams that made the playoffs, and he was on the field in no fewer than four of the "100 greatest games of the nineteenth century," according to SABR's Nineteenth Century Committee.[10] In addition to the sporadic attention from hardcore baseball devotees, a highly fictionalized but still recognizable McKean does make cameo appearances recently in a historical novel by Luke Salisbury and a book for young readers by Bill Bildner and Loren Long.[11] Still, chances are that until now you'd never heard of Ed McKean.

So, why does Ed McKean matter?

McKean was the exemplar for the major league slugging shortstop before either Wagner or Boudreau. From his rookie season in 1887, when McKean played every game of the American Association Blues' schedule, through his final tour of the National League as a full-time player with the 1898 Spiders, McKean rarely missed a game. In 1892, he accidentally shot off part of a finger and still missed only 20 games of the regular season. That was the year the shortstop came back to lead his team in runs batted in, and then hit .440 in what was the first postseason playoff for a Cleveland team. No player in history had 600 official at-bats in a National League season before Bull McKean, according to Lee Sinin's *Complete Baseball Encyclopedia*. The warrior's lifetime offensive accomplishments rank him among the elite players before the turn of the century: McKean, John Montgomery Ward, and Jack Glasscock are the only shortstops before 1900 to record 2,000 hits—but only McKean was a .300 hitter over his career.

Also, by Sinin's calculations, no shortstop in the major leagues from 1887 through 1898 had more plate appearances, at-bats, runs, hits, singles, doubles, triples, runs batted in, walks, and total bases, played in more games, or reached base more times than Ed McKean in his 12 full seasons; he ranks behind only Herman Long in home runs and George Davis in slugging percentage. He accumulated at least 10 triples in 10 seasons, including a high of 24 in 1893. His 283 total bases in 1895 established a record for shortstops. In his best seasons, from 1892 through 1896, McKean averaged 130 games played, 16 triples and 117 runs batted in, and his Spiders teams made the playoffs three times. The shortstop who is sometimes dismissed today for an infamous 105-error season was applauded by sportswriters who watched him play for his always daring—on occasion, brilliant—fielding, for years accomplished without the aid of a glove.

Beyond the stats, Ed McKean was a genuinely Whitmanesque figure, a blue-collar tough who embraced his own contradictions while living large. He worked variously as farmer, Greco-Roman wrestler, ghostwriter of sports columns, barkeeper, referee for professional boxing, semi-pro football player, and Cleveland alderman. Even though McKean was actually smaller (by three inches and, when he was young, by 15 pounds) than his deer-like teammate Jimmy McAleer, Big Ed used his impressive presence and strength to make himself one of the era's great "heavy hitters" and to intimidate the opposition, which included all umpires. The man feared as the enforcer on the riotous Spiders teams of Patsy Tebeau, Jack O'Connor, and Jesse Burkett[12] probably prepared for a life in the clergy before he set his mind on baseball.[13] Some have claimed that McKean was the author of at least one book of poems originally attributed to him by Cleveland sportswriter Elmer Bates.[14]

Rethinking McKean has taught me the story of a popular hero who, in his soaring trajectory toward arête, could be brought to earth at any moment by a workingman's stubborn hubris. The story of Ed McKean's life reenacts the Irishmen's struggle to win a significant place in *fin de siècle* America. Its hero is the son of an Irish immigrant family, who leaves the farm in Ohio to reimagine himself as one of Cleveland's original sports heroes. It is the story of the so-called rowdy game, played with championship success by the Hibernian baseball teams led by John McGraw, in Baltimore, and Patsy Tebeau, McKean's manager in Cleveland. It is finally the tragic lesson of a charismatic player, fueled by his heritage to fight to win on the field, but equally driven to make friends for success and fulfillment outside of baseball. McKean's is the cautionary tale of a championship athlete who too soon found an early death, from the effects of long-term alcoholism, in his retirement from the game. His story is also the complex story of organized baseball organizing itself. In its drive to cleanse the game of its frequent violent attacks on umpires by teams, its tactics of rowdyism, and threat of outright fan riots, the National League owners were, in effect, reclaiming what they were calling "the national game" from a decade of dominance by Irish players, managers, and umpires. Unfortunately, the process of cleaning up the sport has also marginalized the story of the once-famous Ed McKean, the Spiders, and Cleveland's first baseball championship. Patsy Tebeau and company sent their funeral barge flaming into the lake; because the Spiders didn't build an ark, only Jesse Burkett and Cy Young are progenitors. I invite you to read this book as an open letter on McKean's behalf to the Veterans Committee of the National Baseball Hall of Fame.

Prelude

October 11, 1895,
187 Superior Avenue, Cleveland

> "It seems a shame," the Walrus said,
> "To play them such a trick.
> After we've brought them out so far,
> And made them trot so quick!"...
> "O Oysters," said the Carpenter,
> "You've had a pleasant run!
> Shall we be trotting home again?"
> But answer came there none—
> And this was scarcely odd, because
> They'd eaten every one.
> —From stanzas recited by Tweedledum and
> Tweedledee in *Through the Looking-Glass*

Over three hundred were assembled for the banquet at Elks Lodge number 18 that Friday evening in Cleveland.[1] Seated prominently among the officials and privileged guests, baseball cranks in the room outnumbered by the socialites and politicians who attended in order to see and be seen, the keystone partners for the newly crowned Temple Cup champions might have conjured up images of the Tweedle twins from the widely popular novel by Lewis Carroll.[2] Just maybe some wag like Elmer E. Bates, who loved to josh his pal Ed McKean in his sports columns, did the conjuring himself for the amusement of the crowd.

Plump and cherub-faced, McKean's second baseman was nicknamed Kid and Cupid for the obvious reasons. Taunting sportswriters in Cleveland's 11 rival cities called him Fatty Childs, while conceding his remarkable skills on the ball field. Before the start of the season, when New York passed

Cleveland Elks Lodge 18, scene for the celebration of the Spiders' Temple Cup triumph over the "Oysterville" Baltimore Orioles, which was adjacent to Trinker's Oyster and Chop House (Cleveland Public Library).

on signing him to the Giants, a writer dubbed Clarence Childs "his fatlets" in the *Sporting Life*.[3] "What a funny little fat man," a young lady remarked upon seeing Childs at-bat. Then, when he delivered a double, she added: "He's a perfect angel, anyhow." It had been Childs' first plate appearance before the home crowd in League Park.[4] On this night five years hence, only the most hyperbolic of compliments were tossed out to him, like a whole month's worth of fat pitches to prey on.

Privately, Childs may have felt the press had let him off easy. His was the era when O. P. Caylor, a leading voice in organized baseball, felt free to brutalize the Phillies' diminutive second baseman, Cub Stricker. For the pages of the canonical *Sporting News*, he wrote: "Talking of high things, reminds me that I read of 'Cub' Stricker's heroic action in trying to save a lady whose clothes were in flames. The sad sequel is told that the woman died in spite of 'Cub''s efforts. I suppose Stricker saved her as high up as he could reach."[5] Readers of sports pages seemed never to tire of the fun poked at Pete Browning's handicap. In towns throughout the country, Fat Men versus Skinny Men baseball games remained popular amusements. National League opponents found nothing funny or bizarre about the bare-handed dexterity with which Childs and McKean dispatched them by turning the double play, applying the hard tag at second base, or holding onto a runner's belt when the game's lone umpire wasn't looking. In Cleveland, the cranks (or fans) soon learned to celebrate Cupid Childs for his remarkable patience at-bat, his gift for getting on base, and, in disregard of his girth, his penchant for scampering around the bases when brawny Ed McKean drove him home. Childs' career on-base percentage positions him precisely between Stan Musial's .417 and Wade Boggs's .415, and he averaged better than 117 runs scored a year for the Spiders.

Cleveland was a perennial contender when Baltimore native Cupid Childs played second base beside shortstop McKean (author's collection).

Childs was vain, a dandy of a dresser, most at home when out on the town. He liked to think of himself as an untapped talent for the minstrel shows.[6] In the room's gaslight, Cupid Childs' close-cropped hair only added to the cherubic aspect of his face and bow-shaped lips — in photographs he maintains a perpetually impish expression without regards to circumstances. Childs was a ladies' man, his ego apparently untouched by nicknames, and his keen batter's eye was no doubt turned tonight on the bevy of slim, wasp-wasted Cuyahoga beauties crowned by fashionable pompadours in the Gibson-girl style, must have been secretly flattered by his briefest attentions. Tomorrow morning would begin the long offseason in Baltimore, where many of his 10 siblings congregated, and his work as a maker of tin cans. After his baseball career, he lived permanently in Baltimore and drove a truck for a local coal company.[7]

For years, Tweedle Kid and Tweedle Ed had worked the middle infield in unison behind the artful twirling of Cy Young and Nig Cuppy. Cleveland had become a contender when Childs joined Ed McKean, who was already in his fifth season as the Spiders shortstop and RBI specialist. Cupid's 33 doubles, with Syracuse in 1890, had led the American Association the season before he came to the Spiders. With the two middle infielders in place and hitting at the top of the lineup, the Spiders won 679, lost only 439, and played for three postseason championships. McKean, Childs, and left fielder Jesse Burkett were all left-handed hitters, and each stood 5-foot-9. The trio would finish as the Spiders' all-time leaders in most meaningful hitting statistics. Tuesday afternoon's championship clincher in Baltimore must have been savored by Cupid Childs, after a bitter contract dispute with his hometown Orioles four years before. But during this season, Ed McKean had begun to show tell-tale signs of slowing. It was becoming hard to remember the rookie shortstop who was credited with 76 stolen bases.[8] Only four years before, *Sporting Life* had observed that McKean "is getting a reputation for beating out hits to the short stop and third baseman and is pushing up his batting average thereby."[9]

McKean's Just So tobacco card, 1893 (Old Cardboard).

Ed McKean would have been seated nearby his partner Childs. In fact, about the only thing that had kept the two teammates apart over the last five National League seasons was their politics; the Republican Childs was a staunch supporter of Ohio governor William McKinley in the 1896 presidential election, while McKean voted for William Jennings Bryan, and any other Democrat on the ballot. McKean never did get along with his first partner, Cub Stricker, who vowed never again to play beside him following the Brotherhood War of 1890.[10] The striking features of Ed McKean's visage were his high cheek bones and unexpectedly sensitive blue eyes, beneath a large brow tending toward a widow's peak. The sides of his mustache turned down, giving his face a natural melancholy look belied by two ruddy cheeks. His firm mouth could have been a row cut by his father's plow. But in company, like tonight, and private moments of affability, his mouth could be the very fount of blarney. The Rochester press, the season he was the toast of the International League, took to calling him Smiling Ed McKean. In uniform, he was Big Ed McKean, one of the early game's most threatening sluggers. McKean played baseball as a blood sport. He was "deep of chest and wide of shoulder" and, less fortunately, "the kind that ran to stoutness."[11] Even at dinner, the son of Irish immigrants seemed always to be fighting, fighting to keep below the 200-plus pounds his body wanted to be, and fighting the bottle. Ed Delahanty's biographer blames a night of drunken revelry, with McKean and Deacon McGuire, for the start of the fated Delahanty's reputation as a drinking man.[12]

But Ed McKean looked smaller tonight, in his suit and stiff collar and relegated to a table. McKean appeared less like one of the game's 200-pound intimidators, and more like his 5-foot-9 self. Ring Lardner recalled, in *Some Champions*, "the toughness of ... Jim McAleer and Ed McKean, with whom I became well acquainted in after years, was something that could be put on or taken off at will, like bridge work."[13] The only rough treatment of the evening was reserved for his teammate Chief Zimmer. Because the catcher was not a brother Elk (he was a member of the Knights of Pythias), he'd received a good-natured jostling upon entering the building.[14]

During the beckoning offseason, the baseball hero led the life of a mere mortal. Ed McKean looked forward to an extended stay at the family homestead in Grafton, Ohio, only a short train ride but a whole other world away from the city's cranks and reporters. By winter, there would be little work to do on his father's farm. After he'd had his fill of hunting, he could sneak back into Cleveland for workouts at the Cleveland Athletic Club. He could challenge his manager, Patsy Tebeau, at handball. He'd heard that his longstanding mate Jimmy McAleer planned to spend the winter touring with the theatrical company he'd bought.[15]

The Spiders' recent Temple Cup triumph, the banquet speakers would have reminded whoever was listening, had come at the close of a most historical season. The 1895 season was the silver anniversary season of the National League. And the country was in mourning for Harry Wright, one of professional baseball's founding fathers, since his death on October 3. Furthermore, thanks to the Cleveland Spiders, this was the first postseason since 1887 that a non-eastern club had won a major league championship.

For this historical night, there were heroes in the chambers of the Elks. But America's new breed of hero, the sports star, certainly didn't operate according to the strictures laid out earlier in the century in Thomas Carlyle's *On Heroes, Hero-Worship and the Heroic in History*. You could hardly classify

Ed McKean as divinity, prophet, poet, priest, king, or man of letters. The American sports hero was a relatively recent invention spawned by the public's adoration of boxing figures. Bare-knuckle boxer John L. Sullivan was the first to be elevated to the status of hero; matinee idol King Kelly was probably the first baseballist to sign autograph requests. By helping to create sports celebrities, organized baseball was testing its newfound power to validate an individual like Ed McKean and, in turn, a whole minority of Irish-Americans. Neither was Ed McKean among the new antiheroes like Kelly or Browning. (In a week, on the same day Elmer Bates' report of the banquet appeared in *Sporting Life*, the New York *Times* reviewed Stephen Crane's antiheroic novel *The Red Badge of Courage*.) Perhaps Ed McKean and the new American hero more resembled the western hero Owen Wister had begun to write stories about. Wister created The Virginian as a composite figure, as he freely adopted Old World formulas from *The Odyssey* and the Arthurian legends. Tonight's Elks Club audience was capable of seeing Cleveland's team of nouveau heroes, in light of Homer via Wister, only just returned in triumph to its polis from their Temple Cup odyssey after a siege of Baltimore. In Homer's *Odyssey*, popular reading in McKean's day, the banquet scene provided a formula by which the hero was defined and the audience taught lessons.

The Temple Cup, awarded to the winner of the National League postseason series, for the years 1894 to 1897 (National Baseball Hall of Fame and Library, Cooperstown, New York).

From time to time, there rose from the head table the latest speaker in the interminable order of orators introduced by toastmaster Davis Hawley. A prominent banker and longtime promoter of local baseball teams, Hawley had dreamed of bringing home a championship since 1887, when he became secretary for the Cleveland Blues of the American Association. It had been Hawley's decision to make rookie McKean the Cleveland shortstop, and then, in 1890, he signed Cy Young from Canton, two big steps toward realizing that championship. Hawley was one for details: the Spiders secretary had taken care to buy Dent Young a new suit when the raw rookie arrived in town wearing clothes he'd outgrown.[16] How long ago now it seemed that Patsy Tebeau had been the first to speak a few words, halting at first—apparently finding he'd left his famous histrionics on the field—but warming to his appreciative audience.

The celebration had been grandly launched by a reading of the letter of congratulations William Temple had sent, in his stead, for the occasion. The $800 loving cup in his name, reflecting the room's gaslights when player-manager Tebeau carried it to the podium, was an ironic symbol of the professional game's woes. Now nearly forgotten on its shelf in Cooperstown, the Temple Cup is every bit as old as ice hockey's internationally famous Stanley Cup. Of course, Lord Stanley's venerable hardware has been awarded all these many postseasons, while William Chase Temple withdrew his trophy after only four years of competition. His frustration was due to team disinterest in playing for the prize, poor attendance at championship games, and even acts of violence by cranks in host cities. The Temple Cup series was baseball's second crack at establishing a postseason tradition. Its predecessor, the Dauvray Cup, was commissioned by the actress Helen Dauvray (Monte Ward's wife) and fashioned by Tiffany. That cup had been permanently retired to Boston's trophy case, the club winning it the requisite three times, including the 1892 championship over the Spiders. That same year, in 1893, Temple sold his stock in the Pittsburgh ball club; he also sold his big idea for a best-of-seven series between the first- and second-place finishers in the League. The Temple Cup had initially seemed like the solution to a dilemma; as it turned out, it was a lesson in patience. Ever since the American Association had folded, the 12-team National League had had no team to play in a "world's series." Ten years later, with William Temple's legacy spoiled, the Pittsburgh Pirates played in the first World Series between National and American League teams.

Making themselves conspicuous among this evening's auditors were recently elected mayor Robert Erastus McKisson (Robert Bliss had gotten Ed McKean's vote, in spite of His Honor's Irish surname), the city treasurer, and the county sheriff. Occupying the table of Spiders club owner Frank Robison were vice president M. Stanley Robison, treasurer Wilbert Robison, and secretary (or business manager) J. Howard Robison. Pittsburgh-born Frank

DeHass Robison briefly attended the University of Delaware before going into the streetcar business in Cleveland with his father-in-law. At one time, he was business partners with President-maker Mark Hanna. Robison used his earnings to build the original League Park, at East 39th Street, for his American Association Cleveland Blues, and to gamble on Rochester's unproven 19-year-old shortstop Ed McKean. Given the opportunity to enter a franchise in the National League, in 1889, he created the Cleveland Spiders. His brother Stanley Robison had associated himself with baseball since his student days at Northwestern, when he was made team captain.[17] By 1891, the Robisons' Spiders opened a brand new League Park, at East 66th Street, with Cy Young pitching the inaugural game. Over the last four seasons, the club had gone to two championship playoffs, with a third in the cards for next season. Throughout it all, Ed McKean was Frank Robison's shortstop. In return, McKean had been loyal to the Robison brothers. Howard Robison would be dead by Christmastime next year, with Ed McKean one of only three Spiders attending the funeral. (Jimmy McAleer and Charles Zimmer were the other two mourners from the team.[18]) McKean and Zimmer had been two of the players who, in the end, did not desert the Robisons' Spiders for the Cleveland Brotherhood team six years before. McKean finally left Cleveland to become a reluctant Perfecto, in St. Louis, only when Frank and Stanley dismantled the Spiders in 1899.

Luminaries from the Cleveland newspapers in attendance make an impromptu sportswriters hall of fame. There was Charles W. Mears, whose scrapbooks are the foundation for the treasure of the Mears Baseball Collection in the Cleveland Public Library. John B. Foster had served, since 1889, as the official scorer at League Park games, sitting in a box with Hawley when the latter was team secretary. At 18, Foster was

Frank DeHass Robison, president of the Cleveland Spiders and builder of League Park (Rutherford B. Hayes Presidential Center, Fremont, Ohio).

October 11, 1895, 187 Superior Avenue, Cleveland

Stanley Robison, co-owner and treasurer of the Cleveland club (Library of Congress).

appointed the postmaster in his hometown Norwalk, in McKean's part of Ohio; when he lost in the next election, he moved to Cleveland and made his name writing for the *Leader* and the *Press*. John Foster, after writing for the *Leader*, made himself a powerful national figure in baseball, for years chairing the rules committee and editing the *Spalding Guide*.[19] There was also Frank Brunell, whom David Nemec endorses for "us[ing] his desk at the Cleveland *Plain Dealer* not only to tout the local [team], but as a platform for his trenchant comments on the game."[20] F.H. Brunell had championed the rookie Ed McKean during his controversial signing in 1887, and he defended McKean in 1890, even though he was probably offended by the shortstop's jumping between the National League and the Players' League. This season, Brunell had written article after article promoting Ed McKean's stardom. Bespectacled Elmer E. Bates, whose pen name was the Little Old Man, had followed Tebeau and the Temple Cup to the rostrum, to say a few too many well-chosen words about the health of the game. Bates and Ed McKean had made fast friends, in spite of their fundamental differences. Both men had gone to theological seminaries, but the newspaperman from Madison,

Ohio, was a Baptist and a Republican. (The year following McKean's death, Elmer Bates was a delegate to the GOP Presidential convention that nominated Ohioan Warren Harding.) Ed McKean retired twice from baseball and was dead at 50, whereas Bates' distinguished career lasted 50 years. He was still a working journalist in 1930, for the *Lake County Republican Herald*, on the day he died. "The supper," as Bates afterward effused for the benefit of his *Sporting Life* readership, may very well have been "a dream of epicurean bliss, and everybody was happy," but many who were within earshot of his words that October night in 1895 were thankful for the guest who'd brought the home-brewed beer.[21]

And so Ed McKean and Cupid Childs, now cheering and now silent, endured the banquet as if it were some game gone into extra innings—only here they had no hope that an umpire would call the proceedings, on account of the darkness outside. The boys could be forgiven if they were a bit weary of victory fetes. They'd just survived a banquet for winners and losers at another Elks Club (or was it the same room in every city?), before the Spiders escaped Baltimore. Winning ball games was much to be preferred to toasts and speechifying. The post–Cup delirium, carrying McKean's celebrity on its shoulders, would burst through the doors and spill out into the streets of Cleveland over the ensuing days.

After Patsy Tebeau had presented the Temple Cup on behalf of the team to the city of Cleveland, it was no longer the center of attention. Instead, the 30-inch trophy was visually dominated by a floral arrangement. This elaborate, four-foot-square centerpiece on the head table depicted "a base ball diamond, with a spider on each base, a spider for a pitcher and an open oyster symbolic of Baltimore, lying midway between home plate and first base, with four spiders walking over it and eating it up." Its design featured nine floral arachnids in all, representing the Spiders team in the field, plus four more to mark the winning four of the five games in the series.[22] The centerpiece would have spoken to the celebrants in what popular dictionaries of floriography called "the language of flowers."[23] The spider mum, a bloom of autumn, was generally considered to mean triumph and renown. To our critical eye, their ornate and overdone designs, melding naturalism with symbolism, appear like specimens of late–Victorian aesthetic confusion. But the centerpiece also tells us a cautionary tale, which is the subtext of this biography of a second-generation Irish-American celebrity: that is, the oyster has been opened, but there is no prized pearl of reward. Instead, in the scene the Irish are at work devouring the Irish. It is a business worthy of Brian Boru. Even in their victory over Oysterville, the Spiders were losing.[24] For these seasons marked the historical height of the Emerald Era, its best lineups dominated by Irishmen who played the rowdy style of baseball they best understood.[25] By this point in Ed McKean's career, manager Patsy Tebeau had become the guarantee of his fame and the model for his inner elan. Before the end of the decade, Tebeau would be disgraced for his "dirty-ball" strategy and McKean would struggle in a restless retirement.

Tonight's witty designer of the floral piece had innocently reduced Hibernian competitiveness to its primitive state, one not far from the League owners' revisionist view of the rowdy elements in its game. The monolithic National League's vested interest was increasingly to package baseball as a gilded mirror held up to the so-called national character. Organized baseball was even then at work on self-consciously cleaning up the game for mass consumption, meaning to attract ladies and children as badly needed paying customers. As a result, even the feared Mugsy McGraw became gradually assimilated (although not fast enough to Ban Johnson's liking) into the mainstream of "scientific" baseball; and his star teammates, Hugh Jennings and Wilbert Robinson, reinvented themselves with McGraw as World Series managers in the next century. The justly proud Tebeau and his Spiders remained unreformed, anachronisms before their playing days were over. Next time the team would celebrate following a Temple Cup final, next October in Baltimore, they would be party to an Irish wake upon the sudden demise of the Emerald Era. Tonight's pearl, the newly polished Temple Cup, would be withdrawn from competition after one more season. And the Spiders franchise, which represented the city of Cleveland in postseason playoffs in three of five years in the 1890s, would soon be usurped in the popular memory by the coming of the American League Blues and Naps. For most Clevelanders who are fans today, baseball history begins with the Indians.

Ed McKean's personal success story seems paradoxically at odds with the creation of a genuinely national game. His America was rapidly restructuring, from its agricultural roots to its industrial future. Its leaders were fearful of enfranchising a cheap immigrant labor force and, at the same time, perpetuating the frontier myth of The Garden that had attracted immigrants (like McKean's father) in the first place. Within the span of his brief life, the venue for baseball evolved from farmer fields and bowling greens, to urban grounds with wooden grandstands, and ultimately into steel-and-brick stadiums. Ed McKean played in the opening games for both League Parks, and his last hour on the field, an old-timers exhibition in 1909, was one of the final games before League Park II was renovated in brick and steel.

Mercifully, all of this remained in the imponderable future. No one raising his or her glass to toast the Robisons, McKean, Childs, Patsy Tebeau and the victorious Spiders could have surmised that it would take another 25 years—

and a Cleveland team by another nickname, in a new major league—for the next championship.

At some juncture in the evening, did Ed McKean brood through the public orations that were as florid, in the style of the day, as the centerpiece? McKean had helped to bring home the Cup, but his mood was in danger of giving way to something personal. How did the devout Catholic feel to know that James Cardinal Gibbons had recently favored the opposition, both John McGraw and shortstop Hugh Jennings, with crucifixes blessed by Pope Leo and gold medallions he'd had struck for them?[26] Yes, it was no doubt best for a man like McKean to turn to the more imminent concern. There was an off-season to get through, a looming wintertime of five hard months of bills and expenses before a player could petition Wilbur Robison for a cash advance on next season's pay.

The floral centerpiece, like the party-goers, had no doubt already begun to droop. Even now, Ed Delahanty, a guest of the Robisons, was flagging down that elusive waiter with the disappearing drinks.

ONE

The Fields of Ohio (1884)

> My head arises above the cornfields. I stand up among the new corn...
> Now—from now—from to-day I shall do deeds of fiery meaning.
> —Sherwood Anderson, *Mid-American Chants*

McKeans have lived in Lorain County, Ohio, in and around Range 16 of the Connecticut Western Reserve, at least since the unborn ballplayer's parents settled in Grafton, about the time of the Civil War. Neighboring towns, such as Medina, Lodi, Oberlin, and Elyria, had been constructed according to memories of New England villages, "with their broad central greens, clapboard churches, and neatly tended public squares."[1] But when Martin McKean helped his wife and their two-month-old son Martin B. McKean, the ball player's older brother disembark from the wood-burning train, Grafton Station featured no green that he could see, and no public square; both were rendered irrelevant by the railroad tracks that defined the place. In the days when men played barehanded baseball, the railroads splayed like fingers across the plain leading to this place; and Grafton made the toughened palm of a fielder's catching hand. Over the family's lifetimes, the rails would come to describe an iron diamond at the village's heart.[2] Railroad, grist mill, and rock quarry interests had generated a boomtown at the confluence of what is now State Route 57, already a road on the first maps of Ohio, and the Black River, which becomes northrunning hereabouts. How the river got its inscrutable name remains a matter of speculation for historians.

The decade of the 1850s had seen the opening of the Grafton Stone Company, which tapped limestone deposits left by the prehistoric inland sea that bequeathed Lake Erie. By 1853, the merger of several local lines produced the Cleveland & Toledo Rail Road Company. Grafton was large enough to become incorporated on the first day of 1877, when our baseball player Eddie McKean was seven. The spanking new town boasted of 25 commercial buildings, featuring two hotels convenient to the railroad tracks for salesmen and travelers.[3]

On Mechanics Street, which intersected the unpaved main drag, the flour mill assembled farmers from the outlying townships. In outlying stone quarries, unskilled workers cut sandstone blocks for as little as 50 cents a day.[4]

Crossing Black River proved to be a Rubicon for more than one notable man. Some 50 years after Martin McKean crossed the stream and, at length, into the backstory of baseball in Ohio, the writer Sherwood Anderson left his business office in Elyria, on Thanksgiving Day of 1912, crossing the railroad bridge over the Black River, and walked into Cleveland and literary fame.[5] To be sure, McKean *fils* had set himself in determined pursuit of a more practical dream than writing the great American novel. His was the Irish immigrant's dream, the dream of owning land. He meant to farm the clay-based soil, as famously arable as it was notoriously hard to work, in what would come to be known as the Corn Belt.

The McKeans were welcomed into an Irish community already well-established in Grafton and neighboring townships. Eddie McKean's Irish-born maternal grandparents had settled in Eaton Township, directly northeast of the fledgling town, where his mother Margaret Moran McKean was born in March of 1836. (Growing up, it may have amused her to be the junior of three Margaret Morans living in Eaton. The widower Margaret Moran, born in 1810

Ed McKean's hometown of Grafton, Ohio, circa 1895 (courtesy Doris P. Wildenheim).

ONE. *The Fields of Ohio (1884)*

in Ireland, kept her own house on a small parcel of land. A young relative of the old lady's from the homeland, one Mabel Moran, born 1858, roomed in the house when she taught at the nearby schoolhouse where Eddie McKean was a student.) Eddie's grandmother, born in Ireland in 1817, was also a Margaret Moran. By August 29, 1850, at the time of the U.S. census, her husband Thomas Moran was deceased, leaving the 33-year-old single parent with eight children, all born in Ohio between 1835 and 1844, and the house valued at $900. The shortstop's mother was her second born, arriving a year after her older sister and ahead of four sisters and two brothers. The story of Margaret Moran McKean's childhood, how the household survived without a father, and the circumstances of her courtship with Martin McKean, is not known. It is worth noting here that Eddie McKean, in 1895, married himself a Moran girl from Ireland. He and Belle Moran McKean built a house and raised a family in West Cleveland.[6]

For the McKean and Moran families, the most important building in Grafton was its Catholic church. Only the year before Martin McKean brought his wife back to Grafton, parishioners had "carefully hauled St. John's chapel ... down the road and placed it" on a lot on Erie Street, beside the church under construction.[7] Immaculate Conception Church, erected at a cost of

Immaculate Conception Catholic Church in Grafton, Ohio (author's collection).

$10,000 and dedicated by 1871 (the year Eddie turned two), is also significant in the history of the Cleveland diocese, as the first cathedral built between Cleveland and Sandusky. Generations of McKeans were christened, married, instructed, eulogized, and sustained there. For the last one-hundred years, a stained glass window in Immaculate Conception has memorialized the initials of Martin McKean and his first-born child, Martin B. McKean. Throughout Eddie's childhood, the church was a center for a thriving Irish population. By the time he was 11 years old, the 10th annual St. Patrick's Day parade in Cleveland attracted so many celebrants from Grafton that, on the following "Monday[,] the quarries and the railroads were hard put to meet production, with so many off for illness."[8]

The record is unclear, but Eddie McKean may have initially left the farm life in Eaton for a career in the church over baseball. "Few people are aware of the fact that shortstop McKean at one time contemplated joining the ministry," the *Cleveland Press* informed its readers at the start of the 1894 Spiders season. "He studied theology for a time and came within one of being a sky pilot."[9] In those days, a devout Catholic boy from Lorain County could choose from one of the colleges nearby, Mount Saint Mary's of the West Seminary, then in Cedar Point, or Saint Mary's Theological Seminary, in Cleveland. Both enjoyed traditions in Catholic education dating from the late 1840s.[10] It is possible that Eddie acquired, however brief his curriculum might have been, instruction in English composition that would prepare him to ghostwrite pieces on boxing for revered Cleveland newspaperman Charles W. Mears.[11]

We do know that Eddie's father, Martin McKean, was born in Ireland, on the 10th of November in 1829, to Thomas McKean and his wife, a Clark. Martin was not a young man when he came to Grafton in 1866. Already in his mid-30s, he was betting on Ohio for a lucky third chance at success. It must have seemed to him a lifetime had passed since he'd forsaken his Irish homeland, where he and countless men like him were destined by a decade of famine and English law to live out lives of destitute poverty toiling in absentee landlords' fields. For such men and their families, North America promised a second chance—at the risk of an early death on the transatlantic passage, or in the customs quarantine. The Irish Family Memorial, a granite Celtic cross recently erected at Cleveland's Heritage Park, asks us to remember why folks like Eddie McKean's father dared take the risk.

The English called it the Irish Famine, but the Irish knew it as the Great Starvation. By either name, the Irish diaspora begins with the onset of the potato blight, in summer 1845 (when patriarch Thomas McKean's son Martin was an earnest lad of 16), and worsens over the next six years. Within the decade, *Phytophthora infestans* had caused the destruction of the potato crop at a time when the starchy tuber was the staple of the peasants' diet. Ireland's rural population, as a result, was reduced to nearly one-half.[12] The official British response to the crisis, in the form of parliamentary relief bills, was to put the Irish to work, building roads and bridges to nowhere, qualifying peasant families for rations of maize meal. In order to qualify, however, men like Thomas McKean and his son Martin were required to part with all their land above one-quarter acre. As the bitter saying went: "God sent the blight; but the English landlords sent the Famine!"[13] Within five years, Ireland lost one-quarter of its population to death and blight flight; by 1855, two million emigrants—Martin McKean among them—had fled to England, Australia, and Canada, but mostly to America, in an ironic reversal of the path of Sir Walter Raleigh's introduction of the potato, in 1586, from the New World to Ireland.[14] Part of what Martin would never leave behind in Ireland was a considerable heritage that linked him to McKeans in County Cork as far back as the 17th century. Their name is derived from the given name Ian, or John; McLain, the early form of McKean, means "son of John." McKeans are first discovered in Scotish records in Argyllshire, a family seat.[15] The Scotch McKeans in America produced Governor Thomas McKean, a signer of the Declaration of Independence, who was born in Chester County, Pennsylvania, in 1734.[16] Another part of the McKean clan moved to Ireland.

Ivan Knox has recently traced a McKean *sept* (an Irish term for "clan") emigrating from Ireland to New Brunswick in the 1800s.[17] According to family lore, Eddie's father Martin entered North America through Canada. Many Irish chose to book passage aboard sailing ships to Newfoundland because it was a cheaper ticket than one to Boston or New York City. Canadian customs was set up on Grosse Isle, Quebec, or in Montreal, in the summers, and at St. John or Halifax, for winter passages when the St. Lawrence River was frozen over. Those who survived quarantine took one of the overbooked ferries to the Midwest, where they at length settled. Unfortunately, since the so-called St. Albans lists were kept by Canadian customs offices starting only in 1895, we have no documents that track Martin McKean's progress through Canada to Wisconsin.[18] We do know that, in the two decades before the American Civil War, the Irish comprised the largest English-speaking group to relocate in Wisconsin, second in minority population only to the Germans. But by 1860, the great influx of Germans, who competed with the Irish for unskilled jobs as well as for the best tracts of land, and the pursuit of a longer growing season by those who farmed, led many Irish, like Martin McKean, to leave Wisconsin.[19] If he ventured to Grafton as a farmer, he was fortunate. Most of the area's Irishmen had chosen the area for the opportunity to gain steady, albeit back-breaking, work on the railroads or in the stone quarries. Before

Martin and Margaret McKean left Wisconsin for Ohio, they were married in a Catholic ceremony on the 24th of August, 1863. Two months after Martin B. McKean's birth, on January 14, 1866, the young family moved to Eaton Township.

By March 27, 1866, Martin had purchased a half tract of land on Capel Road, where he built the house in which Eddie would be born in June 1869. For a mortgage of $3,380 (about $170,000 in 2011 dollars), Martin was deeded the middle part of Lot 63, some 96.6 acres from the old Watkins farm, in addition to "all the firewood, rails, loose lumber and manure" on the premises. A witness for the signing of the deed was John Moran, probably Martin's brother-in-law. The house Martin McKean built at the front of that property was the only home Eddie knew growing up.[20] And the farm continued to be sanctuary and refuge for the Cleveland ballplayer during his stardom. While older brother Martin B. stayed in Eaton and ran the family farm, Eddie chose to roam the cities of the major and minor leagues (perhaps their father had made it clear the oldest son was to inherit the farm) and reside in Cleveland after his retirement from baseball. His career track almost certainly went contrary to his father's expectations, and must have been the source of family disputes over the years. The low point probably came when the Nashville club sent Eddie home, after a handful of games in the summer of 1885, to work beside his brother and father in the Eaton fields. It would be happier to think that Martin McKean recognized in his second son something of the quality of persistence that had made him prosper. It may be that Margaret favored her Ohio-born son, and defended him. On her death, Elmer Bates wrote that Ed "McKean was as devoted to her as a young man could possibly be to his mother, and his winters at the home in Grafton were the happiest hours of his life."[21]

His parents would always live in the house on Capel Road. Margaret Moran McKean passed away first, on December 12, 1895, at the height of her son Ed's celebrity. Martin McKean survived until November 13, 1910, dying three days after his 80th birthday. The retired farmer had stayed at the homestead with Ed's sister, Mary E. McKean, who was at the time a teacher at Grafton High School. According to his obituaries, he died a wealthy man.[22] The McKean property grew over the years to about 150 acres before it was partitioned, following the deaths of Mary, in 1925, and Martin B., in 1929.

The baseball references will tell you wrongly that Ed McKean grew up in Cleveland—his hometown was Grafton. Eddie must have attended the one-room schoolhouse that still stands today (now a residence), where Capel Road dead ends into Durkee Road, during an academic year relieved by spring plantings and fall harvests. It's easy to picture Eddie, a strapping farm boy, trudging

ONE. *The Fields of Ohio (1884)* 25

past his teacher's house on his way to school, then dashing past on his way home or off to play ball in town. What was everyday life like for an Irish lad in Grafton? Historian Thomas Gallagher argues that naturalized Irish families like the Morans and McKeans weren't so much assimilated into the American culture as they were caught up in its work ethic:

> The Irish in the Midwest, surrounded by land whose fertility exceeded the wildest stories they had heard in Ireland, ... simply became too busy with and rooted in their new land to cling so tenaciously to the horrors and causes of the famine. They would go on being as faithful to Ireland and their loved ones as the easterners, but they would at the same time become more engulfed in America, in the entire continent surrounding them, in the work they had to put in on what they could at last call their own land, with no religious tithes attached and no pig needed for the absentee landlord's rent.[23]

The familiar sounds of Eaton Township must have stayed with Ed McKean all his life. From the copper tower of Immaculate Conception there rang The Angelus Bell announcing mass, and sometimes the Toll Bell, a rarer sound.[24] His childhood memories must have featured trains: earliest, the noises of the Cleveland-Columbus-Cincinnati line coming and going from deep in his father's fields, and later the excitement of the trains when he was old enough to play and work beside the tracks. The boy must also have internalized the sights and sounds of commerce emanating from the quarries and mills that defined Grafton and village life.

The ballplayer's birthday depends on whatever source you happen to be consulting. My research has led me to believe that Edward John McKean was born on June 20, 1869. Ed's headstone, in Cleveland's Calvary Cemetery, marks 1869 for the year of his birth. All the standard baseball references and encyclopedias prefer a June 6, 1864, date. U.S. census records for 1880, when Eddie was still a dependent on his father's farm, indicate 1864, and the census for 1900, the year following Ed McKean's retirement from the major leagues, specifies June 1865. The adult Ed McKean consistently remembered the date and place of his birth as June 20, 1868, in Grafton, Ohio, which makes better sense of both his brother Martin B.'s earlier birth in Wisconsin and their parents' wedding anniversary. A June 20, 1868, birthdate is in agreement with Ed McKean's state of Ohio death certificate (file number 47354), the "U.S. Census of Ohio Deaths 1908–1953" report, as well as correlating with his obituary in the *Cleveland Plain Dealer*, on August 17, 1919. However, when we consider the fact that the McKean family headstone in Grafton's St. Mary's Cemetery memorializes 1868 as his sister Mary's year of birth, then Ed McKean's birth a year after hers—on June 20, 1869—makes the best sense of all.

Even his name is a matter to be established. Baseball references routinely recite the player's name as Edwin John McKean. His vintage baseball cards, and the *Cleveland City Directory* over three decades, identify him simply as E.J. McKean. All available census records for the ballplayer, his parents, and his wife and family, declare his Christian name was Edward. The misnomer Edwin may have its origins in mistaking the brother's Martin for Edward, or a misreading of the abbreviation for Edward, in handwritten documents. But this is largely speculation. At any event, the mistaken Christian name has been perpetuated, much like the error of McKean batting right-handed. By whatever name, Edward John McKean is best identified through his life in baseball.

His was the first generation of American kids that grew up playing baseball. Eddie's father had abandoned the ravaged fields of Ireland to farm the rich fields of the Midwest at the same time that Union soldiers were returning from the killing fields of the Civil War. The veterans brought home, to pastures and bowling greens, their newfound passion for "base ball." The game was played in nearby Oberlin as early as 1865,[25] and Harry Wright's Cincinnati Red Stockings barnstormed 11,000 miles across the country for 57 wins and a tie in the summer of 1869, when Eddie was a newborn. Clarence Darrow, growing up in another small town in Ohio, called baseball in those days "the one unalloyed joy in life."[26]

Just when, where, and how Eddie came to learn the game is apparently lost to history. We have no family stories of the boy's first strides in the game that would make his name. It's as if Eddie McKean arrives full grown in Youngstown, Ohio, an 89-mile train ride east of Grafton, where his professional record starts in 1884.

Of course, the shortstop didn't invent himself. Life on the farm would have contributed to Eddie's strong back and arms, but the daily routine of chores wouldn't have left much, if any, time for playing a game like baseball. Regardless, the country boy would have been presented an array of formative venues for watching baseball and honing his own skills. Oberlin College continued to be a hotbed for the game throughout McKean's childhood. Twirler Lee Richmond, author of the first perfect game, was a member of the Oberlin College nine, as were Fleetwood Walker and his brother Weldy, pioneers of black enfranchisement in baseball. By the time Eddie McKean was a teenager, at least two dozen towns in northern Ohio were fielding teams.[27] The Elyrias, a strong independent club from Lorain County, played a rigorous schedule in 1880 and 1881.[28] There was, by 1879, a proliferation of sandlot teams in the Cleveland Amateur Base Ball Association. Playing on fields nearest to Grafton were the Elyria Southern Rocks, the West Side Reds, and the memorably named Whiskey Island Shamrocks. Joe Neale, a phenom who came into prominence in 1884 when he won an Ohio state championship for Bucyrus, and later pitched in the American Association, hailed from Wadsworth, just down Route 57 from Grafton. He was a longtime resident of Akron.[29]

The dominant figure in Western Reserve baseball also lived in Akron, two counties removed from Lorain. Samuel Washington Wise was the man who organized and captained the Akrons, the semipro team famous for beating the Louisville Eclipse in 1881. No fewer than 14 future major leaguers graced the Akron roster that year, most memorably Hall of Fame second baseman Bid McPhee. Ed McKean competed against both Wise and McPhee in the big leagues, but he may have been introduced to them as an amateur. Modoc Wise was a player strikingly similar to McKean. A left-handed slugger better known for his hitting than his fielding, he was stocky, especially for a middle infielder. A typical Akrons lineup in 1881 featured Cyrus Edward Swartwood at first base or in right field, Ed Andrews at first base, Charlie Morton at shortstop, and Tony Mullane in the pitcher's box. Harry Wright himself signed Ed Swartwood to his first contract, initiating an eight-year career in the majors. Swartwood was a graduate of Western Reserve College in Cleveland. Before joining the Akrons, George Edward Andrews had been a member of the 1880 Elyrias. His 56 stolen bases led the National League in 1886. Charlie Morton's family, like the McKeans, claimed to be descended from a signer of the Declaration of Independence. Like Sam Wise, Morton made Akron his home throughout his long association with baseball, beginning with the Cleveland Forest Citys and including stints as a player in the American Association and as manager for the Southern League's Savannah club. Charles Hazen Morton was a gifted third baseman but a light hitter, whose true genius would be revealed in his careers as a manager and executive. Charlie Morton would die in the Massillon, Ohio, state mental hospital where pitcher Cy Voorhees died. Cork, Ireland–born Anthony John Mullane cut a legendary swath through Akron, Toledo, and Cincinnati. The pitcher they called the Apollo of the Box and The Count had already claimed 285 big league victories by age 33, when he won his last, as McKean's teammate with the 1894 Spiders. McKean would face Tony Mullane for his first major league at-bat, in 1887. When Eddie McKean was a first-year player with Youngstown, he also batted against a much-lesser-known pitcher from the old 1881 Akrons, Harry Arundel, who proved good enough for 16 major league decisions.

Of course, there was the practical way for a farm boy growing up in Grafton to learn about baseball. Eddie may have played, after the long work days on his father's farm, for one or more of Grafton's company teams. The game was passionately practiced by workers from the railroads, mills, and quarries. Also, Grafton would have fielded its own nine to compete against nearby LaPorte, Oberlin, and Elyria, and against other town teams as far away as

Akron and Kent. It is difficult to concoct a scenario that does not bring together Eddie McKean and Pit Gilman during their formative days in baseball. Their names originally show up in a few box scores, when the two boys were teammates with Jimmy McAleer on the minor league Youngstowns of 1884. But Eddie McKean and Gilman almost certainly were opponents, if not teammates, dating all the way back to their first amateur games on Lorain County fields.

Pit Gilman was born, in LaPorte, five years before McKean's birth a few miles away. Jonathan H. and Miranda Pitkin Gilman christened the last of four children and only boy Pitkin Charles Gilman, passing down the distinguished maternal family name.[30] The father's side of the family, as in the McKeans' case, traced its inheritance back to a Founding Father. The two boys may have been aware of the historical coincidence that Pit's ancestor, Nicholas Gilman, was commissioned as a captain in the Revolutionary army by President of the Continental Congress Thomas McKean himself. Captain Gilman was later a delegate from New Hampshire at the framing of the Constitution.[31] Pitkin Gilman was a bright young man; at the age of 19, he was teaching winter school in Elyria, and he taught again four years later in LaPorte.[32] As a player, Gilman was a speed-burner—relatively late in his career, *Sporting Life* still identified him as "the sprinter" in spring 1887[33]—so the outfielder and sometimes leadoff man matured early. In

Sam Wise was one of northern Ohio's seminal baseball figures from McKean's developmental years (Library of Congress).

September of the 1884 season, when he and McKean were with the Youngstown club, 20-year-old Pit was summoned to the majors by the Cleveland Blues for two games. But his shortcomings at the plate—he managed only a single, and struck out three times, in his 10 at-bats for Cleveland—relegated him to a career in the bush leagues.

Eddie McKean would have to be more patient for his own call-up to Cleveland, which would come in 1887, but the younger boy had to have been inspired by the success of his Lorain County neighbor. And he could bring the news home to Martin McKean, evidence that there was some kind of future in playing a game. At the very least, Gilman's cup of coffee tells us that somebody in Cleveland was watching the Youngstown team and its teenaged second baseman. Years after their retirements from baseball, the career paths taken by Pit Gilman and Ed McKean continued to bring them together. During the time that McKean worked for the M.J. Hinkel Company, a wholesale distributor of whiskies, and managed a tavern in Cleveland, Pit Gilman was a salesman in the city for the Robert F. McKenzie Candy Company.[34] McKenzie Candy, famous for its "blue bell kisses," filed 12 patents for candies in a single year.[35] Gilman never cut his ties with Lorain County. He and his wife, Marie, a LaPorte girl, returned to live in the county in the 1920s and lived there until his death, in Elyria, in 1950. Pitkin Gilman is buried in North Eaton's Butternut Ridge Cemetery, not far from the old McKean farm.

When Eddie McKean said his tentative good-byes to Grafton and the rural life, it must have been the spring of 1884. He was free of the farm, and on his own recognizance, for the summer that stretched out ahead like the railroad tracks he rode for 90 miles to Youngstown, probably the longest trip in his life. But what the big Irish kid found there may have caused him second thoughts. Everywhere he went in the city was dominated by the belching smokestacks of the great steel mills, the prospect even from the ball grounds. Eastern Ohio was then an unrecognized mecca for early baseball personalities, in most part because the burgeoning steel mills brought their immigrant fathers to the Mahoning Valley for work. Deacon McGuire was born in Youngstown and made it his home as an adult. Hall of Fame umpire Billy Evans grew up there and wrote for the local paper. Bonesetter Reese practiced an early form of sports medicine from his Youngstown office. Future big leaguers McKean, Jimmy McAleer, and Ed Cartwright broke in with the Youngstowns and made teammates.

Such had not always been the case. The March 1, 1878, *Vindicator* sounded less than baseball-friendly when it declared: "The first man that proposes to organize a base ball club in Youngstown should be set to work in the streets with nothing but boiled balls for food."[36] In 1882, the Mahonings gave the city its first taste of the pro game, competing in the Ohio Valley Base Ball Association, but the team lasted only from July 19 through September 18 before it disbanded. Jumbo Cartwright was the bare-handed catcher for the Mahonings, and homegrown boy Jimmy McAleer patrolled left field. There is some evidence that Eddie McKean played that year.[37] The next year, in 1883, McAleer and Cartwright played for Youngstown against New Castle's Fleetwood Walker. For the 1884 season, the Ohio Valley Base Ball Association changed its name to the Oil and Iron League.[38] Second baseman McKean's name appears on the tentative roster for the Youngstown team, released by the new league in April.[39] Here begins Ed McKean's documented life in professional baseball. He was playing as a 15-year-old, probably having told the club he was 20.

In Ohio, 1884 is on record as a stormy weather year. In February, the Enigma Tornado outbreaks wreaked chaos in the Ohio Valley. And the map of baseball that season looked like a tornado had hit it. With the creation of the Union Association, big league baseball was being played in 24 cities, including entries in the unlikely venues of Altoona and Wilmington (Union Association), and Richmond and Toledo (American Association). The Union Association declared itself to be a major league but refused to recognize the National Agreement, which had been regulating the clubs of the National League and the American Association, as well as the Eastern, Northwestern, Ohio State, and the new Oil and Iron minor leagues.[40] Back in November 1883, representatives from Ohio and Pennsylvania clubs had met in Youngstown, intending to form a new low-minor league to be run according to American Association rules and regulations, right down to the adoption of Spalding's official baseball. Concurrently, the National League Cleveland Blues had plans to run a so-called "reserve team," or precursor to the modern-day farm team, in either Akron or Youngstown.[41] But the Blues' ultimate decision to keep their "colts" in Cleveland cleared the way for the creation of the Oil and Iron Association, and its Youngstowns—and a spot on the roster for an inexperienced kid from Grafton who could throw and hit a baseball a country mile.[42] The rest of the clubs in the fledgling league would be fielded in Pennsylvania towns: New Castle (the Neshannocks, nicknamed for the creek that runs through the town), Franklin, Johnstown (to be replaced by New Brighton on August 1), Oil City (to be disbanded August 4), and East Liberty (the latest club in the borough to be called the Stars). Managerial chores in Youngstown fell to T.P. Brownlee, who had no professional experience, playing or managing. His career resume is limited to this season, plus Youngstown's aborted 1885 season and a return for the 1894 revival of the club.

The typical sports fan in Youngstown at the time followed the city's

ONE. *The Fields of Ohio (1884)*

Cannon Ball Bill Stemmeyer gave up Eddie McKean's first base hit in professional baseball. McKean's feat was recorded, before his 15th birthday, with the 1884 Youngstowns; three years later, McKean would notch the first of his 2,084 career hits in the major leagues (Library of Congress).

cycling team, anyway; the local baseball team was granted precious little ink in the local newspaper and never had a nickname, as Richard Worth confirms in *Baseball Team Names* (p. 331). So box scores for McKean's Youngstown team are hard to come by and largely unstandardized. Furthermore, the league in its inaugural season doesn't seem to have kept official statistics. It is as the starting second baseman for Youngstown that McKean's name originally appears in the box scores, if at times misspelled "McKeon" or "McKeown," or worse, by scribes in Pennsylvania towns. He may have played against his first big league lineup when Youngstown hosted the Cleveland Blues and their star shortstop, Pebbly Jack Glasscock, in a mid-season exhibition at the new West Federal Street grounds, on July 10, 1884.

McKean's debut in professional baseball took place in New Castle, Pennsylvania, where his Youngstowns played their season opener on April 5, 1884. Straddling the Ohio-Pennsylvania border and separated by only 16 miles of railroad tracks, the towns made natural rivals. A crowd of about 600 curious people, some traveling from Youngstown on the train, ventured to the old baseball grounds to witness the Neshannocks handily turn back the Youngstowns by a score of 8 to 3. New Castle's Bill Stemmeyer goes down in history as the first pitcher that Eddie McKean faced. The writer covering that day's contest for the *Pittsburgh Commercial Gazette*, innocent of history, mangled the twirler's name, spelling it "Sheminger."[43] Cannon Ball Stemmeyer struck out 10 Youngstowns that afternoon. Two years later, he would win 22 games for Boston and lead the National League in batters fanned and fewest hits per nine innings. But the pitcher, who writer Billy Kinney later dubbed "Stemwinder,"[44] also threw 63 wild pitches that season, still a record. From day one, Stemmeyer exhibited a habit for losing his head and balking, according to Deadball Era rules, batters to first base.[45] The talented but erratic Stemmeyer never regained his effectiveness in the pitcher's box following his great year of 1886. He soon wound up his major league career, with two bad starts (both losses) for his hometown Cleveland Blues, in 1888. James Egan's retelling of "Stem's story" affords some insight into the pitcher, and also into what McKean's life was like, when they were briefly teammates with the Cleveland Blues:

> His first game as a Cleveland pitcher was that disastrous 28–7 loss in Philadelphia.
>
> Before that road trip was over, Manager [Jimmy] Williams told Stemmeyer to go home. As soon as the rest of the team arrived home, Stemmeyer found the team's ace pitcher, "Jersey" Bakely, and talked him into accompanying him on a little business trip to the west side. A saloonkeeper had borrowed $100 from "Stem," and he went to the tavern to collect his money. The story told is one of

ONE. *The Fields of Ohio (1884)* 33

Bakely and Stemmeyer shaking dice at the bar, and some customer interfering with their fun by repeatedly insulting Stemmeyer until he lost his temper. Whatever the truth might have been, Stemmeyer was fined $25, and required to pay another $75 for the insulter's doctor bill to repair a leg broken in two places. So much for "Stem's" $100. Bakely went on to get very drunk, and in the game with St. Louis the next day gave up 18 runs on 26 hits.[46]

The Neshannocks shortstop behind Cannon Ball Stemmeyer that April afternoon back in 1884 was Heinie Kappel. Like Eddie McKean, he was seeing his first action as a professional. Henry Kappel made the majors with the Cincinnati Red Stockings in 1887, the same year McKean broke in with the Cleveland Blues. But Kappel spent most of his long career languishing in the minors. Legend has it that Kappel was baseball's original "Heinie," a nickname broadly applied to players of German descent, or thought to be.

On May 8, the East Liberty Stars soundly drubbed the visiting Youngstowns by the lopsided score of 14 to 6.[47] McKean, his name misspelled "McKeon" in the *Pittsburgh Commercial Gazette* box score, batted sixth in the lineup, behind Jimmy McAleer; his dubious contribution to the loss was four of his team's whopping 14 errors on the day. Eddie McKean's major league career would be linked with that of the hometown kid who was playing left field for Youngstown. James Robert McAleer would develop into the best fielding center fielder of his time in the National League.[48] The more experienced player regularly batted ahead of McKean in the Youngstown lineup, but, like Pit Gilman, he would never develop as much of a hitter. A few years later, Elmer Bates, making an impassioned hot stove argument against the Cleveland Spiders trading away the light-hitting defensive whiz, figured that "McAleer saves ten games [a season], by the marvelous accuracy with which he gauges a ball and the lightning-like rapidity with which he gets under it, to one that he loses by his failure to hit safely when a hit would win a close game."[49] Fellow Youngstownian Billy Evans once claimed Jimmy McAleer was the first outfielder to take his eyes off a batted ball to run to the spot for the catch.[50] He'd earned the nickname "Loafer" for his effortless style. It was probably no coincidence that McAleer's career year at the plate was 1895, the Spiders' best season. When he eked out 87 hits in 1898 (three of them doubles) he called it quits as a regular player. His distinguished second career in baseball also started with Youngstown, when he managed its team in the Interstate League. Soon, he was called back to Cleveland to manage its first team in the new American League. Jim McAleer worked alongside Ban Johnson to help found two original American League clubs, in Boston and St. Louis, and he was the Red Sox president when they won the World Series in 1912. When Johnson sent him to manage the Browns in 1902, McAleer signed a trio of former Spiders (Jesse

Burkett, Jack Powell, and Bobby Wallace) and a future Cleveland Nap (Red Donahue). It was probably McAleer's idea, when he was manager of the Washington Senators, to ask President Taft to throw out the ceremonial first ball in 1910.

Jimmy McAleer was born and died in Youngstown. He learned to play baseball on the sandlots of West Youngstown, in the shadow of the rolling mills where his father worked as a boilermaker. His parents, Owen McAleer and Ann Keenan, were married on January 7, 1838, in the parish of Tyholland, Ireland, and the couple immigrated to Canada in 1839, anticipating the route into the New World that Martin McKean was later to follow.[51] He married Annie Durbin (whose own parents were born in Ireland) on March 28, 1898, at the time when she was the private secretary for Youngstown's mayor. McAleer's impressive resume of offseason jobs in Youngstown included a position with the national bank, home furnishings store-owner, streetcar stock-owner, and politician. Jimmy's teammates had already been calling *him* the Mayor of Youngstown for years.[52]

Jimmy McAleer was McKean's teammate and confidant. "No one but McAleer could have made it," Harry Wright once lamented, after one of the center fielder's catches beat his Phillies (Love of the Game Auctions).

Most of the 500 in attendance in New Castle on May 10, 1884, exited the grounds after the first inning when the visiting Youngstowns had batted around, but a scribe for the hometown *News* has preserved from that game a picture of the teenaged McKean in his days as a fearless baserunner. When McKean, batting seventh, came to the plate, Bill Stemmeyer needed one more out to get out of the disastrous inning. But the rookie determined to make it tough for the twirler: "McKean made a safe hit, went to third on a pass[ed ball by the catcher], and walked half way up the line from third to home, and as the catcher played the ball to the pitcher came very nearly scoring." McKean finished the game, a 12–8 win for The Only Keenan, with two base hits, a run scored, and two errors playing first base.[53] Brownlee promptly returned the kid, a work in progress in the infield, to his regular position at second. Two weeks later, the Youngstowns played New Castle in a home-and-home doubleheader on Decoration Day. "Brownlee's Beauties" dropped the morning slugfest at home, 13 to 11, to a pitcher remembered only as Hofer. Eddie McKean, batting sixth for Youngstown, hit safely twice and scored a run. He played an errorless second base. Then the two teams travelled to New Castle to play the afternoon game before 2,000 fans. All the hits must have been left back in Ohio, as Keenan lost the contest, 2 to 1; McKean batted fifth and went hitless and errorless.[54]

With McKean, who was still a growing boy, and a young Jumbo Cartwright in the lineup, the Youngstowns could boast of two of the early game's most athletic big men. Cartwright, at 5-foot–10-inches and 220 pounds, regularly batted leadoff this season.[55] And Eddie McKean was known to be fast, particularly going from home to first, as well as a dashing baserunner. Ed Cartwright, originally a catcher, had been converted to third base for the 1884 Youngstowns. He finally got his chance in the major leagues with the American Association Browns; the 30-year-old rookie, in a game on September 23, 1890, drove home seven runs in one inning. His best years in the majors were with Washington in the National League, where he was an RBI specialist much like his buddy McKean. In 1895, the Washington players elected the good-natured Cartwright to serve as team captain. That year, the rotund Cartwright stole 50 bases, mostly on his good judgment. (Gus Schmelz, who managed the Senators that year, spun the vote as a denouncement of teams that played the rowdy game eschewed by Cartwright.[56] Gus Schmelz never played a game of baseball, but he was a manager for 11 big league seasons.) In the end, Jumbo Cartwright was released by the Minneapolis Millers, according to *Sporting Life*, "for no other reason than an accident that befell him while riding a wheel," so he went to work in a Minneapolis rolling mill.[57] When last heard from, Cartwright was still playing semipro ball in 1901, in Minneapolis.[58] He and Jim McAleer are buried in Youngstown.

In another holiday doubleheader against New Castle, Eddie McKean took part in what have been billed as two of baseball's most unique games ever. Youngstown's ambidextrous pitcher, Owen Keenan, celebrated his Fourth of July, legend has it, by winning both games—one from each side. In the early 1880s, when teams mostly went with a single pitcher who was expected to finish most of his starts, it wasn't unknown for a starter to win a doubleheader.

There were prominent switch-handed pitchers. Larry Corcoran was the star right-handed twirler for Cap Anson's famous Chicago Colts, until he hurt his arm; afterward, he attempted a comeback in the minors as a left-handed pitcher. Ice box Chamberlain was much-coveted by Patsy Tebeau but wound up pitching only two games for the 1896 Spiders. He probably threw left-handed when his right arm was tired.[59] One of the outstanding pitchers of the 1880s, Chamberlain is best remembered for serving up all four of Bobby Lowe's home runs in a single game. Among The Count Mullane's many talents was his ability to pitch with either hand. In those days, it was also not unheard of for a pitcher to change throwing arms during the course of a game.[60] But the feat attributed to Owen Keenan that July 4 twin bill was different, even for him: it was said that he threw right-handed and won the morning game, then won the afternoon game as a southpaw.

I find no evidence in the sparse newspaper record that McKean played out the 1885 season with Youngstown after being cut by Nashville. What the *New Castle Daily News* does tell us is, the only baseball game in New Castle for July 4, 1885, was an amateur contest between the Neshannocks and the local college team. A few days later, New Castle and Youngstown met in a home-and-home doubleheader, but that date's morning game occurred in Pennsylvania (McKean's Youngstowns did win it, 12 to 3) and the afternoon game was staged in Ohio (New Castle took that one, 7 to 4).[61] Is this the doubleheader McAleer remembered? Most likely, the Keenan doubleheader took place on the Fourth of July *of 1884*. The reporter for the *New Castle News* provides little more than the score of the morning game, which suggests he may not have witnessed Keenan's victory in Youngstown. The details of his account of the afternoon game, contested in New Castle, fail to support McAleer's specious story. Instead, Owen Keenan appears in the box score as the right fielder, batting seventh behind McKean, and starting pitcher Darrah (his given name is unknown) is charged with the Youngstown loss. McKean's base hit in the second inning was the second and last hit off winning pitcher Jim Hyndman all afternoon. If Owen Keenan came in to relieve Darrah, the box score does not show it.[62] Of course, it's feasible that Keenan's feat may not have seemed worth noting in the next day's newspapers, since The Only Keenan started and finished most of Youngstown's games against New Castle, as he did against the four other teams in the Oil and Iron League in 1884, and considering that ambidextrous players were not especially newsworthy. If the local reporter hadn't seen Keenan pitch that morning, he may not have even been alert as to which arm he'd employed.

As far as I can determine, the apocryphal story originated in the *Suburbanite Economist*, a Chicago newspaper, in an August 28, 1908, interview with

ONE. *The Fields of Ohio (1884)*

Jimmy McAleer, who might be forgiven a soft spot for the twirler who shared his father's given name, his mother's maiden name, and his own baseball origins. McAleer was the manager of the Browns, and McKean was in his last days as a player in the minors, at the time he recalled a legendary game: "When Ed McKean and I were with the Youngstown, Ohio, team in 1885 a pitcher named Keenan beat New Castle righthanded in the opener of a July 4 doubleheader, then won the afternoon game lefthanded." McAleer's remark was picked up by the *New York Times* and became the stuff of legend, or at least baseball trivia.[63] Owen Keenan had been out of baseball for two decades by then. He was living in downtown Pittsburgh and working as a musician in a dance orchestra.[64]

The big news at the time, back in 1884, was that New Castle had halted a Youngstown winning streak on July 5, Keenan losing to his nemesis Neshannocks. The previous week, the Youngstowns had beaten the Oil City Exchange, the Meadvilles (twice) and, only the day before, shut out the Johnstowns.[65] For this midseason game, McKean was moved up to the cleanup position in Brownlee's lineup, as he had been earlier in a June 22 loss to New Castle.[66] He usually batted low in the lineup, sixth or seventh, but the extant box scores show no evidence of the extra-base power that will be Ed McKean's trademark in the National League.

The professional game was catching on in Youngstown this year, even while the New Brighton and Oil City teams were disbanding. In the last week of July, Youngstown started construction on a ball park, and it was ready for a July 31 opener, against Oil City, followed by a baseball tournament to help foot the bill for the new venue.[67] My research failed to unearth either the final standings for the 1884 Iron and Oil League's six franchises in eight cities, or the record for McKean's first team. The *New Castle News* did print the standings, as of the games on July 1: Franklin 16–7, New Brighton 17–8, Oil City 11–12, New Castle 10–13, Youngstown 13–17, East Liberty 8–16.[68] We can be sure that Eddie McKean was getting plenty of game experience; somehow, his team had managed to play the most games by far in the circuit.

Two

The Best Shortstop in the International League (1885–1886)

> "Watch me!
> In me you see all the movements of the game."
> —Sherwood Anderson, *Winesburg, Ohio*

Ed McKean was familiar with railroads. He'd grown up in a train town, where his friends' immigrant fathers supported their families by working for the railroads, and his own father's fields were crossed by rails. As a child, he must have heard stories of the midnight hour when Abe Lincoln's funeral train passed through Grafton.[1] And his own trip the year before, half way across Ohio, gave the boy his first taste of travel. But nothing in Ed McKean's early life would have prepared him for either for the long train journey to Nashville, or the Southern culture awaiting him. His stay in Nashville would be only the briefest of interludes, but it meant something greater than an early test of the soon-to-be 16-year-old's ability on the diamond.

Nashville amounted to a challenge of an innocent Irish-American's fundamental assumptions about living, right down to the levels of food he had never tasted, a brand of religion alien to his Catholic upbringing, and a spoken dialect he couldn't always understand. Intrepid Ed McKean had signed on with the brand new Southern League, which was scheduled to play exclusively in the Reconstructed cities of the Confederacy. Baseball had been introduced to Nashville, in 1862, by Union soldiers of the occupation. Lincoln's army played at Sulphur Spring Bottom, future home field for the 1885 Nashville Americans.[2] A mere 20 years after the Civil War, the good citizens of Nashville were careful when they chose the name for their ball club; the city's newspaper was renamed the Nashville *American*, at the same time.

Two. Best Shortstop in the International League (1885–1886)

Then, too, the Southern League marked a big jump in competition over the Iron and Oil League, McKean's previous stop. No fewer than 15 men on the Nashville roster had played, or would soon play, at the major league level. His Nashville teammate Norm Baker had pitched previously for Pittsburgh, in 1883, and spent part of 1885 with Louisville, before following McKean to Rochester in 1886. Baker's final season, 1890, was with the Baltimore Orioles. Like McKean, Norm Baker played in the Oil and Iron League in 1884. However anxious he might have been, Ed McKean must have felt equally good about his prospects. He was earning $50 a month[3] to hold down second base and bat second in the lineup behind Leonard Sowders, a player so good he would lead the Southern League in hitting and play for the American Association Baltimore Orioles the year after. Sowders' ability to reach base seemed almost certain to pay off in plenty of chances for McKean to drive in runs all summer.

Nashville released McKean before summer descended on the ball fields, however.

The Southern League was the first minor league to play a 100-game season[4]; Ed McKean lasted only six games and 27 at-bats. He managed a .185 average, and no extra bases, while committing four errors in the field. On April 22, Ed McKean's trial (in both senses of the word) was over, two weeks before Nashville's home opener.[5] One of the era's great pull hitters never got a crack at Sulphur Dell's 262-foot right-field wall, or the local merchants' prize given to the first Nashville American to hit a home run.

After plans for a Southern League were announced in fall 1884,[6] Will Bryan secured McKean's services early in his creation of the Nashville team. McKean's manager found himself in charge of his second club of many in what turned out to be a long career in the minor league circuits; Bryan was still organizing franchises in 1901, when McKean wrote him for the first-base job on a proposed American Association club for Washington.[7] However, in June 1885, Nashville's local ownership—which included league secretary Deadrick—was disassembling the very team they'd hired William C. Bryan to organize months earlier. Why?

A late May *Sporting Life* affords some insight, in the form of two short items about the Nashville club. The first piece gossips that "the Nashvilles are accused of too much boozing," and below it, implying a causal link, a second notice delivers the news that "Nashville has released Manager Bryan, McKean and Rhue."[8] Players' drinking problems and rumors of drinking weren't very newsworthy, much less sufficient reason to break up most nineteenth-century teams; and, in the aftermath of the housecleaning, no opprobrium would be placed on the banished Bryan and George Rhue. Macon's Alexander Proudfit, who also served as the president of the Southern League, didn't hesitate to hire Bryan on the rebound to manage his team. Also, Rhue, Bryan's left fielder, cleanup hitter, and sometimes pitcher, stayed in the league, immediately catching on with the Augusta Browns. (Rhue would spend time with 14 teams over eight minor league seasons. He eventually surfaced in Columbus, Ohio, where he went partners in 1895 with a former Cleveland Spider, Milton "The Cigar Store" West, in a scheme to build a ball park in the capital city.[9]) Most likely, Will Bryan resigned in protest when the Nashville owners jumped at the chance to bring in three of Cap Anson's discards.[10]

Enter Nathaniel Monroe Kellogg.

Whatever the reason, the Nashville front office had panicked. Bryan's Americans were 7 and 4 at the end of April, but it was the owners' peremptory decision that the fledgling club needed a more experienced manager, and a second baseman. They got both when they signed Nate Kellogg as Nashville's new playing manager. To be sure, Kellogg was still in his first season in pro ball, but he'd survived spring training with Chicago, hitting behind Cap Anson in the lineup. And he was good; he'd be back in the National League for the last month of the coming season, this time with Detroit. Without a doubt, the ex–Colts were offering a talented trio of ball players. Oliver Perry Beard made it to the big leagues, two years after McKean, as Cincinnati's regular shortstop, and he finished up a third season, at third base, for Louisville. Lefty Marr played outfield and third base for three big league clubs, starting with his hometown Cincinnati in the American Association, in 1886, and ending with the Reds and Kelly's Killers, in 1891. He hit over .300 in his two full seasons, and one year stole 44 bases.

Ed McKean hit well enough to start in every spring training game, and the team won early. Manager Bryan faithfully stuck with him as his second baseman and two-hole batter in his lineups. The Americans' spring schedule started on the road, with exhibition games against Western League clubs in Indianapolis and Cleveland. Nashville dropped its first two games, on March 30 and 31, to the Hoosiers. Indianapolis was loaded; at every position, the club fielded a player who could, or would, claim time in the majors. Most conspicuous in their lineup were two baseball legends: Youngstown-born catcher Deacon McGuire, and slugging outfielder Sam Thompson. McGuire and Thompson would establish major league records for endurance and runs batted in, respectively. According to BioProject author Don Thompson, when the Western League ceased operations the following year, "Many of the Indianapolis players were taken by the Detroit Wolverines. In those days," he explains, "a team had ten days to claim players from teams that had disbanded. The owner of the Wolverines had eight Indianapolis players kept on a steamer in Lake Huron until they all agreed to terms with the Detroit club and the time had passed. By this time the players were seasick and would have agreed to any terms."¹¹ Big Sam Thompson's arrival in Detroit coincided with the ousting of Akron, Ohio's, Charlie Morton, who had been managing the Wolverines. Taking the overnight train to Cleveland after the Indiana games must have felt like a homecoming for a homesick McKean. The Southern League team played inspired ball and won twice over the Cleveland Cardinals, on April 1 and 2. Notably, the Cleveland roster included Moses Fleetwood Walker and his brother Weldy Wilberforce Walker.¹² One can only hope that an entourage from Grafton attended the games at the old Kennard Street grounds.

McKean's debut in Southern League play came in Nashville's April 6 exhibition loss at Chattanooga; he went 0-for-4 at the plate and was charged with an error. Perhaps McKean's best games were back-to-back Nashville wins in Montgomery. On April 14, McKean contributed two hits in five at-bats, but also made an error at second base, with Nashville outlasting Montgomery, 10 to 7. The following afternoon, the Americans embarrassed the home team, scoring 18 runs to Montgomery's 5. McKean went 3-for-5, but collected another error, this one as the right fielder.¹³ The personal highlight of Ed McKean's spring had to be the April 10 exhibition game, before a crowd of 4,000, against Anson's Chicago Colts, baseball's best and most feared team. In Nashville's 5 to 4 win, McKean recorded a hit against the great John Clarkson.¹⁴ That summer, Clarkson would pitch the Chicago Colts to a National League pennant, win 53 games, and lead the League both in strikeouts and shutouts. John Gibson Clarkson won 326 games in a 12-year career. Before it was over, he would be Ed McKean's teammate on the Cleveland Spiders club that was the champion of the National League's "second season" of 1892. (His brother, Dad Clarkson, twirled a few games for Baltimore teams, when the Spiders and the Orioles contended for the Temple Cup.) Batting against Chicago teams was considered so daunting that some sportswriter coined the term "a Chicago game" to indicate a shutout.¹⁵ Nate Kellogg, Anson's third baseman for that preseason game but the team's regular second baseman, posted a box-score line that mirrored McKean's hit and an error. Less than a month into the future, Kellogg was to replace Ed McKean on these Nashville Americans.

McKean and the whole team hit well coming out of spring training. Nashville opened the regular season early in 1885, on April 15, winning 11 to 9 at Columbus, Georgia. McKean had one hit in his four at-bats but made an error at second base, his characteristic box-score line with the Americans. The following day in Columbus, Nashville was again victorious, this time by a score of 6 to 2. Ed McKean went 2-for-5, with two more errors. On April

18, Nashville lost for the first time, 5 to 1 to Columbus. McKean continued his modest three-game hit streak with a single, and he played errorless ball. Then he fell into a mini-slump and wasn't allowed to recover. April 20 brought another loss on the road, 7 to 4 in Birmingham; McKean was held hitless in five times at the plate. His team scored 11 times in an eight-run victory in Birmingham, on the 21st, but McKean was struggling (1-for-5, with an error). At length, Nashville took the series, allowing Birmingham only two runs in the April 22 rubber match. McKean hit for the collar and watched his team push across eight runs on the day. It was Ed McKean's last game for the Americans.[16] Within another month, the Nashville organization made a fresh start to their still young season: the team had a new manager and second baseman, and its players are decked out in "old gold" uniforms.[17] It should be noted that, years later, W.C. Bryan got the last laugh. He would dryly remark to a reporter, in the weeks after Cleveland's first appearance in a playoff series: "I am 'kinder' interested in [the Spiders], as McAleer played for me in Charleston [for the 1886 season] and McKean played for me in Nashville, and both of them were released over my head by obliging officials as being too slow and no good."[18]

Ed McKean, unlike Bryan and Rhue, dropped out of the baseball record books for the rest of 1885. He must have played after his release from Nashville, surely performing well enough for Providence to sign him, well in advance of the 1886 season, to start at shortstop, a demanding position and a new one to McKean. Jim McAleer always remembered McKean playing for the Youngstowns in 1885. At any rate, Youngstown disbanded on June 11, while the Oil and Iron League was tottering, after the franchise failed to gain admittance to the New York State League.

Among the last games the Youngstowns played that truncated season were three exhibitions in Kansas City. The visitors won the first contest but dropped the next two because the team's catchers were disabled. So that the series could continue, Kansas City manager Ted Sullivan furnished, after the fashion of the time, a catcher for game two, spare outfielder Conny Doyle. Cornelius Doyle made a number of intentional errors to throw the game to Kansas City in 11 innings.[19] David Nemec calls the aptly nicknamed Con Doyle "one of the most extraordinary con artists ever to don big league garb." In 1887, "he purportedly was held up on a train and got the drop on the robbers, at which point he revealed that he was a Pinkerton detective named Dan Shaw in disguise, who was working undercover as a ballplayer. Unhappily for Doyle, one of the 'robbers' produced proof that *he* was the victim and Doyle was the robber."[20] Another player on that Cowboys team, Joe Visner, would soon be McKean's teammate with Rochester in 1886. In 1901, Visner attempted to organize a semipro team in Minneapolis, along with McKean's old friend Ed

Cartwright.[21] Nemec speculates that it may have been Visner's Chippewa ancestry that kept him in the minors for most of his career. Joe Visner died, in 1945, on Minnesota land he claimed by invoking Native American rights.[22]

In the aftermath of Nashville, and possibly Youngstown, McKean could easily have caught on with one of the many amateur and semipro teams in northern Ohio. Elmer Bates counts 75 amateur ball teams, in Cleveland alone, by 1893.[23] A January 17, 1911, article in the *Sandusky Star-Journal*, "Some Stories of Baseball in Sandusky During the 80's," would locate the humbled McKean sometime in 1885 trying to catch on with the local team, "but [he] couldn't hang on so fast was the company." No baseball records seem to exist to confirm or dismiss the claim.

Ed McKean's next stop in the minor leagues proved to be almost as fleeting as his Nashville experience had been. However, he was at last a shortstop, or at least learning to become one, and he was situated in a comfortably small northern city with a big-league baseball tradition. The old Providence Grays, behind the pitching of Charley Radbourn and the managerial skills of Frank Bancroft, had won the National League pennant, and defeated Tim Keefe and the New York Metropolitans in the first "world's series," only a year and a half before. The Grays' championship didn't keep them from bankruptcy. Cleveland, another small-market franchise, suffered a similar fate: following the final game of the 1884 season, which Cleveland lost in Providence, Cleveland dropped out of the National League. Providence lasted through one more major league season after 1884. During the winter months of 1886, lawyer George J. West and the other stockholders were working to bring baseball back to Providence, minor league baseball this time, by joining either the New England League or the proposed Eastern League. Their plan was to parlay the minor league club into a major league franchise in the near future.[24] Subsequently, Grays general manager J.J. Piggott signed Ed McKean in February 1886, even before the new club was officially organized at Providence's Narragansett Hotel, on March 18.[25] McKean was ticketed to start at shortstop. A decade later, Piggott could boast: "I signed him ... and predicted a great future," but at the time of the contract it must have been a gamble.[26]

Teen McKean rapidly advanced through the minors, seemingly oblivious to setbacks, eased by the competition among clubs for players in an era of rabid league and team expansionism. His clubs in Youngstown, Nashville, Providence, and soon Rochester, were all in their first years of operation in newly formed leagues. When Ed McKean rose through the ranks to arrive, after parts of three minor league seasons, in time for the Cleveland Blues' inaugural team in the American Association, his preparation at the shortstop position consisted of 96 games, all coming in his final year in the minors, patched together between Providence and Rochester. The big-chested farm boy's entire minor league career consisted of about one full season's worth of games. More significant in his case than the number of games played, McKean's involvement with the Grays brought him to the attention of Frank Bancroft. By the end of the 1886 season, under manager Bancroft's mentoring in Rochester, the unproven teenager became Ed McKean, the slugging shortstop.

John Doyle was the player-manager of the new and revised Providence Grays, after Bancroft's departure along with the National League franchise; at least for the time being, Ed McKean was his second baseman. Doyle was 10 years older than his double-play partner and comparatively a man of the world. John Aloysius Doyle was born in Halifax, Nova Scotia, and played college ball at Fordham University. Doyle went 20–20 in 45 minor league starts in the pitching box and then, after four seasons, prolonged his career by filling in at second base and in the outfield. His perseverance paid off with two weeks, in July and August 1882, up with the St. Louis Brown Stockings, for whom he started and lost his three games in the majors. McKean's Providence team would be Jack Doyle's single foray into managing. After the collapse of the minor league Grays, Doyle came back for a few games, in 1889, with Auburn in the New York State League. A good citizen of Providence, the gentleman the city entrusted with its new Eastern League franchise, would live there until his death in 1915. First base for the 1886 Grays was Otto Schomberg's territory or, rather, hitting was the stone-handed first baseman's domain. The following year, McKean's infield partner would hit .308 for last-place Indianapolis, rap out 16 triples, drive home 83 runs—and make 53 errors, the record of futility for first basemen. The peerless Jack Glasscock was throwing across the infield to first that season, or Otto Schomberg just might have collected even more E-3s.

Ed McKean's record with the Grays was anemic. He batted .221, amounting to 19 hits in 86 at-bats in 20 games, and he had to be dropped in the batting order from leadoff to the second slot. He was a station-to-station runner (one stolen base). He was still a singles hitter; his only extra-base hits were three doubles, resulting in a paltry .256 slugging average. Worse, even when he hit well in a game, he continued to be prone to errors. May Day was opening day in Providence, and the Grays celebrated by beating the Hartford Dark Blues, 4 to 3 in 14 innings. McKean, leading off, contributed two hits in three at-bats. At shortstop, he started a double play, recorded seven assists and three putouts. He also made three errors in a long day. The Grays visited Hartford for the May 3 game, and again won 4 to 3 for Bill Corrigan. Providence seemed destined to bring another pennant to the city after they won yet again, in

Two. Best Shortstop in the International League (1885–1886) 45

Meriden, Connecticut, on May 4; McKean's hit was a double, his first extra-base hit of the season. Alas, the wheels fell off in Meriden, on May 6. Providence pitching gave up 12 runs and McKean's 2-for-5 day at the marble was spoiled by his three errors and six passed balls. (At the scorekeeper's discretion, a passed ball would be any ball that eluded the fielder but was not counted an error.) Starting at short for Providence, from May 17 to his and the team's last game on June 2, McKean committed eight errors; three of them came in one awful game, a 16 to 1 loss at Jersey City, on May 25. In those nine games, his base hits were a single and two doubles in 46 at-bats.

It was a team collapse. After winning its first three games, and a fourth on May 7, the Grays stumbled the rest of the way to finish at 7–13. Cancelling the rest of the planned 36-game schedule, Providence ceased operations in the financially wobbly Eastern League. There would be no professional baseball in that proud city until 1891.[27]

The team's only strength was the two hitters at the top of the lineup around McKean, Tommy McCarthy and Schomberg. Since Jack Doyle played most of the time at second base, the infield play was not improving. Adding to the team's difficulties, manager Doyle was never allowed the luxury of settling on one starter: the pitching staff was an ongoing tryout for the likes of William Corrigan, Doc Landis, Edgar Smith, and also a boy from Cleveland with a bright future, Ed Seward. Frank Bancroft was to pluck Seward, along with McKean, off the Providence roster to play in Rochester.

It would be an overstatement to say Ed McKean had found himself in Providence. But the experience he gained, both as a shortstop and a professional, proved invaluable. He had performed in a high minor league beside and against quality players. Bancroft took Ed Seward with him when he managed the Philadelphia American Association team in 1887. In three seasons, Ed Seward won 81 games, and regularly pitched against his former shortstop Ed McKean. McKean would square off against his old teammate Tommy McCarthy, most significantly when Cleveland played Boston for the National League championship of 1892. As a Gray, Ed McKean played against Hartford's Hugh Duffy, the outstanding hitter in that 1892 playoff series. Both McCarthy and Duffy are enshrined in the Hall of Fame. Other notable players around the Eastern League its first year were Bridgeport Giants shortstop Tommy Corcoran, Newark Little Giants Oyster Burns and Phenomenal Smith, and Waterbury Brassmen Moses Fleetwood Walker and Joe Battin. (The latter was a member of the original Cleveland Forest Citys of the 1870s, and he is buried in Akron, Ohio.)

After Providence, Ed McKean was a man without a club—reminiscent of the year before, when Nashville cut him loose early in the season—and

Frank Bancroft's Rochester Maroons needed a shortstop. The manager had released his starting shortstop, the veteran Ed Caskin, 15 games into the International League season. It would have been routine for Bancroft, who had managed the Grays just two years before, to send word of the vacancy to Jack Doyle, back in Providence. Wherever he went, Bancroft always maintained his social and business networks in Cleveland, dating from his 1883 season at the helm of the Blues, one of the manager's seven stops in his nine-year career. And McKean was a bargain pickup, eager to sign so far into the season. McKean would replace a shortstop who owned an impressive resume from six big-league seasons with New York, Troy, and St. Louis. Caskin was nearing the end of his playing career. He'd never been a good hitter, but now that raw minor league twirlers were knocking the bat out of his hands, it was time to go back home. So after his release by Rochester, Ed Caskin played out the season with Lynn-Newburyport. First-year shortstop McKean had the great fortune to play for Rochester beside Walter Hackett, a former major league shortstop who was winding down his career at second base. In Providence, McKean's double-play partner Jack Doyle had had to play out of position; Hackett was a seasoned infielder from Boston's Union Association and National League teams. In 1884, he'd led all Union shortstops in fielding percentage. McKean's mentor was a born baseball man: Walter Hackett was a cousin of John Clarkson.[28]

Seventeen-year-old McKean joined a Rochester roster loaded with 22 individual big-league success stories. Lon Knight, the team's captain and right fielder, had worked under Frank Bancroft on two National League clubs, Worcester in 1880 and Detroit in 1881–1882. The season after Bancroft left the Grays, Alonso Knight's big-league playing career was over, as well. Now in Rochester, captain and manager were reunited, to the benefit of Ed McKean's development. Knight had experience all over the baseball field. As a pitcher for Philadelphia in 1876, he had the distinction of giving up the first base hit in National League history (to Orator O'Rourke). Four years later, right fielder Knight made the defensive play that saved Lee Richmond's perfect game, when he charged a ball off the bat of Cleveland's Bill Phillips and fired to first base for the out. Lon Knight knew what it took to win baseball games in the Deadball Era: he was Philadelphia's leadoff hitter and manager when the Athletics won the American Association pennant in 1883. Knight's second baseman on the championship team had been Cub Stricker, McKean's first double-play partner in the big leagues. Also, one of the pitchers on Lon Knight's staff in Philadelphia had been Jersey Bakely, who was Rochester's biggest winner and least dependable player in 1886. An Edward Enoch Bakely baseball card is one of the strangest in the Old Judge series; in the miniature picture, the pitcher's windup obscures his face from the camera, as if he'd rather be incognito.

He was the nominal ace of the Rochester staff, when he was sober. Bancroft, alternately disciplining and propping up his pitcher, coaxed starts out of the carousing Bakely. You have to wonder just how enthused McKean was to be reunited with Jersey Bakely on Cleveland teams in future seasons. The influence of Francis Carter Bancroft would have extended to the young Ed McKean's personal conduct, too. If McKean had been a drinking man in Nashville, he would not be one while in Rochester. His latest manager was a teetotaler during the baseball seasons, and he was known to swear his players to temperance pledges.[29]

Frank Bancroft, at age 40, was still a go-getter. He'd been organizing baseball teams beginning with his service in the Civil War. Bancroft was one of a new breed of baseball men, who had never played a professional game. On the bench, his walrus mustache, dark suit and shirt collar made him look like a businessman in a time of playing managers. Throughout his nomadic career, Frank Bancroft was ever the visionary—he'd taken teams on barnstorming tours of Cuba and Hawaii—and the innovator—his agreement to release Hoss Radbourn from his reserve contract probably led to the Grays' championship. After managing teams, Bancroft settled into the front office of the Cincinnati Reds for his last 29 years in baseball. But before that, Banny's resume is one unfoldable road map through the great age of the proliferation of professional baseball leagues and the expansion of team rosters.

Since 1876, the National League monopoly had survived challenges from rival leagues (American Association and International Association) and was in the process of steeling itself for more tests upcoming (Union Association and Players' League). Moreover, from 1882 to 1887, the National League increased the number of reserved players allowed each of its teams from 14 (that meant five were permitted to sit on bench), to as many as 23 per roster. Sixteen major league teams struggled and fought to fill their rosters in 1887, which would also be a year of labor disputes and rules changes. Baseball in Ed McKean's breakout years was a fast-track training environment, ruled by mentors like Bancroft, Knight and, later in his career, Patsy Tebeau, before the controls of farm systems and player unions. Starting at Rochester, McKean demonstrated the qualities of character and ability that enabled him to triumph in the game, under entrepreneur Bancroft and scrappy Tebeau alike. He learned to adjust—something he'd failed to do in Nashville.

Envious International League clubs complained all season about what they called the unprincipled way Bancroft assembled his winning team; they cried foul when he paid top-dollar salaries to attract players like Ed McKean.

FRANK C. BANCROFT, Manager, has a record in that onerous position during the past two seasons that he can refer to with pardonable pride. He was born in Worcester County, Mass., in 1846, and has been an enthusiastic disciple of baseball from his youth. In his early days he pitched for an amateur club of his native town, and during the late war he spent the leisure hours of a four years' service in playing baseball. In 1876 Mr. Bancroft, who had been proprietor of a hotel at New Bedford, Mass., for several years, organized an association in that city, and established a ground which was made a paying institution by exhibition games. In 1878 the New Bedford Club was organized, and under his management they played 130 games during that season—the greatest number ever played by any club, and including victories in four out of five games with the strongest League clubs. The result at the end of 1878 was the gaining of the championship of New England. During the past season he managed the Worcester Club of Worcester, Mass., with acknowleged credit, bringing out Richmond, a phenomenal pitcher, and enabling his nine to play 125 games—the greatest number credited to any one club in 1879, and also including an almost unbroken succession of victories over all the prominent professional clubs. The fact that he is highly esteemed by the citizens of Worcester, Mass., is practically illustrated by his re-engagement as manager of their representative club. His executive qualities and business tact peculiarly adapt him for the position of manager, and the advantage of an officer of his value is proved by the pecuniary success of the New Bedfords in 1878 and the Worcesters during the past season. Personally, he is a man of good address, sharp and alert, is deservedly popular with his own nine, and has given great satisfaction in his business relations with all clubs. He has been engaged to manage a nine mainly composed of his last season's players during a trip to Cuba and the South, returning in the Spring of 1880, and assuming again the position of manager of the Worcester Club.

Baseball entrepreneur Frank Bancroft was Ed McKean's first experienced field manager, while playing for the Rochester Maroons, when the 17-year-old shortstop emerged into stardom (*New York Clipper/Old Cardboard*).

Two. Best Shortstop in the International League (1885–1886)

Bancroft had also wanted to sign Otto Schomberg from the Nashville team, but, when Utica claimed rights to both McKean and Schomberg, the dispute was settled by each club taking a player. The Utica Pent Ups (named for the local penitentiary) picked Schomberg and eventually edged out Rochester for the International League pennant.[30] When Toronto beat the Maroons on July 20, the city's correspondent to *The Sporting News* gloated: "Manager Bancroft, of the Rochesters, sat on the players' bench during Tuesday's game, and had the melancholy pleasure of seeing his very crack, six hundred dollar, left-hand, National League pitcher thoroughly punished."[31] The new Rochester pitcher was Charlie Parsons, who had thrown a few innings in May for the National League Boston Beaneaters. Bancroft had somehow talked Boston president Arthur Soden (the inventor of the reserve clause) into releasing Parsons at the end of June for $600 of his $1,400 contract investment.[32] Naturally, the Syracuse Stars felt justified in shelling out the money to bring in Charlie Sweeney, all the way from San Francisco, to pitch in their own August drive for the pennant.[33] Charlie Sweeney was soon back in California. Before releasing him, the Syracuse directors recovered some of their investment by loaning out Sweeney on the sly to pitch a game for the local town team in Constableville.[34] Ironically, it was Frank Bancroft who had made Sweeney's reputation, teaming him with Hoss Radbourn on the championship Providence team. Ed McKean would be teammates with the once-great Charlie Sweeney, for three games on the 1887 Cleveland Blues, at the finale of the then 23-year-old's major league dalliance. Left-handed Charlie Parsons would one day be McKean's teammate on the Spiders.

The umpiring at Rochester's Culver Field was roundly criticized by visiting teams, even more than usual for the Deadball Era. When Syracuse was swept there, in a three-game series in late June, they contended that the crucial games "were undoubtedly taken from them by the umpire. The treatment they received in Rochester is the most disgraceful ever received by a visiting club." Stars team captain Charlie Householder was still livid days later when interviewed for *The Sporting News*. He swore the first game was lost due to collusion with the umpire, although his story seems inadvertently to finger the Syracuse catcher who fell asleep in the rain.

> It was so dark that I couldn't see the ball when it was thrown. There was a big black cloud right over our heads and the rain was falling from it in a pretty good shower. There were three Rochester men on bases. As the rain increased I shouted out, "Time," and approached the umpire [Harrington]. Just as I reached him I heard him say to Bancroft, the Rochester manager, "I'll do just as you say." Then the man who was on third came in. [Stars catcher Bill] McCloskey was standing, ball in hand, at the plate, but didn't offer to touch him. "Why didn't you put that man out, Mac?" I asked. "Because it was that umpire's duty to call

time," he replied. Then the other men on bases started for home. I snatched the ball out of McCloskey's hand and was standing ready to touch them, when [Stars second baseman Harry] Jacoby seized me about the body and pulled me away from the plate. When the three runs had scored the umpire called time.[35]

As the other International League teams watched the Maroons climb steadily in the standings, the charges piled up. In early August, readers of *The Sporting News* were told: "The Rochesters are the worst principled team in the League. In Oswego, [Jack] Horner was charged with deliberately trying to hit a man who hit his pitching, and he was nearly mobbed when he knocked him senseless."[36] At the time, Rochester was in second place, only percentage points behind Utica. The objective fact is Bancroft's team was playing well at this point in the season; they were second only to Utica in batting and fielding and their novice shortstop McKean was leading the league in fielding.[37] Jack Horner's 15 wins for Rochester were second best on the team. His career was a grand tour of minor league clubs, from California to Canada, stopping long enough to win 154 games and lose 152. When Horner died, at 46, he'd been living in New Orleans. That Binghamton player that Jack Horner intentionally beaned in the July 24 game was Bobby Gilks, who had invoked the pitcher's ire for doubling in his previous at-bat. Gilks was knocked unconscious on the field. The league's best utility man, employed by the Crickets in the outfield and infield and even in the pitcher's box on occasion, recovered nicely to team up with Ed McKean on several Cleveland teams. Gilks retired as the storied Toledo Mud Hens franchise leader in games played and had a long second career as a major league scout.

It was at Rochester that Ed McKean became a star. His body was maturing at the very time he came under the tutelage of his first experienced manager, coach, and double-play partner. Bancroft started McKean at short stop for 74 games (also one at second base), and he responded with the third-best batting average on his team, and the sixth-highest average in the International League among players with at least 300 at-bats. Emerging from obscurity and failure, McKean became a standout fielder and a threat on the bases. The Rochesters made a spirited run for the pennant on the shoulders of their unofficial rookie of the year. He was the best shortstop in the International League. He'd become Ed McKean.

Rochester's club was nicknamed the Maroons, perhaps in admiration for the St. Louis Maroons of Union Association fame. For some in this liberal-minded city, an important stop on the Underground Railroad in past decades and hometown to Frederick Douglass and Susan B. Anthony, the name also defiantly echoed a term for Creoles. Rochester, whose ball club had just joined a league with international aspirations, was prepared to embrace the Irish shortstop. McKean played well starting with his first game as a Maroon, on June 8, the same day Bancroft claimed him.[38] The manager batted him seventh in the lineup against Utica's Billy Serad, the best pitcher in the league. In the ninth inning, McKean started a rally by singling, advancing to third on a double by catcher Ed Warner, and scoring on Jersey Bakely's sacrifice fly to center field. He also started the game's only double play. McKean's day was spoiled by Rochester's 6 to 4 defeat, and an error in the field. Ed McKean's debut before the hometown fans took place the next afternoon, when his team beat visiting Hamilton, 3 to 2. He went hitless in the cleanup spot in the lineup, but was praised by the Rochester paper for his fielding: "McKeon [sic], the Rochesters' new shortstop, distinguished himself by several remarkably quick stops."

June 11 saw the Maroons hosting the Detroit Wolverines, who were to finish in second place in the National League that season, in an exhibition. Two-thousand cranks got to see Detroit stars Hardy Richardson, Deacon White, and Dan Brouthers "in action," or at least in person, at Culver Field. The center fielder that day was Ned Hanlon; the rest of the visitor's lineup was comprised of something like their second team—their battery was pitcher Lawrence and catcher Ball, two amateurs—and Detroit mailed in an 11 to 4 farce. The local scribe once again singled out Ed McKean for his play at short, and once again misspelled his name. He further observed that McKean "in the eighth inning almost made a home run, but the ball reached the plate before he did." From his first games with Rochester, Ed McKean was known as a good shortstop. His error in a June 15 win over Buffalo was dismissed in the Rochester newspaper, which lauded his range instead: "He muffed a pop-up fly, but as he takes every possible chance he must make some errors." As it turned out, an aggressive style, regardless of miscues, was exactly the kind of shortstop manager Patsy Tebeau would one day demand of him in Cleveland.

By June 26, McKean's offense had become so essential to the Maroons' attack that Bancroft moved him into the third spot in the batting order. The team was jelling and making a strong run at the pennant. A July 20 victory in Oswego launched the Maroons into second place, as infielders "Hackett and McKean played a brilliant game for the Flower Cities." Bancroft rewarded McKean's timely hitting by bumping him up in the lineup behind leadoff man Joe Visner. The slugging of Visner and first baseman Doc Kennedy, the former Western League Cleveland Cardinals team captain, had carried Rochester up to this point; McKean would contribute from that key position for the remainder of the season. McKean seemed to always put the ball in play, and he usually pulled the ball behind a runner at first base (two reasons why managers in his early years in the big leagues liked to bat him second). After Rochester prevailed, 6 to 5, over the visiting Hamilton Clippers on July 21, the club was in first place. In the fifth inning of that game, McKean singled and eventually scored from third on a rundown, when Lon Knight ran between first and second bases to attract a throw. Joe Visner's rebel yell could be heard in every part of Culver Field at his team's feat. On July 22, in Syracuse, McKean scored in the fifth inning and knocked in Rochester's third run in the 12th inning to beat the Stars and Lefty Marr, whose career had crossed McKean's in Nashville. At the season's halfway point, Rochester perched atop the International League standings, with a record of 33–17. Ed McKean was enjoined in his first pennant race.

"Bancroft's Beauties" won four straight in early August, playing at home against Hamilton, Syracuse, and Oswego, and then McKean and company ran into a roadblock: Utica swept the Maroons in a series on, August 4, 5, and 6. In the third game, McKean made a costly mental error. With the score tied in the seventh inning, he stayed put on third base instead of scoring on the Utica right fielder's fumble. Rochester fell back in the standings all the way to third place (36–24), behind the Utica Pent Ups and the Toronto Canucks. The Maroons continued to play flat-out ball, no matter. On August 9, Rochester started Charlie Parsons in both games of a doubleheader in Hamilton. Facing the Hamilton Clippers was always special for McKean; of all people, his counterpart at short for those games was Nate Kellogg, and the team's nickname must have reminded him of the clipper his father took as a young man across the Great Lakes to Wisconsin. In the morning loss that day, McKean had two hits and scored three times, but also made one of the Maroons' three fatal errors. The afternoon game drew as many as 8,000 spectators, so many that hits to the outfield were only good for ground-rule doubles. Jersey Bakely roused himself to throw a no-hitter against first-place Utica, on August 17. His shortstop McKean banged out three hits, including a triple, scored two runs, and was responsible for one of four Rochester errors. Rochester remained mired in third place.

It was in Utica on August 18 that Bancroft furnished the press with a letter signed by Ed McKean and all but one of the Rochester players. The faithful signees attested that they knew of no dissatisfaction among the team with Bancroft, even though they were losing ball games. Frank Bancroft had read articles critical of him in the three Utica papers (the *Sunday Herald*, the *Morning Herald*, and the *Post-Express*), and presented his resignation to the club's president Winne and director Katz. Although the stockholders chose not to accept their manager's resignation, in view of his player sentiment, the furor wasn't over. When McKean's name didn't appear on the list of players' signatures sent to the Associated Press, he was questioned by all the newspapers

Two. *Best Shortstop in the International League (1885–1886)* 53

for their August 20 editions. So it came to pass that Ed McKean was baptized by fire into clubhouse politics and public relations. Perhaps the grilling by the press unsettled the rapidly maturing shortstop; that same day, he was "caught napping at second," after singling to lead off the ninth inning in Utica. His mental lapse negated what would have been a run scored on Lon Knight's subsequent double, which instead could only tie the game that inning. Utica won, 8 to 7, with a run in their half of the ninth. Frank Bancroft's punishment was to drop McKean to eighth in the batting order for the next day's game; instead of brooding there, he singled and stole a base in the 10th inning of the Rochester victory.

Ed McKean saved his best baseball for the Maroons' late-season drive. Things turned right for McKean when Rochester stiffed the visiting Oswego Starchboxes in both ends of an August 31 doubleheader. After going hitless in the first game, he stroked two hits in the afternoon contest, initiating a remarkable consecutive game streak in games of significance. Rochester shut out the Binghamton Crickets on the following day, as the man the hometown newspapers were now calling "Smiling 'Mac'" collected two more hits. McKean also hit safely twice, stole a base, and scored three times in the Maroons' 10 to 1 domination of Binghamton on September 2.[39]

Rochester kept nipping at Utica's heels. Before a home crowd on September 3, the Maroons beat the Pent Ups, 7 to 5, for their sixth win in a week. Ed McKean made his presence known with an RBI hit in the eighth inning. Rochester made it seven wins the following day, regaining second place; Bancroft had his team playing .612 ball on the season. McKean recorded three hits, scoring twice, in this 9 to 4 win over Syracuse. He walked in the first inning, reached second on a wild pitch, and got to third base on a passed ball by the catcher. Then he came home on the front end of a double steal with Lon Knight. He still wasn't finished. "McKean started the other half [of the first inning] with a wonderful assist," enthused the *Rochester Democrat and Chronicle* on September 5. "He stumbled and nearly fell, but fielded the ball to first in remarkable and sufficiently quick time just the same."

The personal height of the International League's first pennant race came, for McKean, in the September 6 contest against Utica. So many fans thronged into Culver Park that all the standing room along the foul lines was occupied before 8:00 am for the afternoon game. Rochester cranks had turned out to be a part of the series opener between the two contenders for the pennant. In the third inning, a "smiling McKean brought down a torrent of applause that echoed to the Four Corners by a clean home run, bringing in three men. It was fully five minutes before the applause subsided," reported to the September 7 *Democrat and Chronicle*. He did not disappoint. "McKean made the best assist of the game on [Jim] Halpin's hot liner" in the sixth, and he wound up with two hits in the 5–2 win." The inspired home team nearly shut out the Pent Ups the next afternoon, winning persuasively, 6 to 1, to tie for first place. Ed McKean, now called "Mac the hustler" by the Rochester press, was good for two hits and, in the second inning, "a clever assist." When Rochester played the Buffalo Bisons on September 8, McKean was still hustling. He opened up the sixth inning with one of his three hits in the game, took second on a wild pitch, "and came bounding over the plate" to score on a poor throw over to first base. He ran out his other two hits for triples.

Regardless of McKean's heroics, Utica was back in first place to stay on September 8, when Rochester lost at home to Buffalo while the Pent Ups were idle. The Bisons shut out the Maroons, 2 to 0, on that decisive day, after a one-man rally by McKean fell short in the seventh inning. With the score 1 to 0, he was stranded on third base after his hit and steal, and a passed ball. Buffalo managed to win only five times all year in its 14 meetings with Rochester, but two of those victories came in the crucial month of September.

The Maroons played an exhibition game of some note at Culver Field, on September 10, versus the Boston Beaneaters. Although the Rochesters pulled off a triple play in the fourth inning that did not involve McKean, it was still "'Little Mac' at short" whom the newspaper singled out for kudos. Frank Bancroft showcased his kid shortstop by batting him leadoff against the great Charlie Radbourn, who was only two seasons removed from posting a record 59 wins for him with Providence. McKean showed something of how far he'd come as a hitter, solving Old Hoss' specialty "out-curves" for a triple and a single.

Bancroft gave the ball to reliable Charlie Parsons for the September 15 home game with Hamilton. The Clippers scored five runs off Parsons, who was a solid 15–10 that year for the Maroons, to win in the ninth inning. McKean opened the scoring with a single, a stolen base, and a run on a hit by Lon Knight. He finished the game with three of Rochester's six hits off 19-year-old Mike Morrison. (The following season, Morrison would be McKean's teammate and start 40 games for the Cleveland Blues.) The next day brought another loss at home to Hamilton, and McKean's error led to the visitors' first run of the game. Even in its report on a disappointing loss, the local newspaper rhapsodized: "Probably the most interesting feature of the game was McKean's wonderful stop of Kellogg's ferocious grounder. Everybody thought it good for a base, but providence 'Mac' made a great running stop, and recovered in time to field it to first. He was heartily applauded." One can only imagine how satisfying it was for Ed McKean to rob Nate Kellogg of a hit, after Nashville had released McKean in favor of Kellogg only the year before. The reporter's pun on the city and the providential makes a neat epithet for the up-and-coming player. He continued with a rare early glimpse of the shortstop in the field: "McKean probably covers more ground than any other player in the nine. He runs in every corner of the field, and looks at a foul tip in a disappointed way, as if he wanted to run behind the batter and catch it."

During the pressure of the pennant drive, Ed McKean had hit safely in all 14 games from August 31 through September 14, amassing 27 base hits over two weeks. In the end, it was not enough—Rochester didn't have the starting pitching to take the pennant. Utica's team was led by Billy Serad's 30 wins, tops in the International League; Douglass Crothers was next with 27 victories for Syracuse. Bancroft miraculously coaxed and threatened 18 wins out of the wayward Jersey Bakely. Ensconced in second place with a week to play in the season, Frank Bancroft conceded the pennant to Utica and released some of his best players in a move to reduce the club's expenses.[40] Utica defeated Rochester in the season finale at Culver Field. The home crowd applauded just twice, both times for brilliant double plays that went McKean to Hackett to Kennedy. Veteran first baseman Doc Kennedy led the Maroons with his .341 batting average. He'd played on Cleveland clubs as far back as 1879; growing up in Grafton, McKean had undoubtedly known his name even then. Cleveland would be Ed McKean's next destination.

He was highly recommended by the stats he'd racked up in just 76 games for Rochester: 97 hits, 62 runs, a team-leading 29 stolen bases, and 109 total bases. McKean's final batting average of .305 placed him one point behind Toronto's batting champ, Jay Faatz; the two were destined to be teammates with Cleveland in 1888 and 1889. Next spring, *The Sporting News* pronounced Ed McKean "the best shortstop in the International League" for 1886, and nothing less than "the peer of Glasscock in the shortstop position."[41]

Directly following the last game of the exhausting season, Bancroft left for his New Bedford, Massachusetts, home for the offseason. Frank Bancroft would return to the major leagues in 1887, as the Philadelphia Athletics manager. Edward J. McKean's name does not appear on the list of Rochester players reserved for 1887, although the *Rochester Democrat and Chronicle* for September 25 reported he had already signed with the Maroons.[42] McKean's contract will set off the first of the two acrimonious contract disputes that were low points in his life in baseball. For the present, the new celebrity announced his plans to winter in Rochester.[43]

1895 Temple Cup: October 1, Cleveland

"All the time you're eating your breakfast,
I'll repeat 'The Walrus and the Carpenter' to you;
and then you can make believe
it's oysters, dear!"

—Lewis Carroll

Manager Hanlon and his Orioles weren't much interested in being in Cleveland. Baltimore had just won its second consecutive National League title in 1895. Three weeks earlier, the club had trounced the runners-up Spiders in a much-anticipated September series that effectively decided the pennant race. They'd vanquished the heralded Cyclone Young for one win, and his cohort Nig Cuppy for another, confirming the fabled superiority of the eastern teams (Baltimore, New York, Boston, Philadelphia, Brooklyn, and Washington) over the western (Cleveland, Chicago, Pittsburgh, Cincinnati, Louisville, and St. Louis). Many around the baseball world agreed. The game's two championship trophies, the Dauvrey and the Temple Cups, were in the possession of Boston and New York; Brooklyn had entered the 1890s as a powerhouse. Even perennial second-division Washington was empowered: Washington-based Nick Young happened to be the National League president. Meanwhile, Chicago and St. Louis, the dominant western franchises from the previous decade, had gotten old, along with the acts of Cap Anson and Arlie Latham. Baseball's civil war between East and West was reflected in battles in print between the *Sporting Life* of Philadelphia and *The Sporting News* of St. Louis.

During the regular season, on Saturday, September 7, the scheduled four-game showdown started out well for Cleveland. Cupid Childs threw out Kid Gleason, with the bases loaded in the ninth inning, and Nig Cuppy had outlasted Sadie McMahon, 4 to 3. The Spiders had performed ably in hostile

Union Park, where a playoff atmosphere prevailed. Every game in the series drew a better-than-Temple-Cup-average gate of more than 10,000 paid, many spectators travelling from considerable distances to stand among the overflow crowd in the outfield. Back in Cleveland, a city notorious for its poor attendance at baseball contests over the years, some 3,000 cranks packed the Euclid Theatre daily to follow the play-by-play of the away games over the telegraph.[1] After all, Cuppy's win put the Spiders 31 games over .500 for the season, just a game behind the first-place Orioles.

Cleveland supporters had reason to feel confident when the series resumed in Baltimore on Monday: 28-game-winner Denton Young was in line to take the ball for the Spiders. Young's blazing fast ball, following nine innings of George Cuppy's unsolvable slow pitches, was a formula almost certain to keep the Orioles hitters out of sorts. Young and Cuppy were the most successful pitching duo of the decade, garnering 381 victories between them in eight seasons.[2] But on this day, Wizard Hoffer was Cy Young's better, as he outpitched the Hall of Famer, 4 to 1.

Hoffer was on his way to 31 victories in his rookie season; after two more outstanding seasons with Baltimore, he was all but finished in the major leagues. The Spiders dropped to two games behind the Orioles, but still had a chance to tie for first place when they played a doubleheader at Union Park on the following Tuesday. Umpire Bob Easlie had a short fuse that day. A Farmer Young fastball had knocked him senseless, and he had had to be removed from the previous day's game in the second inning. So early in the first game of the doubleheader, he ejected Patsy Tebeau—in a stroke, effectively retiring Cleveland's manager and first baseman—for the offense of kicking. "Kicking" was the term in Ed McKean's day for arguing a call or decision, but it frequently meant the player also landing kicks and blows on the umpire. Tebeau was a master practitioner of both. Minus Tebeau, Cleveland lost this game to Sadie McMahon, whose chronically sore shoulder had kept him on the sidelines until deep into the season. Ed McKean's single was the only hit the Spiders could manage off McMahon, who wasn't even particularly sharp (he walked five batters). McKean also contributed two of the Spiders' five errors behind Nig Cuppy, as his team self-destructed to the joy of the afternoon tilt's overflow crowd. The final score might well have been worse. When the Orioles loaded the bases in the eighth inning, the game was called for darkness. Ned Hanlon and Patsy Tebeau couldn't even agree on how to divvy up the considerable gate, so the scheduled fourth game in Baltimore had to be cancelled. The Spiders departed for the friendlier confines of League Park three games behind in the standings, never to recover first place. Instead of settling matters between the two clubs, the head-to-head series and the suspended game resulted in conflicts that would be taken unresolved into the postseason. It all amounted to yet another contributing cause of Baltimore's profound ambivalence to playing this Temple Cup; the Spiders, on the other hand, looked to avenge their humiliation.

You could look it up. Baltimore had won the bragging rights; they were the best team in the League after dominating the nominal 132-game schedule. The Orioles felt they had nothing much to gain if they won the Temple Cup (maybe a split of another paltry series gate), but much to lose (another tarnished championship), just like last year. Hanlon's men had repeated as regular-season champions, but they weren't in the mood for a repeat performance of last postseason, when they'd unenthusiastically agreed to play the second-place New York Giants—and promptly got swept in four games. The winningest team in the 12-team National League wouldn't win a game in the Temple Cup until game four this year, when Cleveland was already in firm control of the series.

Moreover, the Orioles were bone tired. They had been sorely challenged to repeat as pennant winners. Baltimore had started the season slowly.[3] The ace of the 1894 staff couldn't pitch. In fact, veteran John McMahon's shoulder was so sore that Hanlon had to depend on Bill Hoffer, an untested rookie discovery from the Eastern League. Hoffer surprised by leading the team in wins. When slugging first baseman Dan Brouthers proved himself finished at age 37, his replacement Scoops Carey, another rookie, fielded brilliantly to earn his nickname and solidify the League's number one defense. No matter that second baseman Heinie Reitz broke his collarbone—manager Hanlon converted Kid Gleason, who had won 15 of his 20 starts for Baltimore the previous season, to the infield. Catcher Wilbert Robinson (like McKean) lost part of a finger to amputation—Ned Hanlon became an early practitioner of platooning. The champs got a boost when Sadie McMahon recovered in August; his four shutouts led the League in a customized warm-up for the playoffs. The Baltimore manager further bolstered his pitching staff by bringing in the brother of the famous John Clarkson, in a trade with St. Louis. Arthur Clarkson, who was called Dad in spite of the fact that he was the younger sibling, won 12 of his 15 decisions for Baltimore the rest of the way. Star third baseman John McGraw, the sparkplug of the Hibernian Orioles, suffered all season from hand injuries and attacks of malaria, so the irrepressible Hanlon ran a makeshift trio of Gleason, a mended Reitz, and Frank Bonner in and out of the lineup for 41 games—and Baltimore kept right on winning. All of Foxy Ned's moves turned to gold for the 1895 season, but the silver Temple Cup had so far escaped his grasp.

Edward Hugh Hanlon was a proven winner. His Orioles clubs took five

National League pennants from 1894 to 1900, including three consecutive. As a player, he had captained the Detroit Wolverines to their championship in 1887, and eight years before that he was a starter for an Albany team that claimed a minor league pennant. Ned Hanlon had been a standout defensive center fielder, breaking in with the Cleveland in 1880. He still holds the distinction of being the only NL Cleveland Blue in Cooperstown, but the light hitter made the Hall as a manager. Hanlon found himself when he came to Baltimore to manage at the start of 1892 season. He assembled an Orioles' dynasty in part by masterminding trades for shortstop Hughie Jennings and corner outfielders Joe Kelley and Willie Keeler, and then purchasing the contract of center fielder Steve Brodie. There was one conspicuous flaw in those Baltimore teams: Hanlon never was able to add an ace to his pitching staffs to match up against Cleveland's Cy Young or Boston's Kid Nichols or New York's Amos Rusie or Chicago's Clark Griffith.[4] Instead, Hanlon brought in fresh pitching talent on a conveyor belt—he somehow found Joe Corbett when he was pitching on the distant Pacific Coast—and his teams outhit, outfought, and fielded better than the opposition. Ned Hanlon was a pioneer of the new "scientific" or "inside" baseball. He employed innovative tactics, including the hit-and-run and the double steal, to give his teams a competitive edge.

But Hanlon's strategy for winning always remained the same—for the Orioles, along with Tebeau's Spiders, were the most successful practitioners of unreformed rowdy ball. Hanlon's teams intimidated umpires and opponents, without discrimination. In *The Irish in Baseball*, David L. Fleitz observes:

> Almost any decision [by an umpire] against the Orioles, no matter how mundane, could instigate a wild, unruly protest that sometimes involved the fans as well as the players on the field....With the umpires sufficiently cowed, [Hanlon's] Orioles directed a steady stream of rough, physical play against their opponents, especially on their home field. Tripping, shoving, and blocking base runners were daily occurrences, and [his captain] McGraw perfected the art of interrupting an opponent's progress around the bases by grabbing the runner's belt and holding on. On offense, the Baltimore players, urged on by [captain] McGraw's command, "Get at 'em!" slammed into and trampled over infielders and catchers, often with spikes flashing dangerously, leading to a large number of on-field brawls.[5]

Going into this Temple Cup showdown, the Cleveland Spiders were a tired team, too. All the way back in March, Ed McKean had half-jokingly indicated to Elmer Bates that he was already looking ahead to an offseason trip around the world—and then McKean, Jesse Burkett and Jimmy McAleer went on to play all 131 games of the Cleveland regular season. (Around the League, only Baltimore had multiple ironmen in 1895, shortstop Jennings and all three outfielders, Kelley, Brodie, and Keeler.) Indeed, the Spiders shortstop hadn't missed a game since his accident-marred 1892 season. That was the fall McKean performed so well in his first championship playoffs; but early in the regular season, his fielding and slugging had been hampered by a self-inflicted injury when he accidentally shot himself in the finger with a pistol teammate Jake Virtue had brought into the dressing room. McKean must have felt he'd let down his teammates and admirers in a moment's negligence. He rushed himself back into Patsy Tebeau's lineup, playing hurt, and pursued each game like a man on a mission.

Led by a rededicated Ed McKean, Cleveland was the best team in second half of the National League's "split season," and the franchise appeared in its first postseason that October. McKean hit .440 and accounted for six of the Spiders' 13 RBIs, but his team didn't win a game in the best-of-five tournament. Cy Young lost twice in a week, after pitching Cleveland to a tie in the series opener. All that was three years ago now, ancient history to McKean, who was coming off a banner 1895 season, his ninth in Cleveland, in which he averaged .342, with 17 triples and 119 runs batted in. He was weary but primed to perform on a winning playoff team this time around. He'd outhit the Boston shortstop, the talented Herman Long, by almost .220 in batting average in the 1892 "world's series"; this year, he'd worked himself back into a position to win what Baltimore's shortstop Hugh Jennings had failed at last year: William Temple's Cup. Ed McKean had willed himself to become one of the game's dominant shortstops. Yes, he and the Spiders were tired, through and through—but they were also driven, for once everybody in the same winning direction, by McKean's personal vendetta against losing, and the club's collective need to drum up revenue to meet payroll and keep the franchise in Cleveland.

Uncle Nick's schedule-makers gave Cleveland a week off before winding up the regular season with two games in Louisville. So they waited for the Baltimore to play out their season, the Spiders picked up exhibition games, in Finlay and Detroit, ostensibly for the players to earn pocket money and stay in game shape—but also to contribute to owner Frank Robison's purse. Accordingly, the Spiders took the field in Detroit, on September 23, and were unceremoniously beaten, with Bobby Wallace pitching, 10 to 8. Next day, Cleveland saved face by winning easily, 10 to 3.[6] Future Hall of Fame shortstop Wallace had performed well enough to win 12 games as the Spiders' number three starter in 1895, but he was not to touch a ball or a bat in the upcoming Temple Cup.

Robison's finance-minded scheduling was roundly criticized in *The Sporting News*:

> If the Spiders lose [this year's Temple Cup series] it will be owing to the fact that they are bundled about from one town to another to play exhibition games instead of being given a chance to rest up on days when a league game is not

scheduled, and because they have been hustled to other league cities to play Sunday games which they have invariably lost. Sunday games are not played in Cleveland, and Tebeau's warriors have been rushed onto trains after the Saturdays' games and carried to St. Louis, Chicago, Cincinnati or Louisville to play Sundays throughout the season. Riding all night and half the day, as they were compelled to in order to play in St. Louis or Louisville, naturally militated against the Clevelands' chances of victory, and the return ride did not land them rested up for Monday's game, by any means. But one or two of these Sunday trips have resulted favorably to Tebeau, and, in addition, he has been compelled to play countless exhibition games between league dates. Of course, this is due in a great measure to the poor support accorded the Spiders in their own town, but it would have been a good stroke of policy to let the dauntless Clevelands get a little rest-up occasionally. They are beyond all question the pluckiest nine in the league ... and despite criticism of the severest character have never shown the white feather, nor the slightest sign of discouragement.[7]

The newspaper's commentary does raise the intriguing possibility that the Spiders might have taken the pennant over Baltimore in 1895, and drawn more paying fans for League Park games, if the team had played at home on Sundays. Baseball on the Sabbath, of course, was still illegal in Cleveland, and, as we shall see, its opponents were busy organizing.

To salve the rigors of playing out the long season, the barnstorming Spiders created their own fun distractions along the way, which evidently included the spinning of tall tales. In his famous career, Jesse Burkett incited fans, baited umpires, and ruthlessly razed opposing pitchers from the coaching box; Harvey Frommer properly calls him "a one-man riot."[8] However, The Crab, not known for his sense of humor or his fielding, "set a new fashion out in Indiana," as the tall tale was relayed by *The Sporting News*:

When Cleveland was on one of its barn-storming tours a game was played in Elkhart. It was in the eighth inning, and the Cleveland scores had almost reached three figures, while the locals hadn't made a run. The best batsman of the Elkhart team was at the plate, and the crowd yelled for him to save them from the disgrace of a shut out. He whaled away, and by sheer luck sent the ball sailing far over Burkett's head. Jess happened to spy a fellow in the near-by crowd with a bicycle. He tore the machine from his hands, mounted it in hot haste and chased down the sphere in time to hold the runner on third. Then he convinced the umpire that he had a right to use a bicycle to chase flies with and assured him that it was often done in the big league. Now every ball player in Elkhart is getting measured for a machine.[9]

At times, it seemed as if the National League were treating the playoffs as a joke. Most recently, the League trumped even the Baltimore club's indifference to the Temple Cup games. James F. McDonald, one of four umpires who would be officiating the playoff games in teams of two, received a telegram during his final ball game of the season. It contained President Young's last-minute orders for the first-year ump to report to Cleveland, on October 1, ready to help officiate the Temple Cup.[10] And, starting in July, the awarding of the Temple Cup had itself been the subject of an especially divisive debate as to whether the trophy should even go to the winner of the playoffs each year. The brouhaha was initiated by Dodgers president Byrne, who argued that the Temple Cup should stay in New York, with last year's trophy-winning Giants. Charles H. Byrne was fed up. Three years ago, his Brooklyn Trolley Dodgers took the American Association pennant into a "world's series" against the National League Giants; since then, the Amercian Association (and the Players' League, as well) had collapsed, leaving the 12-team NL monopoly that would be the shape of baseball for the decade—and providing no system for playoffs. Now Byrne was boldly asserting that this year's NL pennant winner must play the 1894 champions (which happened to be the club in his neighboring borough) for the honor of the Temple Cup. Byrne's scheme was transparently self-serving—it set up the possibility for a playoff series between the two New York teams—but not so easy to dismiss by Nick Young and the League, who were interested in fielding a national postseason series that would be more popular with the fans. The Temple Cup was a loser: at the gate, with the club owners, and their players. But the biggest failure was the National League's, for not coming up with a playoff plan. Of course, the League was also once again exhibiting its unofficial bias, in favor of its eastern clubs.

John Montgomery Ward, who had played for Byrne's Dodgers and retired as playing manager of the Giants after their 1894 Temple Cup victory over the Orioles, came out forcefully against Byrne's plan a week before the playoffs were set to begin.[11] A the end of that week, *The Sporting News* could definitively announce:

> It is settled beyond question that the two clubs ending one and two will compete for the Temple cup and the accompanying gate receipts. In view of the controversy that has been going on among the various clubs on the subject, "Uncle Nick" Young, in his semi-official capacity [as league president and first among owners], wrote a letter to Mr. Temple, the donor of the trophy, a few days ago for his decision on the subject. The reply has just been received at League headquarters [so, in effect, Temple took the decision, at Young's urging], and the substance of it is that the prize is to be competed for by the two teams standing one and two in the championship column at the close of the season.[12]

Nick Young got around to officially settling the debate by conveying William Temple's final decision in a document to club owners on September 7—only three weeks before Cup play.

Now that the regular season was over, and a playoff scenario was at last in place, Ned Hanlon knew the Temple Cup games would be written up in the newspapers as a clash of the Hibernians and, once the teams were on the field, played for blood. They were bound to be a repeat of the September matchup between the two contenders for first place. Back in early September, *The Sporting News* preview of Cleveland's series in Baltimore sounded like today's NASCAR fan wishing against a crack up, while at some deep level, hoping to witness one:

First as team captain and then as manager, Ned Hanlon won six National League pennants, including three consecutive with Baltimore (1894, 1895, and 1896). His rookie season as a Cleveland outfielder in 1880 qualifies him as the only member of the National League Blues who is enshrined in Cooperstown (Library of Congress).

> When the Baltimores and Clevelands meet for their last series, which starts in Baltimore next Saturday, there will be fur flying sure enough. These will be battles well worth traveling miles to see. When such scrappers as Patsy Tebeau, Jack O'Connor, Jesse Burkett, Ed McKean, Joe Kelley, "Tough" Brodie, "Mugsy" McGraw, and Clarke are on contending teams and fighting tooth, jaw and toe nail for such an honor as the league championship there is bound to be fun and lots of it. Every true friend of the game hopes nothing will occur to make one of these violent exponents of the game lose his temper and control to such an extent that an outbreak will start a free fight. The Baltimore bleacher habitués are notoriously the worst behaved of any in the Eastern division cities, and it would not take much of a spark to start a row there that would hurt the game for years to come. At the first sign of "dirty" ball playing by either side the bars will be let down, there will be a turning of tricks at which the players on these two teams are particularly adept, and if in the working of one of these a Baltimore player should get a hard dump to terra firma or a spike slicing, the trouble will start.[13]

In fact, the "row ... that would hurt the game" *would* come to pass, the following month, with the riot by Baltimore fans at game five of the Temple Cup.

The rowdy game, with its potential for hooliganism on the field and rioting in the grandstands, was not without its proponents. Albert Mott, the Baltimore columnist, regularly defended the Orioles' take-no-prisoners style for the ginger it added to contests. "We don't want any dirty ball playing and rowdyism, most assuredly," he wrote in the middle of the 1894 season, "but it is absolutely necessary that the players should have their feelings worked up to a strong point in order to furnish the public good sport and an honest[ly played] one. The 'I'll-do-my-duty-and-earn-my-wages' sort of players in a team will neither win games nor please the general public. As soon as a game is quiet it is tame and *lifeless*," Mott contended. "You can howl at Tebeau, Tom Tucker and little McGraw, but whenever you succeed in entirely suppressing these types of innocently scrapping ball players you will at the same time suppress your spectators."[14]

Indications are that fans in Cleveland appreciated their home team's rowdy play, as well. Back in 1894, the Spiders were holding their spring training at the Cleveland Athletic Club when the latter staged a burlesque at the Euclid Opera House, entitled *Moses Cleveland Up to Date* and featuring a number of Spiders players in a brief skit. Jesse Burkett, playing himself, hits a home run only to be called out at home plate; the umpire's decision ignites a row, The Crab's teammates joining in.[15] The popular reception of this low-comedy sketch suggests there was a self-conscious entertainment side to the rowdy style, something Clevelanders could identify with and chuckle about. However, the apologist Mott was dead serious about the impact in the won-lost column of rowdy techniques. Writing days before the first game of the 1895 Temple Cup, Mott attributed a decisive Baltimore victory, the September 10 rematch against Nig Cuppy, to a dirty tactic associated with the rowdy game.

> When Cuppy pitched that invincible game at Baltimore [the Spiders' win on September 7], and when [Boileryard] Clarke and [Frank] Bowerman and [Joe] Kelley and everybody else had failed to move the nerve of the cool Clevelander, McGraw proved by perfectly legitimate means to become such an irritant that for the first time Cuppy looked toward the coacher, displayed the slightest temper in the delivery of the succeeding ball, and it was hit out hard and safe. There was not another man in the whole National League that could have attracted the attention of Cuppy from his work that day.[16]

A decade later, during the startup of the Indians and the "sanitized" American League, Cleveland sportswriter Ed Bang would blame the chronically poor attendance at League Park on the rowdy game favored by the Spiders. "Unquestionably the use of billingsgate, foul language and offensive pantomime as a means of rattling opposing pitchers or batsmen reached its greatest development in the days of the old Baltimore Orioles and the Cleveland Spiders under Patsy Tebeau. Both were great teams and the chances are," Bang postulates, "each would have been just as successful with the offensive tactics eliminated." As for why this did not occur, Bang writes:

> But the club owners could not be convinced of that. They considered foul language and indecent gestures the very embodiment of "aggressive" ball playing, and they were cordially supported by the press of their own towns.... In encouraging these tactics, the owners ... showed they did not understand the character of their own patrons, who emphasized their condemnation of rowdy ball ... by staying away from the grounds. Baltimore, with a three-time winner, became a minor league town ... and it took years and years for the management of the Cleveland Club to induce the fans of the Forest City to forget the methods of Tebeau, McKean and the rest of the bunch."[17]

It's fair to say that Tebeau could spout more profanities and swear words than his contemporaries J.S. Farmer and W.E. Henley could collect in their seven-volume *Slang and Its Analogues* (1890–1904). It's also true that Cleveland ranked 11th among the 12 National League clubs in attendance from 1894 through 1896, including the two Temple Cup contenders. Cleveland was last in the League in attendance for 1897 and 1898; the infamous 1899 Spiders, their best players having been transferred to St. Louis, played only a handful of games at home.[18] On the other hand, in his anatomy of a traumatized fan base, Bang doesn't take into consideration two salient facts: Cleveland was one of the smallest markets in the National League, and the ban on Sunday baseball made it possible to play only one game on a weekend. The population for the city of Cleveland was higher only than that of Pittsburgh, and nearly two million less than New York.[19] Baseball clubs drew fans in the nineteenth century mostly from inner-city workers and dwellers; games began at 3:00 or 3:30 in the afternoon to facilitate the working man. On weekends, Cleveland could do no better than hope to interest those fans from the surrounding area who were fortunate enough to work only half a day, and were willing to travel for hours round-trip on the train, for its handful of Saturday games.

Franklin Lewis, the author of the first book-length history of the Cleveland Indians, blames McKean personally for the Spiders' poor finish in 1897, the season after two straight Temple Cup appearances: "The Spiders were fifth, largely due to a policy of argument instituted by the team captain and shortstop, Ed McKean[, and the team's] constant squawking to the umpires." According to Lewis, the moral of the tale comes when "finally McKean's tongue was curbed and the team settled down ... to take on the manners and appearance of a big-league team."[20] Lewis was writing to a Cleveland readership flush from the triumph of the 1948 World Series and innocent of the nineteenth-century club. The writing of history can be a way of forgetting. Both Bang and Lewis dismissed the pagan Spiders from the tradition of the modern Indians, and discounted the first Cleveland baseball championship.

But all this was in the unborn future. On October 1, 1895, Ed McKean and the bawdy, bulldozing, boisterous, belligerent, bullying brigands who called themselves the Cleveland Spiders were on the eve of their Temple Cup debut, a fateful match between the two National League rosters "with the highest percentage of Irishmen." As David Fleitz points out, the Orioles and Spiders were also "the most disorderly, and games between the two clubs often featured fights, beanball wars, and fan violence. Mobs of fans in both cities turned out early to pelt the opponents with garbage, rocks, and bottles as they arrived at the park, and at game's end those same fans would often storm the field and attack the players and umpire." In Fleitz's considered opinion, "The 1895 season may have been the worst in the game's history for player and fan behavior with the Orioles and Spiders as the main offenders."[21]

Five or six players in the Spiders regular lineup were Irish: McKean, Burkett, McAleer, Chippy McGarr, Jack O'Connor and, if we count self-identity over genetics, Patsy Tebeau. Ned Hanlon and six of his championship Orioles starters were Irish, when either Sadie McMahon or Dad Clarkson pitched. His lineup featured Joe Kelley, Willie Keeler, John McGraw, Kid Gleason, and McKean's counterpart at shortstop, Hughie Jennings. Catcher Wilbert Robinson's wife was born in Ireland. It has also been said that Baltimore's "eighth Irish teammate" was Thomas Murphy, the groundskeeper at Union Park. Murphy's covert contributions to the Orioles' home-field advantage included sprinkling soap flakes around the pitcher's box, after warning his team's infielders to assiduously avoid the slippery spots.[22]

What was pretty much an open secret in Ed McKean's day was baseball's bigotry. Two weeks before the playing of the 1895 Cup series, *The Sporting News* ran an article on "the relative success of ball players of Irish and German descent." McKean is listed therein, alongside Irish shortstops Corcoran, Reilly, Sullivan, and Coogan (but omitting Jennings, who was the son of immigrants). "There has always been an amicable dispute among ball cranks as to the relative value of Irish and German players. Each nationality has it warm adherents," the writer explained, "and each faction can see all the good points in its own race and all the failings of the other. Germans, being heavy, solid, enduring men, make good catchers. The Irish are more active and possess better heads for action—think more quickly and devise plans and schemes better."[23] To be fair, it must be remembered that Irish players, managers, and even umpires had earned their reputation around the League as fighters. On the field of competition, Ed McKean was an inveterate umpire hater and an intimidator of teams. We can only wonder how much of his combativeness (tempered by his after-hours conviviality) was inherited from an Irish father's code of fighting for what will not be given willingly.

An *Atlantic Monthly* article from 1896 presents a blatant account of what Ed McKean, and his fellow Hibernian players, encountered as baseball's original racial barrier. In "The Irish in American Life," Henry Childs Merwin surmised that Irish-Americans were subservient by their nature and social conditions. The openly contemptuous Social Darwinist portrays the Irishman as a "notoriously a passionate, impulsive, kindly, unreflecting, brave, nimble-witted man; but he lacks the solidity, the balance, the judgment, the moral staying power of the [Englishman]." Furthermore, as a result of "long and cruel subjection to [England] the Irish character has ... acquired a quality of deceit, of unveracity," as well as "a morbid sensitiveness, a readiness to take offense." Merwin's Irish immigrants pose a specific threat to American democracy because "as Catholics,...they owe allegiance first to the Pope, and only secondarily to the government of the United States." The essayist concludes the Irish—no better than poor farmers—are best suited for domestic servants, or Democratic politicians![24]

Ed Andrews, who joined his quondam Akron teammate Ed Swartwood to umpire in the National League after their playing days, swore that he quit the profession out of disgust with the hooliganism of three managers: Patsy Tebeau, Ned Handon, and Buck Ewing, a non–Irishman who had played for Tebeau.[25] Some of the most successful umpires during the period often retaliated in response to the rowdies. Irish umpire Tim Hurst gained Tebeau's respect and admiration that way. In an 1898 interview, the Spiders manager spoke sentimentally about his off-the-field comrade and now managerial adversary Hurst: "Yes, I long for the return to the diamond of that roguish, circular, Hibernian visage and those bold hazel eyes that snapped like flint. I mean my friend Tim Hurst, one of the quaintest characters the game has ever produced. We have been mixed up in some odoriferous cross-talks on the ballfield." Patsy went on to give readers a PG taste of the salty gamesmanship the manager and umpire enjoined, in a game at League Park in the 1895 season:

> The Orioles were the attraction and there wasn't standing room in the deep field. We roped off the grounds and went to work. In the first inning, Tim sent Billy Keeler to first on balls, and catcher Chief Zimmer argued that Tim had remained blind to a strike. "Go on, you odor of rare Limburger," said Tim. "If you don't quit shootin' that Swiney con into me, I'll give you a kick in the chest." I broke into the conversation and offered to send a right into Tim's face. "You're a chesty little Mick," said I, "and if you don't give us what's coming to us in this game I'll cut down the ropes [holding back the overflow crowd] and let that mob have it out with you." "T'hell with the mob," said Tim, "and, just to show you that I

won't renege on you or the crowd, I'll just give them a chance." The next man at-bat was Joe Kelley. Joe sent a liner 20 feet to the foul of the third base line. "G'wan and take your base, Joe," yelled Tim. "It's fair this time." Then he threw his cap on the grass, doubled his fists, took a hop, step and jump, and let his Owney McGinty howl from that falsetto of his. "Yes, b'God, it's foul, Tebeau, you big pimple head! It's a foul and let's see what that mob will do! Cut the ropes, Pat Tebeau! Cut the ropes! I don't care for anyone in your Salvation Army burg from the sheriff to the dogcatcher!"[26]

McGinty was the Irish mobster behind the Mounds Casino, conveniently located outside the Cleveland city limits. The Catholic boy McKean was seldom known to swear when he "kicked." He left that duty to the capable lungs of his teammates Burkett, O'Connor and, of course, Tebeau.

Hanlon's managerial opponent, Oliver Wendell Tebeau, "was an Irishman by choice, not by birth." When Oliver was a lad in St. Louis, the Irish construction workers he idolized christened him Patsy; he grew into the nickname and became more Irish than the Irishmen.[27] Tebeau learned the rowdy game when he played first base for the Peach Pies, a Mound City semipro team that included Jack O'Connor catching the legendary Silver King. The notoriously quick-tempered, foul-mouthed Peach Pie O'Connor's nickname seemed ironic. He was also known as Rowdy Jack. Patsy Tebeau employed his friend—in right field, at first base and behind the plate—on every Spiders team he managed. Nearing the end of his 21-year career, O'Connor was still fighting. As a member of the Pirates, in

Rowdy Pat Tebeau fashioned the "Hibernian" Spiders after his own image, and made McKean his team's enforcer. Led by playing-manager Tebeau, Cleveland teams posted a .570 winning percentage during the regular season, and played for three postseason championships over a six-year span from 1892 to 1896 (*The Sporting News*/Mears Auctions).

a July 26, 1901, game, "he started a brawl in St. Louis reminiscent of Ireland's infamous old Donneybrook fairs. He punched the Cardinals' playing manager, Patsy Donovan, then pitcher Ed Murphy of the Cardinals decked Jack."[28] Addie Joss always remembered the verbal abuse O'Connor and Burkett showered on him from the coachers' boxes in his debut game in 1902.[29]

The yannigan Tebeau had secured a 20-game tryout with Cap Anson's Colts toward the end of the 1887 season, at the time Ed McKean was capping his successful rookie season on Cleveland's American Association Blues. By 1889, the Cleveland team (now playing in the National League as the Spiders) needed a third baseman and signed Patsy Tebeau. In the Brotherhood year of 1890, he jumped across town to the Players' League Cleveland Infants, along with most of the Spiders lineup except for McKean and Chief Zimmer. Tebeau got his first crack at managing when Ted Larkin was fired by the seventh-place Infants in late July. The team floundered to a 21–30 record under the novice manager, and finished seventh in the standings for the Players' League's only season. Tebeau was welcomed back to play for the Spiders for 1891, following the collapse of the Players' League, and, on July 11, he took advantage of another of that club's mid-season firings, when Frank Robison appointed him to manage in place of Bob Leadley. He was all of 27 years old and already confirmed in his ways.[30] "My instructions to my players are to win games," Tebeau proclaimed, "and I want them to be aggressive. A milk and water, goody-goody player can't wear a Cleveland uniform."[31]

Among the newly appointed manager's initial moves were to make Ed McKean his team captain—replacing Charlie Zimmer, a calm man on the field, and never known to take a drink or smoke—and add two more Irishmen, Jack O'Connor and Crab Burkett. The Hibernian Spiders infield worked best when Patsy Tebeau's legs and ailing back allowed him to play first base. He and Ed McKean played together particularly well. Elmer Bates remembered a patented 3–6–3 double play he claimed Tebeau and McKean pulled off at least "fifteen times" in 1896:

> The play was practically invented by Tebeau, as no other first baseman I have ever seen play has ever made it more than once or twice in a season. With a base runner on first and a right-handed batter up Pat would play in for the assist, nailing his man at second by a quick throw to McKean and then getting the ball back with an even quicker throw from McKean and putting out the batter ... [It was] a double play that has to be made in in chain lightning time and yet has to be made so quietly that many of the dolts who attend games never appreciated it.[32]

Manager Tebeau proved to be popular with the Cleveland fans (presumably the dolts and baseball-smart alike), right up until his last year at the helm of the Spiders, because his teams won ball games. In the view of at least one "poetical correspondent," it was Patsy Tebeau and his rowdy game that put the city on the map.

> The United States is very large,
> And full of varied fun;
> Yet Cleveland town is dying;
> Its mourning has begun.
> Amid the nation's progress,
> It was never known to nap,
> But Patsy Tebeau is the man
> Who has put it on the map.
>
> The pines [bleacher seat patrons] were never heard from
> Until Tebeau did appear
> Upon a Cleveland diamond
> Unconscious of all fear.
> The nerve and vim of Patsy,
> And his great desire to scrap,
> Have been the means of placing
> That jay town on the map....[33]

Patsy Tebeau had fought alongside his Hibernian Spiders all the way to the national arena of the Temple Cup, and the now the cranks in Cleveland closed ranks behind him. The 1895 playoffs, advertised as a blood match between the two most feared teams in baseball, were contested at the precise apotheosis of the Emerald Age. Just a season later, following the calamity of the fans' riot in Baltimore, would arrive the disastrous after-shocks of the baseball riots in Louisville, and Tebeau's assault of a Cleveland reporter. Irish baseball, and the legacy of McKean, would soon be in ruins.

Three

The Invention of the Slugging Shortstop (1887–1888)

> Perhaps McKean was the harder hitter
> ...when it came to driving them out.
> —*Pittsburgh Press*, September 7, 1919

Arguably, Ed McKean invented the slugging shortstop. Before McKean's emergence in the big leagues, a club generally filled the shortstop position with a good defensive player who hit a little. Beginning in the late 1880s, a handful of other shortstops, most notably Jack Glasscock and Herman Long, also brought a new dimension to their team's offense. But no early shortstop was able to fashion the dozen power-hitting seasons that McKean did. You might say, in terms of offensive production and physical build, Ed McKean was the original Honus Wagner. Upon his death, the *Pittsburgh Press* remembered that McKean, along with Jack Glasscock, Hugh Jennings, and Wagner, had been "classified in their day as the greatest shortstops in the game. Wonderful infielders and great-batsmen they were." Honus Wagner's hometown newspaper went even further in its final judgment of Ed McKean's slugging: "Perhaps McKean was the harder hitter of the four when it came to driving them out."[1]

McKean and company changed the shortstop's function. Back in the days when baseball was a gentleman's club sport, Dr. Daniel L. Adams was probably the first shortstop.[2] The pioneer was mostly utilized as a fourth outfielder, or "short fielder," but he was sometimes brought into the Knickerbockers infield. Dickey Pearce, shortstop for the Brooklyn Atlantics teams in the 1860s, was primarily an infielder who could also range into the outfield to make a play. It was left to light-hitting Arthur Irwin to introduce the fielder's glove to shortstops, when he performed with the Providence Grays in 1885.[3] Boston's George Wright regularly set himself beyond the restrictions of the baselines before the pitch. Probably the heaviest-hitting shortstop before Ed McKean, Wright was the 1870s' equivalent of the slugger.[4] Soon after McKean's Cleveland club joined the National League, the shortstop position was attracting some of the game's great "heavy hitters," including Ed Delahanty, Ned Williamson, Hugh Jennings, and Bill Dahlen.[5]

Ed McKean brashly announced his coming of age in the majors by going on a 23-game hitting streak before his 18th birthday. That's according to the rule for the 1887 season only, which counted a walk as a hit. In any year, the rookie shortstop can be said to have begun his career in view of the Cleveland cranks by getting on base for nearly two dozen games; and he hit safely, according to modern revised rules, in his first 19 big league games. Major league baseball had not been played in Cleveland since its franchise was dropped by the National League two years earlier. The city was eager to welcome the reconstituted Cleveland Blues, who were replacing the Pittsburgh club in the American Association, and its boy phenom from Lorain County. It was common knowledge that McKean had come perilously close to spending another season in Rochester.

Before McKean could play ball for Cleveland, a vexing matter had to be settled: Had he or had he not already contracted with Rochester for 1887? What the newspapers in Cleveland and Rochester bandied about as The McKean Case was more or less your typical contract squabble in an era of players "jumping" teams and leagues, and owners invoking or ignoring the rules they'd made. In September 1886, elated after their rousing finish to the International League season, the Rochester front office overlooked the National Agreement deadlines, and signed their star shortstop early. McKean, all of 17 years old and successful for the first time in his baseball life, would have been eager to re-sign with the Maroons and play a full season at shortstop. Two months later, when the American Association granted Cleveland the new franchise, McKean saw the opportunity to return home to northern Ohio, and play in a major league (albeit, for the same $1,400 minimum pay observed by both the American Association and the International League). And so it came to pass that Ed McKean inked a contract with Cleveland. Rochester management was quick to remind McKean that he had signed not one but two contracts with them. As February 1887 came around, and with it plans for spring training, Rochester club secretary S.D.W. Cleveland charged that the Blues had no legal claim to McKean, whatsoever. He apparently stretched the truth by adding that a four-member arbitration committee for professional baseball had confirmed his view; in fact, both clubs were awaiting Nick Young's word on where Ed McKean would play in 1887—if anywhere.[6]

At least part of the confusion in the newspaper reportage came from mis-

THREE. *The Invention of the Slugging Shortstop (1887–1888)*   73

taking Cleveland the city for Cleveland the Rochester secretary.[7] In the second week of February, *Sporting Life* reported that McKean was blacklisted, meaning he could not play professional baseball, "under provision of Section 33 of [the] American Association Constitution."[8] One week later, recently hired Cleveland manager Jimmy Williams spoke for the club: "The case of McKean is in the hands of the American Association. It can reinstate him if he complies with the Association's rules and signs a Cleveland contract. Rochester's recourse is to take the matter to the Arbitration Committee." Williams added that he was willing to abide by an arbitration committee's decision; the Blues stood ready to reinstate him with Cleveland, or release him to Rochester. Ed McKean had been in Cleveland on Wednesday, February 9, to talk with Williams.[9] The would-be player maintained that he'd signed only once with Rochester—before December 18, 1886, or the day of his agreement with Cleveland—and that the Rochester contract was dated November 1, although he'd signed it on September 25. McKean went on to visit Youngstown—he would have sought Jim McAleer's council there—before returning to Grafton to wait out the decision on his baseball future.

    The local sportswriter who built the case for Ed McKean, and for the American Association in Cleveland, was the same innovator who would later originate horse racing's daily form and attempt to organize a Players' League club. It was F.H. Brunell, in his column for *Sporting Life* on February 23, who made McKean's best case. Brunell wrote to brush aside recent criticism by two of baseball's most influential commentators, Henry Chadwick and Oliver Perry Caylor, both men charging the Cleveland club with acting too extremely in McKean's instance. At the time, Chadwick was commonly referred to as Father Chadwick, in deference to his formative influence on the sport, as well as his continued pronouncements, which were taken by many as baseball gospel. O.P. Caylor had launched into careers in law and journalism before he'd masterminded the building of the American Association team in his native Cincinnati. Caylor was sitting editor of the influential *Reach Guides*. When Chadwick and Caylor spoke, they spoke for the baseball establishment.

    Undaunted, Brunell went further to address Rochester's latest threat, having found baseball law unjust, to pursue the case in common law courts. In fact, Brunell pointed out, since Rochester was a chartered member of the International League, it was not entitled to sign players for the 1887 season until November 1, 1886, *one week after* McKean was claimed to have signed with them. At length, after five anxious weeks for McKean and the Blues, *Sporting Life* ran two stories on March 16, one from its correspondent in Rochester and another by Brunell. The first piece refers to letters from McKean in which he indicated his desire to play in Cleveland; however, the Rochester reporter backs McKean's version of the timing of the contract. This reporter establishes that McKean did, indeed, sign the one contract with Rochester, written by F. R. Winnie (then Maroons club president) and entrusted, on September 25, 1886, to S.D. Cleveland (who became secretary for the club on November 1). The so-called second contract that outgoing team secretary J.A. Ware produced—drawn up by S.D. Cleveland and signed by McKean on November 1—was actually a pay voucher now in the hands of Nick Young, complete with a seven-page affidavit and statement of the known facts.

In the second article, printed under the headline "How McKean's Case Was Settled," Frank Brunell had the happy ending of the story to tell: Rochester had granted McKean's release for $300 and his return of the $150 pay advance; the player would soon be reinstated by the American Association; afterward, McKean would get to sign a fresh contract with the Cleveland Blues. According to Brunell, "McKean settled the case himself" by writing Rochester president Howe and demanding his release on the grounds that the club had "duped" him by the ploy of his December advance. It was clear that McKean decided to accept Rochester's terms rather than spend time and money to go before Young's arbitration committee. Brunell happily closes his article with the heady prediction that "McKean is another Glasscock and [Germany] Smith."

The McKean signing was just one indication of a ball club having to scramble to assemble a 12-man roster at the 11th hour. There was, in 1887, no expansion draft of designated players from the other American Association clubs, and the National League wanted to run the whole league out of business, anyhow. In his analysis of the American Association, David Nemec charges that "The Cleveland club had money and brains behind it but little luck." The wealthy Robison brothers left personnel decisions up to club secretary Davis Hawley.[10] It was Hawley's decision, for one, to hire Jimmy Williams to manage the Blues. Williams had previously managed in St. Louis, but his genuine talent was for organizing—he had served as the first secretary of the American Association, and he later aided Ban Johnson to reorganize the Western League.[11] Williams was poor at handling the "hard cases" on the roster and, in Cleveland, he was immediately tested by pitchers One Arm Daily and Charlie Sweeney. To Hawley's credit, he did discover and sign up-the-middle stability for Cleveland teams, in McKean and later Chief Zimmer and Jimmy McAleer, but that became evident only in the long term.

The first spring training for the Blues was "short and sweet," reported *Sporting Life*; it consisted mostly of three games in Cleveland with the local Malleables, Electrics, and Shamrocks, followed by away games at the Mansfields, the Akrons, and the Cantons.[12] In the April 11 warm-up exhibition in

Irish-born Ohio baseball legend Tony Mullane (left) served up Ed McKean's first base hit in the major leagues. Three years earlier, he'd teamed up with Hank O'Day (right) to constitute the entire Toledo Blue Stockings pitching staff. O'Day also pitched against McKean, and later umpired many memorable Cleveland games (courtesy John Husman/Toledo-Lucas County Public Library).

Cleveland against Toronto, major leaguer McKean must have savored his two hits in seven at-bats against an International League team, more than reason enough to overlook his error in the field. The Torontos were trying out a boy named Barrett, fresh from the Alliance, Ohio, club, and it turned out to be a baptism by fire; Cleveland amassed eight home runs on the day, two by Pete Hotaling but none by McKean.[13] McKean's initial plate appearance for the day must have been the first time he couldn't call for a high or low pitch, due to this season's change in the rules.

He found it easy enough to adjust to the new rule and the new league. Ed McKean hit safely in his first month in the majors. His first four games were multi-hit performances. In 84 at-bats during the streak, McKean made 29 hits, good for a .345 batting average. (By my count, he was awarded a "first base on balls," popularly known as a "phantom" hit, an additional six times—it took five balls for a walk, four strikes for a strikeout in 1887—so fans at the time figured he was hitting .372.) Those base hits included a double, two triples, and a home run.[14]

Ed McKean's regular season debut as a Blue, on April 16, was Cincinnati's season opener. McKean batted second in the lineup, behind Pete Hotaling, and both players had three hits off Tony Mullane. But the Redlegs won easily, the first batters of the game tallying five runs off George Pechiney, a native of the Queen City, and two more in second. It was a sloppy game, performed in the cold before only 3,000 onlookers; of the 22 runs scored, only 11 were earned. The Blues rookie shortstop made one of the team's five errors on the afternoon. Both pitchers showed the effects of the raw weather: winner Mullane walked seven and threw a wild pitch; loser Pechiney also walked seven and surrendered 18 hits in the 16 to 6 shellacking. The catchers were victimized for 11 stolen bases, two by White Wings Tebeau, Patsy's older brother.[15] The next day, McKean recorded the first of his 158 career triples, and added a single against Jumbo McGinnis, the winning pitcher. George Washington McGinnis was a seasoned veteran, starting his career back in the old National Association in 1873. In the final game in Cincinnati, on April 20, McKean stroked two more hits in five at-bats against Mike Shea, but made his second and third errors in the early going. The Blues lost again, 14 to 6, as Billy Crowell was saddled with one of his 31 losses for the season, second most in the American Association. Crowell had pitched in the Southern League in 1885, winning 14 games for Nashville in the wake of Ed McKean's release. (Another McKean teammate on the original American Association Blues, outfielder Scrappy Carroll, was with both Southern League Memphis and the Western League's Cleveland Cardinals for 1885. Also, Blues utilityman Jim Toy had played for New Brighton against McKean and the Youngstowns in 1884, then briefly

THREE. *The Invention of the Slugging Shortstop (1887–1888)* 77

with Oswego and Utica in the International League in McKean's breakout year of 1886. Toy made a toy-sized first baseman at five-foot-six. James Madison Toy was among the first Native American players.)

The box score for Ed McKean's fourth game, this one in Louisville, looks nearly identical to the one for the day before: the consistent McKean went two-for-five, the erratic McKean committed two miscues, and once again the Blues starter lost badly. Cleveland did jump out to a 3 to 0 lead in the first inning, but poor George Pechiney was slammed for nine Colonels runs in the third. In the loss to Colonels lefthander Toad Ramsay, McKean stole his first big league base; his keystone partner swiped three. Stricker and McKean ran loose on the base paths in 1887—stealing a combined 162 bags, 76 by McKean—the season a runner taking an extra base was given a stolen base. On April 23, McKean was credited with two more hits in six at-bats against Louisville's Ice Box Chamberlain, although one of the "hits," a "first base on balls," is no longer officially recognized as a base hit.

McKean's initial game in St. Louis (where he would end his career as a Perfecto in 1899) was notable for his first career double, recorded against the esteemed Silver King on April 27. Nineteen-year-old Charles Frederick King was destined to win 32 times that season, as the Browns took the pennant by 14 games. King was part of a troika of a rotation, with Bob Caruthers and Dave Foutz, deployed by playing-manager Charles Comiskey. His outfielder Tip O'Neil was the league's best hitter, retrospectively awarded a Triple Crown. He also led the American Association in hits, runs, doubles, triples, and slugging. In the last game of the series, McKean notched his first career home run—off a pitch by Foutz—and scored three runs, but Cleveland continued to lose on their way to a last-place finish. Even when the Blues scored 13 runs against the mighty Browns, on May 1, they lost the game by a run, undone by Comiskey's home run and triple. St. Louis scored a total of 74 runs in their four-game sweep of the road-weary Clevelands.[16]

At the middle of May, the team was 3–18 and never recovered in the standings. The Blues' pitching was substandard and, even with all the opposing runners on base, the Cleveland infield wasn't turning double plays for the pitchers; the first one of the season—from Stricker to McKean to Charlie Sweeney at first—wasn't recorded until April 28, in St Louis, in the team's ninth game. Their next double plays came in one game, on May 9 in Cincinnati; McKean started one and handled the pivot for another. McKean was charged with 17 errors in his first 20 games. In truth, the hastily laid infield in League Park was tough on infielders, Cleveland having one of only three "skinned" or dirt diamonds around the American Association. Oyster Burns, playing home games on Baltimore's skinned infield, made 101 errors at short one year. (Chippy McGarr, the shortstop for Philadelphia and McKean's future mate at third base, also played half of his schedule on a dirt field.) *The Sporting News* for June 13 reported the "ball grounds will be re-graded" while the Blues played away games. There seems also to have been a physical reason for McKean's early season rash of errors. On April 30, *The Sporting News* reported, "Just now he is suffering from a lame arm so that he is not playing up to his real form."

The team was so severely lacking in major league experience that newspapers soon gave them an alternative nickname, the Cleveland Infants. Cleveland claimed one victory in its first 14 games, having beaten Louisville's Peekaboo Veach, 6 to 4, back on April 26, in the fourth game in the Kentucky series. It had been Veach's debut appearance in the League, after which he was returned to the minors. In 1890, he was Ed McKean's teammate in the Spiders infield, at first base. Winning Blues starter Morrison had to provide his own margin of victory, by hitting a two-RBI triple in the sixth inning. (Ed McKean had batted against both Mike Morrison and Ice Box Chamberlain in his season in the International League.) The Louisville Colonels had put together one of the most colorful rosters in all of the colorful Beer and Whisky League. Joining Peekaboo on the pitching staff were Elton Chamberlain (32 wins for St. Louis in 1889; two seasons of more than 200 strikeouts) and Toad Ramsey (38 wins in 1886, with 499 whiffs). (Wadsworth, Ohio, phenom Joe Neale also threw a few innings in 1887.) Starting in the Louisville outfield were James van Winkle Wolf and Hub Collins. David Nemec identifies Hubert Collins as one of baseball's best bunters and strongest arms. His career and life were foreshortened as a result of a collision with Oyster Burns in pursuit of a pop fly. The team's most extraordinary outfielder, the iconic slugger Pete Browning (.457 batting average, 118 RBIs this season), had the most ordinary name.[17]

For Cleveland's home opener, against the Red Stockings on May 4, the Blues were decked out in their new uniforms of white flannel, with navy blue belts, stockings and caps. The first game in the new ball grounds attracted a big crowd of 4,000. One of the gala day's "features" was Ed McKean's "long drive," a ninth-inning triple. It was the home team's first extra-base hit off Tony Mullane. Umpire Ned Cuthbert was late for the historical occasion, finally showing up five minutes before the scheduled 3:30 start for the game.[18] In fact, Frank Robison's new house for his Blues came close to not being ready. It was nearly April, less than a month before the game, when construction on the stands was finished, and League Park's infield took even longer because of rainy weather.[19] Cincinnati spoiled the day's festivities, once the game finally got underway. Going into the eighth inning, Cleveland was behind by only a run, 6 to 5; then McKean misplayed two routine ground balls at short, leading

THREE. *The Invention of the Slugging Shortstop (1887–1888)* 79

to all the insurance runs the Reds needed to win the contest, 10 to 6. Mike Morrison, the losing pitcher, finished the season with a 12–25 record and 205 walks, the most free passes in the American Association. McKean almost redeemed himself in the ninth inning by knocking in Hotaling and eventually scoring himself. His two hits on the day extended his hitting streak; his two errors were costly.

McKean batted second in Jimmy Williams' lineup, behind Monkey Hotaling.[20] The acrobatic center fielder's nickname seems to have originated from the agility he showed as a catcher in the minor leagues.[21] Pete Hotaling had come back to Cleveland, where he'd played for three seasons, from a stint as playing-manager with Charlie Morton's Savannah team in the Southern League. The Savannahs he left behind were packed with major-league-ready players the likes of Hub Collins, Joe Neale, The Only Nolan, Hank O'Day, and Sy Sutcliffe. In 1887, Hotaling would hit .299 and lead the Blues in doubles, triples, and runs batted in.

Desperate for a win in front of its fans at home, Cleveland lost a tough one to in-state rival Cincinnati on May 7. *Sporting Life* commiserated: "Rain and the trickery of the visitors deprived the home team of a victory. [Cleveland] had scored five runs in the sixth inning, with two men out and Hotaling on second, when the visitors raised a wrangle and delayed the game until it was called on account of rain. This gave the Cincinnati Club a victory in a five inning game," since, according to the rulebook of the day, a called game reverted to the score for the last complete inning.[22] It isn't clear, but Ed McKean may very well have been the batter, with Hotaling in scoring position for him, when umpire Cuthbert stopped the game. Shortstop McKean acquitted himself well enough on the muddy infield, making no errors but only one assist. Cleveland's first win at League Park finally came on May 10, when George Pechiney turned back Brooklyn, 8 to 7. In the ninth inning, doubles by Hotaling and McKean, followed by a base hit off the bat of Fred Mann, plated two runs and put the home team Blues ahead for good. It would prove to be Pechiney's one win of his farewell season; Cleveland's opening day pitcher finished with a 1–9 record and an ERA of over seven runs. Davis Hawley also cut ties with the journeyman Mann, after he'd logged 62 games in a Blues uniform; at the time of his release, he was the only .300 hitter on the team.

Ed McKean's hitting streak came to a halt, at least by post–1887 standards, against pitcher John Harkins and the Brooklyn Trolley Dodgers, on May 14. McKean was playing the game out of position—for the 20th Blues game of the season, Jimmy Williams had McKean swap positions with Cub Stricker—perhaps in consideration of the rookie's sore arm. The change may have thrown McKean off stride. Just to switch things up, Williams would also put McKean

The 1888 Cleveland Blues of the American Association. McKean stands far left; Chief Zimmer stands third from the left; Cub Stricker sits far left. Jimmy Williams (center, in suit) was McKean's first manager in the big leagues (Legendary Auctions).

at second base for the games of July 8 and 9, but he was never a good fielder there. Cleveland fans were plenty familiar with Harkins, who had broken in with the National League version of the Blues, in 1884, and struggled to a 12–32 record. Over four-plus years, John Harkins won just 51 of 134 career decisions. Ed McKean's streak of consecutive games reaching base was still alive, though; Harkins allowed him a "first base on balls."

McKean's fielding problems continued to mitigate his heavy hitting. Throughout his 19-game hitting streak, he was charged with 17 errors and had a hand in only three double plays. On May 23, at League Park, the Philadelphia Athletics beat Cleveland, 13 to 6, for one of the once-great Charlie Sweeney's last big league wins, on a McKean error. The shortstop's wild throw in the first inning helped the visitors to eight runs. And yet, Ed McKean was playing so well overall that Frank Brunell was moved to write, as May dropped off the Cleveland schedule, that McKean "is, without doubt, as great a general ball player as ever played here."[23]

Jimmy Williams was asked to preside over a boardinghouse pitching staff of drifters. Although Frank Robison had made what moves he could to

THREE. *The Invention of the Slugging Shortstop (1887–1888)* 81

improve the situation by late June, he was hampered by a severe shortage of able arms in this expansion era. During the crisis, it got so bad that

> Charles Sweeney, the pitcher, was called to Philadelphia, on a dispatch by Manager Williams, on [a] Tuesday. He left at once. On Wednesday Pechiney, with a lame back, and [Myron] Allen, with a strained leg, returned. The Clevelands got in a week ago Friday morning and tackled the Louisvilles that afternoon and as your score columns show Hugh Daily, the one-armed pitcher is now with Cleveland. Manager Williams signed him on Monday in Baltimore, and used him Wednesday against the Athletics with fearful results...Manager Williams is likely to leave the team in the hands of [catcher Pop Snyder] and go away on an angling trip, with cash as bait and men the game. The Cleveland club is playing good ball for its speed, but isn't strong enough to more than make trouble. So Williams is going away to get men either by begging, borrowing or stealing them.

Frank Robison took emergency measures and bypassed Davis Hawley and "wired manager Williams on Monday to the effect that in future he was given full authority, without consulting any one, to buy, engage or release any player he saw fit and at any terms."[24] Hawley, who had built the team for Robison, was kicked upstairs before his creation had played half a season. There simply was no good pitching out there for Williams to land. *The Sporting News* reported the results from one stopgap signing: "Cleveland's high-priced pitcher, John Kirby isn't doing anything remarkable so far. He came here with a lame arm and has been hit very hard in the three games in which he has pitched. On Wednesday, Baltimore trimmed him up for nineteen hits. He is expected to improve. There is plenty of room for it."[25] Kirby spent most of his time with the Blues "up in the air," compiling a record of no wins and five losses, and an earned run average of 9.00.

In Cleveland, on the last day of June, McKean hit a triple and three singles in five at-bats against the Reds' best pitcher, Elmer Smith, who would win 34 games on the year and lead the league in ERA. Still, Cleveland was struggling along at a .250 winning clip. Jimmy Williams sent out McKean to play left field in Cincinnati and his new outfielder responded with two hits. McKean was back at his regular shortstop position on July 2, and slashed two more hits. At home against the Trolley Dodgers for a Fourth of July doubleheader, McKean made five base hits, four hits and a walk coming in the morning game off Adonis Terry, and he might have had more. With the game deadlocked at 7 to 7 after 12 innings, the unusually sympathetic umpire Jack McQuaid called the contest so players on both sides could rest before their afternoon game. The tie game was supposed to be played out, restarting in the 13th inning, the next day, but it was never completed. Cleveland's One Arm Daily won game two, with the Blues scoring all eight runs in their first at-bats. Hugh Ignatius Daily would finish his major league career with Cleveland on August 22. As a National League Cleveland Blue, Daily had authored one of baseball's first no-hitters, on September 13, 1883, in Philadelphia. He won 10 consecutive games in late June and kept Cleveland in that year's race for the pennant into September. The following season, he struck out 20 batters in a game in Boston.[26] The Irish immigrant was a mere teenager when a musket shot in the left wrist permanently rendered him one-handed. His biggest handicaps, though, were his advanced age—he didn't pitch in the major leagues until he was 34—and his well-documented black temper, not necessarily in that order.[27]

Although Williams was doing a good deal of experimenting with his lineups and batting orders, he was never able to settle on winning combinations. On July 9, leading off and playing back-to-back games at second base, Ed McKean belted a triple and two singles off Athletics pitcher Gus Weyhing. Cannon Ball Weyhing won 264 games in the nineteenth century but never adjusted his curveball to the overhand style late in his career. The proud McKean may very well have felt humiliated in front of the Cleveland fans when he was moved, during the August 16 game against the Browns, from shortstop to left field. It was one of two times that manager Williams used outfielder Myron Allen at short. Simply put, the Blues lacked the talent and depth to win this season. "The Louisville-Cleveland game this afternoon was totally devoid of interest," was *The Sporting News'* succinct comment on the Blues' September 21 game. Late in the 16 to 8 Cleveland loss, it came Cub Stricker's turn in the pitcher's box.[28] McKean's old International League opponent Bobby Gilks was pressed into emergency service after Hugh Daily was released, and he posted a winning record in 13 starts for Jimmy Williams. The multi-talented Gilks also filled in around the infield and in the outfield.

Toward the close of the long season, *The Sporting News* stayed optimistic about the Blues, choosing to believe that "it is very likely that the Clevelands will be a very much improved team before this season of 1887 comes to a close."[29] The Blues' best months were August (10–18) and September (8–13), so they did show slight improvement but still wound up with a record of 39 victories against 92 defeats, and a winning percentage below .300. The Blues finished dead last in the American Association, 54 games behind the pennant-winning Browns, who beat them in 18 of the 19 games between the two teams. Cleveland managed a winning record against only New York, who came in four games ahead of them. True, the Blues were getting stronger up the middle, if for no other reason than McKean, who wouldn't turn 19 until next June, was a budding star. In his rookie year, he led his team in at-bats, hits, and walks. He also finished second on the Blues in stolen bases and third in runs scored. Cleveland was last in team batting but still averaged .305 according to the 1887 rules. By the same reckoning, McKean was listed seventh among qualifiers

THREE. *The Invention of the Slugging Shortstop (1887–1888)* 83

for the American Association batting title, one of the league's eight ".400 hitters." He was credited at the time with 201 base hits in 126 games played. McKean's 60 walks led all major league rookies in 1887, and his 13 triples tied Mike Griffin and Darby O'Brien for top honors in the American Association, according to the *Baseball Rookies Encyclopedia*. After a slow start at short, he'd shown steady improvement as the season progressed; official league statistics had him seventh among shortstops in fielding percentage, at .851. He was one of the better defenders on the Cleveland team, which finished above only the New York Metropolitans in fielding percentage.[30]

Another reason for optimism was the purchase, in mid–September, of Chief Zimmer's contract from Rochester. Although the franchise backstop of the future would get into only 14 games for Cleveland, he "revolutionized the art of catching when in 1887 he became the first catcher to station himself directly behind home plate for every play," according to *Baseball: The Biographical Encyclopedia*.[31]

In a potentially significant development for 1888, Frank Robison found a way to circumvent Cleveland's ban against baseball on the Sabbath by playing one of his team's "home" games at the Cedar Avenue race track, on August 21, 1887. Some 3,000 paid to watch the contest in the rain, a measure of the revenue the club had been missing out on, whereas many other clubs in the association regularly scheduled Sunday home games. Going into the new season, Robison knew his club needed to draw an average of 1,400 paying fans to home games; by season's end, the average was about 900.[32] A club of "Infants" that won 22 of 58 home games had proved to be not much of a draw in Cleveland, and the prohibition of Sunday baseball further hurt the attendance totals for the Blues' inaugural season. In the Cedar Avenue preview game, Ed McKean drove a ball over the carriages parked in the race track's makeshift outfield, and he raced all the way to third base before the New York Metropolitans' outfielder could retrieve it.[33]

Changes in Cleveland helped to improve the team that was beginning its second season under Jimmy Williams' management. This version of the Blues would play winning baseball in front of the home patrons, going 34–27 in a team effort to more firmly reestablish the big league game in Cleveland. The boost in the final standings would be marginal, from the cellar to sixth place in the eight-team American Association, and the Blues still came in 40½ games behind the dynastic Browns. Two non-roster changes were a factor in 1888. The league office favored Cleveland by scheduling a homestand to run 28 straight games, longest in the league. And the field conditions at League Park were significantly upgraded over its inaugural season.[34] In March, the Robison brothers hired Tom Lawrence to redesign the playing field. Lawrence had been the groundskeeper at old Kennard Park, and he also knew the game from his experience as manager of the Cleveland Cardinals. Lawrence's makeover was radical. He began by eliminating the late-afternoon sun field problem on the left side of the infield—no doubt, a factor in Ed McKean's non-throwing errors at short the previous season, and the cause of many dropped balls and even collisions between defensive players—by reorienting the diamond toward the south; he graded the dirt base paths and re-sodded the grass. The club did not move to change the dimensions of League Park. The nearest outfield wall, 470 feet out in left field, was a rumor from home plate.[35] McKean, of course, was a dead pull hitter so his natural power was to right field, where triples went to die.

Naturally, last year's finish in the cellar demanded changes to the team's roster. Cleveland management's plan for rebuilding its pitching staff upon the bar stool of Jersey Bakely (whom McKean knew all too well from their days in Rochester) looked suspiciously like a hot stove gamble. The lenient Jimmy Williams and the intemperate Bakely seemed an unpromising match. Amazingly, the acutely unstable pitcher stabilized the Blues pitching staff by having his career year. Jersey Bakely was good for 60 complete games, 533 innings, and 25 wins. His four shutouts were three more than the rest of the staff, combined. He allowed fewer than three earned runs a game. Frank Robison also brought in John O'Brien, who completed 30 starts as the number two pitcher. Still, the Blues were to employ 11 pitchers over the course of the season, the same fat number as last year. From the 1887 staff, Billy Crowell returned for only 18 starts, and Mike Morrison pitched four times. Newcomer Ed Keas was brilliant; his loss to arm troubles after six starts was a blow to Cleveland's chances to finish in the first division.

The Blues everyday players never really established themselves in 1888, with the exception of Cub Stricker. No outfielder appeared in as many as 100 games, and third base was the answer to a trivia question all year long. A team strength was in the developmental stages behind the plate. Veteran receiver Pop Snyder was slowing down. The catcher who had led the National League in fielding for three straight seasons was bowing out as a mentor to rookie Chief Zimmer when he wasn't catching. The club also brought in Deacon McGuire to catch a few games and sit beside Charlie Zimmer when it was Snyder's turn in the lineup. Ed McKean, one of the strongest Blues hitters again this season, was in jeopardy of becoming a player without a position. He was mostly exiled to left field but still batting second in the lineup. Manager Williams had begun to lose confidence in McKean's play at short last season; now he moved McKean around his infield or tried to hide him in left field.

THREE. *The Invention of the Slugging Shortstop (1887–1888)*   85

Despite the various tweaks to the club, the Cleveland Blues must have felt doomed to repeat the history of last year—once again, they lost nine of their first 10 games. In fact, Cleveland surpassed its bad start of last year by dropping 10 of 11 games, the lone victory coming in Philadelphia, on April 26, on a day when the offense made up for the pitching, 10 runs to 9. Williams prolonged his stay in Cleveland because the team won six of seven games at the start of May. However, the 10 to 1 pounding by the Athletics on opening day for Cleveland, May 2, was witnessed by only 1,000 fans in League Park. Things would get worse. Perhaps 300 bothered to show up at the May 14 game, a loss to Brooklyn this time. Jimmy Williams was fading into a well-earned obscurity, and Cleveland baseball fans were losing interest. *The Sporting News* had taken to derisively referring to the team as Cleveland Remnants.[36] Some began to wonder if the club hadn't been downright doomed to failure from the get-go. Cleveland couldn't play a spring training game without causing trouble for themselves. Team captain Faatz kicked so vociferously during an exhibition in Wheeling that he was arrested afterwards for disorderly conduct.[37] The fans and the constable on Wheeling Island couldn't have known that Jay Faatz and his wife were mourning the recent death of their little son. Wheeling should have been lucky territory for Cleveland—it was hometown to both Jack Glasscock and Jesse Burkett. In contrast, the stars were in alignment for the Nailers' kid second baseman from Cleveland, Ohio, Ed Delahanty. After Al Buckenberger managed Wheeling to second place in the Tri-State League, he sold Delahanty to the Philadelphia Quakers, where Delahanty began his legendary career. Buckenberger led the Rochester Bronchos to two Eastern League pennants before Ed McKean took over, with disastrous results, as player-manager in 1902. The bad luck persisted. In July, Jimmy Williams resigned as Blues' manager on the very day his father died.[38]

Cub Stricker went down with an ankle injury in the first weeks of June, and Williams temporarily restored McKean to the infield, where he played an errorless second. The team had been enduring loss after loss. On June 14, Pop Snyder was appointed team captain in place of poor Jay Faatz, who was judged to be "too easy with the men."[39] It was a sign that the powers in Cleveland had finally come to find Jimmy Williams himself too lenient. The club needed to restore a sense of discipline among its players. Hard-nosed Ed McKean, after a year in the manager's dog house, was named a team baseline coacher.

McKean's effectiveness may have been muted as one of the many new rules for the 1888 season was being enforced during these weeks. On the books was a rule prohibiting a team's coachers from addressing (i.e., heckling) anyone but his own base runners. The June 13 *Sporting News* reported "In three of the last eight games played" in Cleveland, "coaching was barred by agreement between the captains of the clubs," with the result that "the quiet game was just as preferable to the Cleveland people as the whoop-la wild west games."[40] Cleveland was involved in another innovation, on June 18 at Philadelphia, when two umpires were deployed for the first time in a regular-season game. The two-umpire system had been unveiled in last year's postseason.[41] Now Ed McKean had double the number of officials to hate on the field of play.

After Jimmy Williams' inevitable resignation, Tom Loftus became the new manager of the Cleveland Blues, and McKean was his starting shortstop. Lofton was an early advocate of what came to be called "inside baseball," stressing team play and the virtues of the sacrifice bunt.

Loftus proved short on miracles, although initially under his leadership the team improved its record. The turnabout came when Cleveland took three games in Brooklyn, on July 17, 18, and 19, with McKean hitting behind leadoff man Stricker. When Baltimore broke Cleveland's win streak, 3 to 2, on July 20, the Orioles had to score the winning run in the ninth inning. At that, a resilient Cleveland team came back to win the next day in Baltimore, 17 to 11, in a game in which McKean belted out a triple, a home run and three singles. Playing more relaxed baseball after his reinstatement at short, he was finding his power stroke. Another home run, on July 26, was spoiled by the loss to St. Louis. McKean performed particularly well against the Browns in 1888. Earlier, on May 29, Cleveland won in St. Louis on the strength of what *The Sporting News* called McKean's "splendid work with the stick making three singles which brought in runs"; on July 31, McKean singled and doubled in a game in which his fielding drew "honors of the day."[42] And then, on August 13 in St. Louis, McKean's "long home run hit" and two doubles were the only damage off 25-game winner Nat Hudson.[43]

Still in his teens, McKean had established himself as the once and future Cleveland shortstop. He'd not only won back his starting position (from the forgettable Gus Alberts); he'd come to lead the association's shortstops in fielding, as well.[44] By season's end, he'd distinguished himself as the team leader in games played (131), although he was the shortstop for only 78 contests, mostly after Williams' exile. Cleveland's pitching was coming around, too, mostly thanks to Jersey Bakely. In Cincinnati, on August 22 and 23, Bakely became the first American Association hurler to shut out a team on successive days. In the waning days of August, Tom Loftus' reinvigorated Blues moved briefly into fifth place. A nine-game win streak, all at home, was halted on September 10 with a close, 2 to 1, Bakely loss to Brooklyn that took 70 minutes to settle.

The Blues during these transformative days were even *looking* more like an American Association club, playing Sunday dates over parts of three months. Frank Robison sidestepped local laws and scheduled his club for five

THREE. *The Invention of the Slugging Shortstop (1887–1888)*   87

games at amusement parks outside of the city.[45] Three of the games were played at Geauga Lake Park: Jersey Bakely beat Baltimore's Phenomenal Smith there on July 22; the following week, Silver King and the Browns were victorious over John O'Brien; and the Browns triumphed over Bakely and the Blues in a rematch at Geauga Lake, on August 26. At Beyerle's Park, on September 2, when Bakely lost to Louisville, Cleveland, Ohio's own Lave Cross was the Colonels shortstop and the game was umpired by former Blues pitcher Billy Crowell. Ed McKean was awarded a ground-rule home run off Toad Ramsey when his routine fly ball was swallowed up by the roped-off crowd. The following Sunday, McKean was undoubtedly eager to be back at Beyerle Park to swing his home-run bat against Kansas City twirling, but, when the Cowboys refused to play a regular season game, it counted only for an exhibition.

On September 15, an injury kept McKean out of Cleveland's lineup for the one time all year; he quickly recovered to play September 18 in Kansas City. Even with McKean, the Blues season was starting to unravel. Beginning with a loss on September 20, Cleveland won just five times the rest of the season, against 17 losses and two ties in Louisville. Cleveland's ownership quit early on the team and released Pete Hotaling, one of its best players.[46]

Slugging Ed McKean's list of accomplishments is impressive for what would be his, and Cleveland's, last season in the American Association.[47] He finished with 164 hits, third most in the league. The sophomore's 233 total bases were fourth highest. His .299 batting average was sixth best, as were his .425 slugging percentage and six home runs. He was tied for 10th in runs batted in, with 68 to his credit.

Frank Brunell informed the readers of his *Sporting Life* column that the star shortstop would spend the offseason among family and friends "in and around Cleveland, Grafton, and Youngstown."[48]

Four

Ed McKean and the Players' Revolt (1889–1890)

...one of the worst of the lot...—*Sporting Life*, February 26, 1890

When Cleveland replaced the Detroit franchise in the National League for the 1889 season, the Spiders were born. *The Sporting News* lamented that "The old vets do not seem to be in much demand this year," and named Pete Hotaling.[1] Cleveland's center fielder for the previous year had been the last remaining link on the field to the old National League Cleveland Blues. Besides Hotaling, the newspaper's list of original Cleveland players from "just ten years ago" who were still active in the majors included Bill Phillips and Jack Glasscock from 1879, plus Fred Dunlap, Frank Hankinson, and Ned Hanlon from 1880.[2] The National League was already Ed McKean's fifth league in his four years as a professional baseballist. He would remain a National Leaguer for the rest of his major league days.

By the first week of March, Cleveland had contracted its exhibition roster of players, except for Henry Gruber, late of the Detroit Wolverines. The pitcher had been training the ball players at Yale University and holding out for a $2,100 salary; he had, however, taken precautions and "sent on the measurements for his uniform." Cleveland had offered him $2,000.[3] The Spiders, under Tom Loftus, would be competitive from the start of the season. His feisty first-year club made it all the way into second place, on June 28, before falling back to the pack. After a late-season slump, Cleveland would finish half a game behind fifth-place Pittsburgh in the eight-team League. One of the Pittsburgh outfielders was Hanlon, who had caught on with them after the Detroit club folded. Cleveland captured several former Wolverines for its roster, most importantly left fielder Larry Twitchell, pitchers Eb Beatin and the reluctant Gruber, plus Sy Sutcliffe, a backup catcher who threw left-handed. Twitchell, a Cleveland native, led the team in RBIs in 1889 and generated what has to

Four. *Ed McKean and the Players' Revolt (1888–1890)* 89

be the highlight of the Spiders season. In League Park, on August 15, he not only hit for the cycle—*three* triples, a homer, a double, and a single—but he pitched to two Boston batters in the third inning. That was the afternoon that Cleveland set a record when they became the first National League team to score in all nine innings.[4] Unfortunately, Twitchell's big day was one of only three wins and a tie during a 19-game free fall for the Spiders, who finished below .500 for Loftus. At least the team got to play a meaningful game for the season finale, a contest that would help decide the 1889 pennant.

It was in May that the team had acquired its distinctive nickname. Sportswriters had initially relied on the default sobriquets for a first-year team, calling them the Babes or, sometimes mockingly, Babies. F.H. Brunell bestowed the moniker that would stick, as he watched some Cleveland players practicing. "They look skinny and spindly, just like spiders," he was overheard to remark. "Might as well call them Spiders and be done with it."[5] Brunell was the first to use the nickname in print, in his columns for the *Plain Dealer* and *Sporting Life*. *Sporting Life* further attributed the inspiration behind the Spider nickname, "so called on account of their particular appearance in their suits of black and blue," to how McKean and his mates looked in their new uniforms.[6]

The Spiders became admired around the League for their hustle and spirited play, as Loftus brought a degree of stability to the team. The bench manager settled on an everyday lineup and, barring the inevitable injuries, mostly stuck with it. The entire infield and outfield played at least 110 games, and Chief Zimmer handled the bulk of the catching. Loftus brought in Patsy Tebeau from Denver, where he'd made a reputation as best-fielding third baseman in the Western League. Newcomer Tebeau solved what had been a perennial problem at that position, and rookie Jimmy McAleer starred in League Park's spacious center field. Out of spring training, McKean was Tom Loftus' third batter in the order, his pick for a dependable run producer to hit behind his fleet men on the bases, Cub Stricker and McAleer. McKean, however, was the one Spider whom Loftus would occasionally bench for what he thought to be selfish play. The clash between manager and shortstop was a fundamental disagreement, one that would necessarily limit McKean's offensive production in his early years in Cleveland. Loftus' concept of team play, with its emphasis on the sacrifice bunt, helped to bring order to the Blues, but it could not have endeared the manager to his slugger in the long run. Ed McKean liked to swing hard at pitches. His greatest attribute as a batter was his ability to consistently drive the ball to the outfield. McKean was a power hitter who would eventually be depended on to drive in runs or, at the least, move base runners by putting the ball in play—his rate of one strikeout in every 29.0 at-bats is second only to Cub Stricker's career record on Spiders teams. Loftus, to his credit, also established an orderly pitching rotation, anchored by Cinders O'Brien, Jersey Bakely, and Ebenezer Beatin, counting on each man for over 300 innings.[7] Henry Gruber contributed another 200 innings pitched.

The new manager and his team, gathered at the Plateau Hotel in Hot Springs, Arkansas, were tested before a baseball had been thrown in spring training. First baseman Jay Faatz, only recently reinstated by Loftus as team captain, was in Hot Springs for a week when his wife died following an illness of seven days.[8] It was almost exactly the one-year anniversary of the crushing news of the passing of the couple's boy. Somehow, Loftus found a way to rally the men, seizing the occasion of his first training camp with Cleveland to set a winning tone for the young team. In their opening exhibition, in Hot Springs on March 19, Cleveland took on a Picked Nine made up of local players and a few Spiders including starting pitcher John O'Brien. The contest was memorable for a triple play in the eighth inning that went second baseman Stricker to first baseman Sy Sutcliffe to Tebeau at third. McKean was a bystander at short.[9]

On the road, Saint Joseph's pitcher Bill Crowell held the Spiders to one run in an April 3 game. Bobby Gilks, Crowell's brother-in-law, played first base for the Spiders because the luckless Jay Faatz had been hit by a pitch the game before and broke a small bone in his wrist. The roster for the Western Association St. Joseph's Clay Eaters was an indication of the growing community of ball players of which McKean was a member: besides former Cleveland teammate Crowell, there were McKean's old Youngstown teammate Ed Cartwright and Joe Ardner. Ardner, who had played in the International League in 1886, would be McKean's second baseman in 1890. Pete Hotaling and Chippy McGarr did not play in the exhibition against Cleveland that afternoon, but they too were with the St. Joes later in the season. Tom Loftus himself took the field with his boys for an exhibition at Canton, Ohio, on April 19. (He'd had six hits in nine career games with St. Louis teams, in 1877 and 1883.) The Spiders were celebrating the conclusion of a busy training schedule of 16 road games, having won 11 out of 15, and playing to a tie in Louisville. Loftus had led the team across the map and back, from Kansas City to St. Joseph to St. Louis to Columbus, Ohio, and Cincinnati, down to Louisville, back to Ohio in Mansfield, up to Milwaukee, and finally on to Canton.[10]

The championship season was a challenge from the start. Ed McKean started slowly this year. He couldn't buy a hit all spring, and, two weeks into the regular season, hometown sportswriter Charles Mears was doing his best to sound patient: "McKean has not found his last year's home run suit of

FOUR. *Ed McKean and the Players' Revolt (1888–1890)*   91

clothes yet, but when he does the outfielders will not have a chance to doze."[11] Through it all, Loftus stuck with his number three hitter. The hits, when they came, came in bunches. McKean polished off his debut season in the National League with at least 35 multiple-hit games.[12] And yet, when the Spiders arrived in Indianapolis on the eve of the regular season opener, they were a team beset with injuries; in addition to Faatz's wrist, McAleer's leg, and Gruber's and Charlie Sprague's sore pitching arms, a catcher on a tryout from Houston, Joseph Lohbeck, hurt his throwing arm, and reserve catcher Pop Snyder had yet to join Loftus' thin ranks.

At Athletic Park in Indianapolis, on Wednesday, April 24, the Cleveland Spiders played their first game in the National League, a Jersey Bakely loss to Pretzels Getzein.[13] The box score shows Ed McKean doubling in four at-bats, with a sacrifice bunt for Loftus and the team. McKean's counterpart, Jack Glasscock, went 2-for-5, and tacked on a stolen base for Indianapolis. In this first of many head-to-head meetings between the two greatest shortstops in early Cleveland baseball, neither made an error. Next afternoon, Eb Beatin shut out the home team after the third inning to win, 10 to 4. Beatin had been the first Spiders pitcher to win in spring training; he'd hit the first homer by a Spider on the year, in another preseason game; and now he'd recorded the first Cleveland victory of the championship season. Both shortstops went 2-for-4 at the bat—McKean was credited with a triple and a stolen base; both of Glasscock's hits were doubles—and McKean committed an error. For a lopsided April 26 loss, McKean was held out of the lineup by Loftus and replaced by Bob Gilks. Jack Glasscock scored four of the 14 Indianapolis runs in support of another Getzein win. Patsy Tebeau made three errors at third, as the Cleveland infield fell apart. McKean's return to the lineup was a key to John O'Brien's victory in the last game of the opening series. His pair of doubles outshined Glasscock's seven assists like a new three-dollar gold piece did an Indian-head penny, and this day O'Brien shut out Indianapolis into the seventh inning of a briskly paced game, in the books after 80 minutes. O'Brien's second victory on the early season came on May 2, in a game featuring what was to become a winning combination in Cleveland for years—McKean's slugging (3-for-4) and Jim McAleer's fielding—although, in the first inning, McAleer fell down rounding third base and failed to score on McKean's triple. O'Brien's third win, still without a defeat, was the occasion of Cleveland's May 6 home opener. To the joy of the crowd, the Spiders evened their record at 6 and 6 that glorious day, beating Cap Anson and Chicago, 11 to 8. McKean hit safely three times in his five at-bats, and his double-play partner Stricker went 4-for-6. About this time, Charlie Comiskey said admiringly about Tom Loftus, "There's the livest manager to-day in the League."[14]

The upstart Spiders' first trip east was a learning experience. Ed McKean continued his good play, slashing out five hits in the first three games he played in New York and outplaying the Giants' Monte Ward, on May 3, at short and at-bat. But in the series finale, manager Buck Ewing showed his disrespect for the Cleveland Babies when he started himself in the pitcher's box and won. A deflated Spiders club escaped to Boston for a two-game visit. Ed McKean's four hits in the May 17 game, including a clutch three-run homer in the ninth inning, were overshadowed by two Cleveland defeats. Going into Philadelphia, the Spiders' mood darkened; in the seventh inning of a May 22 loss, Patsy Tebeau ignited the kind of angry altercation that would later characterize the Spiders' rowdy play when he was manager. Jack Clements had made a wild throw and, when Philadelphia third baseman Bill Hallman obstructed Cub Stricker, coacher Tebeau decided to push his base runner toward home. Clements tagged Stricker for the out and Tebeau went wild, delivering a punch to the catcher's neck. When the diamond dust settled, umpire Watch Burnham fined Patsy $10 for fighting—and Faatz $50 for his language.

McKean did bang out five more hits in the first two games in Philadelphia. His on-the-field reunion with Ed Delahanty turned out to be unfortunate for the Philly rookie, who broke his collarbone on a slide into Cub Stricker, as McKean stood by. Buoyed by taking three of four games in the City of Brotherly Love, Cleveland ventured on to Washington—and into more controversy on the field.

Tom Loftus was in danger of losing control of his team. In the Spiders' May 28 victory at the capitol, a stunt by Patsy Tebeau—and not Loftus' disciplined "inside baseball"—proved to be the game changer. The Senators had loaded the bases against John O'Brien in the first inning, when Tebeau intentionally let George Shoch's popup fall to the ground. This was years before the infield fly rule, so Tebeau threw to McKean (who had alertly kept Sam Wise standing on second and hustled over to cover third base) for one out, and McKean relayed the ball to Zimmer for the double play. In the bottom of that inning, McKean singled and scored; with two outs in third inning, he singled, stole second, and eventually scored. The Spiders prevailed, over Wise and catcher Connie Mack, 5 to 3, for O'Brien's seventh win. The following day, umpire Wallace Fessenden was transparently quick to even things out for the home team, ruling a non-catch by McKean that wiped out a Cleveland double play in the first inning of the game.

Crafty Patsy saved Jersey Bakely's one-run victory against Hank O'Day and the Senators, on July 2. Bakely had already surrendered three runs in the ninth, and slugging Walter Wilmot stood on third base with just one man down. With Jack Carney at-bat, Chief Zimmer went into a delay but never

Four. Ed McKean and the Players' Revolt (1888–1890)

called time. It was the catcher's prearranged signal to third baseman Tebeau. When Wilmot wandered off the bag, Tebeau tagged him out with the hidden ball. Tebeau's quick thinking and bad temper had been keys to any number of Cleveland's wins of late, and he was displaying career-best power at the marble in his first season as a Spider. Before an overflow crowd in New York, on July 13, Tebeau won a cash prize put up by James J. Coogan for the next player to hit a homer in the Polo Grounds. Coogan was the real estate merchant who had sold Giants owner John T. Brush the land for the Polo Grounds below what was known as Coogan's Bluff. So it came to pass that Patsy Tebeau walked away with Coogan's $100, plus another $10 bet from the pocket of pitcher Mickey Welch.[15] It was one of Tebeau's team-leading eight homers on the season. For the record, Ed McKean's 64 lifetime home runs are almost twice as many as the next highest Spiders batter; his number for home runs per at-bat is also tops.

Jack Glasscock broke in with the original Cleveland Blues in 1879. Pebbly Jack was the class of the bare-handed shortstops; he also hit .352 one season for the Indianapolis Hoosiers. Like McKean, Glasscock played in Springfield (Ohio) and Fort Wayne, in addition to Cleveland (Heritage Auctions).

Even counting Tebeau and McKean, Robison and Hawley had not assembled one of the League's better-hitting clubs. It was when Cinders O'Brien asserted himself as the ace of the staff, and he established his curve ball as one of the National League's most effective pitches, that the Spiders became surprise contenders for first place. In the month from June 5 through July 6, O'Brien enjoyed winning streaks of four and seven games. At Independence Day, his winning percentage and ERA made him one of the three best pitchers in the League, along with Welch and John Clarkson, both of them bound for Cooperstown. Upon O'Brien's 18th win, on July 6, Cleveland held second place in the standings, a lofty 18 games above .500

John F. O'Brien was two years removed from pitching a team from Grafton, Ohio's neighbor, Lima, to the state championship. The previous June, his Lima Lushers were in first place in the Tri-State League when the American Association Cleveland Blues purchased his contract. O'Brien's best year would be for these 1889 Spiders, when he won 21 games despite his acute wildness (167 walks, 27 wild pitches, and 24 hit batters). Cinders O'Brien's high point on his personal winning tear must have come in League Park, on June 19, when he beat New York's Smiling Tim Keefe, his boyhood idol. As *Sporting Life* recalled, "In 1882 Tim Keefe was pitching for the Troy team and took enough interest in the young schoolboy to give him several points on how to handle the sphere."[16] After O'Brien's victory that day, he'd won 12 of his decisions and Cleveland was in possession of second place, at 29–16. "His delivery was, without any doubt, the most peculiar of any right hand pitcher who ever played ball," recalled one obituary writer three short years into the future.[17] It seems John O'Brien was the Deadball Era's Luis Tiant: "With his face turned toward center field, he would get a grip on the ball and with an elegant swing of his good right arm he would send the sphere with lightning speed over the plate. Seldom did his face turn toward the plate until the delivery was completed and on this account all batsmen feared him for none knew where to expect or receive the ball."[18]

Charles Mears gloated in a late June column for *The Sporting News*:

Star-crossed John O'Brien won 21 games for the original Cleveland Spiders team, pitched the next year with the cross-town Cleveland Infants, but passed away before the 1892 season (negative plate courtesy Huggins and Scott Auctions: print by Hillary Flexer).

Well! Well! Well! Who, at the beginning of the season would have thought that Cleveland, with a club composed of Class C players, could have reached second place by June? No one! Not a one! Bold thinkers only gave it sixth place, but here we are, and are constantly decreasing the gap between ourselves and first place.... The Spiders are playing the game of their lives and a very lively one at that.... The papers all over the country are praising Cleveland's playing.[19]

In an afterthought, the still-enthused Mears returns to earth a bit, and accurately foretells the Spiders' future even as he describes the city's present appetite for the team:

> Manager Loftus will be satisfied with sixth place, and has not expressed the least-murmur with regard to the pennant.... The city is ablaze with excitement over the teamand the question, "What is the score?" is being asked by everybody from the boy indresses, nearly, to the old gent who used to play when a catch on the first bound was out. Score boards are appearing daily in all parts of the city. Fire engine houses are using their official blackboard for a score board.

The firehouse was a social center for Irishmen, and boys like Ed Delahanty, in cities like Cleveland in the Emerald Age. "The Y.M.C.A. has erected one for the benefit of those people who dislike to enter a saloon to find the score. It was an act approved by all. The news depots, throughout the city, have them also and each and every one is patronized to the full extent of the law."

Through it all, "McKean is the same popular and well liked 'Mac' that he ever was."[20] Part of Tom Loftus' success with the men was his reliance on coach McKean and captain Faatz as "he directs all the field work through Faatz and McKean."[21]

Ed McKean's leadership, hitting, and fielding were such a vaunted part of the Spiders' ascendancy that, during the June 6 game, his followers presented him with flowers. In that game, McKean tripled off Kid Madden. One month later, O'Brien's July 6 win at home against Boston positioned Cleveland to overtake the first-place Beaneaters the upcoming week in Boston. McKean boomed another triple, in the first game in Boston, adding a single and a double as Beatin won. Unfortunately, it would be the only Cleveland win in the series. Worse, John O'Brien's season (and ultimately his career) took a severe downturn; he suffered losses in his next four decisions, and won only three more times over the next three months.

McKean was out of the lineup for O'Brien's July 13 loss in New York. And when McKean's replacement Bob Gilks went down with an injury on July 19, Loftus had to resort to starting left-handed Sy Sutcliffe at short. During the tailspin, some Cleveland papers advocated trading away McKean because Gilks played so well at short. Bob Gilks was never more than a utilityman in the majors after in his one season as a regular leadoff hitter in 1890. But the doubts and recriminations were mounting against the players who were heroes to Clevelanders only a month before. The local press was searching for reasons behind McKean's recent power outage. "McKean hits the ball hard away from home and not while here. His plea against the black center field fence is good. It throws out his eye."[22] Disappointed cranks replaced bouquets with boos, targeting the veteran, who was suddenly showing signs of immaturity, as a figure of the franchise's familiar losing ways. "Saturday, McKean, who thought he was the only player in the club and was sent home to rest in consequence, took it upon himself to visit [the Case Hall] bulletin [board for a game update]. Gilks had done good work, making five assists and one putout, when a small sized crank in the gallery yelled 'Good boy, Gilks! We don't need McKean,' whereupon the only arose and left."[23] It must have doubly wounded the sensitive McKean to read about his humiliation.

McKean's fielding was popularly considered responsible for the Spiders' slide into the second division even though, at the start of August, his .899 average ranked him a respectable fifth among National League shortstops, and he'd made eight fewer errors than the model Jack Glasscock.[24] McKean's performance was seldom depreciated in rival League cities, where he may have played under less pressure. After a 2 to 1 win in Chicago, on August 3, the report back to Cleveland was that "Chicagoans say they've never seen anyone play shortstop like Ed McKean does today. He handles 11 chances flawlessly and has two hits...."[25] In a doubleheader in Boston, on September 13, McKean ranged all over the infield for 16 chances with only one miscue. The Sandusky *Register* for August 19 offered a precise analysis of the shortstop: "He often plays in the most brilliant manner, but slow grounders bring him misfortune."

McKean continued to start at shortstop and, soon enough, the sentiment in Cleveland once again favored him. On August 10, one reporter conceded: "Even if the Babes *are* on the toboggan, Ed McKean and Eb Beatin remain as lively as in the spring."[26] It was in spite of McKean's seven hits in back-to-back losses to Chicago's 41-game-winner Bill Hutchinson that the team fell below .500. The day John O'Brien garnered his twenty-first victory, 3 to 1 in Washington on September 3, McKean singled and scored in the first inning, and his second hit of the game drove home the winning run. Since July 6, the Spiders had gone 17 and 43.

By far, the most poignant cause of the team's demise was John O'Brien's health. *The Sporting News* noted, on August 17, how "O'Brien is virtually useless in these days. He dumps his game in one or two bad innings, and it is because his weak stomach affects his speed and makes it impossible for him to keep in fine physical condition." In the same issue, the weekly reported that Cleveland also lost the services of its starting catcher, struck in the neck by a foul tip. The gritty journalism of the day recreates the frightening scene in Philadelphia:

FOUR. *Ed McKean and the Players' Revolt (1888–1890)* 97

As [Jim] Fogarty struck there was a click, a gurgle and a dull thud, and Charlie Zimmer was on the ground helpless. By the kind hands of his clubmates he was restored to consciousness and sent home. He was so badly injured that his uniform was not removed until he arrived home. On Friday the club's admirers were pained and shocked by the report that he was dead and great was their joy when they heard the later news to the contrary. Scores of people visited his home and inquired on the streets with regard to his condition.

McKean's sidekick Jimmy McAleer was the next to succumb. In a September 9 game at the Polo Grounds, Cleveland's "best fielder and fastest base runner" ruptured a ligament in his leg, after repeated pickoff tosses intended to catch him napping at second base. The Spiders had no viable replacements for the three players.[27]

Bull McKean battled on till the end. In an October 1 loss to the Beaneaters, he collected three hits off John Clarkson, who was pitching nearly every day during Boston's race for the pennant. Eb Beatin notched his 20th victory, in Cleveland on October 20, over 48-game-winner Clarkson. That was the day McKean had to witness the sorry spectacle of King Kelly, drunk and muttering on the wrong bench. The Boston Parnell had to be forcibly removed from the sidelines by the police. Upon the fall of the biggest Irish star in baseball, let us draw a veil over the 1889 season.

Cleveland agreed to play a postseason benefit against the Pittsburgh Alleghenys to raise money for the new ball park in Youngstown. The game meant a return to McKean's original baseball home and Jimmy McAleer's boyhood neighborhood. McAleer, still recovering from injury to his ligament, agreed to umpire. In the seventh inning, McKean's triple drove in the winning run in Cleveland's 4 to 3 victory. So West Side Grounds had its money, and Cleveland had the beginnings of the series with Pittsburgh that would engage the Naps through the turn of the century. The Spiders were still an active team through the middle of October, engaged in an Ohio postseason series that had them hosting Columbus then playing Cincinnati in Akron before traveling to Columbus, where the three teams played a round robin. The postseason games dragged on into the offseason until the end finally came in Cincinnati, where the Spiders lost before 50 spectators in the cold.[28] Ed McKean had played 123 regular season games in 1889, all but one at short, and led his team with 159 base hits. He was the only Spiders regular to hit .300 (.318), and the only one with a .400 slugging percentage (.418). His 34 extra-base hits tied Patsy Tebeau for team honors. He scored the second-most runs for Cleveland and drove in the third-most runners. McKean also won his turf battle with Tom Loftus, who would not return to the club for the next season. Before then, the great war that was the players' rebellion of

1890 would threaten to destroy both the Cleveland Spiders and Ed McKean's career.

Days after his New York Giants prevailed in the 1889 "world's series," shortstop John Montgomery Ward officially formed a new baseball league. The Brotherhood of Professional Base Ball Players (commonly known as the Players' League), owned and operated by former National League and American Association players, ignited a civil war among owners, players, and cities, and divided the loyalties of national newspapers. Overnight, the Spiders' already insufficient fan base had to be shared with the Brotherhood's Cleveland Infants. The National League Spiders drew 47,478 fans at League Park in 1890, down from the previous season's modest attendance of 144,425.[29] Spiders ownership reacted to the players' revolt by an act of entrenchment. The Robison brothers and Davis Hawley persisted in their quest for the ideal manager who could win with a minimum of talent (good players were a rare commodity with so many competing teams and leagues), in a historically small market even further diminished by local competition. At the same time, Cleveland Infants owner Al Johnson assumed the role of an unwise Solomon, who *did* wind up cutting the Cleveland baby in two.

Ed McKean must have been profoundly disappointed with Frank Robison these days. McKean had come back to the Spiders, re-signing in November 1889, after he'd impulsively jumped the previous month to the Brotherhood Infants. Now, in the long hot stove season, he was regretting his decision. Cleveland lost Tom Loftus to the Cincinnati National League club, and Frank Robison replaced him with another Tom Loftus, also from Cincinnati (the American Association club); as a result, McKean was facing the prospect of another year on a team run by yet another baseball innovator. Like the departed Loftus, Gustavius Heinrich Schmelz, the Spiders manager in 1890, was a devout believer in team play based on strict discipline and—McKean would have rolled his eyes at the mention of it—the sacrifice hit. Schmelz was Loftus redivivus, but with a difference: he was even more a theorist of the game. Robison's latest proponent of "scientific baseball" had never himself played baseball, and the rigorous training the former gymnast Schmelz brought to the Spiders' spring camp never translated well into the regular season. Schmelz constantly experimented with his lineups, trying McKean, his best hitter, at leadoff or in the third slot, or sometimes second.

The *Sporting Life* correspondent for the Columbus Solons, the American Association team Gus Schmelz managed after he left Cleveland, openly complained about his management:

> Manager Schmelz's system ... consists of a surfeit of sacrifice hitting, the frequent indulgence of which has combined to lose many games where a bit of hard hit-

FOUR. *Ed McKean and the Players' Revolt (1888–1890)* 99

ting might have resulted differently. But this is not the worst result of sacrifice hitting. It is also claimed by some of the players that the manager has forced them to engage in sacrifice hitting to such a profuse extent that it has ruined them for hard hitting, and that where they formerly went up to the plate with confidence and ability to hit the ball out they now have neither, and are absolutely powerless to make a safe hit, unless it be of the "scratch" order.[30]

It could be argued that Cleveland's slugging shortstop was misused by ordering him to sacrifice so many times in 1890. Still, according to *The Sporting News* at season's end, "Short Stop McKean of Cleveland did not play for a record this year, but for the good of his club. He made seventy sacrifice hits, leading the League in this respect."[31] The new manager, also like his predecessor, failed to win in Cleveland. Gus Schmelz would be replaced by midseason, having theorized the Spiders to the reality of a 21–55 record. Cleveland fans had to wait until the middle of 1891 for Patsy Tebeau to undertake the building of a hard-hitting championship Spiders club around McKean's power game.

In the weeks after McKean had "flopped" and then renegotiated with the Spiders, he was made increasingly aware that the new team in town intended to field a wide-open offensive team. Al Johnson valued the spectacle of scoring, and he laid out Brotherhood Park to his batters' advantage. Charles Mears, who favored the National League Spiders, wrote unapprovingly of Johnson's plans for his park:

> The batter has the advantage all around. If he hits a ball hard[,] over the fence it goes and a home run is the result. If the catcher passes a ball the back stop is so far away that a player on first could easily make second. And again if a player hits, say to third base and the baseman throws high to first, the stands at the side are so low that a block would be the result and the runner would get two if not three or four passes on it. Al was sharp when he laid that plot of ground out! He knew Cleveland wanted hitting and he was bound to make it appear as though they could hit even if they can't.[32]

The new grounds at East 55th Street featured notoriously short fences in the outfield. Infant Pete Browning enjoyed a monster year, rattling the left field wall—where a house sat at the end of the foul line, a mere 200 feet from home plate!—with a bucket full of his league-leading doubles.[33]

This restless offseason, Ed McKean further agonized between his loyalty to the Spiders and his desire to earn more than the National League was offering to pay a man. His contract with Robison for the upcoming season was for $2,500, a healthy increase over the League minimum $2,000 he'd made in 1889.[34] The National League, to compete with the Players' League, had upped its basic salary to $2,400; the additional $100 to McKean was probably compensation for coaching duties. Ed Delahanty jumped from Philadelphia to the Cleveland Infants, on March 21, for a $3,500 contract, $1,000 in advance.[35]

It's reasonable to assume that Al Johnson was offering McKean even more money. Delahanty's biographer sums up the situation: "Three years older than Ed Delahanty...McKean already had three solid years in professional baseball. As a player, he had advantages over the unproven and often-injured Del, who had no experience at the shortstop position he coveted."[36]

The public furor over his contract for 1890 must have felt to McKean like a recurrent nightmare from 1887. The 21-year-old ball player was facing his second contract fight in three big league seasons. Newspapers across the country would render McKean as a modern Buridan's ass, stuck deciding between the National or the Players' League. And yet, the case of McKean's multiple jumpings and floppings is not unique; rather, it is one illustrative story from the landmark players' revolt.

The players' revolt was, in many significant ways, a Cleveland story. Hawley House, Al Johnson's Cleveland headquarters and the actual birthplace of the Players' League, was owned by Davis Hawley of the Spiders. And Albert Johnson, like Frank Robison, was a streetcar magnate in the city. It was Ned Hanlon, the former Cleveland player now managing for the Brotherhood, who originally contacted Johnson to determine if Cleveland had a site for a ball park near one of his street car lines.[37] For a time, Johnson's Infants had under contract both McKean and Delahanty. The high drama of the two Cleveland teams and their two Cleveland boys played out daily in the newspapers, which took up sides. Baseball newcomer Johnson proved to be a master of diversion, signing veterans to big contracts long before his club had a park to play in. He freely issued bravado for publication to keep the cranks entertained: "Cleveland has the cheapest franchise in the [National L]eague, and I won't be at all surprised if the magnates decide to drop these people. I met Frank Robison ... last night [February 5] and he bet me a case of wine that I'd never build a stand on my grounds. I'd like to bet him a hundred cases to ten that I'll have the finest stand in America."[38]

Ed McKean may well have joined up with the fledgling Brotherhood club originally out of an abiding sympathy for unions and the workers' movement in general. As we know, he was raised in a town dependent on the Irish-American labor force, in a region where the Granger movement flourished. Inside Cleveland's Brotherhood Park read a sign "WE ARE THE PEOPLE," and the players in the league commonly called themselves "workers."[39] These divisive days, McKean watched as every one of his teammates from the Spiders, except for Chief Zimmer, Bob Gilks, and Eb Beatin, was choosing to join Ed Delahanty on the Players' League Infants; all but Gilks had at one time or another negotiated with Al Johnson. Jim McAleer's signing with the Players' League team would have been especially hard on McKean. Gone too from the

FOUR. *Ed McKean and the Players' Revolt (1888–1890)* 101

1889 Spiders were their sparkplug Tebeau, McKean's double-play partner Cub Stricker, RBI specialist Larry Twitchell, and the entire pitching staff of John O'Brien, Henry Gruber, and Jersey Bakely. Both reserve catchers, Sy Sutcliffe and Pop Snyder, also agreed to play for Johnson.

The black headline announced "M'KEAN HAS JUMPED." Below it, the February 8 article brought *The Sporting News* readers up to date on events, with no attempt to spare its target the sarcasm. "Last fall, McKean thought that Al Johnson was good enough for him, but on November 20 he concluded that Mr. Robison's aggregation was his best friend. Now, when Judge O'Brien rendered his decision against the temporary injunction, McKean has come to find out that Al Johnson is again No. 1 in his estimation. McKean was always somewhat of a jumping jack as far as contracts are concerned." The writer did not neglect to rehash the old news of McKean's contract struggle with the Cleveland Blues, taking pains to cite his *Reach's Guide of 1887*.

Each successive week, the latest revelation of the McKean case made the newspapers. On February 12, *Sporting Life* reported Ed McKean met with Al Johnson, with the result that the Players' League reinstated him, even after he'd broken his contract with the Infants and had subsequently been blacklisted. Johnson's latest reasoning was that, since McKean had signed with the Brotherhood before re-signing with the National League, his first contract was "therefore the legal one." In a separate article in the same paper, PL secretary-treasurer Frank Brunell, who had been McKean's champion during his contract row three years previously, makes McKean the exception:

> Under no circumstances will any man who has once signed a contract with the Players League and then flopped over to the old League be taken back. Yes, there will be one man only—E.J. McKean, of Cleveland. He went to Al Johnson in a manly way, said he had committed an error, and was willing to refund to the old League all the advance money that was paid to him. But no man like Del[ahanty], who, since the injunction against Ward was refused, has been running around the City of Cleveland and almost praying to be taken back ... will ever be allowed to play in the organization with my consent.

A week later, *Sporting Life* reports McKean in Cleveland had "again expressed a determination to fulfill his Brotherhood contract." Meanwhile, Davis Hawley remained publicly confident that his shortstop would return to the Spiders.[40]

From this point on, an unsympathetic press expressed increasing impatience with McKean's plight. "McKean is flying around the country getting interviewed just for the fun of the thing but Mr. E. J. is at present letting off too much 'gab' for any good whatever," *The Sporting News* charged on February 22.

> At Pittsburg he told two reporters that he would be among the [National] League players next season and to another he said that he would stick with the

[Brotherhood] boys till the last. He seemed to think that he was not in a very favorable position and was troubled over the numerous changes his mind has made. He will probably turn up in California next[,] swearing that he is out of base ball for good.

It wasn't so implausible to imagine the beleaguered McKean escaping to California, where his confidante Jimmy McAleer was skiing himself back to health.

Sporting Life ganged up on the equivocating shortstop. In late February, R.W. Wright published an article there, under the provocative headline "McKean's Unenviable Position—Both Factions Soured on the Slipping Shortstop," about a recent "little escapade at Pittsburg." According to Wright, after two or three days of "telling a different story to every reporter that came along, McKean lost more Cleveland friends than he will be able to make in five years." Certainly, McKean's position was untenable. He was called by some a "traitor" for jumping from the Players' League back to the National League, while others commended him for his "good sense"; for his subsequent flop back to the Players League, many branded him "a knave."

McKean stuck it out in Cleveland for part of a week before he had to retreat "to his rural fastness at Grafton." He then resurfaced in Pittsburgh, where Al Johnson reiterated his faith in McKean and accused the Pittsburgh papers of distortion. In a separate article, a close friend to Al Johnson claimed the blacklisted McKean was, in fact, "formally reinstated" by the Players' League. The correspondent villainized McKean as "one of the worst of the lot" of double-dealing contract jumpers, "still endeavoring to carry water on both shoulders."[41] Cleveland fans took their frustrations out on Ebenezer Beatin, who would be the Spiders' opening day starter, and the Players' League was hardest on Charlie Zimmer, ultimately threatening him with a civil suit. It is interesting to note that, precisely one decade after the failure of the Brotherhood, Zimmer would join Hugh Jennings and Clark Griffith to launch the Protective Association of Professional Baseball Players. Although Ed McKean's reputation was widely besmirched—Joe Pritchard, for example, lampooned him in a national publication, assigning him to sing the song "What Need Have I to Tell the Truth" in his nasty musicale—he seems to have remained one of the most popular baseball figures in Cleveland.[42]

All the protracted squabbling continued right into the spring training camps for the two Cleveland teams. For McKean, the breakthrough finally came from an unexpected source. Spiders manager Gus Schmelz personally escorted McKean into Hot Springs, reeling him in by means of "some tall hustling."[43] While the wrangling over his services still went on around him, McKean had made his definitive commitment to remain a Spider. To *Sporting Life* at the end of March, Al Johnson made the claim that he was in possession of a telegram from McKean, which informed the owner that he would report to the Infants' New Orleans camp. A follow-up article printed the contents of a telegram of unconfirmed provenance, purportedly sent from inside the Spiders camp: "HOT SPRINGS, ARK., March 21. *Al Johnson*—Cleveland, O., will report Sunday in New Orleans with Beatin. Notify me if satisfactory. Answer at once. E.J. McKean."

Sporting Life counted this "the fifth somersault that McKean has turned since the close of last season, first from the [National] League to the Brotherhood, then from the Brotherhood to the League, once more back to the Brotherhood, then again back to the League, going to Hot Springs with the League Club, accepting the captaincy of the team and now to the Brotherhood again." R.W. Wright's conclusion was harsh stuff: "This young man is the most notorious flopper in the business and should be made an example by both sides."44 If Al Johnson couldn't have McKean for his shortstop, he might at least turn Clevelanders against the Spiders star player and the establishment National League. For years, the leading financier of the Players' League and Frank Robison had been friendly competitors in the streetcar business; Al and Tom Johnson, like their enemies the Robison brothers, had dedicated themselves to the people of Cleveland. Tom Johnson would make a famous mayor in the city's near future.45 Now, all was fair among the warring businessmen who were in love with the same girl.

Unfairly, the headline in the April 2 *Sporting Life* accused the "Vacillating M'Kean" of "Still Another Flop," even though the beleaguered McKean had not reported to the Infants' training camp. McKean was challenged to deny authorship of the spurious telegram to Johnson printed in the previous issue of the weekly. The anti–McKean article goes on to quote Ned Hanlon, a Players' League manager this year, as saying, "I can conceive of a man making one mistake in such a matter and repenting, but for the life of me I don't know how McKean can have the hardihood to ask for a second reinstatement." Hanlon is quoted as advocating the banishment of "men like McKean" from both leagues. (One can only imagine McKean's feelings, five years later, when the Spiders met Hanlon's Orioles in Temple Cup competition.) A front page article by Wright in the same issue targeted McKean in the newspaper's campaign against the practice of jumping. "The McKean-Beatin Episode" gives Al Johnson's view priority ("McKean has a contract with us, which calls for his services commencing April 1, 1890.") over concerns voiced by Spiders secretary Hawley about the authorship of the Johnson telegram. Wright concludes erroneously: "McKean's vacillating course has completely disgusted even his friends in this city."

The engineering of the Players' League made it impossible for the Spiders to build on what successes they'd worked to realize in their inaugural season in the National League. Eb Beatin, last year's number three pitcher, was forced into service as the Spiders' ace. In 1890, he threw 474 of his total 946 career innings and lasted only one more season in the majors. Bob Gilks, the previous year's super-sub, was made the regular left fielder and hit a subpar .213. Charlie Zimmer would have caught every game if not for a late-season injury to his neck, but he hit just one point better than Gilks. Ed McKean played every game. In all, 25 men wore a Spiders uniform in 1890, eight of them pitchers; only five everyday players saw action in over 100 games. Ironically, the Brotherhood made for lifetime animosity among some players. Cub Stricker swore he'd never again play with McKean, on any club, in any league. Buck Ewing was never accepted by his Spiders teammates, even during his tremendous 1894 campaign with Cleveland, in the wake of his Brotherhood shenanigans. F.H. Brunell, the man who had named the Spiders, worked in the Players' League front office. Others, like Jimmy McAleer and Patsy Tebeau, found it easy enough to resume with the Spiders in 1891, after the collapse of the Brotherhood. At a later stage in McKean's life, in 1902, when he was the manager and his best player, a young man, defied him by threatening to jump the Rochester team, Ed McKean would be a hard-liner and disciplinarian—he would not play the role of the conciliator.

Gus Schmelz ran the Spiders' training camp like a boarding school. *The Sporting News* ran a telling anecdote about conditions under the new manager.

> It was his custom to assemble all the members of the team in his room at the hotel in the morning and put them through a lesson on the signs. Down at Hot Springs he called the roll promptly at 10 o'clock each morning, and the ball players lined up like the scholars in a class. One morning ... the young gentlemen ... agreed it would be a most excellent scheme to surprise the manager with a few original answers. One of the signals was communicated by the manager from the bench, and consisted in two raps upon the ground by a bat. It either meant to steal a base or sacrifice or something of the kind...
>
> Gus had his scholars toe the mark and seating himself in front of them picked up a bat and rapped twice upon the floor. No one said a word. "What is that, Beatin?" said Schmelz.
>
> "A bat," was the interesting rejoiner. The manager glanced with a peculiar significant expression at Beatin and passed on to the next. "What's that?" he said to Parsons, rapping again.
>
> "Two beers," said the player without a smile. Schmelz stood erect. Again he rapped.
>
> "What's that, Dailey?"
>
> "A noise," was the reply.
>
> Another duet of raps and a similar question of explanation to Veach.

FOUR. *Ed McKean and the Players' Revolt (1888–1890)* 105

"Spirits," replied Veach with his nose elevated as though he sniffed them.

By this time Schmelz could talk in five different languages with one motion of his vocal organs. He made a last attempt and thundering the bat on the floor yelled to the third baseman, "What's that, Smalley?"

The poor Californian, considerably flustered, could neither think what the true significance of the sign was nor what he had intended to answer. He stared vacantly at the wall for a brief time and finally managed to utter, "I don't know."

The expression on Smalley's face was too much for the manager and his temper, which had been crawling above boiling point, dropped to something normal at once and he had to join in the general laugh. The members of the team, however, rehearsed those signs about an hour longer than usual that morning.[46]

It's easy to picture team "elder" McKean among the bad boy instigators of this mini-revolt against their by-the-book pilot, and Schmelz pulling red hairs out of his fastidiously coiffed beard.

Fitness fanatic Schmelz placed a huge amount of importance on his team's spring training. He "arranged a grand exhibition tour" for Cleveland to "invade territory that has never before been covered by a regularly organized League team," according to *The Sporting News* on March 8, "the Spiders have the opening game in no less than five cities on their forthcoming Western trip." It was a forced march, beginning after two initial weeks of "boiling out" in Hot Springs, Arkansas, and dragging on until March 26, when the Chicago Colts took over the facilities. On St. Patrick's Day, March 17, in Hot Springs, a big crowd attended the exhibition "between the Cleveland League Club (all Irish) and a picked nine (all American)." Pitchers Ezra Lincoln and Jack Wadsworth, outfielders Bobby Gilks and Tom Dowse (normally a catcher), and catcher Chief Zimmer played for the nine; on the League team, "McKean showed up well."[47] Next, Schmelz roadtested his Spiders, starting with a three-game series in Kansas City against the Cowboys, then moving on to Omaha and Denver and back to Omaha, before dates in Sioux City and Des Moines, and, at last, on April 17 and 18, running aground in Evansville.[48] Schmelz was already at work experimenting with his lineup. For example, in the first Kansas City game, he penciled in McKean to bat third in the order; by April 12, McKean was his leadoff hitter.[49]

A bad incident marred the March 29 game in Denver, on the occasion of the minor league team's third straight win against the embarrassed National League visitors. In the eighth inning, with the score 2 to 0 in the Mountaineers' favor, Cleveland's Vince Dailey hit a triple. The outfielder returned the ball to third baseman John T. McGlone, "who played the dirty trick, which he attempted time and time again to perform while he was with Cleveland in 1888," shoving Dailey off the bag and tagging him. When the umpire called Dailey out on the play, team captain McKean kicked and, at length, took the

Spiders off the field. Schmelz subsequently thought it necessary to apologize on McKean's behalf to Mountaineers manager Dave Rowe, an act that undercut his captain.[50] McKean was overly familiar with McGlone's tricks, having played beside the third baseman in two seasons with the Blues. In the Patsy Tebeau era to be, McKean could count on his manager to back his on-the-field decisions.

The official results of Schmelz's ambitious exhibition schedule were inconclusive: in its six wins and six losses, Cleveland had scored a total of 85 runs, or over seven runs a game, to the opposition's 73. At the conclusion of the preseason, *The Sporting News* pronounced McKean to be "the same great player he always was," although his leg and ankle were "bothering him." Taking naturally to his added responsibilities as captain, "he braced the young pitchers up nicely."[51]

Mac was a force in the opening game of the regular season, a 10 to 6 drubbing of Cap Anson's Colts in Cleveland, on April 26. Batting leadoff and "wearing a white flannel uniform trimmed with black hat, belt, and stockings," McKean recorded the first hit of the 1890 campaign and scored the first run.[52] On the afternoon, McKean added two more hits, another run, and two stolen bases. He was also responsible for three errors and Joe Ardner, his new second baseman, contributed two of his own. The Spiders had Cleveland all to themselves for the day. The Infants opened on the road and wouldn't play their home opener until June 6.

It was natural for Cleveland fans to keep track of the comparative performances of hometown shortstops Delahanty and McKean as their seasons progressed. As play in May ended, McKean was leading his team, with a .358 batting average, and outplaying his Brotherhood counterpart at short, committing 50 errors and averaging 2.25 putouts and 3.10 assists per game to Delahanty's 1.78/3.35/.82.[53] *The Sporting News* reckoned "McKean fields better than ever."[54] On the down side, McKean suffered through five double-play partners on the year, and even played second base himself. The whole Spiders infield was in flux. Converted pitcher Peekaboo Veach was installed at first base, his only everyday job with a major league team, which kept the power-hitting Jake Virtue out of the lineup for half the season. And the loss of Patsy Tebeau to the Infants proved irreplaceable. His replacement Will Smalley played every game on the schedule and led the League's third basemen in chances, but he batted .213 with just 12 extra-base hits. Meanwhile, Tebeau, "one of the most popular players who has ever played in the Forest City," was "regarded by many as the best third baseman in the Players League."[55] Fortunately, George Davis was playing a spectacular center field and establishing himself as the Spiders slugger to complement McKean, so the outfield didn't miss McAleer.

Four. *Ed McKean and the Players' Revolt (1888–1890)* 107

Simply put, the Spiders had not assembled a competitive team—they'd been 10 or more games under .500 since June 6—and Schmelz was losing both games and his clubhouse. Two weeks before Gus Schmelz's resignation, he made Chief Zimmer team captain, replacing McKean, an indication of the widening divide between the manager and his best player.[56] Schmelz had been the one who personally coaxed his reluctant shortstop into joining the Spiders for 1890, even going so far as to leave with McKean on the train for Hot Springs in advance of the team.[57] Charles Mears reported the passing of the Schmelz regime for the August 2 *Sporting News*. In his autopsy, Mears unfavorably compared Gus Schmelz to Loftus. "Tom Loftus was a man who thought that a man who did not make an error occasionally was a record player while with Schmelz ... when a man makes an error ... he is sure to be overhauled for it and that kind of treatment only makes the case worse." Here one wonders how the proud yet sensitive McKean would have taken Schmelz's criticism.

Mears also took the occasion to revisit the issue of the sacrifice hit, under debate since Loftus' teams, this time siding with the sluggers. "Schmelz's idea of sacrifice hitting is ... rather antiquated. If ever a Clevelander is lucky enough to reach first the next man is told to bunt the ball and allow the runner to advance a base. This method is gone through again and then the Clevelands have a man on third, with two out and as one witty fellow said to me the other day the next man also sacrifices and the side is out." One wonders if the witty man was Ed McKean, who was known to have Mears' ear. Playing for Loftus, McKean continued his practice of sacrificing his at-bat instead of hitting away, the mark of a team leader rededicated to winning. McKean had never ceased his slugging. He hit two home runs off Pittsburgh left-hander Fred W. Osborne in an August 13 game, a three-run homer in the seventh and a two-run homer in the eighth.[58] McKean's blasts were two good reasons for the Alleghenys to send Osborne from the pitcher's box (where his record was 0–5) back to left field, and then down to the minor leagues.

It's entirely possible that McKean or Zimmer ran the team until Schmelz's successor could arrive from Detroit. In any event, Ed's mood had lifted. The same article that reported McKean's two-home-run day hints, tongue in cheek, that the self-reliant shortstop was bringing his own good luck to the ball yard of late. The Spiders' bats had gotten well—even Beatin and Zimmer at the bottom of the order were hitting—ostensibly because of a water cure:

> They are all using McKean's Grafton water which Mac claims helps a man's hitting like sixty. It is imported from Mac's home at Grafton in kegs, and it greatly reminds one of the Weddell House ginger snaps which so greatly aroused old Anson last year. Drink! Manager Leadley has ordered several hundred kegs of this wonderful beverage which he will have patented or copyrighted (under

which head it will come nobody knows) so that no other clubs will catch on to his little snap.

A copyright for either Mears or McKean would be most appropriate for such a tall tale! Perhaps McKean had been inspired, looking back to spring camp, by the commercial possibilities of the throng of tourists "taking the waters" at Hot Springs. We do know that mineral baths were discovered, the source of G. Hogan's commercial Devonian Springs mineral water, not far from Grafton, in 1887.[59] The writer would have us understand our man McKean was celebrating the new start to the season with libations of Devonian water in lieu of the bad luck Hot Springs variety or toasting the departed health nut Schmelz with a healthsome drink of his own concoction, instead of the customary rot gut. McKean worked as a distributor of liquor for the decade following his retirement from baseball.

The Spiders had been losing fans to the crosstown Infants, and Eb Beatin was badly overworked, when Davis Hawley brought in a southern Ohio farmer who had been making a lot of noise in Canton, Ohio. The papers

A gloveless McKean in the popular "action" pose of catching a studio popup. Over his big league career, McKean made 2,820 actual putouts at shortstop (National Baseball Hall of Fame and Library, Cooperstown, New York).

FOUR. Ed McKean and the Players' Revolt (1888–1890)

called him the "Canton Cyclone," or Cy for short.[60] Before Cy Young's debut, in Cleveland on August 6, Cap Anson dismissed the kid as "just another big farmer"; after the Colts managed just three hits in their loss to the raw rookie, Anson offered Hawley $1,000 on the spot to buy Young's contract. Outfitted in a Spiders uniform too small for him, Dent Young had outpitched Bill Hutchinson, who would win over 40 games on the year after losing to Cleveland on opening day. *The Sporting News* would say of Young's performance that day: "His curves were all unsolvable to all but [Malachi] Kittridge, [Howard] Earle and [Tom] Burns," those batters who accounted for the three Chicago hits off Young. "He pitches a very speedy ball that gets past a batter before he realizes what is happening and the result is that when the ball is hit it is either a pop-up fly or an easy chance to an infielder." Overall, "He was as cool as though he were home at Canton, instead of making his initial bow before a National League audience."[61] The game also marked the first time Charlie Zimmer caught Cy Young, the audition for one of the game's most memorable batteries. Over the rest of 1890, Young dominated at home and pitched poorly on the road, perhaps the result of a country boy having to adjust to rail travel between major league cities and to live out of hotel rooms. In an away game on August 16, the Red Stockings abused Young for 10 runs as the Spiders were shut out in a merciful 100 minutes. When the Spiders played Cincinnati, McKean's counterpart at short was usually Ollie Beard, one of the Chicago players who came to Nashville when McKean was ousted. Beard was a defensive-minded shortstop, one more fit for manager Tom Loftus's kind of game. The two shortstops' parallel careers make one way to evaluate just how far McKean had come.

With Young's inspired pitching and the manager Hawley had brought in earlier, the Spiders had the feel of a new team. Whereas Schmelz had shuffled the batting order like a deck of bad cards, Bob Leadley was quick to establish Gilks as his regular leadoff man and bat McKean behind him. Manager Leadley brought his own sense of discipline to the club, as well, fining workhorse Beatin $125 for poor pitching.[62] The skipper also showed unusual confidence in a player he'd inherited. He stuck with Zimmer during his consecutive game streak, in an age when starting catchers rarely caught 100 games in a whole season. Chief was going strong in his 109th straight game, on August 27, when he twice threw out Sliding Billy Hamilton. Hamilton, on his way to leading the League in stolen bases, had been gunned down only two times before all season.[63] It was Zimmer's own call when he did abandon his intention of catching every game, in consideration of his wife's serious illness.[64] It was not really a new team, of course; only the manager was new. *Sporting Life* sniped that "the Clevelands played like amateurs," when they went scoreless in Boston on

August 21.[65] His teammates made errors all over the park, eight in total, and yet the fielding of McKean was considered the game's feature. McKean was exciting to watch, a fearless shortstop who went after every ball. That year, he led League shortstops in errors with 75, but he was also third in putouts, fifth in assists, fifth in range, and fifth in fielding percentage.[66]

Individual statistics aside, the Cleveland teams lost four games in a single day, on September 1, the Spiders to the Giants and the Infants to the Boston Reds.[67] But the Spiders under Leadley's direction would give Cleveland followers reason to wait till next year—they entered play in October victorious in 12 of their previous 16 games and became the talk of the town once more.[68] The extraordinary season of parallel clubs ended at home for both Cleveland teams, on October 4, against the two teams from Philadelphia. For the Spiders, Cy Young pitched both games of a doubleheader and won them both; his burden was somewhat lightened when the second game was called for darkness after seven frames. In the coming season, Young would have the distinction of starting the first game ever played in Frank Robison's new League Park, at Lexington Avenue and East 66th.

Ed McKean's decision to remain a loyal Spider during the Brotherhood season was ultimately a happy one, for player and team. He was the club leader in games played, hits, triples (fifth in the National League), homers (also fifth in the League), walks (a career high 87), on-base percentage (fourth-best in the League), stolen bases, and slugging. His final batting average was .296. McKean regularly batted ahead of George Davis and came in second to him in runs batted in on the team. A star player nearing the height of his powers, Edward McKean had just completed the first third of his major league career.

1895 Temple Cup: October 2, Game One

"I generally hit every thing I can see—when I get really excited."
"And I hit every thing within reach," cried Tweedledum, "whether I can see it or not!"
Alice laughed. "You must hit the trees pretty often...."
—Lewis Carroll

An overflow crowd 7,000 strong turned out to watch the opening game of the Temple Cup. Average attendance at League Park for the regular season had been about 2,200 faithful—and a ticket cost one dollar for the postseason exhibition, instead of the usual 50 cents—so this gate had all the promises of healthy shares for the players at the conclusion of the best-of-seven series.[1] Certainly, the 1895 Spiders were no strangers to performing before big crowds: precisely one month before, some 21,000 cranks shoehorned themselves into New York's Polo Grounds to witness Nig Cuppy, master of the soft toss, go face to face against Amos Rusie, whose fastball rivaled Cyclone Young's.[2] Even the Spiders' away games had become a sensation among Cleveland's fanatics. Earlier in September, when the games in a Baltimore series were "reproduced by electricity" and a talented telegraph operator, the Cleveland Lyceum had to turn away "several hundred people."[3]

This day's postseason contest with the Orioles was a showcase for the two best shortstops in the game. Fresh off a season in which he generated 204 hits, drove across 125 runs, stole 53 bases, and led all shortstops in fielding chances and percentage, Baltimore's Hugh Jennings played wonderfully in the losing cause. Cleveland cranks were rooting for Jennings' complement, and hometown favorite Ed McKean didn't disappoint. The visiting scribe from the *Pittsburgh Press* wrote that "Ed McKean monopolized the applause [starting] in the second inning. He participated in the three plays made beginning by making a running catch of Brodie's line drive. McKean did the best batting, but his double and triple were wasted, and only his single helped to boost Cleveland's score."[4]

It took until Ed McKean's ninth year as the Cleveland shortstop, and a Temple Cup championship, for his infield play to be widely acclaimed in the papers. One observer, who had had the advantage of playing outfield behind McKean since their days at Youngstown, supplied the most memorable appreciation of McKean in the field. At the height of McKean's popularity, in October 1895, Jimmy McAleer described what we might think of today as the prototypical modern shortstop and slugger:

> Season after season he has gone along in his steady gait, winning game after game for Cleveland, either with his bat or in the field, and yet there is no fuss made about him. When he makes an error there is the usual groan; when he makes a brilliant play there is usually nothing but large wads of silence. And after all these things are a compliment to McKean. They show that the people expect him to play good ball as a natural course. There is no surprise and applause when he does well, but there is plenty of the former when he does poorly. Records on this point are hard to get, but it is safe to say that McKean has batted in more runs for Cleveland this season than any other player. Others may reach first base oftener than he, but who in the team is there who has the confidence of the Cleveland base ball lovers more than McKean, when a hit is necessary to win a game.[5]

Runs batted in was not an official statistic in the Deadball Era, but the reconstructions of Ed McKean's career, box score by box score, confirm that he led his Cleveland teams in that category six times. (See Appendix B.) His bat accounted for a career high 1.06 RBIs per game in the 1893 season. McAleer's tribute to his teammate continues:

> McKean never was and never will be a showy player in his position. This is because of his throwing style. Players like Hugh Jennings and Fred Ely appear faster than McKean. This is because they have the long-arm style of throwing the ball. After getting the ball these players, and many others, pull their arms back as far as they will go and let the ball drive toward first base. This pulling the arm back of the shoulder loses valuable time and the throw must be fast to catch the runner. But it looks nice. McKean's style is the short-arm or side-snap throw. It isn't pretty to look upon, but it catches the runner and is safer.

Ed McKean's name frequents the lists of historically worst seasons by shortstops. The easy, but misleading, conclusion would be that he was one of baseball's all-time bad fielders, certainly not the kind of player one would enshrine in Cooperstown. It is a bit of a technicality, but Ed McKean did not commit the 105 errors that record books show for his 1887 season. He made 99 miscues—bad enough to tie Cincinnati's Frank Fennelly for most errors that season among American Association shortstops—plus half a dozen more in eight games at second base. Of course, McKean was learning the position by playing nearly every day in his rookie season.

McKean finished fourth in the Association in range among shortstops in 1887.[6] By 1888, his .909 fielding percentage led all American Association shortstops, and he came in second in 1889. Ed McKean was steady: he logged the most games at short in the National League for 1891, 1894, and the Temple Cup seasons of 1895 and 1896.

Errors back then were about as common as bases on balls are in today's game. In that same season of 1887, Louisville shortstop Bill White made 96. And 100-error seasons were not unheard of in the Deadball Era: 16 shortstops between 1884 and 1893, including Hall of Famer Monte Ward in 1890, hit the century mark in errors. Ed Delahanty's biographer Jerrold Casway makes it clear that, by 1890, McKean was held to be a model for "the perceived quick-thinking Irish infielder," not a defensive liability.[7] It's also clear that the Spiders owner favored aggressive play, the kind Patsy Tebeau demanded and Ed McKean practiced, over fielding percentages. "The game can be improved if the fielding averages are abolished," Frank Robison calculated in 1896, adding:

> That would prove a remedy for the record players who are seeking the bubble reputation through the medium of figures which do not mean facts. The secret of the success of the Cleveland team is that there isn't one record player on it. The fielder who is afraid to take a chance on a ball for fear of making an error is a coward, and he can be cured of this cowardice if fielding averages are done away with.[8]

No one in McKean's day could accuse him of being a record player, a fact that makes him all the more difficult to evaluate today. Writing upon the occasion of McKean's death, in 1919, the *Pittsburgh Press* unequivocally recalled that the shortstop "had a life's average of .900 in fielding in the days when gloves were unknown as part of the equipment of infielders. Only four other shortstops of the old school can boast of a record which carried their names in the .900 class—Jack Glasscock, George Davis, Herman Long and Bill Dahlen."[9] In McKean's case, the writer's personal memory would seem to trump our sabermetrics.

After being shuffled between the outfield and shortstop in his sophomore season, McKean became an ironman shortstop—fourth in games played among all pre-1900 shortstops—and did average well above .900 over the rest of his career (.005 above the average shortstop in his period). Ed McKean's strengths at short were his strong arm, and his aggressiveness tempered by baseball intelligence. The level-headed F.H. Brunell once attested to the rookie's impressive athleticism: "McKean throws with either hand, and will be up with [Chippy] McGarr and George Smith, unless I'm a wild guesser."[10] In the time before fielders wore gloves, a talented shortstop could use both hands for throwing. His weaknesses was always his range. It was never better than average for a major league shortstop; in mid-career, McKean became slow afoot and his range got to be more and more limited. We can surmise, from a compilation by Baseball-Reference.com of total chances, that McKean's range among major league shortstops for the seasons from 1887 through 1891 was average. Then, starting with his finger-injury season of 1892, McKean ranked dead last in total chances among National League shortstops for six of his last seven years as a regular. When he got to a ball, he was sure handed. His fielding percentages rose steadily through the second half of McKean's career, probably upon his adoption of a rudimentary fielder's glove.[11] After game one of the Temple Cup, a Cleveland paper noted that "McKean and Young fielded extraordinarily," as did Baltimore's Jennings and McGraw.[12]

The Spiders were a formidable team in 1895, especially when playing at League Park, where they won 47 of 60 games. Jesse Burkett won the batting championship, averaging .409, and his 225 hits topped the League. Ed McKean's 283 total bases were good for fourth among National League hitters, ranking him just behind Burkett. McKean and Willie Keeler managed an improbable tie, after a schedule of 130 games, with a League-high 565 at-bats apiece. Cy Young (35 wins) edged out Baltimore's rookie Billy Hoffer for the most victories in baseball; Nig Cuppy was fourth (26 wins). The National League was a hitter's delight in 1895, three seasons into the ruling that moved pitchers back to 60 feet, six inches: Young's healthy .294 on-base percentage was the lowest, and Chief Zimmer, famous for his defense, belted .340 that season. Bill Hoffer finished the season third in ERA (3.21) to Cy Young's fifth (3.26). The Orioles were the best defensive team in the game, if we judge by fielding percentage. Jennings led shortstops in both fielding percentage and chances; rookie first baseman Scoops Carey and receiver Wilbert Robinson completed the regular season with the highest fielding percentages at their positions.[13]

The lineups deployed by the managers in game one remained set for the whole series, with the exception of the starting pitchers, and Boileryard Clarke catching for Robinson in game two:

Baltimore	*Cleveland*
McGraw, 3b.	Burkett, lf.
Keeler, lf.	McKean, ss.
Jennings, ss.	Childs, 2b.
J. Kelley, lf.	McAleer, lf.
Brodie, cf.	O. Tebeau, 1b.

Gleason, 2b.	Zimmer, c.
Carey, 1b.	Blake, rf.
Robinson, c.	McGarr, 3b.
McMahon, p.	Young, p.[14]

It was no great surprise to Cleveland fans when Cy Young and Sadie McMahon kept the teams scoreless through the first four frames. Young, McMahon, and Bill Hoffer had led the League that season with four shutouts apiece, McMahon's shutouts all coming after his Lazarus-like return to the Orioles staff in August. On the other hand, Ned Hanlon's pick of McMahon was somewhat unexpected, considering the aging twirler's recent history of shoulder and drinking problems and the emergence of Hoffer, a fresh arm who had just gone 31–6 for his freshman year. Or was it just like Foxy Ned to go with his fabled instincts and ride the hot hand one more time?

In the bottom of the fifth inning, Ed McKean drove home the game's first tally, mostly thanks to Chippy McGarr's aggressive base running. McGarr, who also stole two bases on the afternoon, had led off the half inning with a single to left. Cy Young followed with a bunt that went for a base hit. Either Patsy Tebeau ordered two consecutive bunts (in a playoff game), or Crab Burkett (one of the most accomplished bunters in baseball history) tried to lay one down for a hit. The result was a Burkett sacrifice and Spiders on second and third, bringing McKean to the plate. The crowd must have reacted wildly at the prospect as Ed McKean's 119 RBIs paced Cleveland this season, enough for fifth overall in the League. The pitcher won the battle this time—McKean pulled a McMahon pitch but managed only to lift a popout to Baltimore second baseman Kid Gleason—however, an alert McGarr tagged up at third base and scampered home before Gleason could recover and throw to the plate. Had Chippy McGarr, or his third base coacher, determined to challenge Gleason, a pitcher until this season? Did Kid Gleason have to make the catch with his back to the infield?

William J. Gleason opened the season as one of the pitchers Baltimore was counting on, a winner of 136 career games, 15 from the previous season. After he dropped four of his first six decisions to start 1895, Hanlon replaced him on the staff—purchasing Dad Clarkson from St. Louis—and installed Gleason at second base. He enjoyed his career year at the plate, hitting over .300 and teaming up with Hugh Jennings in a memorable infield. Although he competed for 22 seasons as a big league player respected in two centuries for his all-round play and fighting ability, Kid Gleason is best remembered today for another championship series. In the 1919 World Series, he was the guileless manager of the Chicago Black Sox.

In any case, Cleveland had scored first in the Temple Cup.

Baltimore came back with a run in the sixth inning when Mugsy McGraw scored on an infield hit by Joe Kelley. McGraw had singled, advanced to second on Keeler's ground out, and taken third on Jennings' fly to Jimmy McAleer. Neither Young nor McMahon had been scored on convincingly by the offenses, but their armor had been pierced. Cleveland resumed the lead in the next inning, the seventh. Patsy Tebeau singled and Chief Zimmer somehow legged out a ground ball to Kid Gleason. (Keep in mind, a virtual replay of the scratch hit and tardy throw would be decisive in the ninth inning.) Tebeau subsequently scored on Harry Blake's ringing double off the wooden fence in left field. Blake was emerging as one of those otherwise obscure ball players who save their heroics for the big stage of the playoffs. Like center fielder McAleer, right fielder Dude Blake was on the team to catch and throw the ball in the outfield. Patsy Tebeau's Spiders always seemed to be in search of a right fielder; temporary fixes over the years would be Peach Pie O'Connor (a catcher by trade), Buck Ewing (in the Hall of Fame as a catcher), and the doomed Louis Sockalexis. Tebeau found the 20-year-old native of Portsmouth, Ohio, on Southern League Atlanta's roster in 1894 and originally platooned him in the outfield. A season later, Blake was the starting right fielder in the Temple Cup. Harry Cooper Blake was to hit safely in four of the five games in the series, and contribute two big game-winning RBIs. He would enjoy his best season on manager Ed McKean's 1902 Rochester club.

The Orioles weren't finished yet. In their half of the eighth inning, McGraw singled again, advanced into scoring position on Keeler's groundout, and came home on Jennings' base hit. At this crucial juncture in the game, Dent Young's defense came up just short on two plays. A Kelley fly ball fell in front of a charging McAleer, perhaps the only man in the League who had a chance for that ball, sending Jennings to third base. Young induced the next batter, Steve Brodie, to force Joe Kelley at second, but Hugh Jennings scored when McKean's relay to Tebeau was too late for a double play. The Spiders' bad luck continued into their half of the eighth, when Tebeau was not awarded first base after he'd apparently been hit by a pitch—umpires Tim Keefe and James McDonald ruled that Patsy had made no effort to get out of the way of the ball. After his usual bout of extreme kicking, Tebeau finally got back into the batter's box and settled the matter by doubling. He scored on Harry Blake's single, and second run batted in of the game, to knot the score at 3 to 3. It was a new game.

Wilbert Robinson doubled off Cy Young in the ninth inning, and Baltimore led when John McGraw solved Young for a two-out hit to plate his buddy Robinson with the go-ahead run. Uncle Robbie was a good-hitting catcher. Back on June 10, 1892, he had seven hits in seven times at the plate, and drove in 11 runs, in Baltimore's 20-inning win over St. Louis. It was the longest game played in the nineteenth century, and Robinson caught and hit all day long.

So the stage was set for Cleveland's catcher Chief Zimmer and second baseman Kid Gleason to become, respectively, the hero and the goat of the game. Jesse Burkett led off the Cleveland half of the ninth with his first hit of the game, a double. Ed McKean was the next hitter. When he came to the plate in the gathering dusk, it was hard to see the ball come out of Sadie McMahon's hand. He'd already doubled and tripled off McMahon when it was daylight. Now McKean strong-armed a long single into right field, in spite of being fooled by the pitch,[15] chasing Burkett home with the game-tying run. Next, McKean's keystone partner Cupid Childs worked the count, until he found the pitch he wanted, and singled. Jimmy McAleer, batting fourth in the lineup as he often did back in the Youngstown days with McKean, tried to advance both runners into scoring position by laying down a bunt. It was beginning to look like the home team's day when the bunt went for a hit that loaded the bases with Spiders. Ned Hanlon drew in his infielders for a play at the plate, and Tebeau obliged him by hitting a grounder, forcing McKean at home. Then it was Chief Zimmer's turn at the bat.

Zimmer had followed McKean, the year after, from Rochester to Cleveland. He had astonished the baseball world by catching almost every game in the 1890 season, when no National Leaguer had ever caught as many as 100 games for a year. Over the span of three successive seasons with the Spiders, he played in 352 games, handling Cy Young's fastball and Nig Cuppy's off-speed junk, and making it all look equally easy. Nearing the end of his career, Zimmer once claimed:

> Though I have been playing for a good many years, I have never suffered with a sore arm in the spring of the year. I can throw the first ball in the spring just as hard as I can at any time during the season. Furthermore, I have never had a finger hurt since I have been in the league. I was with the Cleveland team for 13 years, and in 12 of the 13 years I caught over 100 games each year, yet I never had a finger hurt nor even a nail bruised. I have but two broken fingers on my hands, and I broke them before I was playing professionally.[16]

Ohio-born Charles Zimmer was especially valuable on Tebeau's clubs—prone as they were to kicking and even losing games because of their abuse of umpires—for his calm, level-headed presence behind the plate. Unlike his teammates, he never swore, drank, or smoked. And yet, Zimmer was a leader of the rough bunch of men who played baseball for a living; in the spring of 1900, Zimmer was one of three stars who proposed a players' union as we know, in the wake of the failed Brotherhood experiment a decade earlier.[17] Patsy

Tebeau had given Zimmer his nickname, not for his dark complexion but because he imagined the catcher's demeanor resembled a police chief's. He and McKean would be reunited briefly in the minor leagues, as manager and first baseman, for Little Rock in 1906.

It was most likely Ed McKean who told Elmer Bates a story that purportedly "dated" Charlie Zimmer's offseason business acumen (at one time or other, he operated a tobacco emporium and was one of the first players to endorse his own brand of cigars, a clothing store, and marketed his own baseball board game) all the way "back to the big catcher's infancy," when Zimmer was was approached one day by a stranger:

> "Here, me foine lad," said the stranger, "could you be after telling me phwat has become of old Mrs. Maloney, who lived about these parts at wan time?"
> "I could if you give me a dime," said Charley.
> "Well, here it is, me boy; now, where is she?"
> "Dead!" yelled Charley, as he legged it for home.[18]

The bases were still loaded when Chief Zimmer stroked the perfect double-play ball, right at Kid Gleason. Gleason easily fielded the slow grounder, stepped on second base to force Tebeau, and threw to Scoops Carey to double up Zimmer. One of Charlie Zimmer's attributes as a star player was not his speed on the baselines. In fact, it was a curiosity for Clevelanders to see Zimmer moving so rapidly when he cycled his bike to League Park.[19] Nevertheless, umpire Keefe ruled the catcher safe at first, just as Childs crossed home plate with the game-winning run. Exiting the park, it struck people that Tim Keefe and Kid Gleason were only four years removed from pitching together on the Philadelphia staff. Whether or not Gleason's relative inexperience at turning the double play had handed the game to the Spiders, it was a memorable play for Cleveland. The first game of the Temple Cup was theirs, by the slimmest of margins, 5 to 4.

The game didn't end there for some cranks. They clustered threateningly around the Baltimore bench and set an angry tone for the rest of the series.

FIVE

The Spiders Make a "World's Series" (1891–1892)

> A milk and water, goody-goody player can't wear a Cleveland uniform.
> —Oliver Tebeau

With the collapse of the Players' League and the rival Cleveland Infants, Frank Robison got his roster back and pushed to add key personnel, sometimes against the wishes of his stockholders, committing the Spiders to a rebuilding process that would take them to three National League postseason series in five years. His players were eager to return to work. In mid–March, club treasurer Davis Hawley spent one whole day writing checks for advance money to players, back in Cleveland from a winter without paychecks.[1] Hawley had to act precipitously to make Jim McAleer a Spider again, since Al Johnson had sold his contract to Browns owner Christian von der Ahe.[2] Ed McKean was "get[ting] first-class pay,"[3] plus a small supplement for endorsing a new line of spiked baseball shoes, a pair advertised for $7.50. Among many other players, McAleer, Eb Beatin, Jersey Bakely, Dent Young, Ed Delahanty, and Clarence Childs also lent their names to the shoes manufactured by Waldo M. Claflin of Philadelphia.[4] Before Cleveland could pluck the stocky second baseman off American Association Syracuse's roster, Childs had to be cleared to play by a court, Judge Phelps basing his decision on the National Agreement.[5] Cupid Childs blossomed into one of the Leagues' hitting stars in his sophomore season with the Spiders. He was McKean's double play partner for the rest of the shortstop's career in Cleveland.

The Spiders pitching would be improved for 1891, if only because the staff would have Cy Young for his first full year in the majors. The ace won 27 games for the 1891 Spiders, the most for a Cleveland pitcher since Jim McCormick's days with the National League Blues. Hawley also attempted to sign George Koppe, although the 22-year-old decided to finish the season with the Meadville, Pennsylvania, team.[6] As Nig Cuppy, he would join Young in Cleveland the following year to form the premier pitching duo in the League. Arguably, the key development at the launch of the new season was the resigning of Patsy Tebeau to play third base and serve as team captain. After Tebeau's eventual promotion to manage the Spiders, in July 1891, Cleveland would be perennial contenders. By August, Ralph Johnson, one of the team's better hitters but a right butcher in right field—*The Sporting News* excoriated him as one of the League's worst fielders[7]—was replaced by Jesse Burkett. The Crab would make a brilliant fit on the Spiders during the time of Tebeau. If he wasn't much of a defensive improvement on the banished Johnson, he was fire-in-the-belly Oliver Tebeau's kind of player. And Burkett hit—he would average over .400 in back-to-back seasons with the Spiders.[8]

Manager Tebeau's one blind spot was George Davis' star potential: he shifted the kid from center field to third base, and let him fill in for McKean at short, before trading him away. Chances are, Tebeau never warmed to the player fans called Gorgeous George, even though Davis was the son of an Irish immigrant father. Tebeau probably sized up Davis, the way he would Jake Virtue, as someone among his "fighting Spiders" who lacked "gravel."

Cleveland signed George Davis from an Albany semi-pro team to replace McAleer in center for 1890, and the rookie wound up leading the League with 35 assists. When McAleer returned to the Spiders from his dalliance in the Players' League, he was relegated to left field in favor of Davis, who was by far the superior hitter. Before the 1893 season, George Davis was sent to the Giants, in return for some much-needed cash for the over-extended Robison plus an aging Buck Ewing to put in right field. Ewing had one of his last great years at the bat for Cleveland

Jesse Burkett, pictured here about 1921 as a coach for none other than John McGraw, was a "one-man riot" in his playing days. For the two seasons the Spiders contested McGraw and the Orioles for the Temple Cup, Burkett averaged .405 and .410 (Mears Auction).

FIVE. *The Spiders Make a "World's Series" (1891–1892)*

in 1893, but he was a Jonah in the clubhouse. Davis responded to the trade by going on a 33-game hitting streak with his new club. In New York, shortstop Davis was to find his position and his mentor, the old shortstop John Montgomery Ward. He even "grew a handlebar mustache that resembled Ward's, making it difficult to tell the two apart."[9] In 20 seasons, Davis led his league in fielding four times, twice in the National League and two more seasons in the American League, and amassed 689 extra-base hits with 1,440 RBIs, on his way to a reunion with Ward in Cooperstown. To his credit, McKean seemed unthreatened by the emergence of George Davis, even managing to be generous about the way Davis played the infield (67 games at third base and 21 at short) when first he, and then Tebeau, went down with injuries. "He's the greatest all-around player living," McKean told the press.[10]

The talk in the Forest City this spring concerned the latest player signings, in contrast to last season's persistent rounds of broken contracts and threats of litigation, and also progress on the new ball park. Having won his civil war with the Brotherhood Infants, Frank Robison reunited Cleveland baseball cranks inside a recently erected League Park at the East 66th and Lexington Avenue stop on his streetcar line. This League Park's memorably short and high right field wall (290 feet from home plate; only 240 feet for overflow crowds)[11] would be tattooed by Cleveland sluggers, from McKean to Lajoie to Speaker and Averill, over the decades. Construction of the field and wooden grandstand, undertaken in February and finished in unseasonably snowy weather in time for the May 1 home opener, was facilitated by recycled sod and lumber from the old park and also by the playing schedule, which had the team start the season with 14 games on the road.[12] Cy Young pitched the first game in League Park II, against former Cleveland manager Tom Loftus' Cincinnati Reds.

Contrary to its many moves toward improving the Spiders for 1891, the front office made the unsound decision to stick with Bob Leadley. Manager Leadley was originally signed in 1890 apparently on the strength of Davis Hawley's fascination with Detroit's success of 1887 and the availability of its personnel after the National League dropped the franchise in favor of Cleveland. The upstanding Hawley proved himself a poor judge of character in Leadley's case, for Robert H. Leadley was a confidence man, with a modicum of managerial experience. He'd been mostly a hanger-on in Detroit, rising from team secretary to interim manager and slinking back to the minor-league Detroit club after his tenure in Cleveland, never to manage again in the majors. Bob Leadley did organize the benefit game, in 1894, for disabled Charlie Bennett—only to wind up defrauding the Detroit icon.[13] In coming years, the man *Sporting Life* once identified as the "ex-manager, ex-magnate and now absconding police clerk of the city of Detroit" ran Ban Johnson's Western League franchise in Grand Rapids into the ground and sold off its players for his own profit.[14] His nefarious financial misdeeds eventually chased him into Mexico near the end of an unsavory life. The most positive thing about Leadley's comparatively benign stay in Cleveland was that he didn't spend as much of the Robisons' money on telegrams as had Gus Schmelz, the previous manager, writing letters instead.[15] Davis Hawley's record for signing managers, before finding a fit in Tebeau, has the looks of a multi-car train wreck. Not one of his four hires—Jimmy Williams, Tom Loftus, Gus Schmelz, and Bob Leadley comprise the rogues' gallery—stayed in Cleveland long enough to complete so much as two full seasons with the Spiders.

This year, Ed McKean seemed particularly keen to play baseball and reverse his poor start to 1890; he was a hot hitter from spring training. McKean homered in an April 1 game against the Gainsville home team, and he and Tebeau led the Spiders' attack with two doubles each during a preseason schedule that had been abbreviated to a fortnight due to Robison's new-construction-depleted budget.[16] Of some note was Cleveland's 6 to 3 win over Pittsburgh in St. Augustine, as it was the very first spring training game between major league teams ever played in Florida. After Leadley's Spiders beat about every team who dared to schedule them, it soon came time for the club to break camp and play its way north. Along the way, Ned Hanlon "conceded" several exhibition matches after Cleveland had "done his team up and down," humiliating his Alleghenys.[17]

Cleveland marched into the 1891 campaign by sweeping Cincinnati, April 22 through 25. Young George Davis was the star of the opening games: "All through the series the batting and fielding of Davis was phenomenal. He made several hairlifting catches and made two singles and a triple on Wednesday, a single on Thursday, two singles and a three base on Friday and three triples and a home run on Saturday."[18] These Spiders had every appearance of being a winner, outscoring the Reds 41 to 18 in their own park. The one source of anxiety might have been four errors at third base early in an injury-marred season for Tebeau. (He was destined to emerge from a hospital to take charge as manager at mid-season.) McKean's first home run of the season came in Pittsburgh on April 26. Before then, Leadley had settled on him to bat second in his lineup, behind leadoff man McAleer and followed by Davis; Cupid Childs hit cleanup, mitigating his lofty on-base percentage.

The Cleveland home opener, which was also the inaugural game for League Park, sustained the Spiders' upbeat spring.[19] The colossal crowd of 9,500 was unprecedented, happily delaying the start of the game to accommodate the overflow in the 6,000-seat park. Howard White helped out with ticket

FIVE. *The Spiders Make a "World's Series" (1891–1892)*   123

buyers; he'd been a Cleveland club stockholder since the American Association era and had to think back to the Fourth of July of 1889 to recall such a crowd. The Spiders rewarded the grand assembly of cranks with a memorable 12 to 3 victory over Cincinnati. Ed McKean's one hit in five at-bats drove in a run, and he scored twice; but the Spiders' hit parade was led by Kid Childs' four RBIs and Jake Virtue's two triples. Arlie Latham's three-run homer late in the contest, when Cleveland already had the game won, accounted for all the runs off Cyclone Young. Latham's eighth-inning blast over the left-field wall was the first home run in League Park. In recognition of the longest visitor's hit of the day, he was awarded a box of cigars. Latham had been a star at third base for the American Association St. Louis Browns dynasty dating back to the mid–1880s. The one the press adored as The Freshest Man on Earth was years later hired by John McGraw to be the first professional base coach; as a player, he'd always been a top-notch agitator from the coaching boxes. Jake Virtue won the host team's box of cigars for his two long hits. The switch-hitter spent his five-year major league career with Cleveland, as its starting first baseman for 1891 and the following season. In his best season, 1892, his bat produced 20 triples and 89 RBIs, but he struck out too much. After he managed only three hits in 24 at-bats in that year's "world's series," Tebeau considered him a utilityman.

Jake Virtue's nickname was Guesses, and baseball historians still guess which hand he threw with, although period newspapers clearly indicate he was a southpaw. John Foster once wrote that Virtue's throwing was "a poem. He draws back that left arm with the ease and grace of a practiced gymnast and then shoots it forward and the ball never misses its mark." Foster recalled "the first game in Philadelphia in which Virtue played," toward the end of the 1890 campaign:

> [Billy] Hamilton reached first safely and then tried to get to third on one of Billy Sunday's short hits. The ball was fielded to Virtue and he slammed it across to [Cleveland third baseman] Smalley. The latter stood on the line waiting for Hamilton to get [to] him and touched him out. A most laughable look of astonishment spread over Hamilton's face. He went back to the bench and said to Clements: "Say, John, are there two balls in this game, or was I dreaming when I thought Sunday hit the ball out?" "Dreaming," said Clements, "didn't you see that left-handed mug over there on first base almost knock Smalley over with the ball? Us lefthanders are dangerous people."[20]

Cleveland's record was 6–3 after Cy Young's May Day victory, and cranks could be excused for dreaming of a finish somewhere in the upper division. Ed McKean had extended his spring slugfest into the regular season. On May 5, he singled, doubled, tripled and drove in a run off Jesse Duryea's curveballs, and Young found a way to win 15 to 12 over Cincinnati. Bob Leadley recognized his shortstop's importance as a leader and made the longest-serving Spider team captain. One of Captain McKean's signature ploys was to call time during a game, ostensibly to tie his shoe laces, and give his pitcher a breather.[21]

The Sporting News for May 30 reprinted a poem which affords us a glimpse of Cleveland hitters from some amateur poet's bleacher seat, so close to the League Park diamond "[he] could have shaken hands with the third-baseman, / And ... also very near the plate." It goes, in part:

> 'Twas in the fourth that Cleveland opened business:
> Viau hit the ball right down between his toes;
> Swift Clarkson made a very pretty pick-up
> And then one of his famous lighting throws
> But Cleveland's pitcher scooted like a race-horse
> And ere tall Tucker could the sphere obtain
> Viau had got landed on first base in safety
> And Powers could not call him back again.
>
> Then McAleer walked up to swat the leather:
> He looked the pitcher fiercely in the eye.
> Next dug two little holes to put his feet in
> And waived his ugly-looking bat on high.
> Three times the ball went whistling toward the catcher.
> It seemed to split the rubber plate in twain;
> "Mac" failed to pulverize the sphere and then the
> Boys on the bench they called him back again.
>
> McKean next walked slowly to the rubber:
> He shut his teeth and stoutly braced his nerves;
> At length there was a deafening crack, and he had
> Removed the starch from one of Clarkson's curves.
> The ball sailed off, pursued by Fielder Stovey,
> Who tried to catch it on the fly in vain;
> "Mac" stopped at third while Viau went home and tallied,
> And Powers dared not call him back again.
> Next Davis squared himself to do some hitting,
> And Clarkson sent the ball right o'er the plate:
> A second later out to left 'twas sailing
> And Lowe o'ertook it just a little late.
> Out of his hands the slippery globule bounded;
> McKean scored and Childs, the cherub, then
> Hit up a fly and started round the bases,
> But Powers quickly called him back again....[22]

This rude verse commemorates the game of May 23, in which McKean went 2-for-5, with a stolen base and a sacrifice hit. All indications are that Ed McKean, who triples in the poem off John Clarkson, was a deadly curveball

FIVE. *The Spiders Make a "World's Series" (1891–1892)*

hitter. Reportedly, Phil "Powers gave an awful exhibition of umpiring that day, at one point Billy Nash simply ignored him when he ordered him off the field and continued to play."[23] John Clarkson and Lee Viau, the game's pitchers, were to switch teams during the 1892 season. But for 1891, Viau was Cleveland's second-best pitcher, starting 38 times and going 18–17, with an ERA bettered on the staff only by Cy Young's. Gus Schmelz always remembered Lee Viau was a matinee idol. "Viau's good looks were written all over the American association circuit [in 1888], and while we [Cincinnati Reds] were on the road scores of women actually came to the train to bask in the radiance of Leon's charms."[24]

In June, *The Sporting News* supplied a few more precious details of Spider batting habits. Ralph Johnson

> complains that one reason he doesn't get down to first any faster is that the hole dug at the plate by the other left handers handicaps him. Childs digs a hole near the plate, McKean makes his about half way to first, Davis a few inches back of Childs', while Virtue and Johnson stand between Davis' and McKean's dug out. After an inning or so has been played, especially when the opposing team has any left handed batters, the holes all merge into one big cavern and it's an impossibility to get a start. McKean, however, manages to get one on account of his standing back so far from the plate.[25]

Although no photographs seem to have survived except for canned studio poses, we can venture a picture of Ed McKean at-bat. His unorthodox batting stance was designed to facilitate both power hitting and putting the ball in play, as the situation dictated. He stood erect and well off the plate so he might extend his strong arms and drive a pitch to the outfield, or spring out of the batter's box on contact with the ball. By July of the 1891 season, the slugger was "getting a reputation for beating out hits to the short stop and third baseman and is pushing up his batting average thereby."[26] McKean's remarkably low strikeout rate—only 31.7 at-bats per strikeout, third best in the whole League, and just 19 strikeouts all year long—is graphic evidence of this team player's willingness to cut down on his powerful swing with two strikes in the count. He kept his hands together, choking up a bit on the heavy wagon-tongue bat held low and close to his belt. Phillips remarks that "Like King Kelly, he used an odd stance, showing pitchers only a part of his muscular figure and often causing them to balk."[27] To postmodern fans, McKean at the plate might have resembled Stan Musial. According to the playing rules of 1885 and 1887, a pitcher balked the batter to first base when he held the ball too long before a pitch, or when he started his pitching motion without delivering the ball. Apparently, McKean's closed stance could deceive pitchers into thinking he was not quite set in the batter's box.

Bob Leadley's Clevelanders were consistently losing, and his team captain

The 1892 Cleveland club, Champions of the "Second Season": (Standing) Cy Young, George Davis, George Rettger, John Shearon, Jack Doyle, Jimmy McAleer, Jack O'Connor, George Davies; (front) Jake Virtue, Tom Williams, Nig Cuppy, Cupid Childs, Patsy Tebeau, Lee Viau, Jesse Burkett, and Ed McKean (author's collection).

was gradually losing it himself on an extended eastern road trip in early June. On June 6, a wrathful McKean stood on the field in Boston and abased John Morrill, a popular former player and manager filling in for the regular umpire, for a strike call on Jake Virtue. McKean pointed a damning finger at the man they called Honest John and spit out his accusation before the hostile crowd: "That's wrong—you know it's wrong. You are doing us wrong and you mean to."[28] In another game, in Brooklyn on June 10, he abused umpire Jack McQuaid to his own satisfaction and a stiff $50 fine. McKean was kicking a safe call at the plate on a throw from Jim McAleer. Increasingly frustrated, the competitive "McKean still holds to his practice of calling down his players when they make a slip," abusing his authority and eroding his popularity among his own teammates.[29] On the positive side of the ledger, as play ended for the month, McKean had hit safely in 38 out of Cleveland's 51 games.[30] The rest of the team had gone cold under Leadley's management and the Spiders seemed content to play .500 ball. Inevitably, the Cleveland sports pages started a campaign to oust Leadley in favor of Patsy Tebeau, a manager of last year's Brotherhood Infants and a sparkplug of a player for the Spiders. Although the most cursory investigation into Bob Leadley's dealings would have been sufficient to villainize him and make Tebeau a hero, the papers got creative.

James Egan recalls, "In one story his fast thinking was credited with saving

FIVE. *The Spiders Make a "World's Series" (1891–1892)* 127

a man from drowning. The man had gotten drunk in the bar at the Kennard house—the players' hotel—and Pat had pulled him out of the lobby fountain just in time."[31] To be sure, Leadley was not to be blamed exclusively for the team's mediocre showing. It took, for instance, until July 9 for the first Spider to homer at League Park, a McKean shot for two runs off Boston's Pretzels Getzein.[32] The breakthrough home run occurred within a week of McKean's two home runs off Wild Bill Hutchinson in a July 3 game in Chicago. McKean notched four career homers against Hutchinson, the Yale graduate who was twice a 40-game winner.

The end for Robert Leadley in Cleveland came after the Spiders split an Independence Day doubleheader against Philadelphia, with two big crowds as witnesses to the team's ineptitude. They scored 15 runs in the morning game but were lucky to win by a single run. Starter Lee Viau squandered a 14 to 4 lead, and Leadley had to call in George Davis from the outfield for a shaky save. Philadelphia scored nine times in the afternoon game, while Cleveland nicked Kid Gleason for just one run. The League Park cranks, 7,000 for the first game and another 10,000 for game two, went home disappointed; with the loss, the Spiders had missed the chance to even their season's record at .500.[33] Patsy Tebeau, straight from a 10-week hospital stay, played third base in both games. A week later, Frank Robison initiated a new era in Cleveland baseball by firing Leadley and hiring Oliver Tebeau as his playing manager. It took little time for the team to be remade after Tebeau's image: the papers were soon calling them "the fighting Spiders." Unfortunately, this year's team was to fare no better with Tebeau at the helm; Cleveland would have to scramble to get back to a 42–42 record in early August. Playing adversity baseball for the rest of the schedule, Cleveland led the League in base hits and looked good at home (40–28 in League Park). Still, they finished in fifth place at 65–74, going only 34–40 under Tebeau. It was widely rumored that a losing streak was caused by the dissonance between McKean and his new manager over control of the team.[34] While we cannot know Ed McKean's aspirations, it would be understandable if he privately held that he should have been given Tebeau's job, in recognition of his career-long loyalty to the Robisons. It is clear that Cy Young at least initially resented the way Tebeau was using him to frequently come into games in relief of Hen Gruber and Viau; Young won only two games in six weeks after August 1.[35] And Jim McAleer had become permanently supplanted in center field by George Davis, even though no less an observer than Harry Wright testified, after a McAleer catch in Philadelphia, "I've seen a great many wonderful catches in my day, but McAleer's effort today beat them all. No one but McAleer could have made it."[36]

Meanwhile, in spite of his build up by the local press, playing-manager

Tebeau was proving himself a mortal, perhaps a bit more Trilby than Svengali. After Leadley's demise, it was the same team and the team was still capable of making problems for itself. "McKean makes errors seemingly easier than any other man in the League on account of his sulkiness. If he drops a batted ball, even though it lays a foot or so away, he'll not pick it up to make the play first intended. Mac is too old a man to act that way."[37] On one play in an August 5 game at the Polo Grounds, both player Tebeau and Ralph Johnson wound up standing on third base instead of loading the bases. Umpire Phil Powers declared both men out, and manager Tebeau could only protest the game to President Young afterwards. Charles Mears wrote that the Spiders, fallen into sixth place, were driving Cleveland fans to drink.[38] At the very time when McKean's batting average bottomed out at .277, George Davis still provided hope—his .323 average was sixth best among National League hitters, and his 121 base hits were the most among the top 10 hitters for average in the League.[39] But the lowest point of the season came in the August 18 game, when the Spiders rioted on the field in Cincinnati. With their sworn nemesis Phil Powers umpiring, Jimmy McAleer chased Arlie Latham across the field while menacing a bat, somewhat on the order of wrathful Achilles chasing Hektor around the walls of Troy. Other Spiders, including McKean, took part in the fracas with their fists. The writer of *The Sporting News* account of the brawl, in the lovingly lurid detail of yesteryear's journalism, placed the blame on dirty ball and inept umpiring:

> All the trouble came in the eighth. In this inning, McAleer, in turning third, viciously kicked Latham twice. Then Latham hit McAleer a hard punch on the jaw and knocked him down. This enraged [the usually pacific] Zimmer, who rushed at Latham like a mad bull. By this time McAleer had partially recovered and he ran to the home plate, where he secured a bat. He was half frenzied with rage, and with the bat brandished above his head in a threatening manner he bore down on Latham. The Reds' captain saw he was in danger of his life and turned and ran.
>
> McAleer pursued him, with nearly all the Cleveland players at his heels. McAleer had murder in his heart. He ran Latham out in center field, and, when he saw he could not catch him, threw the bat with all his might and main. It sped through the air with terrific force, but Latham was lucky enough to dodge it. McAleer continued to follow him. Zimmer, McKean, Viau and Childs were wild, and went on whipping the Reds' captain. The park police at once rushed on the field to stop the row. Four or five members of the city force, who were in the stands, came to their assistance. The spectators swarmed out in the field and players, police and spectators crowded and jostled each other all over left down in front of the club house.

It was a bad call by Powers earlier in that same eighth inning that gave the Spiders five runs to take a 6 to 2 lead in the game, and the play involved Ed McKean. With one out, McKean singled to center. Davis, the next batter

Five. The Spiders Make a "World's Series" (1891–1892) 129

up, hit an easy grounder which Bid McPhee fumbled at second. Tebeau then hit a pop fly which Latham allowed to hit the ground; his toss to McPhee forced McKean at second, and McPhee touched the bag to retire Davis on what would have been the double play which took Cleveland out of the inning. However, Powers ruled that McPhee touched second before he touched McKean, and that Davis was the only out. During the resulting protest by the Reds, Latham ran in to kick with Powers at home plate, leaving Pete Browning with the ball around third base. Cupid Childs, the coacher at third, tore the ball from Browning's hand and tossed it into center field, where Browning usually stood. Both McKean and Tebeau scampered home before the distracted Powers recovered and ordered them to return to their bases. When play finally resumed, Jake Virtue's fly ball was misplayed by Bug Holliday, allowing both runners to score and provoking Arlie Latham to scream at Powers: "Now see what you have done by your miserable decision." McAleer subsequently singled to score Virtue and, when he eventually advanced to third, Latham twice blocked his way on the base path—and the melee ensued.[10]

The riot in Cincinnati would not be an isolated event in the brief history of the Spiders. It can be seen as an omen of what would eventually scuttle Cleveland's run of success at the close of the 1896 season and ultimately close the Emerald Age of baseball.

Late in the season, the Spiders did play significant games, winning a series against the Chicago Colts that dashed Cap Anson's hopes for the pennant. Chicago, in first place since July 22, came into Cleveland having won 17 of its previous 19 games against the Spiders. In the opening game, on September 28, a hit by McKean drove in a crucial run. And his brilliant stop and throw, with two Colts on base in the ninth inning, saved Cy Young's 4 to 2 victory. *Sporting Life* called game two "the most desperately contested game seen in Cleveland. The Chicagos were simply wild to win," and Anson was all over the field exhorting his nine and playing like a much younger man. McKean came to bat with two out in the ninth inning, Henry Gruber anchored on second and Kid Childs on first. His triple scored both runners to tie the game, but McKean was thrown out at the plate trying for an inside-the-park homer. Chicago came back to win the game in their half inning. Ed McKean had four hits in the loss. Cy Young won for the second time in the series the next day, September 30, when the umpire called the game with two Colts on base and Cleveland ahead by seven runs. McKean was Patsy Tebeau's number three hitter in the lineup at this point in the season.[41]

McKean finished strong in 1891, a season in which he led the National League in games played and at-bats. His 170 base hits were good for second in the League. He scored 115 runs (sixth most in the League), slashed out 12 triples (10th most), and totaled 225 bases (seventh best). In the field, his 91 errors were the League high, but his 248 putouts ranked third best among shortstops, and he amassed a career high 463 assists. In a wrap up of the year in baseball, the October 10 *Sporting Life* observed: "This season McKean has shown visible improvement in handling slow ground hits. They were always hardest for him to take care of, and it is probable that he has more errors on hits of that kind than in any other plays."

McKean and Charlie Zimmer were the only Spiders planning to winter in Cleveland; it was to be McKean's first offseason spent in the city.[42] Just two weeks after the close of the grueling season, an already restless McKean was at shortstop for the local Old Leaguers amateur team, and he and some other Spiders played a benefit game at League Park against the Robison-sponsored Cleveland Athletic Club team.[43] Most days, if you were looking for Ed McKean, you could find him at Wood's gymnasium, on Sheriff Street, taking his massage in the Turkish bath, where Ed Delahanty was exercising and Cub Stricker worked out on the horizontal bar. McKean also practiced with a local football team. After weeks of making up his mind, McKean finally decided to join a team of National Leaguers barnstorming in Cuba.[44] Since the ball club that made the tour played from November 1891 through January 1892, it seems unlikely that McKean accompanied it after all—in January, *Sporting Life* reported him spending his time rabbit hunting in the snow in Grafton.[45]

His weight became an issue for the first time in McKean's career during this off-season. Mac's build was naturally stocky, but at age 22 he was as much as 50 pounds above his playing weight of four or five years ago. Some Cleveland cranks were beginning to worry if their shortstop was losing range and foot speed to overweight. Elmer Bates published a story in November about walking with McKean past a nickel weighing machine, when they encountered John Cranley, the manager of the Kennard House café where McKean was a regular. The ballplayer, the story goes, won a bet with Cranley by tipping the scales at 208 pounds. "I'll cut off thirty pounds of that before April," he vowed.[46] In Bates' follow-up story a month later, McKean still weighed 207 pounds but was "making a great effort to reduce" through a breath-taking regimen that includes long walks out of the city, football, gym workouts with dumb-bells and clubs, Russian baths, sprinting, handball, horseback riding, dieting, massage, lacrosse, cycling, running the stairs, sparring, abstinence from liquor as well as butter and tea, and bedtime by 8 o'clock![47] In the manner of an Irish storyteller, a public persona he easily adopted, the star was reassuring his fans and team owners that they would see the same strong and well-conditioned Ed McKean come spring. Bates' update on McKean's fanciful dietary program came at the end of January. McKean revealed to the reporter, "I'm feeling great.

Haven't touched beer or anything since New Years, and am down 15 pounds in weight. At night when 'tis dark and dreary I take a half-mile spin and don't feel out of breath at all. I was never in better form in mid-winter than at the present moment."[48] True to his word, McKean was down to 184 pounds by the end of March 1892, having shed 30 pounds after December 1.[49] The extra weight would be a concern over the remainder of his career and a factor in his premature retirement from the National League at the age of 30.

After fitness came the business of fitting into the team Patsy Tebeau was assembling, intended to be the fastest in the League from home to first base. Tebeau insisted, from his first spring training: "My instructions to my players are to win games, and I want them to be aggressive. A milk and water, goody-goody player can't wear a Cleveland uniform."[50] In other words, the manager would have done with a whole team of Ed McKeans. His Spiders for 1892 featured other talented players who would enjoy memorable careers in the decade. The roster reads like a futures game for Cleveland fans: Cupid Childs, Jesse Burkett, George Davis, Chief Zimmer, Cy Young, and Nig Cuppy. McKean, the franchise player, was to be joined by Tebeau's boyhood friend Jack O'Connor, who would play right field, catch, and provide ginger everywhere he went. Gone were the aging Cub Stricker (who was still living in Cleveland and available for spring training) and prospect Dirty Jack Doyle (whose nickname suggests an affinity for Tebeau's brand of ball), both replaced by the brilliant Childs. At times, the Spiders' lack of experience and roster depth showed. Cleveland was prone to lose close games, and injuries to starters — Tebeau would be disabled for much of the year when McKean suffered his only serious injury of his career — were tough to overcome, but the season provided a testing ground that made possible the triumph of 1895. Of course, the 1892 Spiders are remembered as the first Cleveland baseball team to reach a "world's series." Cleveland made the playoffs via a unique route. The year the National League achieved monopoly status, after the collapse of the American Association (it called itself the National Association for a time, as if the rival leagues had merged), Nick Young and the owners decreed that a split season be played, where, the winning team of the first half would meet the winner of the second half in a championship series in October. And the Spiders, in part on the strength of a near miraculous return to the lineup by Ed McKean, would be the team with the best second-season record.

Tebeau's first spring training as manager of the Spiders opened in Hot Springs on March 20. Chief Zimmer was reluctant to sign, electing instead to stay behind in Cleveland after most of his teammates had left to go south. He was making a good income from his business ventures, which included his commercial baseball board game, and coaching the Adelbert College team.[51]

As it turned out, the backstop would join the club on the road for the regular season opener.[52] Jimmy McAleer was back from the ski slopes of California, an offseason routine of several winters he obviously felt to benefit his chronically ailing knees.[53] The mood in camp was initially depressed by 10 inches of snow on the diamond and the shocking news, from West Troy, New York, of John O'Brien's death.[54] Ed McKean had a personally miserable boiling out period, missing one of the Spiders' 11 exhibition games with an injury, while hitting for the worst average (.171) on the club, making the most errors (11), and shedding pounds. An active rumor mill had McKean practically traded to the Giants, owned by Irishman Andrew Freedman, or to Pittsburgh. Tebeau saw plenty of Nig Cuppy, working his rookie pitcher into four spring games to Cy Young's staff-leading five. The manager started Young against Chicago, on April 1, and then shifted him to first base when he brought in Cuppy to finish the 12-inning win. George Cuppy was the first Cleveland pitcher to wear a fielding glove and may have introduced it this spring. Young had three hits, raising his exhibition average up to .318, and fielded 15 chances that day without an error, perhaps himself donning a glove for his innings at first base. Cy was reluctant to change his habits in the pitching box, though; he would adopt a rudimentary glove for pitching in the 1896 season. Overall that spring, the Spiders won eight of the 11 contests and the local championship over Chicago, who also trained at Hot Springs. "For their victories the Spiders were awarded a silken banner by the ladies at Hot Springs."[55] A spring training footnote involves John McGraw, a lad who had hooked up with an all–American team, when the Spiders came to Gainsville to play them. The exhibition must have been the first time McKean and McGraw opposed each other on a ball field.[56]

Cleveland may very well have lost their regular season opener in Louisville from "overconfidence." Charles Mears declared Ed McKean to have been the hero in the 5 to 2 defeat: "McKean's batting was the feature of Friday's game. It looks as though this would prove Mack's banner year."[57] Following the loss in Louisville, the Spiders traveled on to Cincinnati for two games. McKean hit a ball so hard in the first game, on April 15, the drive froze right fielder Jocko Halligan in his tracks, struck a plank in the right field fence, and rolled all the way back to second base. The long hit only counted for a single, one of two off McKean's bat that day.[58] The Hot Springs' pennant flew jauntily from the trolley car carrying the Spiders into League Park for their home-opening battle with the invading Reds. Nearing the finish of the first month of play, the Spiders were victorious in five of their last six games, having dominated a series against Chicago by scoring 16 runs to the visiting Colts' five. And then came the accident that threatened to ruin Ed McKean's year, nine games into the season, and spoil the Spiders' chances of a first-half pennant in the split season.

FIVE. *The Spiders Make a "World's Series" (1891–1892)*

"McKean shot himself Friday morning, while monkeying with Virtue's 'didn't know it was loaded.' His index finger of the left hand suffers and Mac will take a vacation for about ten days," Charles Mears announced.[59] The accident occurred in the dressing room prior to the Spiders' workout on April 28, an offday before they were to host the Giants in their next series. According to McKean family tradition, Uncle Ed lost all or part of the finger.[60] The injury proved to be more serious than Mears had indicated or wished to believe, absenting McKean from the Cleveland lineup for a whole month of games. Even then, the shortstop returned to play before he was fully recovered.

Jake Virtue's pistol shot big holes in the club, with vacancies for its cleanup hitter and starting shortstop, although it could be argued that it was fortunate to have George Davis to fill in at short. The future Hall of Fame shortstop fielded magnificently from the start—13 putouts, 22 assists, and a single error through May 7— but the Spiders without McKean had fallen all the way down to eighth place.[61] With Davis at short, Cleve-

Jake Virtue, 40 years after a bullet from his pistol altered the trajectory of Ed McKean's career. After he returned from the accident, McKean became one of the National League's most productive RBI specialists (author's collection).

land dropped five in a row, starting with an April 30 defeat by the Giants on the sad day that Frank Robison's youngest daughter died of pneumonia. Cleveland made it six losses in seven contests before stringing together six wins, only to lose four consecutive games on three different occasions through June 7.

As it was, team-minded Ed McKean rushed himself back into lineup for the May 25 game in Pittsburgh, with mixed results. "McKean is back at short," Mears reported, with a qualifier, "and the sixth column of the [box] score makes it look as if Mac's hand was not all right yet."[62] Reinstalled in his familiar fourth position in the batting order, McKean went 0-for-5 against Pop Corkhill, and registered two errors in that sixth column. He made two more errors at short in his next appearance, in the second game of a doubleheader in Baltimore, on May 27. The following afternoon, he got his first hit since April, a double off Baltimore's John Healy, but errored twice. McKean finished out the month by somehow willing himself to play both games of a doubleheader in Boston—he made three errors that day, two in the afternoon game. McKean continued to play, in pain and with limited success, committing at least one error in each of the first five games in June, and seven errors total. Cleveland's record now stood at 20 wins against 22 losses, but it hadn't improved on eighth place in the standings. After appearing in 22 games, McKean was batting .247, on 23 hits in 93 at-bats. He had scored only 10 runs all season and stolen but three bases. Worse, McKean was last in fielding among National League shortstops, with 24 errors and a terrible .776 fielding percentage. George Davis, if we looked over Mac's shoulder, had fielded at .899 in his 10 games at short.[63]

As Ed McKean's health gradually improved so did the team's prospects, as tracked by *The Sporting News*: "McKean's hand still troubles him but his batting is something pretty to see" (June 25); "McKean's hand is getting better and Mac's fielding improves" (July 2); and "McKean's work at short of late has put to sleep all those grumblers who said Mac was no good. Ed's sore hand interfered with his playing but now it appears to be well" (July 9). Over the last half of June, the Spiders had started playing good baseball. Cleveland would rebound to finish the first half of the 1892 split season in fifth place, with a 40–33 record. But, when McKean decided to go AWOL after Cleveland's final game of the first half and a subsequent rainout, even the loyal Mears was disgusted: "McKean went on a drunk Saturday, and Davis played short better than McKean ever did. The club could well dispose of Mr. McKean's services, when he gets so that he finds it necessary to get drunk."[64] It seems the first half had been a severe test of Ed McKean's commitment and his supporters' patience. He had voluntarily played hurt in order to lead by example, and Patsy Tebeau had stuck with his shortstop through his error-plagued return to form; however, by July, McKean was exhibiting symptoms of strain. And yet, Uncle Nick's official statistics for "first season" play showed just how far McKean had come back from his disastrous start. Cupid Childs led all Spiders with his .309 batting average (good for 11th in the National League), and McKean had pulled himself up to second best on the club, averaging .277 after 234 at-bats over 53 games played. His fielding had recovered to .835, on 45 errors, with 72 putouts and 156 assists.[65]

For the "second season," Cleveland was the best team in the League. The Spiders finished in first place, winning 53 games and losing only 23—a

FIVE. *The Spiders Make a "World's Series" (1891–1892)*

gaudy winning percentage of .697. Part of Cleveland's resurgence was courtesy of John Clarkson, who was signed as a free agent pitcher after the "first season" pennant-winning Boston club released him to save money. Frank Robison's insistence on making Clarkson a Spider caused a rift in the Cleveland front office that led to Robison buying out the other owners.[66] In fact, the $5,000 contract was paying a lot for a rapidly aging twirler who, as it turned out, would never be able to adjust to next year's 60-foot-six-inch rule. So Hall of Famer Clarkson replaced George Rettger in Tebeau's pitching rotation, teaming up with Young and Nig Cuppy to give Cleveland a daunting trio of pitchers. Clarkson holds the odd distinction of pitching for both champions of the National League split season, and he started two games against Boston in the "world's series."

As a Spider in the "second season" of 1892, Clarkson won 17 games, including his 300th career win in front of the Cleveland fans, on September 21. That historic afternoon, Pittsburgh starter Adonis Terry surrendered only two hits in a highly contentious loss. His manager Al Buckenberger played the game under protest after veteran umpire John H. Gaffney was persuaded by McKean and teammates to reverse a call. Later, in the ninth inning with the Alleghenys ahead, 2 to 1, Gaffney called the game for darkness but another round of kicking by the Spiders kept the game alive. The reprieve allowed Cleveland to come from behind, scoring two runs in their half of the inning, to win the game for Clarkson after Terry gave up two walks, a sacrifice hit, and a game-winning single to McKean.[67] In addition to adding Clarkson to the roster, Cleveland entered the "second season" with a "new" shortstop— Ed McKean, the team's unofficial most valuable player. Tebeau was able to field a set lineup, featuring a healthy and rededicated McKean as the regular cleanup hitter, behind Childs, Burkett, and O'Connor, and in front of Tebeau, McAleer, Virtue, and Zimmer. McKean's job in the new batting order was made explicit: drive in runs.

"Cleveland jumped into first place," with a 13-inning victory over the visiting Colts in the second game of a July 29 doubleheader. The Spiders, just returned from taking seven of 12 games on a rare successful eastern tour, were "a 'bunged up team'"—Burkett, Tebeau, and Childs were all injured—but they continued to win through the adversity, buoyed by the pitching staff. On the road trip, Cuppy won four of his five games, Young won three of four; Clarkson, pitching in bad luck, went 1 and 3.[68] Jimmy McAleer's play in the outfield was a key to the pitchers' success:

> McAleer's wonderful fielding has been of great assistance to the local pitchers in their games. It has gotten so, nowadays, that a ball must be batted almost to the fence or it will be a sure out if McAleer takes after it...There are no frills or

flounces on McAleer's playing. He goes after everything in sight, and I don't believe that any individual ever saw him undertake a "grandstand" play since he has been in harness.[69]

And when the big hitters came back to the lineup, the Cleveland offense started to win games. By late August, the Spiders seemed to have adopted "first season" champion Boston's formula for success:

There are six men in the team whose batting averages for the second half alone hover close to the .300 mark. Every player but one or two has got sacrifice hitting down to a fine point, and there isn't one of them but is glad to sacrifice at any and all times. Boston won the first half because its players went after runs, and Cleveland is out for the flag of the second half with the same general idea controlling the men.[70]

In September, *The Sporting News* attributed "The success of the Cleveland Spiders ... largely ... to the hustling brainy work of the St. Louis boy, Captain Pat Tebeau. He is the same Oliver P[atsy] Tebeau, who was not good enough for Anson a couple of years back and to-day he is leading the old man and his contemporaries a merry dance showing a clean hand in his excellent work as Cleveland's pilot. Tebeau is of the Ward type as a worker on the diamond."[71]

By the final month of the regular season, Charles W. Mears was driven to hyperbole in praise of Tebeau's inspired management of the resurgent Spiders:

Tebeau has earned a name for himself this season that will endure as long as that of a Comiskey, an Anson, or a Kelly. As a base ball general he stands second to no person. As a con-

Cy Young in his second full season, pitched the Cleveland Spiders to the 1892 "world's series" against the Boston Beaneaters. He won three games in the 1895 Temple Cup series (Heritage Auctions).

FIVE. *The Spiders Make a "World's Series" (1891–1892)*

troller of men he is more of a success than any man now upon the base ball diamond. Where he learned his remarkable methods of keeping players under control is not known. He simply has that knack. His methods are different than any other manager in the country. They are successful because they are common sense methods. Players are not treated like children as most managers treat them, but like men. The result is plain to be seen. It is shown in the work of the men that he manages.[72]

And what work it was. McKean's partner Cupid Childs enjoyed a breakout season, leading the League with heady figures in runs (136) and on-base percentage (.443); his .317 batting average was third best. Cy Young won a career-high number of games, tying him for most in the National League[73]; he led pitchers in ERA and shut-outs. Nig Cuppy never again matched his personal high of 28 wins for 1892, and his ERA was his career low, as well.

McKean's serious finger wound negatively affected his fielding and batting stats for the year. His batting average came in 40 points below his lifetime figure, the worst of his career until his unhappy last season. His .872 fielding percentage tied him with Baltimore's Orator O'Rourke for 13th among 18 National League shortstops, although his final total of 78 errors was a quiet triumph.[74] The fact that McKean led his team in runs batted in is a tribute to both his individual focus and his stellar team play. He was a club leader in the sacrifice hits category, with 51, fourth best in the League and behind only George Davis (the League leader with 56) and Burkett on the Spiders.[75] By playing hurt, McKean was an inning-by-inning inspiration to his teammates, and he learned to compensate for his injury-induced power outage by coming through with clutch hits throughout the "second season" and the "world's series."

Some who watched McKean play in 1892 saw beyond his comparatively modest individual stats in admiration for his character. *Sporting Life* observed: "He has played here six seasons, and has driven more runs over the plate with those sharp cracks at the ball of his than any other Cleveland player," adding an insight into the tough's make up: "Ed is as sensitive as a child, and a hiss hurts him keenly." George W. Howe, a stockholder beginning with the American Association Blues, offered a glowing testimonial:

> He is as intelligent a man as ever put on a uniform. He is, moreover, one of the kindest-hearted, best-behaved men on club trips that ever traveled. The public see Ed's worst side, for he fights for his club and some times talks "sassy" on the field. When the game is over, though, everything is forgotten and forgiven. No player has a warmer place in my heart than Ed McKean, because I know what a thoroughly good man he is.[76]

The individual stats would come over the next four years. (Leo Durocher one day would famously remark they're for losers, anyway.) Right now, Ed McKean and the Cleveland Spiders were playoff-bound.

The first "world's series" game in Cleveland baseball history was played at League Park on October 17.[77] The best-of-nine-game playoff showcased a trio of twirlers who combined for 1,200 victories in their Hall of Fame careers—Cy Young (511 wins), John Clarkson (328), and Boston's Kid Nichols (361)—matched up against lineups that featured another five future inductees—Jesse Burkett, George Davis, Hugh Duffy, Tommy McCarthy, and Mike Kelly. The '92 Beaneaters, the first team to win 100 games in a season, were managed by Hall of Famer Frank Selee. Selee was a baseball innovator. In this series, he platooned three catchers to great effect; otherwise forgettable Charlie Ganzel went 4-for-8 to outhit the legendary King Kelly, while Charlie Bennett threw out Cleveland runners at key points in contests and even contributed a homer in the decisive game of the series. Among the biographical sketches and ink drawings of "The Boys Who Brought the First Pennant to the Forest City" *The Sporting News* published for October 22, Ed McKean is appreciated as "a heavy hitter, a good sacrifice hitter, a clever base runner and a sometimes brilliant fielder."

In game one, "McKean made his great play in the first inning. Duffy was on first with two out and started to steal second. Zimmer's throw was high and to the left of the bag. McKean reached over with one hand, pulled down the ball and put it on the angel child in time to get him out. Mac got plenty of deserved applause for the fine play."[78] Playing aggressively, he also made the only error of the game. Neither Cy Young (36–11) nor John Elmer Stivetts (35–16, plus a no-hit game on August 6) had allowed a run through eight innings, when, as John Phillips writes, "The Spiders came within a foot of scoring in the ninth inning."[79] With one out, Burkett laid down one of his patented bunts and the ball hit the bag for a single. Next, Davis smashed a pitch down the first base line that handcuffed Tucker and went for another single, Burkett becoming the first Cleveland runner to advance as far as second. That brought Ed McKean to the plate. Jack Stivetts, pitching carefully to the Cleveland cleanup hitter, fell behind in the count to three and two before McKean stroked one of the hardest-hit balls of the day—but right at shortstop Herman Long, whose toss to Joe Quinn forced the runner Davis. Second baseman Quinn immediately kicked to the nearest umpire, Charlie Snyder, claiming Davis had interfered with his chance to make a double play.

Burkett had never stopped running.

Suddenly, Quinn came to consciousness and threw to catcher King Kelly, who blocked the plate and tagged Burkett a foot from scoring. In the Boston half of the ninth, the teams nearly brawled. Kelly yelled out "Help!" from the Boston bench, just as Jake Virtue was about to catch a foul ball, and the first baseman and Zimmer collided. Nick Young had decreed a week earlier that two pairs of umpires would work alternating games of the "world's series," but the extra umpire on the field was no match for the trickster Kelly.[80]

He was the most famous player of his era, and the public never tired of reading about his storied antics and accomplishments. Mike Kelly's *Play Ball* (1888, with ghostwriter John J. Drohan) was the first so-called autobiography by a baseball player; the superstar who introduced the hook slide was the subject of the 1889 hit song "Slide, Kelly, Slide." At his prime, Kelly stole six bases in a single game, but he hit only .189 in the 1892 regular season and went hitless in the "world's series." Kelly's last job in baseball was as the player-manager for Al Johnson's Allentown team in the Pennsylvania State League. And then, in 1894, King Kelly was dead, at age 36.

The three-hour game ended in the darkness, a marathon scoreless tie after 12 innings. It would be the only game in the "world's series" that Boston didn't win. Dent Young later remembered the game as his greatest ever.[81] Chances are, Young's effort wore him out; he would be ineffective for the rest of the playoff. Cleveland had a good record in extra-inning games during the season, going 8–3, and the next two games were to be played in friendly League Park—a Spiders' win in nine innings would have made them a good bet to take the championship.

Game two, on October 18, was too much Hugh Duffy for Cleveland. On top of his two triples and a double, center fielder Duffy made a great catch of a fly ball off Virtue's bat in the ninth and also threw out the swift Jim McAleer at second. Duffy had his way with Cleveland pitching the whole series, but he was only warming up. He'd lead the National League in hitting for 1893 and, the year after that, slug 51 doubles, 16 triples, and 18 home runs as he recorded the highest batting average in history (.440). From the 1891 through 1899 seasons, Hugh Duffy drove in at least 100 runs eight times for Boston.

The Spiders outplayed the Beaneaters all afternoon, collecting 11 hits off Harry Staley; however, with two out in the ninth inning, and the home crowd cheering them on, Cleveland could not tie the game when a close call at second base went against them. Good-hitting pitcher John Clarkson ended the Cleveland rally, after Jack O'Connor's single and Zimmer's triple off the left field fence, when he sent Staley's first pitch back the way it had come. The drive glanced off the Boston twirler but, as fortune would dictate, right at shortstop Long, who threw out Clarkson to save the beans for the Beaneaters. Herman Long, the man who made Boston forget Sam Wise, was one of the Deadball Era's best shortstops, a marginally better fielder and a somewhat less productive slugger (2,129 hits, 1,456 runs, 1,055 RBIs, 537 steals, and a .277 batting average in 16 seasons) than McKean. Like McKean, Long has been unfairly judged on the basis of his lifetime errors, a record 1,070 at short, in spite of the evidence that he was considered a good fielder in his time. Similar cases can be made for both players' admission into the Hall of Fame.

A second piece of bad luck befell the Spiders in this game: George Davis sprained a tendon in his heel and had to be removed in favor of Tebeau, whose own bad leg had limited him to about half a season at third base. Rusty Patsy made an error on McCarthy's grounder in the fifth, leading to Boston's go-ahead run. Number-three hitter Davis had to be limited to pinch-hitting duties for the remainder of the series, an irreplaceable loss to the Spiders attack, especially considering Cleveland batters had averaged below .200 against Boston pitching during the regular season. For his part, McKean singled and scored the first Cleveland run in the fourth inning, on Jimmy McAleer's hit. It was one of McKean's two base hits off Staley that day.

The shortstop continued to shine in the field, especially important because the Spiders weren't scoring runs. *The Sporting News* enthused that "the work of McKean in the three games has been the feature of the Cleveland fielding."[82] Game three was a rematch of opening game starters Young and Stivetts but hardly a repeat of the pitchers' dominance, and Stivetts scored his own winning run, after doubling. McKean had staked Young to a first-inning lead in the game by knocking in Childs and Burkett. But, for the second straight afternoon, Cleveland stranded the tying run on third base in the ninth inning. (Game two had ended with Chief Zimmer unable to score after his triple.) This time, Patsy Tebeau ordered lame George Davis to pinch-hit for his pitcher, only to have him break his bat on a hard out to Tommy Tucker. The series moved on to Boston with Cleveland, at best a mediocre road team, down two games to nil.

Selee started Charlie Bennett behind the plate in game four, and he responded by throwing out two Cleveland base runners. (His counterpart Chief Zimmer threw out three Beaneaters, but also allowed three steals on the day.) Bennett led National League catchers seven times in fielding, and he was behind the plate for Lee Richmond's history-making perfect game. He had plenty of previous "world's series" experience, all of it coming with the Wolverines in the 15-game playoffs of 1887. Bennett was a beloved figure in Detroit, where the ball park would one day be named in his honor. Through 1926, Charlie threw out the ceremonial first pitch on opening days at Bennett Park. He was loved by the players, as well. John Clarkson could never come to accept witnessing his friend fall beneath the wheels of a train, when they were on a hunting trip in the 1893 offseason. Bennett was Bobby Lowe's boyhood idol, both of them getting their starts in baseball in New Castle, Pennsylvania, around the time McAleer and McKean were playing for the

FIVE. *The Spiders Make a "World's Series" (1891–1892)* 141

Youngstowns against the Neshannocks. Lowe, playing left field in this "world's series," would be the second baseman and leadoff hitter for many Boston teams. But he is best remembered for a single day, May 30, 1894, when he became the first player to homer four times in a game.

The big parade in Boston on October 21 was for Columbus Day, not for game four of the series. Festivities disrupted the streetcars to the ball field where Nig Cuppy, baseball's human equivalent to avenue gridlock, was matched against fireballing Kid Nichols. Cuppy's off-speed deliveries and delays between each pitch, not to mention his spectacular "hand-ball assist" in the second and another fielding gem in the third,[83] kept the Beaneaters mesmerized and frustrated, and the game scoreless, until Duffy's home run in the fourth inning. McKean failed in two chances for a Spiders' late-game rally. He singled in the seventh only to be thrown out, attempting to go first to third, by Tom McCarthy's outstanding throw. With two Spiders on base in the ninth, McKean made the second out when he fanned.

Even the Boston enthusiasts lost interest in the "world's series" after the fourth game. Attendance for the previous games averaged over 6,000 paid. In addition to the near-capacity crowd in the stands in South End Grounds for the October 21 game, many cranks without tickets had watched from Sullivan's Tower beyond right field. On October 22, game five drew a disappointing 3,466 and the next contest, which turned out to be the clincher for Boston, was witnessed by only 2,300. John Clarkson seemed the logical choice to pitch when Tebeau and Cleveland were desperate for a win. As a member of the Beaneaters, he'd pitched many times at South End Grounds, and, in two "world's series" (1885 and 1886), he'd garnered three wins. The afternoon's starters were two of baseball's best hitting pitchers: Happy Jack Stivetts was actually a part-time outfielder who boasted a .297 career batting average and 35 home runs, and Clarkson's three-run home run over the wall in right would help stake Cleveland to a big second-inning lead. Following Clarkson's blast, Ed McKean lined a single off the right field boards with the bases loaded that tallied two Spiders, just missing a grand slam. Instead, McKean stole second base and took third on Ganzel's bad throw to Quinn, eventually scoring to make it a 6 to 0 game early on. Two errors by Herman Long meant all the runs off Stivetts were unearned until McKean singled in the fifth inning and subsequently scored on Chief Zimmer's hit. That closed out Cleveland's scoring. McKean and McAleer both made errors, and Tebeau added two more at third base, abetting the Boston comeback in the 12 to 7 slugfest.

In game six, two more hits by McKean were mitigated by his two errors at short. It turned out to be a sloppy game for both teams. Cleveland committed four errors on the day to the home team's five, and the Spiders grouped three hits in the second inning but could not score. McKean had led off the inning with a single, only to be thrown out attempting to steal. His second hit of the day, a single to center, chased home Childs and Burkett for a 3 to 0 Cleveland lead in the third. Cy Young, called on to pitch in cold weather with an arm his biographer notes was "bothered by tenderness," squandered another Cleveland lead.[84] Young was victimized for eight runs, highlighted by Charlie Bennett's trot around all the bases in the sixth (yet another home run to right field). In the eighth inning, as Cleveland's hopes were waning, McKean's error and Long's base running cinched a final Boston run and the championship. Winning pitcher Kid Nichols was the last to throw from a pitcher's "box." The following March, the League instituted revolutionary rule changes, intended to make the game more exciting by increasing runs scored in 1893. The new rules pushed pitchers back to where they remain today, at 60 feet six inches from home plate, and the pitching "mound" and rubber were introduced. Over the next half dozen seasons, Ed McKean produced some of the biggest offensive numbers ever for a shortstop. Going into his seventh year in the majors, he would be the happy beneficiary of the League's offense-minded innovations and his manager's confidence in him to be the Spiders' slugger.

McKean was Cleveland's best hitter for Cleveland in the "world's series," averaging .440 and racking up six of the team's 13 runs batted in. He was remarkably consistent in his first postseason; after going 1-for-3 in the opener, he had two base hits in each remaining game. Still, none of McKean's 11 hits went for extra bases, and his teammates managed only six hits for extra bases in the six games, one the homer by pitcher Clarkson; Hugh Duffy alone accounted for six extra-base hits for the victors. Perhaps it was a measure of the lingering effects of McKean's finger injury that the dead-pull-hitter could never take advantage of the short right field walls at either South End Grounds or League Park. Somehow, McKean scored only twice. No mistaking, the Spiders' profound defeat had been a team effort. Three starters—McKean, Chief Zimmer, and Jack O'Connor—struck out three times each. And Jake Virtue, who had fanned the second most in the League during the regular season, struck out at the then-alarming rate of five times in 24 official at-bats.

A disappointed Ed McKean had no taste for the wait till next year. He stationed himself in Cleveland this winter, already preparing body and mind for the next baseball season. Ed Seward, the trainer at the Cleveland Athletic Club, told Elmer Bates admiringly that "no pupil in his gymnasium can hit the bag as hard as McKean."[85] Bates was thinking hot stove baseball, too. Writing his post mortem of the late series, the scribe considered how home field advantage had worked for Boston:

FIVE. The Spiders Make a "World's Series" (1891–1892)

Just how any club wins a game off Boston on the latter's grounds is past finding out. With [Foghorn] Tucker, Duffy and McCarthy defying the umpires, shrieking like madmen at the visiting pitchers, coaching hoodlum style inside the diamond, kicking at every decision, and emphasizing in every way and at all times the disreputable and disgusting side of the game, a team to win a game here must simply hit the ball out of the lot and turn a deaf ear to a howling mob in the bleachers and a typical old American Association team on the lines.[86]

Bates' complaint portends the polemic to come against Patsy Tebeau's Hibernian Spiders and their riotous brand of ball. One would only have to substitute the names McKean, O'Connor, and Burkett for the Boston triumvirate.

Six

Patsy's Hibernian Spiders (1893–1894)

It takes a few oaths to run a ball team.—Oliver Tebeau

During the months of the baseball season, The White City installation at the World's Columbian Exposition in Chicago showcased America's dynamic entry into the modern era. Ironically, the World's Fair coincided with the Economic Panic of 1893, the country's most severe depression to date, and a parallel to this national incongruity can be found in the Cleveland Spiders front office. The franchise that had won the "second season" pennant a few months before was financially strapped. Having bought out his business partners, Frank DeHass Robison was running the club on his own, with the assistance of his brothers Stanley and Howard. Two years before the economic downturn, Frank Robison had built League Park and purchased the 19.5-acre lakefront estate, nestled within Cleveland in the posh one-square-mile village of Bratenhal, he named Villa Hedges. However, the financial reality of the 1893 season in the Forest City undermined all the White City–like opulence on display. In Cleveland, newly appointed treasurer Howard Robison was prepared to pay all the outfielders at least $1,800, and salaries for the rest of the players ranged within $200 or $300 of that base.[1] Ed McKean was among the returning heroes of the "world's series" who were reluctant to re-sign with the Robisons for a cut in pay. When the star shortstop decided to come to the club's terms, in mid-February, he badly miscalculated by moving too soon to sign for $2,000, a base salary that would be only in the middling range of the League's $2,400 maximum and $1,500 minimum in place a month later.[2] No doubt, McKean did manage to settle for at least an added stipend for serving as a coach and captain.

Frank Robison's pocketbook may have been the reason for trading away Spiderling George Davis in return for the hoary Buck Ewing, an ur-DH whose

SIX. *Patsy's Hibernian Spiders (1893–1894)* 145

value was diminished since he was no longer able to throw to the bases from behind the plate at this stage of his vaunted career.[3] To make matters worse, there was disharmony among the players on Robison's team. As if the shadow of the Players' League had reached out of its grave to strangle the life out of the Spiders clubhouse, the re-signing of John Clarkson and the arrival of Buck Ewing—both players who had "sold out" the Brotherhood—were openly opposed by Cleveland's Players' League alumni, especially Jim McAleer and Jack O'Connor. The players' resentment had a pervasive effect, as O'Connor's buddy Patsy Tebeau had approved of the trade for Ewing, and McAleer's friend McKean was in the awkward position of having jumped the Players' League. There was a further point of contention: Clarkson's hefty contract was resented by McKean, who was earning a considerably smaller paycheck after loyal service to Robison's club, and as an everyday player, for six years.

The economic panic and the unemployment it engendered would make it even more difficult for the Robison brothers to sell tickets to League Park this year. And it was the Spiders' bad luck to sputter-start the 1893 campaign, suffering so many rain cancellations and delays that a wag columnist for the *Sporting Life* suggested the team be renamed The Rainouts.[4] Ironically, the club's solution was to turn back the clock and play the kind of all-out offensive game that the Infants had espoused in hopes of attracting fans. Happily, Frank Robison's desire to increase the spectacle of scoring was in sync with the League office's innovative Rule 5 that moved the pitcher back five additional feet from the batter. Both developments suited slugging Ed McKean's taste just fine. McKean attributed the team's success in 1892 to Tebeau's offense-first attack. "My notion is that base ball must not be made too scientific," he argued.

> You take the old-time patrons of the game nowadays, and they can tell just what will be done in the event of a certain situation presenting itself. This robs a game of the element of uncertainty—its greatest charm. I remember one game last summer, when the Louisvilles were here. They made four runs in the ninth inning and tied the score.... In the ninth, with Tebeau on first, Virtue came to bat. Everybody expected him to sacrifice, but instead of doing so he slammed the ball against the right field fence for three bases, and the game was won. It was an unexpected move, and it set the crowd crazy with delight.
> We don't want technical games.[5]

It's worth noting here for Cleveland fanatics that the last man to have pitched to a batter in a regular season game before the advent of Rule 5 lived until 1969, a few months short of his 100th birthday. Lefty John Hollison relieved in an August 13, 1892, game in Chicago against the Spiders, in the books as a 6 to 2 Nig Cuppy victory. The one base hit Swede Hollison allowed in his four-inning mop up was a long home run by Jimmy McAleer. The medical student never pitched another inning of professional ball, enjoying instead a long career as a doctor.⁶ By the way, one Ohio baseball entrepreneur did manage to make a fortune during the Panic of 1893. Colonel Harry M. Stevens was a real-life Horatio Alger success, having immigrated to Niles, Ohio, from England in 1882 and rapidly made himself the king of ball park concessions and seat cushion rentals. In 1893, the scorecards he peddled, in Cleveland and elsewhere around the League, identified each player by a number on a grid, and featured a fine lithographic portrait of a selected player and beer advertisements. Stevens had sold the standard fare of ice cream and lemonade at the old League Park in the 1880s; more recently, his expanded menu included hot dogs, peanuts, and soda pop. He may have been the first to put straws in soda bottles, presumably so cranks could drink without taking their eyes off the action. Scorecard Harry got his start, in 1887, by printing cards for the Columbus team of the Ohio State League.⁷ You might say Stevens served, in addition, as the unofficial public address announcer at Cleveland baseball games in 1893. His typical banter between innings went: "The score is now Cleveland 2, Chicago 1; batteries Clarkson and Zimmer, Hutchinson and Kittridge. McAleer is now at-bat. Will you have a card?"⁸ Stevens Park, in Niles, is named in his honor.

Larger-than-life Buck Ewing drove home 122 runs in his 116 games for the 1893 Spiders but was never at home in the Cleveland clubhouse (*The Sporting News*/Mears Auctions).

Last offseason, McKean had hit upon a singular way of keeping in top shape. He reinvented himself, during the frozen-over months from Christmas to spring training, as a professional wrestler. As risky as this venture may have been for his diamond career, his time on the mat is a clear sign that his finger had finally healed. In December, Elmer Bates rated Ed McKean

Six. *Patsy's Hibernian Spiders (1893–1894)*

and Kid Baldwin to be the best Greco-Roman wrestlers among baseball players, with John Coleman also "very handy."[9] Of the trio, only McKean was still active in the major leagues; both Clarence Baldwin, a catcher, and John Coleman, a pitcher turned outfielder, had last played in the big leagues in 1890. At the end of January 1893, McKean was training in Grafton, and Bates was carrying the $800 purse for his upcoming match with Al Woods, who was Ohio wrestling champion by 1897.[10] *Sporting Life* noted the rules of that much-anticipated contest: "The men will wrestle continually for one hour, no holds barred, and rolling falls do not count."[11] Following all the buildup, we have Bates' lurid first-hand account of his hero's February 6 match:

> Ed McKean's popularity was put to a severe test last night. He went upon a platform before 1000 people to compete in a wrestling match with a popular local athlete. Frank Robison, ... McAleer, Tebeau, [Frank] Knauss, Zimmer and many other ball players were there, and the audience also contained hundreds of the best-known business men in the city. I have heard a few cheers in ten or twelve years' experience in looking on scrapping matches, athletic contests and base ball games, but the yell that greeted the Cleveland short stop outrivaled them all. For an hour the hall had been filled up with cigar and cigarette smoke, and when the wrestlers loomed up, a cloud of poisonous smoke hung over the platform. After half an hour's brilliant work McKean was forced to succumb to the awful condition of the atmosphere and quit, but in that time he had really secured one fall and should by rights have been credited with another.[12]

On February 28, McKean was the underdog favorite against Charley Uhl, recognized at the time as "the Southern champion," in a match before as many as 1,500 spectators in Galion, Ohio, a town on the railroad line to Columbus from Grafton. Uhl was another wrestler who had played a little baseball, catching in the low minor leagues. McKean briefly turned his attention in the days remaining before spring training to boxing, "becoming a clever sparrer."[13]

The Sporting News for April 1 figured that "McKean is 20 pounds lighter and says the task of getting into playing condition is not going to be as burdensome by half" this spring. "He has held a solemn covenant with himself to do two things this season. The first will be to play in his old time form and the second will be to religiously abstain from 'monkeying' with any and all kinds of fire arms." Patsy Tebeau wrote, in a letter to Charles Mears, that McKean was one of just three Spiders, together with Zimmer and Young, who were in shape when the team reported to Cleveland at the end of March.[14] Following an opening exhibition of baseball in Akron, Tebeau took McKean, Burkett, McAleer, Zimmer, Frank Boyd, and pitcher Bill Schellerman on the train to Cincinnati to meet up with the rest of the squad, all of whom then proceeded south to spring training games that had been scheduled in Atlanta and Savannah. The Spiders beat the Savannah Dixies, 4 to 1, on April 1, with

George Davies on the mound and Cy Young umpiring. Manager Tebeau had already settled on a batting order which utilized the skills of each one of his players, with Kid Childs leading off (taking advantage of his high on-base percentage), Jesse Burkett hitting behind him (a great contact hitter and bunter to move the runner over), Ed McKean hitting in the honored third spot and Buck Ewing cleaning up (both accomplished RBI men).

This spring, McKean and Ewing seemed to be shedding years for pounds. Mears enthused that "McKean looks as slick and well-bred as a Cuyahoga County Congressman...Quick? Well, I should build an air ship! In the fifth inning," in an exhibition with Chicago in Chattanooga, "he tapped one down to [Reddy] Walsh, who ran in and fielded the ball to [Jimmy] Ryan in eye-opener style, but Mac was there just one foot ahead of that ball."[15] And Ewing was punishing the ball from the start of the exhibitions. The three-week spring training period came to a happy conclusion in Columbus, Ohio, on April 24, when Cleveland won the so-called state championship by beating Cincinnati, 7 to 4, on another of Ewing's home runs and one by Jack O'Connor, the former Columbus Solon.[16] Meanwhile, John Clarkson remained at Yale, coaching the baseball team; the starting pitcher Tebeau was most counting on, after Young and Cuppy, was the only unsigned Spider.

Cleveland opened the championship season on the road in Pittsburgh on April 27.[17] That day, Cy Young was victorious over Frank Killen, the Pirates' lefty who would lead the League in wins in 1893. The Spiders' convincing 7 to 2 win sent home 4,000 disappointed paying customers. Another healthy crowd of 5,000 turned out in cold weather for the Cleveland home opener, on May 4, against Chicago. This year's Colts featured a top-heavy batting order: center fielder Jimmy Ryan leading off, followed by Bill Dahlen at short, then first baseman Cap Anson and left fielder Little Eva Lange in the cleanup slot. Flamboyant Tacky Tom Parrott regularly perched at third and still pitched a little. Pony Ryan, a five-tool player, and Ed McKean would join forces in minor-league Evansville in the twilight of their playing days; Dahlen was a McKean-style slugging shortstop over a distinguished career in two centuries. In the initial frame that day, the Spiders, choosing to bat first, failed to score when McKean was robbed on a circus catch in right by Sam Dugan. Cy Young eventually dropped the decision, 5 to 3, to ex–Cleveland Infant Kid McGill, another opening-day lefthander.

On the day the New York stock exchange crashed, May 5, McKean's single and triple helped reluctant Spider Clarkson defeat the Colts, 9 to 6, in Cleveland. The following afternoon, Nig Cuppy won over Chicago in his belated first appearance of the season. This time, it was Ed McKean's hustle that was a key to victory.[18] Willie McGill had squandered a 5 to 3 lead in the ninth

Six. Patsy's Hibernian Spiders (1893–1894)

inning and, with two outs, Crab Burkett scuttled home with the tying run as McKean beat out a scratch hit. Ewing's triple brought in McKean with the winning run in the 6 to 5 contest.[19] In the early going, Cleveland was in first place; by mid–May, McKean had collected 12 hits and scored as many runs in the Spiders' first nine games. An inspired Cleveland team scored 49 runs in a three-game series at home against Cincinnati, from May 18 through the 20th. In the first game, a 21 to 4 rout of the Redlegs, mudders McKean and Cy Young shrugged off the rain and made four hits each. John Clarkson won going away the next afternoon, 19 to 5, and McKean offset his two errors in the field by hitting in the clutch for three singles and a double. In the third game, George Cuppy gave up eight runs to the Reds but still won by a run. McKean made two more hits, and three errors. A rejuvenated William Ewing, now 33 years old, led the League in stolen bases at this juncture in the season and even filled in nimbly enough at second base after Cupid Childs was struck in the nose by a ball. First-place Cleveland was averaging 11.66 hits per game, lagging behind only Philadelphia's phenomenal 12.0 pace.

However, the Spiders slipped from first in the standings at the end of May and, upon losing both ends of a Decoration Day doubleheader in Philadelphia before a combined house of 14,000, the team fell back all the way to fifth place. Even when the Spiders stumbled through a marathon 22-game road trip, starting with 11 losses in 18 meetings with eastern teams, Ed McKean continued his torrid hitting. On May 31, his two hits accentuated Ewing's return to the Polo Grounds and Cy Young's win; he also made two hits in the second and third games of the New York series, the first time the Spiders played against George Davis. On June 5, Cleveland salvaged a third game in Boston, a Young victory in relief, by scoring eight runs in the ninth inning. Ed McKean started the rally with a homer off Jack Stivetts, and Chief Zimmer, who had been hitting ninth in Tebeau's lineup of late, capped the 13 to 11 comeback with the most remarkable home run of the game. Zimmer's drive flew out of the park in foul territory, hit telegraph wires there, and dropped fair. It was a day for round-trippers at South End Grounds, where the center field bleachers were a distant 500 feet from home plate but the fences down either line beckoned a mere 255 feet away. Stivetts, Long, and Lowe also homered for the Beaneaters.

William Temple was in attendance at the Spiders' 4 to 3 loss in Washington on June 7 and saw McKean juggle Orator O'Rourke's ground ball in the eighth inning to allow the Senators' go-ahead run. In the Spiders' half of the inning, Dummy Hoy made a fine running catch of a McKean line drive to save two runs from scoring. On June 9, the day Ford's Theater collapsed, killing 22 government office workers, Nig Cuppy beat Washington. One of the decisive moments of the game happened in the very first inning of play, as McKean this time robbed O'Rourke of a hit and neatly doubled Hoy off first base. Whenever the Spiders played the Senators, McKean found himself on the diamond opposite either Sam Wise or Cub Stricker, who were sharing duties at second this year.

Injuries beset the road-weary Spiders and their bench was so thin due to finances that Clarkson and Cuppy had to play right field in successive games when Ewing was out of action. With a June 16 loss in Brooklyn, in which McKean had three hits but made two errors, Cleveland put an end to its tour of the east; the team that had been in second place when it left Cleveland was returning in seventh. Undaunted, Ed McKean racked up five multiple-hit games, from June 12 through June 19, and next celebrated his arrival in western-division Pittsburgh by slashing three triples and nine singles in a five-game series. Two of those triples came in his five-hit game on June 19.[20] Charles Mears took the occasion to write accolades to Ed McKean for the June 24 issue of *The Sporting News*:

> The short stop is one of the best batters that ever played base ball. During the long term of years that he has been a member of the Clevelands he has been the most consistent and persistent batter in the team.... He is not a fungo batter but one of the most scientific men who ever walked to the plate. He does not lunge at the ball but hits it true and accurately.

Back home in the friendly confines of Cleveland's League Park, McKean clustered 11 more base hits in three games: a triple, two singles, and four runs batted in against Washington's Jesse Duryea on June 27, and five singles in an extra-inning win the following day. In that June 28 contest, ultimately a Cy Young victory, McKean's bad throw in the eighth inning spoiled a double play and set up a three-run Washington rally. McKean turned in an instant from goat to hero to goat again in the 12th inning. On first, after lining a single to center, he was caught off base by catcher Duke Farrell's snap throw, but McKean surprised everyone in the park by promptly breaking for second. Henry Larkin's throw struck the running McKean in the back and bounded into the outfield, allowing him to take third on the play. Jake Virtue followed by grounding harmlessly to the pitcher Esper (nicknamed Duke, like his catcher), who finally caught the reckless McKean, this time between third and home. Senators first baseman "Ted" Larkin was a lifetime .303 hitter with 114 triples. In 1884, with Philadelphia, Larkin slammed a record four doubles in a game. He was the Cleveland Infants playing-manager before Tebeau. The catching half of the Duke-Duke battery was Charles Farrell, who played long and well enough to lead the American Association in home runs and RBIs in its final 1891 season and also drive in a run, a dozen years later, in the 1903 World Series. Both feats were accomplished as a member of Boston teams.

Six. Patsy's Hibernian Spiders (1893–1894) 151

McKean was the star of this year's Fourth of July doubleheader, which drew a combined gate of 16,000, and also of the game the day following. The first game of the spangled double-dip was declared a tie by the umpire so there would be time left in the daylight to play the afternoon game. McKean was a force in game two, pulling a two-run home run over the right field fence in the third inning; doubling and driving in a run in the fourth inning; and adding an RBI single in the sixth. Cleveland did win the replayed game, on July 5, to advance their record to 30–21, but the personnel loss the team suffered in the originally scheduled game—Patsy Tebeau reinjured his knee after being spiked, and he was lost until the last of the season—had the club scrambling. In successive games, 18-year-old Eddie McFarland, Billy Alvord, and Jim Gilman, all recruits from the Cleveland sandlots, followed by the left-handed Jake Virtue, were pressed into service at third base, and all of them found lacking. Finally, on July 12, the Robisons purchased the contract of slick-fielding infielder Chippy McGarr from Savannah.

But the Cleveland newspapers these days were all a-buzz about the play of Ed McKean. After the afternoon game of the Fourth, "It's Ed McKean the crowd of 10,900 is talking about. Clevelanders say they've never seen a shortstop play a better game. He becomes the second batter ever to clear the right field fence, and he also had a double and two singles. In the field, he makes six putouts and has 10 assists. Twice he started double plays." After the replayed game, he was again singled out for special praise: "But, again, it was Ed McKean who entertained the 1,800 spectators. Fielding as if inspired, he made two putouts and 10 assists with one error." Following a July 17 win at home over the Giants, it was observed: "Continuing to play wonderfully, Ed McKean earns the cheers of the 2,000 fans by twice lunging to make one-handed stops." He also contributed two of the Spiders hits off New York's Bumpus Jones, a second-year rookie from Cedarville, Ohio. On July 22, *The Sporting News* lionized McKean as "the best short stop in the league, bar none, of late," since "the big hearted fellow has let himself out and the game he has put up has never been excelled in the league." It concluded: "Truly Mac is a corker." McKean was fielding with abandon and corking the ball with authority; he homered in a win in Louisville, on July 21, and again in Cincinnati, three days later. At the end of July, Cleveland was leading the League with a team batting average of .330, with Ed McKean at his apex for the season at .375.[21]

About this time in the summer of 1893, major league home teams were having difficulty finding healthy or suitable umpires to work the games. When John McQuaid was too sick to umpire two Cleveland games in Cincinnati, the teams chose Jim McAleer and Fred Dwyer to officiate in his stead. In the July 25 loss to the Redlegs, umpire McAleer's call on the bases incited a heated argument and the game ended with Arlie Latham, who had a history with McAleer, intentionally getting hit by a Cy Young pitch to force in the winning run. Just a few days later, for a July 29 doubleheader sweep by the Spiders, Browns owner Chris von der Ahe assigned John Clarkson and his brother Dad to umpire, explaining that he much preferred player officials to regular umpire Tom Lynch.

Although the Spiders' injury bug passed over McKean, the iron-man shortstop suffered through sickness and the "enforced idleness" of a League suspension for fighting on Jim McAleer's behalf in the July 25 ruckus in Cincinnati.[22] During Clarkson's July 31 win in Chicago, McKean became ill and had to be spelled by Jake Virtue, who finished the game at short. Bull McKean came charging back 24 hours later with a triple, a double, and a single in Cy Young's 20th victory of the season. He was out of the lineup again, missing three home games, before returning prematurely to play the morning game of an August 7 doubleheader against the Colonels. In that contest, McKean handled 11 chances flawlessly but went hitless. He returned to the lineup for good on August 11, stroking two hits off occasional umpire Dad Clarkson, as the Spiders triumphed over the Browns in League Park. In the first game of an August 12 doubleheader against St. Louis, McKean tripled and scored on Buck Ewing's thrilling suicide squeeze.[23] Tebeau moved up McKean, his best hitter at .356, into the second spot in the batting order (shuffling a bit after Jack O'Connor broke a little finger, and his own disabling injury), and McKean rapped out two hits off spot starter Jiggs Parrott, in a Cleveland win at home over the Reds, on August 14, and two more hits in the following day's rain-soaked loss to Ice Box Chamberlain. Tebeau experimented with McKean as his cleanup hitter on a disastrous trip east at the end of the month. The Spiders' problem had proved perennial: Cleveland could not find a way to win in the east. We can imagine president Robison's state of mind, at the end of August, when he took a determined stand by blocking Nick Young and fellow National League owners from transferring the western team's games to eastern ball parks for September. After a heated exchange of telegrams, made public record when Charles Mears printed them in the September 23 issue of *The Sporting News*, Frank Robison won his case.

Shortstop McKean's throwing errors in Philadelphia and Boston were a factor in 11 Cleveland defeats in 15 games and seven in a row. Still, the offense was working—the club still led the National League in batting average—and had a stubborn hold onto fourth place. Tebeau's walking wounded came home to beat up the Senators in a series beginning with a game, on September 7, in which McKean rapped out three hits. The next day, Youngstown, Ohio's own Jack Scheible made his big league debut, shutting out Washington on six hits.

Six. *Patsy's Hibernian Spiders (1893–1894)*

McKean did his best to pick up Scheible's confidence by leaping high to steal a sure double off the bat of Jimmy McGuire in the kid's first inning of pitching. McKean probably remembered the inning for another reason: he hit into a triple play. Senators starter Al Maul had walked Childs and Burkett, the first two batters he faced. Next up, Ewing lined a ball to right field, where, according to *The Sporting News*, "[Paul] Radford handled the ball so deftly that Childs could get no further than third base." That left the bases loaded for McKean with nobody out. McKean promptly "slammed a liner toward left center that looked good for three bases and everybody started home. But [shortstop Joe] Sullivan, he with the long arms, was in its way. He jumped a mile in the air and pulled it down, threw to [Duke] Farrell at third, who threw to [second baseman Sam] Wise and three Cleveland chances for that inning had gone to join the host in a distant land."[24] In 1893, rookie Sullivan and Herman Long were the last two big league shortstops to make 100 errors in a season. The game was among the last in Modoc Wise's outstanding 12-year career after the Akrons. McKean was hitting in bad luck; moreover, he'd been playing sick, "complaining the last two months of sickness," *Sporting Life* reported on September 23. Whichever the cause, through September, his batting average plummeted another 40 points at the same time attendance at League Park bottomed out to about 300 or 500 lonesome customers per game.

The last week of play in a mostly unfortunate season included a lucky forfeit, a Baltimore gift to Cleveland, on September 16. With the score 16 to 11 in favor of the home team Spiders, it was arbiter "[Tim] Hurst's opinion that there was sufficient light to play the eighth inning of the last game of the season between Baltimore and Cleveland. The Baltimore players, with more vehemence than good nature," in the view of *The Sporting News*, "vouchsafed their individual and collective opinion that it was entirely too dark to finish the inning."

> The row started when good natured Robinson was kicking like a broncho about not being able to see. [Pitcher Kirtley] Baker turned his back on Hurst, and [Steve] Brodie came wandering in from the field. Taylor put in a kick and [John] McGraw, who played in left field, ... came in to exhibit more of his freshness. Hurst took the time on them and told them to resume play. They did so, but only for a moment.

This enabled McKean to fly out deep to right, plating Young.

> Then there was another kick, but finally Baker was induced to pitch. Brodie was wandering back and forth in center like a drunken sailor, and [Bill] Hawke, [Joe] Kelley and [old acquaintance Tony] Mullane, on the bench, lit a piece of paper for light and warmth. When Tebeau came to bat [Billy] Shindle had deserted his post [third base, in place of McGraw], and Robinson was trying to persuade

Hurst that it was as dark as the ways of the "Heathen Chinese," but Hurst could not perceive the enveloping gloom. Tebeau made a hit, but it was turned into a home run by McGraw, who refused to field it, and Jennings, who refused to make an effort to put Tebeau out after McGraw threw the ball, so Childs and Burkett scored with Tebeau. O'Connor placed a single and it was also converted into a home run, although Jack cut third base by a mile. The game had now become a farce, and Robinson refused to catch the ball or throw it back to the pitcher. Hurst refused the ball a few times and then O'Connor placed himself in Robinson's place. When Hurst discovered him he dramatically waved him aside and commanded McAleer to not touch the ball. Three times he directed Robinson to pick up the ball and return it to the pitcher. Three times "Robbin" refused and expostulated. The crisis and "Robbie's" third refusal happened at the same time.[25]

That's when Sir Timothy Hurst, summoning his best Irish elocution, pronounced the game a forfeit. There is still something more to add to the already rich confusion of this game: Don't look for Tebeau's or O'Connor's home runs in the record books. According to the rules of McKean's day, none of the runs in the calamitous eighth inning counted; thus the official score for Cy Young's 30th win, 9 to 0, reverted to the last inning completed.

In Cleveland's September 30 finale, McKean's two errors were decisive for the Philadelphia win. It was the only game Hall of Fame catcher Buck Ewing caught all year. In spite of his late-season fade, perhaps the aftereffects of his July 31 injury, Ed McKean enjoyed his gaudiest statistical season yet at the plate. His 57 extra-base hits were fourth most in the National League, and he tied his nemesis Hugh Duffy for fifth-most total bases, with 258. He led the Spiders in games played, at-bats, and runs batted in (133, the second best in the League). McKean also placed fifth in the National League in doubles (29) and third in triples (24). He hit for an average of .310, or just above the average National League hitter that year. McKean put together at least 40 multiple-hit games in 1893. Fully recovered from his finger injury, McKean's fielding at short returned to career levels; his fielding percentage would never dip below this season's .902 as long as he was a Spider. His 74 errors, third most among League shortstops, were offset by his career best 6.0 chances per game. The team's weakness at third base before the arrival of Chippy McGarr meant that McKean was asked to cover a lot of ground. He came in a respectable fifth in the National League in putouts, and he was able to surpass this year's 55 double plays only once in his career (1896).

Throughout the ups and downs, McKean was his usual self on the ball field. "McKean is a droll fellow," chuckled *The Sporting News*. "When Baltimore was here, Clarke, their catcher, stood over by third coaching. One of his favorite remarks is 'Well, I don't know.' It grew rather monotonous and McKean made some remark to the coacher to which he replied,

'Well, I don't know.' Mac yelled back, 'That's what I'm telling you for, 'cause you don't know.' The gang had a long laugh over Mac's adeptness at repartee."[26]

Patsy's Spiders had put on a distinctly Irish-American face. On paper, Cleveland could now field an all–Hibernian team, if we have Ewing play one of his five games at second and insert Akron's Ed McFarland in right field. The rest of the lineup would be: Clarkson, pitcher, O'Connor, catcher, Tebeau, first baseman, McKean, shortstop, McGarr, third baseman, Burkett, left fielder, and McAleer in center. Of course, not every Spider was an Irishman by heritage or inclination. Elmer Bates told a story about Nig Cuppy (whose birth name, we remember, was George Koppe) going "into a restaurant last St. Patrick's day to get a lunch. While he was waiting for it he helped himself from a big dish at the end of the counter. 'Here,' shouted the proprietor, 'vat you doing?' 'Eating water cresses,' said the Logansport boy, 'They're delicious.' 'Vater cresses? Vy, mine frient, dose are bunches of shamrocks I had put up to gif mine Irish customers.'"[27]

In the end, Boston won another National League pennant with Frank Selee, better than third-place Cleveland by 12½ games this time around. The Pittsburgh club surprised by finishing ahead of Cleveland for second place on the strength of Frank Killen's 36 victories (two more than Cy Young's total), and boosted by late acquisition Jack Glasscock's 74 RBIs in 64 games after Al Buckenberger, looking like a genius, rescued him from St. Louis. The Pirates seemed to have borrowed the 1892 Spiders' formula for success—best home record in the League, plus dominating pitching, plus run production from the shortstop position—although it should be noted that Cleveland did win nine of 12 head-to-head contests with Pittsburgh. It would take the Spiders two more years to return to the postseason playoffs.

Things went so much askew for the Spiders in 1894 that George Cuppy, chronically sore leg and all, was arguably the most valuable pitcher on the staff, more important than Cy Young for a season. As Tebeau's number two starter, Cuppy went 24–15 and led the League in shutouts. Baseball's first great relief pitcher won a record eight times without a loss, and finished other games for a Cleveland team that never did find a credible number-three starter. John Clarkson, the designated third man in the rotation, began the campaign by winning seven of his first eight starts, but his record was only 8–9 come July. Dent Young suffered through a losing streak of seven decisions during August and September, tying his career longest for futility.[28] The low point for Young and the Spiders was the Labor Day thrashing in Baltimore—in six innings of hard labor, he gave up 22 hits and 16 runs—in front of 25,000 onlookers. In all, Cleveland wound up using 14 pitchers on the season, 11 different starters;

Tebeau even had to call on Jesse Burkett for four innings (he'd started his minor league career as a pitcher), and Jake Virtue got to try out his fabled throwing arm against a batter. After 53 games, Buck Ewing, who had hit a lusty .344 with 122 RBIs in 116 games the previous year, was struggling to average .250. Both baseball legends had arrived, at the end of their playing effectiveness, at the same time on the same team. Both were dealt away by midseason. The notable additions of Bobby Wallace, interviewing for a spot in the pitching rotation, rookie outfielder Harry Blake, and seasoned veteran White Wings Tebeau, were to make an impact a year after this lost season, no consolation for the Cleveland cranks, who were impatient to see the uses of adversity.

Ed McKean stayed healthy all season, and he had a career year statistically. Playing all 130 games on the Cleveland schedule, he averaged .357, on 198 base hits, and slugged .509. He led the team in runs batted in (fifth in the National League), doubles, triples, and even in the stolen bases category (33, his most since 1889). His .904 fielding percentage was eighth best in the League, placing him between Hughie Jennings and Herman Long. And yet, McKean's individual accomplishments were pretty much wasted on a team destined for sixth place, with a 68–61 record, the worst finish for a Spiders team since 1891.

President Robison could divide his time for this offseason between mounting worries over how to finance a franchise in Cleveland and the growing sentiment against the kind of riotous baseball that his Spiders practiced. He looked into the prospect of selling off his interests, and quitting baseball in order to devote himself to his transportation empire, only to be told by Nick Young that the National League owners could find no buyers. The League was also not interested in running the Cleveland franchise in 1894, thank you.[29] While Frank Robison was away in New York at the end of January, rumors already had Ed McKean traded in return for Giants shortstop Shorty Fuller.[30] Later, it became clear that George Davis had been urging the Giants to acquire his former teammate, in spite of the fact that Monte Ward maintained a strong personal dislike for McKean.[31] *The Sporting News*, in March, ran a box on page one, under the headline "No Use for McKean," that read: "John Ward has no use for Shortstop McKean, of Cleveland. At least he says so, and adds that McKean is a trouble-maker and that he would not sign him if he could. Notwithstanding Mr. Ward's remarks, the feeling prevails here [i.e., New York] that McKean would strengthen the New York team immensely."[32] George Davis told Elmer Bates: "We would nail the pennant sure, if we had a hard-hitting short stop like Ed. I have played with him for years and regard him as the best all-around short stop in the big League. With men on bases and McKean

Six. *Patsy's Hibernian Spiders (1893–1894)* 157

at-bat you can bet your money safely four times out of five that somebody will be moved around the bags."[33]

Amidst this unsettled atmosphere in February,

> [McKean] came up from Grafton to see a wrestling match, and incidentally to have a chat with President Robison. Mac thinks he has played here quite long enough and argued that it would be better all around to let him go elsewhere, but the Cleveland president could not see it that way, and told him that he would find the same trouble wherever he might go. In addition to this the president told the shortstop that he considered him as good a man at his post as there is in the league, if not better, and that he would not think of trading him for anybody but Long of Boston. [And t]hat deal is very unlikely.[34]

Robison was asking returning players, including his stars Young and McKean (the year after the infielder had driven in better than a run per game for the club) to accept pay cuts for the upcoming season. As a result, the Spiders were among the last in the League to contract a team. Burkett and Zimmer joined McKean and Young in holding out until the last week of March, when they finally signed—instead of sitting out the year without playing—five weeks after rival Pittsburgh had their whole team in the fold for the season.[35] McKean had to have been hurt and humiliated by what he read in Elmer Bates' column for *Sporting Life* on March 24. Bates had leaked what were the purported salaries for the Spiders in 1893. If the figures are accurate, the shortstop had been grossly underpaid, considering length of service to Robison and value to the club—going into a new contract that was, in actuality, a pay cut. McKean and Burkett appeared at the bottom of the published pay scale, earning $1,800 each, significantly below the two high-priced newcomers Clarkson ($2,500) and Ewing ($2,400), as well as Young ($2,300), McKean's partner Childs ($2,250), and his friend Zimmer ($2,100)! Patsy Tebeau was a bargain, drawing a salary of $2,100 plus a supplemental stipend for managing.

Some of the unsigned players took the initiative to work out on their own in Cleveland. One of the more enjoyable ways to get in shape was to play for the In-Door League, a precursor to softball, at the Red Cross Rink.[36] Cy Young pitched for the Pythians team, and Chief Zimmer was said to be the league's star player.[37] As a further cost-cutting measure, Robison was keeping the team in the city for spring training, inside the gymnasium at the Cleveland Athletic Club (where he had financial interests) and playing at least nine games against local amateur teams—without McKean, Zimmer, and Burkett, who were still holding out.[38] Finally, the March 31 *Sporting News* could confirm "Spiders All Signed" by Howard Robison. There were long-term ramifications of the extended contract negotiations. At the Cleveland Athletic Club on March 17, the normally placid Charles Zimmer engaged in a shouting match with manager Tebeau over the backstop's truancy; and Cupid Childs, who had stayed in Baltimore for the duration of the contract squabbles, reported to Cleveland overweight.[39] Frank Robison, at length, did treat his team to a brief spring training tour (no doubt for the extra income of a good gate), to Akron, where they turned back Buchtel College, and as far abroad as Grand Rapids.[40] During the late-winter months without the prospect of a paycheck from the Spiders, some players found secondary sources of income. McKean was employed by the *Cleveland Press* as a ghostwriter for local wrestling matches.[41] Ed McKean could stake a claim as the original Cleveland player-scribe, beating out Addie Joss for the accolade by a decade. Zimmer enjoyed an income of about $4,000, over three years, from his baseball board game.[42]

At whatever salary the Robisons paid McKean for 1894, the veteran was an invaluable presence in dressing rooms, hotel lobbies, and train cars. Beginning in spring training, McKean and Cuppy vied with Patsy Tebeau and O'Connor for team honors in the invaluable art of clubhouse diversion:

> Cuppy is the story teller and McKean is the joker of the Cleveland team. It was at the Hawley House the other night when these two players were surrounded by an interested group that "Cup" started to tell a funny one, of which he was particularly fond. Mac had heard it before and he passed the wink around. One by one Cuppy's hearers disappeared, but George was so interested in his tale that it was not until he had finished it that he found he was without an audience. It was a cruel joke, but, of course, "Cup" bought the cigars.[43]

Around this time, all three McKean brothers were involved in professional baseball at one time or another, making Grafton village a sometimes center for the sports world. In March and April of 1894, older brother Martin was attempting to resurrect the old Tri-State League by forming a stock company. He aspired to run a club himself in Akron.[44] And in 1895, he went about organizing a team in Dayton to compete in the Interstate League. Both plans failed. Martin B. McKean's initial foray into baseball was during Ed's rookie year with the Blues, in spring 1887, when he signed a minor league contract with the St. Joseph Reds but never played.[45] Kid brother Matt did play briefly in the minors. In 1890, the Des Moines Prohibitionists signed him as an amateur for insurance in the event their 35-year-old second baseman Dick Phelan could not return from a broken shoulder.[46] Phelan must have recovered after all, since Matt McKean's name does not appear on the roster for the Western Association team. Six years later, in 1896, Matt was a right fielder for the Carbondale Anthracites.[47] In 32 at-bats over eight games, he scored seven runs on seven hits, none for extra bases.

Through the fall and winter seasons, Cleveland writers had rallied to the defense of Tebeau's Hibernian Spiders against charges of hooliganism from many fronts. New York columnist Joe Vila fired the first volley, in *Sporting Life* on September 2, 1893, attacking "Tebeau's filthy behavior at the Polo Grounds" and condemning the Spiders (the "Ohio hoodlums") for their bad language and epithets. John Foster made the counter case, in the September 30, 1893 issue of *Sporting Life*, coming out in favor of Tebeau's anti-scientific baseball and refuting Monte Ward's attack of "ruffianly and unsportsmanlike tactics," only to be blasted in the pages of the next *Sporting Life* by Vila, who now declared Cleveland had played crude so-called "Association-ball" in the Polo Grounds during that year's Independence Day doubleheader. Vila fingered Ed McKean, accusing one of the most clean-mouthed Spiders of abusing fellow New York scribe George E. Stackhouse when he allegedly "called him the vilest of all epithets" from the diamond. In the January 13, 1894, issue of *The Sporting News*, Charles W. Mears published his defense of the practice of kicking, a salient feature of the Cleveland game plan:

> The brilliant base ball writers of the East, especially Henry Chadwick, have of late devoted much time and no little amount of newspaper space in demonstrating what terrible evil kicking in base ball has become. They appear to believe that base ball should be conducted on a progressive euchre basis, but I, for one, am prone to disagree.
>
> Tame base ball is relished by very few. The kicking, however, must be genuine. None of the thin stage business, simply for effect, but red and green fire flashing from the eyes of the players.
>
> Earnest protest gives the impression that the game is being played for all it is worth and that both teams are out to win. Every detail of the game ought to be at the fingers' ends of the players, and the least infringements by either side forcibly denounced. A game conducted on these lines cannot fail to interest. Tebeau, Anson, Ward, Nash, Comiskey and others who have reached a high degree of distinction on the diamond, owe it not alone to the excellence of their play, but in part to demanding a rigid enforcement of the rules in the playing of their opponents, and knowing when a protest should be made. The most trivial infraction of base ball law is sufficient to set these giants "on end."
>
> They have played base ball long enough to realize the importance of taking advantage of their opponents' errors, not only in handling the ball…Mechanical ball is losing ball….
>
> That's why we love our Pat.
>
> The rules committee will make a grievous mistake if it takes away from the captain the right to fight for their honest dues.

It was at this point in the heated hot stove exchanges that Patsy Tebeau issued his uncompromising proclamation, heartily approved by Charles Mears, about having no use for what he called "milk and water, goody-goody" players.[48] Father Chadwick couldn't let that pronouncement pass, angrily denouncing what Tebeau considered "aggressive hustling" as "a new name for rowdy, kicking ball players." Mears dismissed what he called "Chad's recent mind wanderings" by quoting them as if self-explanatory before insinuating that Chadwick "is getting real old too."[49]

Clevelanders also found it easy enough to poke fun at their beloved and beleaguered Spiders, given a chance. On the Monday following April Fool's Day, just two weeks before the opening of the National League season, Charles Mears was among the audience treated to "a comical burlesque on base ball in the Cleveland Athletic Club's opera, 'Moses Cleveland Up To Date.'"[50] As we already know, in one of four acts on the bill, members of the Spiders team performed a five-minute skit which climaxed in a kick-turned-riot after Jesse Burkett's risible home run is nullified when he is called out at home.[51] Reportedly, Frank Robison, viewing the proceedings from his box, "was more than delighted with the manner the Cleveland boys burlesqued base ball." *The Sporting News* placed Zimmer, Young, Virtue, Childs, and McGarr beside Burkett on the stage with umpire Stage, but James Egan indicated a dozen Spiders participated. It's hard to imagine that extroverted Ed McKean wouldn't have joined that thespian infield for the occasion. Considering that the actor umpire, Billy Stage, would be a real first-year National League arbiter for 1894 belies the seriousness behind the fun.[52]

As inevitably as ball games succeed the offseason, it was on the field of play, and ultimately in the court of public opinion, where Cleveland was losing the debate. The Spiders' bad conduct had fostered a climate of delinquency among some fans, and League Park became the scene of a fan riot on May 26. The overachieving Spiders had been in first place all month when the team was shut out by Pittsburgh that afternoon. An overflow crowd of 9,000, expecting to celebrate another win in a string of victories, besieged the park for Nig Cuppy's start. Unfortunately, Cuppy couldn't save the game by coming in to relieve himself, and so, while Chauncey Fisher surrendered the rest of the Pirates' nine runs and the Spiders could not score, the massive crowd grew restless. For a diversion, a band of unruly kids standing in the roped-off outfield began to toss around Harry Stevens' seat cushions.[53] Finally, when Buck Ewing came to the plate in the ninth inning, at least 1,000 cranks "broke from the stands and behind the ropes that had been stretched about the field." Umpire Robert Emslie judiciously called time, and Spider joined Pirate to implore the mob to return to the stands, but a barrage of more cushions was the only result. After 10 minutes, Emslie could not move the crowd from the field—the home team had provided but one cop for the Saturday game—and he was obliged to call a forfeit of the contest. *The Sporting News* called the game "the most disgraceful affair that has ever marred the history of the national game" in Cleveland. "There was no harm done to person, and the whole affair was in good nature, but that does not make the offense any the less reprehensible."[54]

Riotous behavior by Pirates cranks later on in the season was more dangerous. On August 8, the Cleveland game in Pittsburgh "ended in a small riot,"

Six. Patsy's Hibernian Spiders (1893–1894)

after which Pirates executive director W.W. Kerr petitioned to have Patsy Tebeau blacklisted from baseball. *The Sporting News* was especially disapproving to know that "many ladies were driven from the stand by the vile language of Tebeau and O'Connor." The newspaper considered "Captain Tebeau ... very fortunate in escaping without severe bodily injury."

> As it was, he was chased out of the grounds and into the bus by a mob of 1,000 infuriated sports, who pushed and jostled him in a most uncomfortable way. The bus containing the Cleveland players was stoned by the men, which needed only a good leader to act upon the whole team. The crowd followed the bus clear through the city, pelting them with melons and other delicacies.

A separate notice in the same week's newspaper reported that cranks in the close-by stands had become agitated when Tebeau, from the coacher's box, and Phil Knell (whose entire season otherwise consisted of one pitching appearance of seven innings, six walks, no strikeouts, and an ERA of 11.57) were calling each other names.[55] The August 18 issue of *The Sporting News* blamed Tebeau, O'Connor, and also Jake Beckley and Jack Glasscock, for inciting the riot. By August 23, the great Glasscock found himself released from his Pittsburgh contract, ostensibly for reasons having to do with a "torn hand," and replaced at short by Clevelander Monte Cross.

Round one of the fighting in Pittsburgh had taken place a bit earlier in the day.

> After the game Tebeau called [umpire Willard] Hoagland some vile names and asked him under the stand to fight. Hoagland, who is one of the best boxers in the country, asked Tebeau to lead the way, and both teams then made a dash under the grand stand in the wake of the umpire and Tebeau, while the crowd went wild and tried to batter down the doors.

"Once under the stand Tebeau grabbed a bat," or so *The Sporting News* claimed. "Hoagland pulled off his coat and squared. Tebeau, seeing he was up against it, dropped his bat and ran out of the stand into the arms of the crowd which was waiting for him."[56]

The circumstances of the August 8 game were similar to those in the earlier riot in Cleveland, which occurred in the ninth inning of a blowout.

> The trouble began in the ninth inning, when the score stood 10 to 3 in favor of Pittsburgh. Cleveland had two men out and the team had to catch a train in 20 minutes. Tebeau started to act a bully, hoping to have the game declared forfeited to Pittsburgh by the umpire. He came up to Hoagland when O'Connor was at the bat. The umpire ordered him to the bench, but in an insolent tone Tebeau refused and dared Hoagland to forfeit the game. Hoagland fined him. Then Tebeau rushed up, tore the mask from Hoagland, and another fine resulted. Zimmer, who was on third, tried to steal home in the excitement. [The version

printed in the August 10 *Cleveland Press* indicated that Zimmer trotted in from third hoping to make the last out and save Tebeau a fine.] Hartman threw the ball to head him off. O'Connor, under Tebeau's instructions, caught the ball and threw it over the stand. Hoagland fined each of them $25 and declared Zimmer out on the interference, which ended the game.[57]

There is no record of either the speed of the horse-drawn team bus or whether the team made their train on time, but the Spiders staged an exhibition game in Sandusky, Ohio, the next day and played in Chicago on August 10.

The Sporting News, published out of Tebeau's home town, was clearly aimed at discrediting him at the same time his boyhood buddy O'Connor remained a darling of the St. Louis fans—he was ranked first in the newspaper's "Most Popular Player" poll for months running. However, the Pittsburgh columnist for the same newspaper did spread the blame around. He agreed, and then some, that "Tebeau's actions were disgraceful to say the least and the language of he and Jack O'Connor during the arguments with Umpire Hoagland drove many ladies from the grand stand. The only pity is that Hoagland did not get in a good blow or two on the Cleveland rowdy when they were together under the stand"; however, the writer added:

> Hoagland who umpired the last week of games in Pittsburgh has not pleased the people here. There is no doubt but the man is short-sighted, as his decisions on balls and strikes are something awful...Hoagland has a very bad habit of trying to even matters up on all occasions. When he makes a raw decision which calls out a strong kick, this umpire seems to loose no time until he makes one in favor of the other side equally bad, just to even matters up. Plainly Hoagland will not do for a National League umpire—he lacks both knowledge and firmness.[58]

The 1894 season would be Willard A. Hoagland's one year as a National League umpire.

The Spiders had jumped off to a promising start in 1894, victors in seven of the first nine (all without the advantage of playing a home game); it was the best start on the road by a Cleveland team, by Charles Mears' count, for the last seven years. Things were going so well that McKean was credited with two stolen bases when Cleveland beat the Colts, 18 to 3, on May 8 in League Park, even though he had reached first base only once.[59] And on the Spiders' first trip east, always the most severe test of a Cleveland club, they ambushed Boston, smashing eight home runs in two games, on June 1 and 2. McKean didn't join home run hitters Zimmer (two homers), Tebeau, O'Connor, Ewing, Burkett, and McGarr, but he did go 4-for-5 off Jack Stivetts in the first game and 2-for-4, with a double, against Kid Nichols the day following. In the second game of a Fourth of July doubleheader, McKean hit a two-run homer off Amos Rusie, the National League pitcher of the year. "McKean's playing bor-

SIX. *Patsy's Hibernian Spiders (1893–1894)* 163

ders on the sensational so the New York writers declare," enthused *The Sporting News* on June 9. However, by the end of June, their usual poor record in the east allowed the rest of the League to catch up with the Spiders; also, the crowds in Cleveland had thinned out. McAleer was hospitalized, so Jake Virtue had to be pressed into service in center field, and Robison had to supplement the roster by adding seven new pitchers by June 25.[60] The overly familiar Jersey Bakely brought a barrel of water on board the sinking ship a month later.[61] Patsy Tebeau had to play second base, when Cupid Childs suffered what was feared to be a season-ending injury, on August 13.[62] For a stretch, Mike Sullivan, at the end of his pitching career and soon to be practicing law, was Cleveland's best starter.[63]

Through all the vicissitudes, McKean's performances at home in the last week of July were memorable. Against Lefty Killen and Red Ehret, on July 26, McKean slashed a double and a triple, and turned the game's only double play. Unfortunately for the few Cleveland cranks who had bought tickets, Cleveland starter Tony Mullane gave up nine runs in the loss. Four days later, when Cuppy beat the Colonels, McKean tripled and singled twice against Wellington, Ohio's, Jack Wadsworth.[64] On August 4, *The Sporting News* updated its readership on the kind of season Ed McKean was having.

> That man McKean is playing better ball than he ever did. Mac never grows old. He is now in his prime as a ball player, and it would have been a grievous mistake to have let him gone [sic] to New York last spring when there was some talk concerning that he move. He takes greater fielding chances than he ever did and his batting has been both hard and timely. One peculiarity about Mac, the madder the opposing players make him the better he can hit.

The scribe recalled a game from the end of Cleveland's hot streak back in July when they had taken 15 out of 17 games:

> In one of the games with the Browns Burkett was struck out on three successive balls that came no where near the plate. Mac and Jesse argued with the umpire and then Breitenstein stuck in his little say so and it struck Mac to the quick. The umpire called "play" and Mac went to the bat. "One strike," called Hurst. "Two strikes" and then "One ball" was called. Mac waited a moment and then went for one that came within his reach. Oh, how that ball did go. It went like a shot from a cannon. It landed against the right field fence with a bang and bounced back a hundred feet. In the meantime Mac was going around the bases.

"The man" also hit especially well (perhaps he played mad there, as well?) at Boston's Congress Street Grounds. In a doubleheader on August 24, when Nig Cuppy won in the morning then started and lost in the afternoon, McKean was 3-for-5, with a double, off Harry Staley and Kid Nichols in game one; and 2-for-3, with a triple, facing game two pitcher George Hodson.[65] In the

Polo Grounds, McKean made four hits in five at-bats and Sullivan beat Dad Clarke, on August 30. At Baltimore, on September 3, Sullivan lost, 3 to 2, in spite of McKean's effort, a triple and a single against Duke Esper. And in Brooklyn on the day following, he doubled as Nig Cuppy shut out the Trolley Dodgers.[66] McKean continued his year of heavy hitting to the very end, in contrast to his late-season decline the previous year. He had 11 hits, two of them for extra bases, in his final 23 at-bats. And the Spiders, though they were a second-division team more than 20 games removed from first place, went undefeated in their last four games.

At League Park, on September 27, Cy Young was the beneficiary of 26 Cleveland runs, four scored by McKean, in a laugher over Philadelphia. McKean tripled and singled four times against Gus Weyhing, who took one for the team and, in one day, inflated his ERA for the season to 5.81 as a result. Those same Phillies finished in fourth place, in spite of a team ERA of over five runs a game, on the strength of their outfielders: Ed Delahanty (.407 average, 131 RBIs), Billy Hamilton (League-leading 192 runs, 100 steals), and Sam Thompson (.407, and 141 RBIs). Even their fourth outfielder, Tuck Turner, hit .418. The two clubs scored 30 runs on the afternoon. Cleveland won again the next day, 8 to 6, behind newcomer twirler Bobby Wallace, as McKean had a hand in a double play for the second straight game, and chipped in a double in five at-bats against Kid Carsey. In the final Cleveland home game, on September 29, McKean solved Philadelphia's best pitcher, Brewery Jack Taylor, for two hits in five plate appearances. It was another win for the Spiders, and an invitation for the home fans to wait until next year.

However, the last game for the Spiders of 1894, a tie in Cincinnati, was as inconclusive as their campaign had proved. Starter George Cuppy watched 16 Reds cross home plate by the sixth inning before the Spiders countered with 15 runs of their own over the last four frames to force the 16 to 16 wash. In the ninth with two outs, Jack O'Connor knocked the ball out of catcher Bill Merritt's hands to score the "winning" run for Cleveland, but umpire John McQuaid called him out for interference—and the riotous season ended with a kick, not a bang. The players on both sides played listlessly in the field— McKean committed three of the 15 errors—but McKean enjoyed one last fine day at-bat, going 3-for-6.[67]

After the game, Bobby Wallace and Mike Sullivan returned home, and Patsy Tebeau was off for St. Louis to claim his inheritance of $2,000 from an estate settlement. The rest of the Spiders went on a two-week barnstorming tour. Jimmy McAleer was in charge of the purse—McKean and his mates cleared $92 apiece—and Young and Cuppy earned their cash by pitching all the exhibitions.[68] On the advice of friends, McKean did not pursue his wrestling career this winter, "fearing an injury that would prevent him from playing ball next season."[69] Still, the Pittsburgh columnist for *Sporting Life* was among those who thought "Ed. McKean should have never given up wrestling." He argued that "few men are better put together for that sport than the Cleveland short stop, and he was just getting good when he retired."[70] As it turned out, the news of his retirement was greatly exaggerated.

1895 Temple Cup: October 3 and 5, Games Two and Three

"Four times round is enough for one dance," Tweedledum pointed out....

For the second game of the Temple Cup, Ned Hanlon gave the ball to Billy Hoffer.

Baltimore's kid twirler had been a sensational find for the regular season: The Wizard led the League in shutouts, and his 31 wins are still the rookie record. In the decade to come, Hoffer would bear the distinction of losing the first game in American League history, pitching for the Cleveland Blues. Both Hoffer and Hugh Jennings were discovered by Jack Chapman, who recommended them to the discerning Hanlon.[1] The Baltimore manager would be especially interested in seeing how Bill Hoffer would stand up to Patsy Tebeau and the Spiders. *The Sporting News* for October 12 described the situation between Hoffer and Tebeau as the "one open rupture" in the always "intense" rivalry between the Orioles and the Spiders. "Pitcher Hoffer assaulted Manager Tebeau during the last game" between the two teams, a Cleveland loss in Baltimore on September 10, the day after Hoffer had won, 4 to 1, "but as the Cleveland manager controlled himself, there was no further trouble" that day. "Hoffer claimed that Tebeau tried to give him the 'leg.'" Two umpires, Emslie and Hurst, were deployed on the field to maintain order, and Tebeau lasted only into the sixth inning before they ejected him for kicking. (Ed McKean's single was the only Cleveland base hit off Sadie McMahon on September 10.) As it turned out, Hoffer had the good sense to put off his personal war with Tebeau until game five of this Temple Cup, when all was lost for his team. "In the entire Temple Cup series Hoffer and McGraw were the only players of either team to play dirty ball," in the judgment of *The Sporting News* for October 12.

Today, more than 10,000 cranks thronged League Park—nearly five times the average attendance during the season—intent upon cheering their Spiders and intimidating the Orioles.

President Robison had taken precautions to tighten what went for park security in those days, and he offered policemen $25 for the apprehension of any crank caught throwing missiles onto the field. Many among the overflow crowd took positions on the playing field behind ropes, the first row sitting and the second row kneeling behind, with standing room behind them the length of foul territory from third base into left. In

Nig Cuppy was the wounded hero of Cleveland's Temple Cup defeat (Heritage Auctions).

short, the Baltimores played in the actual shadows of the fans.[2] One can only wonder what verbal abuse John McGraw was forced to endure a good hook slide away from his tormentors around third base. McGraw's biographer reckons that, in an escalation of the first game's unruly behavior, "More missiles— beer bottles, tin horns, cushions—rained on the Orioles" this day, a charge Cleveland sportswriters would always dispute.[3] It was agreed, however, Cleveland's faithful had arrived fully equipped, with even more and improved noisemakers for game two festivities. Added to the fish horns and tin horns of yesterday were fire-engine-sized bells and "an invention of the tin horn species that was fully eight feet long and had a dozen tubes attached through which as many fans blew at once." It required real "team" effort—seven cranks had to blow simultaneously, one jarring note at a time—to sound the homemade horn in McGraw's ears.[4]

The Baltimore newspapers' inflated accounts of the games convinced their readers that Cleveland's home-field atmosphere was an unscrupulous, if not outright dangerous, bending of the rules of sportsmanship. "It was the pelting they received with missiles," a visiting Baltimore scribe complained, "the bold interference of the crowd and the vile imprecations heaped upon them that the Orioles objected to. Robinson, McGraw and Kelley were the worst sufferers, perhaps, as the crowd was chiefly on the left hand side of the field. Pecks of potatoes seemed to have been distributed along the line, and every time Robinson went after a foul fly a shower of them were hurled at him. McGraw and Kelley were hit in the head with potatoes."[5] The unhappy result of such press coverage was that Orioles cranks prepared a counterattack of riotous proportions for when the games came to Baltimore. Elmer Bates swore that the Cleveland enthusiasts did not harass the Baltimore players, contemptuously denying "the idiotic charge that the Orioles were subjected to any unusual treatment here."

> A few farmers came into town from Berea [sic] and brought with them potatoes. These they hurled at each other, and, incidentally, one or two got out on the field. This gave the newspaper boys who came along with Hanlon's men a great chance to shout about [fan] interference. In their eyes the potatoes were "gigantic rocks," and instead of falling harmlessly on the field they "inflicted bad bruises on the players."[6]

In the act of hurling the inflammatory phrases right back at Baltimore writers, Bates got a little loose with language himself, inadvertently slurring McKean's own background with his references to farmers and potatoes.

The gigantic crowd had plenty to toot their multifarious horns about: the home team scored three runs off Hoffer in the first inning and never trailed in the 7 to 2 cakewalk. The scare of the day came in the second inning, when Scoops Carey's smash back through the box tore Nig Cuppy's thumb nail on his pitching hand; the ball was hit so hard it went all the way to McAleer in center field, where he fumbled it, allowing Kelley to score Baltimore's first run. Undaunted, Cuppy completed the game at his usual casual pace. *Baseball Magazine* once described "Nig Cuppy's exasperating delay" like this: "Nig Cuppy stood holding the ball and holding it, and holding it some more. The maddened batsmen fumed and fretted ... the umpires barked and threatened, the fans counted and counted, often up to 56 or 59—and then Cuppy let go of the ball." He also liked to keep runners close at first base by suspending his right foot in the air for an illegal amount of time before delivering the ball to the batter.[7] He was one of the early game's most remarkable control artists; *The Sporting News* marveled that Cuppy had thrown not one wild pitch all season.[8] In addition to throwing a five-hitter, the twirler hit a run-scoring double of his own.[9] Nig Cuppy had already rapped out nine doubles and three triples during the regular season. And back on August 9, Cuppy scored five runs against the Colts, a record for a pitcher, winning the game, 18 to 6.

Ed McKean played a key part in that first-inning scoring outbreak.[10] His single, a liner over second baseman Gleason, scored Burkett for his third RBI in the first 10 innings of Temple Cup play. He didn't stop at first base, but alertly took second on Brodie's tardy throw to the plate, and subsequently scored the second Cleveland run on Tebeau's sacrifice fly to Keeler. The Spiders lacked concentration in the field early on, too. In the second inning, McKean either booted Kelley's grounder (official scorer Hawley recorded an error on the play) or it was a bad hop; either way, Kelley came around to score, all the way from first base, on the ball that nicked Nig Cuppy. The contest remained 3 to 1 until the fifth inning, when Jesse Burkett's slow roller in front of McGraw was as good as

Hugh Jennings was the opposition shortstop as consecutive Temple Cups matched up the game's best shortstops at the height of their playing careers, Baltimore's Jennings and Cleveland's McKean (author's collection).

a bunt. McKean, the next batter, failed to advance the runner—he popped out trying to sacrifice—but the Baltimore defense collapsed after Childs forced Burkett. A pickoff throw from Hoffer was so wide of first base that Cupid Childs rolled into third and then McAleer's hard bounder handcuffed Hugh Jennings, the National League's leading fielder at short, scoring Childs.

McKean made the highlight play of the game for the first out in the sixth, when he ran in and dove to snare Keeler's ankle-high liner, a sure base hit had he played back on the ball. The Orioles' half of the ninth inning was all McKean: he put Baltimore down in order, throwing out Kelley and Brodie and then corralling Gleason's popup. McKean had committed his second error in two games, and he would record an error in four of the five Temple Cup contests, while Jennings' only error came in this game. Still, contemporary observers recognized him as the fielding star of the afternoon (he had eight assists and four putouts) and for the series, as well.

The next day, a Saturday, Nig Cuppy provided the wildest moment in the park. For his stoic effort in game two, he was presented with the gift of a new shotgun prior to game three. From the packed-to-capacity grandstand, which seated boxing celebrities John L. Sullivan and Paddy Ryan, "He raised the gun to his shoulder and each barrel discharged a blast. A young boy," part of the staged entertainment, "immediately ran out of the crowd from the direction Cuppy had fired, and handed the pitcher a recently deceased pigeon. The crowd was delighted."[11]

The record-breaking crowd stretched the confines of League Park for the rematch between Cy Young and Sadie McMahon. Some cranks perched on the roof of the wooden grandstand, their feet dangling from the scoreboard; others flooded the outfield; a few more climbed telephone poles or occupied the trees behind the ball park's outfield. *The Sporting News* reported attendance to have hit "[at] least 12,000," a figure Browning agrees with, while Egan notes that "wild estimates" ranged from 15,000 to as many as 25,000.[12] The two managers fielded the lineups they had deployed for the first two games, with the exception of Robinson returning behind the plate to catch McMahon, the day after McKean swiped two of Cleveland's four bases off Clarke. And for the third straight game, the Spiders scored three times in the first inning and never relinquished the lead. The Spiders offense didn't strand a runner all day; meanwhile, Baltimore didn't hit a ball out of the infield until the eighth inning after Jennings' fly ball was absorbed into standing room for a harmless ground-rule double in the first. The one big change for this game was the level of the fans' harassment of the Baltimore players; a more subdued crowd this afternoon was content to raise their noisemakers in a joyful sound while the home team romped, 7 to 1.

Game three was McKean's weakest showing in the whole Cup series (he went 0-for-4 with another error), but he did score Cleveland's opening run and knocked in another. Time was called when McKean came to the plate in the seventh inning, with one run in and two Spiders on base, so he could be presented with a diamond stud pin. He promptly repaid his admirers' kindness by lofting a long fly to Joe Kelley, scoring two runs on the sacrifice and the left fielder's errant throw. In the eighth, McKean made a fine play on Sadie McMahon's grounder, limiting Baltimore to just one run in the inning. He chalked up four putouts to go with five assists. "The local infield was ... like a stonewall...[and] McKean was a tower of strength. In all his experience on the diamond he never played with the vim and dash that characterized his work in these Cup games. He was every where, getting every thing. In Saturday's game he went away out into left field, picked up a grounder and threw his man out at first."[13]

This time, Cleveland cranks refrained from rushing the Baltimore bench;

instead, the *Cleveland Plain Dealer* reported, "several hundred" fans marched around the diamond tooting their horns in a victory celebration. "With all the crowd and all the noise nothing occurred that need be regretted by the audience or the management," the paper assured its readership.[14] Without regard to the hostile reception the Spiders would face when the series resumed in Baltimore, a cocky Patsy Tebeau instructed his players to pack only one shirt for the trip, since they wouldn't be staying long.[15]

Cleveland's Temple Cup was but a single victory away. But the road to the championship ran through Baltimore.

Seven

Temple Cup Champs (1895–1896 seasons)

Then came a scene for your life.—The Sporting News, May 18, 1895

The 1895 championship Spiders ended their season as the greatest team in a Cleveland baseball history dating all the way back to 1871. Their .646 winning percentage would be the highest ever for a Cleveland team until the 1954 Indians. It was also Ed McKean's personal best year, the finest for a Cleveland shortstop before Lou Boudreau's 1948 MVP performance in a title year. McKean, playing in all 131 of the team's games, was the only Spider to drive in 100 runs. A determined McKean had come into his ninth training camp ready "to play the game of his life next season," already in game shape and, at 170 pounds, within 10 pounds of his rookie-season weight. Having followed McKean's offseason regimen at the Cleveland Athletic Club, Patsy Tebeau also anticipated a big season for McKean, "remark[ing] that he cannot see where the famous shortstop could improve his playing of last year, but if McKean does he is quite willing to be shown."[1]

All the same, things started out badly for the club; coming on the heels of their sixth-place finish in 1894, the Spiders had the appearance of a ball club that had lost its luck. Cleveland couldn't field a regular lineup all spring and well into June, for one reason after another; center fielder McAleer's chronic leg problems had persisted since the end of last season, third baseman McGarr was more fit to play in the outfield, second baseman Childs strained his side and was in and out of the lineup all the while complaining of his contract, and right fielder Blake was a long time in recovering from a rupture. Patsy Tebeau deemed himself able to play on the field only about half the time, so he signed his brother White Wings Tebeau to cover first base. McKean's newest teammate had upstaged him in his debut with the Blues, in 1887: George Tebeau hit a home run in his own first big league at-bat in that game. His nickname, by the way, came from a popular novel by William Black, not from his pedestrian speed. White Wings would retire as a player after this year's Temple Cup and reemerge as the millionaire owner of baseball teams in the Western League. It was the kind of early season when even newcomer George Tebeau had to absent himself from the team, when his child died in Denver. And iron-man catcher Chief Zimmer joined his manager on the bench, resting a sore shoulder. To add to the Spiders' woes, this was the year the National League was committed to blocking the way of the rowdy Spiders. In March, when the owners proposed to curtail rowdy players and kicking coaches for the upcoming season, they'd targeted Patsy Tebeau among the top 10 worst offenders from 1894.[2]

Through it all, manager Tebeau's brinkmanship baseball continued to win games for Cleveland, sometimes at the cost of keeping him out of his own lineup. In a May 9 victory, when the visiting Nationals threatened in the seventh, Tebeau went for the runner instead of the ball, which had been overthrown by Childs, knocking down Deacon McGuire with a shoulder. When play resumed after the brawl, McGuire was so angry with Tebeau that he got picked off first. Gentlemanly Deacon would one day succeed Larry Lajoie as the manager of the Cleveland Naps. McKean chipped in two hits in the 7 to 3 win. On the down side, by the third week of May, Patsy Tebeau was on the sidelines again, benched this time with a bad case of tonsillitis—brought on by screaming vile names at umpire William Betts, no less. The Betts incident occurred in a 6 to 5 loss at home to Washington on May 10. Following "a rotten throw by Childs, who, by the way, has been accused of playing for his release, sent four runs across the plate" to tie the game against pitcher Bobby Wallace in the eighth inning, the Nationals went ahead by a run in the ninth.

> Then Cleveland went in and worked to win. Two men died easy. Burkett singled and McKean followed suit with a safe hit, putting the monkey on third. Childs came to bat prepared to do or die. He waited for a good one and tiring of that, whanged away at a low ball, sending a hard hit daisy-cutter to Joyce. Billy picked it up very neatly and fired it at Cartwright. The throw was high and wide and "Cart" had to leave the base to get it. Childs reached first in safety. "Out," yelled Betts. Then came a scene for your life. The diamond was filled with the excited populace in less time than it takes to tell it, and the miserable umpire was surrounded and jostled by the angry mob in a manner that savored of rough-house. He escaped all right, however, but the game has been protested. Burkett had scored on the play and the score was tied. Had another hit followed Childs' the game would have been won. Verily, it looks as though Betts' time in this vale of tears will be limited.[3]

Betts lasted three years. Most importantly, Patsy's Spiders were buying into Tebeau's leadership, coming to identify themselves as Hibernian. The players were calling pitcher Phil Knell "Kithaug," which was Gaelic for southpaw.

Frank Robison had rethought the decision not to bankroll spring training by which he had launched Cleveland's lost season of 1894. This preseason, his club played an exhibition schedule beginning in Atlanta during the last week of March. On April 5, in Nashville, George Stallings' local minor league team remained undefeated at the Spiders' expense when the game was decided, 4 to 3, by the "sleepiness of the umpire, that individual failing to see [catcher Mike] Trost do the 'cross-cut act' at third base"—borrowing a trick from Tebeau's playbook—"with the score a tie."[4] The Spiders limped into Evansville next, where they finally started to win games through the middle of April, impervious to the cold in Indianapolis, against Western League opposition. On April 16, Cleveland got healthy against Fort Wayne, a Cleveland farm team at the time, running up the score, 32 to 1. Still, the team was not ready for prime time. Commiserated *The Sporting News,* on May 4:

> There is no disputing the fact that the club started out under awful circumstances. The players who were able to get in the game at all were stiff and sore, as the result of their Artic expedition in Indiana, and the hospital list was alarming. Cuppy and Young were almost dangerously sick at Cincinnati, Blake totally disabled, McGarr worse than a wooden man, McAleer like a glass man, Childs like a stubborn child.

Ed McKean made the sick list too, "with his business arm so sore that he could not lift them [i.e., his throws] over to first," although he insisted on playing every game, as usual.

A crippled Spiders club dropped its first four games of the National League season, on the road against the western ball clubs they traditionally dominated. Mike Sullivan, counted on to repeat as a key member of the staff behind Young and Cuppy, was rendered ineffective by stomach problems, and Bobby Wallace, an inexperienced option, lost twice on the trip. The man they would one day call Mr. Shortstop in the American League was never quite successful on the mound; perhaps his "marvelously clever assortment of curves and changes of pace" too much resembled George Cuppy's repertoire to fool the opposing batters.[5] Cleveland lost the season opener in Cincinnati, 10 to 8, to flamboyant pitcher Tacky Tom Parrott and ex–Spider Buck Ewing, who was now the Reds manager and first baseman. Cy Young had pitched poorly in exhibition games and he was not available to start the season, suffering "grip and muscular rheumatism" to go with his bad throat.[6] Sore-armed McKean made a costly error behind Sullivan that afternoon. On April 20, it was Wallace's turn to take a beating; the Reds won, 14 to 2, although McKean, batting second in the lineup, got his first two hits of the year, in five times up. The Spiders lost again on Sunday, April 21, in the Queen City. That day's memorable crowd of 17,436 must have reinforced for Frank Robison the gospel of the financial rewards of playing on

Sundays, and Ewing's home run would have been doubly galling. Since leaving the Spiders, hoary Ewing had turned baseball innovator: he directed the Reds by a system of signs from first base and the coacher's box.

The Spiders lost more in Cincinnati than the ball games. *Cleveland Leader* scribe John Foster was robbed of his pocket watch in the opening day crowd[7] and, much more importantly to everyone but Foster, star second baseman Cupid Childs jumped Robison's winless team in Cincinnati, on April 22. Childs had been playing without a contract through four games and demanding a salary increase; Robison remained determined to pay him last year's salary, especially after Childs had reported to spring training out of shape and 10 pounds above his usual heavy playing weight.[8] The president and the player met in Cleveland, after which Childs rejoined the team in St. Louis for a 12 to 3 victory on April 24. It was a relieved Childs who banged out four hits in his first game back, initiated a hitting streak, and put new life into the Spiders and McKean.[9] Childs' keystone partner was still suffering from a sore throwing arm—he made 10 errors in Cleveland's first dozen games—but Ed McKean could swing the willow one-armed, if need be, hitting .339 over those games.[10]

McKean was dominant at the marble in one five-game streak. It started in St. Louis on April 25, when he missed a bunt sign then drove in the winning run with a two-run homer over the fence, as Cuppy won, 4 to 2, in the rain. In the second game of a series sweep in Louisville, on April 28, McKean tripled and twice singled, and the following day, another Cuppy win, his four hits included another triple. On May 1, the afternoon of Cleveland's home opener, McKean failed to win the game in the ninth inning, when Red Ehret (the pitcher Mears once called "the gentleman with a seraphic smile"[11]) retired him with Burkett perched on third base. He left the game-winning RBI to the next batter, Clarence Childs, and Cuppy won another, this game in relief of Cy Young over the Browns. At 6,500, attendance at League Park was a disappointment, especially after the other Ohio team, the Reds, had drawn nearly three times the gate for their opening game. The Cleveland fans seemed to be waiting to see what kind of team the Spiders might turn out to be this season.

Overcoming the longest list of disabled players since their 1893 campaign, Cleveland was led by the pitching of Young and Cuppy into third place by the end of May. Near the close of the season, McKean would concede: "It is the Cleveland pitching department that has kept the Spiders up where we are all season."[12] A recovered Young won six of seven starts in May, beating the likes of Stivetts and Rusie in the process; seven of eight decisions in June; and then, as the Spiders went 20–6 in July, he allowed more than two earned runs in only one of his eight starts—and the Spiders were in first place. For August, Young won eight of Cleveland's 19 wins on the month. Young and Cuppy were

The 1895 Cleveland Spiders, winners of the Temple Cup: (Back row left to right) Eddie O'Meara, Harry Blake, Jimmy McAleer, Cy Young, Chief Zimmer, Jack O'Connor, Cupid Childs; (middle row) Chippy McGarr, Frank DeHass Robison, Patsy Tebeau, Davis Hawley; (front row) Nig Cuppy, Phil Knell, Jesse Burkett, Bobby Wallace, White Wings Tebeau, Ed McKean (author's collection).

basically a two-man pitching staff, starting and relieving for Tebeau in the last month of the season. Down the stretch, Cyclone had even pitched on the Sabbath, choosing to overlook the stipulation in his contract. On September 30, against the Browns, Young won his 30th game.[13] Charlie Zimmer is justly renowned for his work behind the plate as Cy Young's first catcher; few remember Ed McKean's contributions to Young's victories for Cleveland. McKean, in the magical season of 1895, tended to hit his very best when Cy Young started.

- —On May 15, the Spiders split a doubleheader in Cleveland. McKean had three hits and Young won game two over Jack Stivetts, a rematch of the pitchers from the famous 11-inning tie in the 1892 "world's series."
- —Two days later, Young spoiled Ed Delahanty's return to Cleveland, beating Philadelphia, 8 to 7. McKean had two hits off Tom Smith.
- —Young beat Amos Rusie, 7 to 4, on May 28 before a crowd of 5,000 at the Polo Grounds. The game was poorly played. Patsy Tebeau, at second base in place of an injured Kid Childs, made two of the nine errors on

SEVEN. Temple Cup Champs (1895–1896 seasons)

the afternoon, and Giants center fielder George Van Haltren's drop of McKean's fly ball in the fifth inning, which let in two runs, proved decisive. McKean's three safe hits led Cleveland batters, who were mostly mesmerized by Rusie's fastball, striking out 10 times.

— In Young's June 7 victory in Washington, McKean had four hits against Win Mercer.
— On June 11 in Philadelphia, McKean hit a two-run home run off Kid Carsey in the seventh inning of Young's 7 to 6 win.
— Young shut out the Giants in New York on June 14, a scoreless game until another Van Haltren error allowed Jimmy McAleer to score in the seventh. McKean was good for two hits.
— In the second game of a double dip in Boston, on June 17, McKean hit a home run off Jim Sullivan, and Chief Zimmer hit two homers off Kid Nichols, in a Cy Young loss.
— Only 500 turned out to watch Young best lefty Bert Inks in Louisville, on June 24. McKean tallied two doubles and a single. Critiquing the Cleveland team for the June 22 issue of *The Sporting News*, Charles Mears pronounced: "McKean still plays short as he always played it—excellently."
— McKean solved Bill Hutchinson for a pair of doubles when Young beat the visiting Colts on June 27.
— McKean made two base hits off Dad Clarke as Young beat the Giants in League Park on July 13; however, a key to the win was not a hit but rather McKean's acting job in the eighth inning. Down two runs to none against Clarke, and Blake on first base, umpire Hank O'Day "got in a deep trance."

Young had four balls called on him. O'Day said three, but changed his mind and the pitcher went to first. Burkett bunted near the plate and he and Clarke collided at first and the first baseman dropped the pitcher's assist, Blake scoring and Young taking third. Then again O'Day got crazy ... in Cleveland's favor. McKean's bat was hit by a pitched ball. Mac rubbed his back and the umpire sent him to first, filling the bases. Clarke left the box and refused to play and the umpire sprung his watch on him. The pitcher's bluff did not go and the game went on. Tebeau flied to right, Young scoring. Childs singled and Burkett scored...Three runs, and...Cleveland had won.[14]

— In game two of a July 16 doubleheader, McKean singled into left field to score Young in the fifth inning with the only run of the day as Cyclone whitewashed the visiting Orioles. It was the most important of McKean's three hits off Duke Esper. Young's victory meant the Spiders had swept the doubleheader and, in the process, moved up to fourth place in the standings. The very next day, Cleveland hosted Baltimore for *another* doubleheader. If McKean was tired, he didn't show it; he produced three hits in the morning, and two more that afternoon. At the end of the day, the Spiders had knocked the Orioles out of first place for the time being.

— McKean went 0-for-4 facing Brooklyn's Ad Gumbert in Cleveland, on July 20, but Young won a 2 to 1 gem and the Spiders won their seventh straight game to regain possession of first place. After the Saturday game, the team hopped an overnight train to Kentucky to play on Sunday in Louisville. Robison's club won only two of seven Sunday games this season.

— Back in Cleveland on Monday, July 22, Young won in relief of starter George Cuppy, in a reversal of roles. Ed McKean's hitting once again proved critical. With the bases loaded in the fifth inning and Cleveland behind 4 to 2, McKean sent a ball so far that not even Win Mercer, the pitcher playing right field, could throw out Charles Tebeau at the plate. In the seventh, McKean's sacrifice bunt set up a two-run inning. And against Otis Stockdale in the eighth, his single with two outs put the winning run on third base for Jack O'Connor's RBI. Cleveland stayed atop the standings by sweeping a July 23 doubleheader from Washington. In the third inning of game one, McKean hit another sacrifice fly to again score Charles Tebeau. Pussy Tebeau had joined his older brothers on the Spiders on July 11, after his Portland, Maine, team in the New England Association couldn't complete its season. In his two-game big league career, he reached base five times in eight plate appearances (three singles and two walks), scored three runs, drove in one run, and stole a base; he also recorded an assist from right field.[15] Contemporaries found it difficult to differentiate between Patsy, White Wings, and Pussy in person: "The Tebeaus bear a very close resemblance to each other, and were it not for the mustache which ornaments George's lip the spectators would be kept continually guessing."[16] Harry Blake's temporary replacement vanishes from baseball after a few games in the minors in 1896. Ed McKean, playing like the go-to man on a team in a pennant race, counted two deep sacrifice flies and a bunt in the contest. McKean had been held without a hit only twice in Cleveland's first 33 games, according to *Sporting Life* on July 20.

— When Dent Young beat Kid Nichols in Cleveland, on July 25, McKean was a modest 1 for 3, but he scored two runs and stole a base. "McKean is playing the best ball he has ever shown us," commented *The Sporting News,* on July 27. "His batting and fielding are wonderful. He plays with a vim and dash that has a wonderful effect on the fellows around him and he is never too busy to laugh. In fact Mac's laugh is a feature these days."

- —Young's 20th win came on August 2, in Pittsburgh, McKean leading the charge with a triple and two singles off Brownie Foreman.
- —Subsequently, Cy Young recorded two wins in three days against the visiting Colonels. McKean had two hits in five at-bats in the August 5 decision, and three singles in support of Young in the second game of an August 7 doubleheader.
- —At home on August 12, Young beat the Browns, 5 to 4, in relief of Zeke Wilson. McKean had two base hits off Red Ehret.
- —Five days later, Young treated a League Park crowd of 6,500 to a shutout of the Reds; McKean had his customary two-hit game.
- —The first day of an eastern road trip, in Washington on August 20, Young was shellacked but did not lose, as Wilson replaced him. In the eighth, McKean sent a Win Mercer pitch into the twilight, what would have been a harmless fly in daylight became an inside-the-park home run, when Hank O'Day ruled him safe at the plate. The home crowd thought McKean was out by six feet. McKean's gift run opened the gates for three more Cleveland runs in the inning, making the score 8 to 7—at which point, O'Day called the game for darkness. Washington cranks kept the umpire captive in the dressing room afterward, but O'Day was back the next day to umpire a doubleheader. Charles Mears wrote glowingly about McKean's performance in the Washington series: "McKean put up the prettiest game at short ever seen in Washington. Some of the stops and throws he made were little short of wonderful."[17]
- —Young won twice in three days in Boston, on August 28 and 30. In the first contest, shortstop McKean made an early error, but persevered to earn "fielding star" of the game. In the second game, McKean homered in the seventh against loser Jack Stivetts, accounting for two runs. This day, his hitting—four hits—was the game "highlight." By the dregs of August, Cleveland was playing a heady 30 games over .500.
- —A Labor Day doubleheader, however, stalled the Spiders' drive for the pennant. Both Young and Cuppy lost to the Giants, McKean committing one of Cleveland's five errors behind Young, to fall behind Baltimore in the torrid pennant race.
- —Young and the Spiders rebounded on September 5 in the Polo Grounds. McKean recorded three hits, and Cy won his 28th. Then it was on to Baltimore for McKean and company.
- —In Young's 29th and 30th wins, on Friday the Thirteenth and September 14 in St. Louis, McKean came through with three- and two-hit performances in support of the ace.
- —In the Spiders' final game before Temple Cup play, in Louisville on Sep-

tember 28, McKean contributed three hits to the winning cause, 9 to 8, behind Young.

Half of McKean's home runs this year were hit in support of Cy Young wins, but all eight of them proved memorable. Six of them came in the seventh inning or later (representing almost a quarter of his career total of 25 in late innings), and he drove in 18 runs on round-trippers. Only one of his homers was a solo. Here are some home run highlights:

—In a June 17 doubleheader at Boston's South End Grounds, Zimmer won the morning game with a grand slam in the eighth inning, and McKean followed with a grand slam of his own, an opposite-field blast, in the afternoon game.
—Fans in Washington, on August 20, were convinced that McKean and the umpire stole the game. The slugger launched a three-run homer into the dark, which gave Cleveland a one-run lead, and Hank O'Day promptly called the game.
—In Cleveland's last home game of the regular season, on September 21, McKean said good-bye and thank-you with a home run and two singles off Pittsburgh lefty Sam Moran. Elmer Bates expressed mixed emotions about McKean's big fly: "Just as Ed came to bat a crazy fan behind me shouted, 'Five dollars that Mc [sic] hits it over the fence.' I thought this good time to pick up five, and took the bet. Just as I was putting up my money there was a crack, a shriek from the crowd and the new white ball went sailing over the right field fence. I have lost $5 many a time in a game of chance, but I never lost that sum quite so willingly. It was worth at least $4.75 to watch the antics of the crowd."[18]

The June 1 *Sporting News* noted that 1895 was shaping up early as a record year for home runs in League Park. After a month of play, seven players had launched home runs in Cleveland, including Ed Delahanty's blast over the left field fence on May 18; he would homer four times in a game this year. Still, it took until a May 24 game, in a Mike Sullivan win against the Giants, for the first round-tripper for the home crowd by a Spider; bow-legged Harry Blake hit it out into left field bleachers and, in the same game, McKean cleared the right field fence for a quick number two. Although McKean was a power hitter and led the team in homers in 1895, he was yet to strike out after Cleveland's first 15 games.

Frank Robison was eager to retain the services of his established slugger and, by the middle of October, he signed McKean to a new contract for a good raise in salary.[19] This fall, the beloved Spiders were in evidence everywhere

SEVEN. *Temple Cup Champs (1895–1896 seasons)*

one looked in Cleveland: "elaborate photographs of the Temple Cup are shown in about half the store windows in town," by *Sporting Life*'s count, and, as late as November, "the store window in which the Temple Cup is being exhibited [continued to be] surrounded all day by an admiring crowd."[20] After the Temple Cup romp, the great championship team broke up and the players were once again left without the prospect of a baseball paycheck until spring. Jim McAleer's creative solution was to join the De Haven Comedy Company tour for the winter; George Cuppy and Chief Zimmer formed the battery for a Bucyrus, Ohio, team which played Galion, on October 13. Cuppy allowed no runs and struck out 11 in the Sunday game.[21] Patsy Tebeau took some of the time off to move his family into a house on Dunham Avenue, a few blocks from League Park, and to play handball regularly at the Cleveland Athletic Club gym, sometimes with McKean for competition.[22] Ed McKean's earlier retirement from professional wrestling ("to save himself for baseball") proved to be a mere hiatus. McKean never did retire well—after his release from baseball in 1899, he attempted a series of comebacks over the next decade—and the income from purses and betting was welcome in the winter months. He was justly proud of what he'd accomplished in the sport. "Many a man who thinks he's a wrestler," he once quipped, "can't even throw dice."[23]

In the days after Christmas 1895, Mac challenged the winner of the upcoming January 15 Jenkins-McMahon match.[24] Tom Jenkins, an illiterate former millworker living in Cleveland, was the U.S. catch-can champion by 1903 and retired two years later to instruct wrestling at West Point. John McMahon was the renowned wrestler from Vermont.[25] Wrestler Farmer Burns once told *Sporting Life* that Ed McKean was "one of the toughest propositions he ever tackled."[26] McKean's engagements in wrestling continued at least into the winter of 1896–97. *Sporting Life* covered McKean's decision over Frank Henry in Painsville, Ohio, on December 28, 1896. Things started badly that night for the shortstop grappler. Richmond, Ohio, native Henry pinned McKean on his back within the first 30 seconds of this best-two-of-three catch-can. However, after 62 minutes, Henry refused to continue unless a better mat was provided—the wrestlers were being punished by working on "simply a Brussels carpet stretched over a platform"—so the match was awarded to McKean, who was not so particular.[27] McKean did not make good on his resolution to give up wrestling, but he probably cut back on his engagements during the 1897 baseball season.[28] Maybe his poor showing in the field that year required him to focus on one sport; or perhaps he'd taken up wrestling again to distract himself in the weeks following the death of his mother.

Next, follows one of the lacunae we must deal with as best we can when we piece together McKean's life. We know that Ed McKean's mother died, in

Grafton, on December 12, 1895. She had lived to hear of her son's greatest exploit, the winning of the Temple Cup. It would be happy to think Margaret Moran McKean also celebrated his marriage, but the story of how McKean came to marry an Irish-born Moran girl remains to be told. Church documents from Cleveland and Grafton were not made available for this biography. And it was a surprise to learn that no news of the baseball star's marriage made the newspapers; even indiscrete Elmer Bates is silent on the topic. In the absence of information about McKean's sentimental life, we might speculate that Edward John McKean and Belle Bridget Moran McKean were wed in Cleveland sometime in the offseason months before or after his mother's death. The few facts on hand point to an arranged marriage between the Moran and McKean families.[29] A low-visibility wedding would have still privately honored Ed's mother, and made his bride a naturalized citizen. His wife was born in Ireland to Michael Moran (born in 1855; died, in Cleveland, in 1921) and Bridget Ruddy Moran (born in 1857; died, also in Cleveland, in 1925), one of nine children. Bridget Moran's father, Pat Ruddy, was born in Dever, Ireland, in 1829; her mother's name was Mary. Belle's parents immigrated to America about 1881, when she was about two years old. Ed and Belle McKean began married life in the Lakeside Apartments on Summit Street, the present site of City Hall. Their union lasted the rest of Ed's life and produced three sons and a daughter. Marie, the youngest of the brood, lived until 1988.

Toward the end of the season, an inconspicuous note appeared in *The Sporting News* in the "On the Fly" column, concerning a ballplayer at Holy Cross College, where Jesse Burkett and Chippy McGarr were coaches. One Louis Sockalexis reportedly "threw a ball 129 yards, 9 inches against a strong wind at Bangor, Me., recently."[30] Already, the Native American was being credited with legendary acts, two years before he would briefly occupy center stage for a national media circus.

It remains one of the game's great ironies — the infield at Louisville's Eclipse Park had been rebuilt that spring into a heart shape.

The riot by Louisville Colonels fans, on June 26, 1896, put into eclipse the last great season the Hibernian Spiders put together. Cleveland's reign as Temple Cup champions proved fugacious. Following a turbulent regular season in 1896, Cleveland returned the Cup to Baltimore after four straight losses, then went into a steep decline. In 1897, mostly the mania over Louis Sockalexis averted the disapproving public eye from Patsy Tebeau and "the riotous Spiders," granting him two more years in Cleveland. By the time Eclipse Park burned to the ground, in the early morning hours of August 12, 1899, the Cleveland Spiders were a decimated franchise in its last weeks of play in the National League, Patsy Tebeau was the manager of the St. Louis

Perfectos, and Ed McKean had been released. Even the most ardent among Spiders supporters abandoned Tebeau, days after the humiliating Temple Cup defeat, upon hearing the news of his brutal assault on a Cleveland sportswriter.

Public opinion concerning the Spiders, which had run from admiring to tolerant, was now, rounding third and coming home, belligerent; cheerleader Chadwick researched and forwarded all anti–Cleveland materials to the readers of *The Sporting News*. Cleveland managed to finish second behind Baltimore again, but this time 9½ games back, in spite of a League-stingiest team ERA and Jesse Burkett's second straight batting championship. In this year of opprobrium, the veterans persevered. Cy Young paced the circuit in strikeouts, and ranked second in wins and innings pitched. In the meaningless games before the Temple Cup, Burkett turned down his manager's offer to sit him and protect his batting average; Crab went 12-for-16 over the final four games and hit .410 for the season. And Ed McKean played in all of Cleveland's games but two and batted .338. He topped the 100-RBI mark (112 total, fourth most in the League) for the fourth consecutive season, and the last.

The beginning of the end, for the first-place Cleveland Spiders and for George Weidman's career, came in a June 26 game with last-place Louisville.[31] Weidman had umpired the previous day's game, when Jesse Burkett shook him by the shoulders after being called out on a play at third base. In spite of the incident, Nick Young allowed Weidman to officiate the next day's contest, with a predictable result: the players argued so many of his decisions that darkness overtook Eclipse Park after three and a half hours and a 4 to 4 stalemate. George Weidman had umpired Cleveland games back when they were the American Association Blues and Jack Glasscock was their shortstop. The young Weidman had been signed right off the University of Rochester campus to pitch his first professional game for the local Hop Bitters team. Buck Ewing was his batterymate in those days. Stump Weidman was a talented twirler and wore the National League's ERA crown for 1881. His greatest day as a pitcher was an 18-inning complete game win over Monte Ward's Giants, on August 17, 1882; right fielder Hoss Radbourn's home run was the only score.[32] He won 100 other games in the major leagues, lost 156, and was still playing as late as 1888 as a pitcher and an outfielder. Although it was only natural that he would keep in the game (after all, Weidman was Silk O'Loughlin's brother-in-law), 1896 was his only year as a major league umpire.

Coming into the 10th inning, Jimmy McAleer had already homered when Fred Clarke lost his fly ball in the gloom. It was at this propitious moment, according to James Egan's game account drawn from the Cleveland newspapers, "McKean decided that Louisville was playing for darkness in order to have the game called, in order to revert to the score of the last full inning, and get off with at least a tie. He hit an easy grounder to [Chewing Gum John] O'Brien at second who let the easy chance elude him," but McKean declined to run to first base. Weidman gathered the courage to call the game in the next half inning, after Nig Cuppy loaded the bases full of Colonels, in a show of standing up to Patsy Tebeau, who had been bullying Weidman, for innings, into continuing the game. So it was that enraged Spiders *and* Colonels surrounded Weidman; in a flash, the crowd of 1,000 rushed the field. A reporter for the *Louisville Courier-Journal* recorded the ensuing pandemonium:

Inept game calling by pitcher-turned-umpire Stump Weidman sparked a fan riot in Louisville, on June 26, 1896, embroiling the Cleveland Spiders in legalities and an unwinnable public controversy over how the game should be played (Library of Congress).

"Wow! Wow!" roared Jack O'Connor. "Patsy! Patsy! Come here! He's called the game! He's called the game!" he yelled at Tebeau, who was playing first base. Then from all about came the Spiders. McAleer, from deep centerfield, reached Weidman first by running fast. As his comrades gathered about Weidman, McAleer struck at the umpire, a terrific righthand swing. Weidman dodged and turned his back at the same time, the blow landing on his left shoulder. In justice to Tebeau, it can be said that he tried to catch McAleer's arm, but failed.

This blow was the signal for the riot. Previous to Weidman's action in calling the game the men [fans] on the bleachers hung over the fence in front of the seats, ready at a moment's notice to make a grand rush on the Spiders. They had been wrought to a very high pitch. When McAleer's fist struck Weidman, 300 men [from a crowd of about 1,000] fell out of the bleachers and rushed across the diamond like some big football team with the

SEVEN. Temple Cup Champs (1895–1896 seasons)

ball. Many men tumbled out of the grandstand to the ground, 15 feet below, and all made a concentrated rush on the Spiders. Tom Lansing, the local welterweight pugilist, led the procession almost at the side of half a dozen private policemen...Lansing's elbow pushed men right and left until he got in the thick of it. He ran up to McAleer and said, "What did you hit him for?"

"It wasn't me; it was him," McAleer said, pointing at the huge form of shortstop McKean.

McKean ran backward saying, "It wasn't me. It was him," pointing to McAleer.

Lansing evidently concluded McAleer was the guilty man, for he made a break for the centerfielder. McAleer dodged and caught a lefthanded swing on his shoulder, which sent him to his knees. While on his hands and knees he scrambled between the legs of men until he got away from Lansing and was on the outskirts of the mob. As he passed along, his hands came in contact with a bat. Grasping this, he struck a short, stout young man with blond hair, who wore a light suit of clothes and carried a cane. The blow from the bat evidently did not hurt the young man much for he brought his cane down over McAleer's head with a resounding whack...In the meantime private policeman Collins and Patsy Tebeau were having an argument 10 feet away. The big policeman was pushing Spiders right and left...Tebeau moved back from the policeman, saying, "What is your number? All I want is your number. I'll see to it that you are fixed."

...Leftfielder Burkett was the second Spider to get to Weidman. He tried to hit the umpire, but a spectator gave him a short-arm punch in the mouth, which made his lips swell as if he had been fighting bumblebees. The crowd gave way and formed a circle in order that the pugilist Lansing could get at Burkett, but the leftfielder escaped between two small men. At this point Jack Ropke ran up, having come from the director's box. He yelled at the crowd: "Don't interfere with the police! Don't get in the way of the police. Let the officers do their duty."

Someone hit Mr. Ropke a terrific blow in the jaw and he decided to let the police attend to their own business. The spectators said they wanted blood and that they were going to have it, but manager [Bill] McGunnigle, captain [Doggie] Miller, the private policemen and others finally guarded the Clevelands to their omnibus, which was surrounded by a jeering, howling crowd of some 200 boys and men. The crowd followed the bus to 28th street and Broadway, throwing stones as fast as possible. The driver of the vehicle whipped his horses and tried to get away from the crowd but failed until he turned up Broadway. It was a pathetic sight to see half the brave Cleveland team laying, stomachs down, in the bottom of the omnibus, dodging flying brickbats and boulders, while the other half were also dodging. Between dodges and swears, Tebeau was raising sand with McAleer for having struck Weidman.[33]

Cleveland accounts made it clear that Louisville players joined in rushing the umpire. *The Sporting News* indicates that one Louisville crank knocked down McAleer with a punch in the face, and does not mention a McAleer blow to Weidman.[34] All reporters agreed that Stump Weidman's incompetency was to blame for the outbreak. "This game was almost a riot from start to finish. The players of both teams made a football of Weidman."[35] The box score as it appeared in Cleveland newspapers, did not show Jimmy McAleer's home run; just as he had feared, the calling of the game erased the feat.[36] For the record, Ed McKean was 2-for-4, with a triple, in Louisville. He made one error, in addition to the one he made by showing up to play that fateful day.

Fortunately, game three of the series was rained out the following afternoon, turning back the 2,000 fans who had come to hiss the Spiders. Considerable action was carried out indoors, however. Louisville owner Dr. Thomas Hunt Stucky secured a warrant for the arrest of Cleveland players and subpoenaed newspaper reporters and others affiliated with the club. Meanwhile, the Spiders were trying to leave town to play an exhibition game in Logansport, Indiana, George Cuppy's home town. Instead of meeting their train, they were taken by Louisville policemen, who had commandeered the team bus, to face a special Saturday police court. As Reed Browning notes, "It was deemed a particularly humiliating turn that they were not even given the opportunity to change from their uniforms into civilian clothes before being hauled off to the courthouse."[37]

The players weren't especially aware of the significance of the moment in their careers or Cleveland sports history; they treated the proceedings mostly as a lark. Harry Pulliam, the National League treasurer, described the farcical courtroom scene:

> Jack O'Connor was the comedian. When he took the stand the judge asked him if he knew umpire Weidman. "Know, nothing," said Jack. "He don't mingle in my society. I travel in a set that lives too far uptown for Weidman, see?" said Jack. Every other question that Jack answered would wind up with "See?" and "D'ye see?" There was no evidence against Jack, but the judge said he'd like to fine him on general principles because he didn't like the tough way that Jack said "See?" "You don't, eh?" retorted Jack. "Well, I'll tell you, Judge, if you heard Dad Clarke say 'See?' you'd give him six months."[38]

O'Connor was a verified tough, but the fearless McKean was the overriding influence in the Spiders clubhouse. He played the roles of enforcer or peace-maker with equanimity. Rugged Tim Hurst never forgot the time he saw McKean intervene between two teammates, before a game in Pittsburgh. "Jack O'Connor's temper had been aroused by an article in the Pittsburgh paper, in which Zimmer was spoken of as the Cleveland team's star catcher." O'Connor was, in fact, a backstop of considerable merit; he'd been the first catcher in a season to catch 100 games, make 100 hits, and hit .300, back with the old Columbus club in 1890, the same year he led the American Association in fielding percentage.[39] But on the Spiders, Chief Zimmer was the starter. Recalled Hurst:

> "Chief," holding a big bat in his hands, was sitting at one end of the bench;

SEVEN. *Temple Cup Champs (1895–1896 seasons)* 187

O'Connor, empty-handed, at the other. Suddenly I heard O'Connor say to Zimmer: "If you didn't have that stick in your hand I'd knock your head off." Like a flash, Ed McKean darted over and yanked the bat from "Chief's" paws. "He hasn't got the stick in his hands now, Jack," said the big short-stop. "Go ahead and knock his head off—if you can." And then, something unusual happened— something unusual on the diamond, at any rate, where sentiment is seldom displayed. "Rowdy Jack" started to get up, settled back on the bench and began to cry like a child. A little later he and "Chief" were shaking hands, and the prospective fight ended in the establishment of a friendship that has never since been disturbed.[40]

That day in police court, Magistrate Thompson wound up releasing all of the Spiders but McKean, Patsy Tebeau, Burkett, and McAleer. Tebeau was fined $100 for disorderly conduct, McKean and McAleer $75 each, and Burkett $50. These players declined to pay their fines out of pocket, so they were released on bond, a hearing set for Cleveland's return to Louisville in August. The date, and the storm of legalistic maneuverings it set off, hung over the clubhouse like a threatening cloud for the rest of the season.

The aggressor in the case had been on edge all year. Jimmy McAleer's strained left leg never fully recovered from late last season; he probably harbored concerns for his career.[41] Following a home game against the Browns, on September 12, McAleer jumped Patsy Tebeau, who was washing up in the clubhouse, and blackened his eye. Tebeau had offended his center fielder by calling for Harry Blake to catch a fly ball in front of him, thinking to take advantage of Blake's superior arm on the anticipated throw to home plate.[42] The Cleveland players felt they were being roundly persecuted, or "given the book," by baseball and public officials, for behavior that had, after all, won ball games for half a dozen years. Elmer Bates gave voice to what he heard of the Spiders' mood of self-pitying indignation in this bit of doggerel for *Sporting Life*:

> Getting fined for squealing
> When an umpire's bad.
> Playing 'gainst policemen,
> Toughest to be had.
> Targets for a Lally[43];
> Isn't he a beaut?
> Bless me, this is pleasant
> Riding down the chute.
> Roasted by the magnates,
> Hopped on by the press.
> Not allowed to whisper
> On the field, I guess.
> Marks for crazy pitchers,

> And the runners' boot.
> Bless me, this is pleasant
> Riding down the chute.
>
> Dangerous to holler:
> "Say, please git 'em down."
> Liable to loosen
> All the cops in town;
> When you get the "hookies" [i.e., fans playing hookie],
> How they howl and hoot.
> Isn't it a picinic
> Riding down the chute.[44]

Indeed, in these days before numbers were sewn on uniforms, the Spiders seemed to be playing the season with bulls' eyes between their shoulders. The old agitator Tebeau was becoming a liability on the diamond. At the Spiders' next scheduled stop, the following Monday, Chicago president Jim Hart made sure to pack the foul lines with extra police. The visitors quietly took the first two games of the series, Young and Cuppy winning on June 29 and 30, without incident. And then, in an attempt to rouse his team in game three, Cap Anson intentionally spiked Tebeau from knee to ankle. The Cleveland club took notice when Anson was not hauled into police court on charges of assault, and the League owners chose to overlook the incident. Cleveland was an easy victim to a piling-on effect, during a period when all the old animosities and fears were freely vented. The Boston correspondent to *The Sporting News*, under the headline "The Tactics of Tebeau Have Done the Game Great Harm," reasoned that "the work of the Clevelands at Louisville simply followed up their riotous proceedings in Boston." He went on to list the Spiders' most recent offenses against the Boston team: "First, Tebeau throwing a ball over the fence in Boston; second, Tebeau spiking a ball in Boston; third, Tebeau calling Keefe a name reflecting on his parentage; fourth, the use of profanity by Tebeau, Burkett, McAleer, McKean and O'Connor, plain enough to be heard in the Boston grandstand; fifth, the breaking in of a door in Brooklyn; sixth, the throwing by Burkett of a ball out of the lot in Brooklyn. Never mind Louisville."[45] A week earlier, this reporter had published the opinion that "The Cleveland Club deserves to be boycotted by every respectable patron of the game."[46]

For the time being, Cleveland fans stood steadfast behind their Spiders. A Cleveland group raising money by volunteer subscriptions, all under $2 each, made the Spiders a gift of more than $200 "in appreciation of the splendid work the boys have done in the face of it all."[47] And, on Friday, July 3, the city turned out to welcome back its beleaguered team from Chicago. Frank Robison and the Spiders were treated to a downtown parade of carriages. Their

SEVEN. Temple Cup Champs (1895–1896 seasons)

own tally-ho dropped off the players at the Forest City House, where Mayor Robert Erastus McKisson and Patsy Tebeau addressed the crowd from a balcony. The team seemed to be weathering the fallout after the Louisville blowup, victors in 21 of their 34 games (tying two) and 2–0–1 against archrival Baltimore.[48]

Hitting out of the third slot in the batting order, Ed McKean carried a hot bat, especially in hostile territory on the road, in the weeks before and during the controversy.[49]

— On May 30, in Boston, McKean homered and singled off the great Kid Nichols in the second game of a doubleheader.
— On June 3, in Washington, he made two hits off Win Mercer in a tie game called for darkness.
— On June 4, McKean's two hits helped Cuppy beat Sadie McMahon in Baltimore.
— On June 5, McKean enjoyed another two hit game against Charlie Esper, as Cy Young wins.
— On June 8, in Philadelphia, Young held on to win, 8 to 7, aided by a McKean homer off Brewery Jack Taylor.
— McKean fashioned a five-hit performance in Philadelphia, June 9, tripling once and singling four times against Al Orth in a Zeke Wilson win. Orth was known by two nicknames: Smilin' Al, for his demeanor, and The Curveless Wonder, for his pitching style. A soft-thrower like George Cuppy, he went on to notch over 200 wins in the majors.
— On June 11, in Brooklyn, McKean singled twice off Dan Daub, a fellow Ohioan. McKean recorded 70 base hits in Cleveland's first 44 games.
— In Louisville, on June 17, McKean collected three hits off Chick Fraser, Fred Clarke's son-in-law.
— McKean led Cleveland batters with two more hits the following day against Adonis Terry, and Cy Young won.
— McKean slammed three hits against Cold Water Jim Hughey as Cleveland beat Pittsburgh in League Park on June 24.
— In Louisville on June 25, the eve of the fan riot, McKean went 3-for-5. After the game, Colonels cranks blamed the umpiring of Weidman for the loss to Cy Young.
— On June 29, McKean played fearlessly, in spite of policemen on the Chicago field, making three hits off loser Clark Griffith.
— On June 30, McKean homered, doubled and singled twice as Adonis Terry lost again to the Spiders, this time to Nig Cuppy.
— On the first day of July, McKean doubled and tripled in a come-from-

behind win in Chicago. This 19 to 7 victory was the high point in Cleveland's season. He also turned a double play behind winning pitcher Wilson. In the Spiders' last 20 games in August, Ed McKean recorded 42 base hits. At the time, he ranked fifth overall in the League in batting at .369.

This summer, the venerable John B. Foster offered Ed McKean to his readers as a model of strength, agility, and nonchalance: "To see him swing on the ball you would think he might be playing racquets. At the same time with a motion no more vigorous than that, I have seen him rap the ball over the right field fence in Cleveland, and I want to say that is something of a hit."[50] McKean was the first Spider all season to clear League Park's right field fence, achieving the distinction with a two-run home run off a Red Donahue pitch, in the seventh inning of a September 9 match against the Browns.

Inevitably, McKean's individual brilliance was thrown into the deepening shadows of the debate over Oliver Tebeau. Meeting in Pittsburgh, on June 29, the National League board of directors voted to impose a fine of $200 on Tebeau for "gross misconduct" in the Louisville game of June 26 and ruled him ineligible to play for 10 days from its official July 3 notice, unless either Tebeau or Frank Robison appealed in court for an injunction.[51] Robison and his manager had clashed in spring training over the issue of which man would run the team.[52] Tebeau won, and in May and he brought Harry Blake back from Fort Wayne (where he'd been banished to George Tebeau's team to learn to hit the curve ball) to play right field instead of Robison's pick, John Shearon, and he reinstalled Chippy McGarr at third base over local favorite Tom Delahanty. Now, Robison was defending Patsy Tebeau in an action that redefined civility on the ball field and caused a realignment of the League office, when Robison's friends Charles Byrne and John T. Brush abstained from the vote against Tebeau but were slow to publicly support the Cleveland cause.[53] The League had rushed to judgment, exclusively considering the testimony of Dr. Stucky as to what happened in Louisville three days before, and not bothering to hear from Tebeau in due process. Robison declared he would pay "not one cent" of the $200 fine and instructed the attorneys for the club to file, in Cleveland common pleas court on July 28, a notice dissolving the temporary injunction against Tebeau so the fine could not be collected by the League.[54]

Frank Robison was worried that his Spiders were being made the exception. The fact was, Cleveland was not alone among National League teams under scrutiny for practicing rowdy play.

> The disgraceful riot at Pittsburgh, Friday [July 17], in which the Philadelphia players attacked Umpire [William] Betts was a good thing for Cleveland and

Tebeau. Base ball writers are willing to admit now that Tebeau is not the only one, and that there are worse than he is drifting around the country...The Pittsburgh riot was worse than the one at Louisville. And yet Tebeau was disciplined double quick, and nothing is being said about the Pittsburg affair.[55]

Even if our Cleveland correspondent was right about his fellow writers, it was also known that Nick Young's office, some National League umpires, and plenty of cranks around the League all remained firm in their opposition to the Hibernian Spiders and their scapegoat manager.

The battle was enthusiastically joined by the newspapers, with Father Chadwick at the front of the ink columns. For the July 25 issue of *The Sporting News*, Chadwick coined the term "Tebeauism" in an invective launched against Tebeau, identifying the Cleveland manager with drunkenness, dirty ball playing, and blackguardism, what he called "The Three Evils in Baseball." "Not

Delegates to the National League and American Association meeting, February 25–26, 1897, at Baltimore's Hotel Rennert: (Standing left to right) E.C. Becker, Chris Von der Ahe, Ned Hanlon, Frank Robison, H.R. Von der Horst, James Hart, J.W. Spalding, H.M. Pulliam, Dr. T. Hunt Stuckey, Col. J.I. Rogers; (seated) John Brush, A.J. Reach, F.A. Abell, Nick Young, J.E. Wagner, Stanley Robison, C.H. Byrne. On their agenda was the issue of sanctions, framed by Stuckey of Louisville, against Patsy Tebeau for his behavior (author's collection).

since the players' revolt in 1890," Chadwick declared, "has there been so serious a blow given the league as that by President Robison of the Cleveland Club in his bringing the force of the law courts into action in defence of blackguardism in the ranks." Meanwhile, Tebeau continued to play—being what Homer calls a man of strife, he'd heard the charges for years now—and it was a laughably simple expediency for him to serve papers against the opposing club, its manager, and the umpire at the start of each series. Meanwhile, the fans of the game were reaching their own verdict on Tebeau, and in Cleveland the cranks were beginning to turn against other prominent Spiders: the *Cleveland Recorder* was campaigning hard to drive McKean off the team, as an answer to problems in the standings.

His popularity eroding among the fan base, Patsy Tebeau was starting to feel the pressure at home games as well as on the road. He had only to turn to page one of *The Sporting News* for August 15:

> The old feeling against Pat Tebeau is cropping out again. Two seasons ago Tebeau was not a popular man in Cleveland. There was a little knot of fellows that infested the third base bleachers who did not like him and at every opportunity they hissed and abused him. Pat paid no attention to this, but went on playing ball and when the Spiders under him last season, succeeded in winning the Temple Cup he became most popular. Now, however, he is being jumped on again. Monday he dropped a thrown ball, and there was an immediate call for O'Connor from the stands. The cry was kept up all the afternoon.

In that homestand against the Pirates, the Spiders lost twice and tied a game. That same week, on August 11, Tebeau spent a whole day in a courtroom, with Robison present, where "much more base ball talk was indulged in by lawyers in Judge Noble's court Monday than the most noisy 'coach' or enthusiastic 'rooter' may ever aspire to." Tolles, the attorney for the club, presented his petition to dismiss the owners' fine, but it was attorney Francis J. Wing, representing the National League, who roundaboutly won the day for Tebeau, arguing eloquently that professional baseball should judge its own business.[56] One week later, Judge Noble held in his decision that Section 28 of the National League by-laws, providing the president the power to fine players and teams, had not been followed. "There is no record of a fine. The directors asked N.E. Young as president, to fine Tebeau, and Mr. Young, as secretary, notified Tebeau, of this request, but Mr. Young, as president, never levied a fine on Tebeau."[57] In effect, Tebeau had never been fined in the first place, but the debate over Tebeau stands as baseball's defining moment in its policy against the rowdy game. From this day on, Patsy Tebeau was more of a distraction than an inspiration, and the Hibernian were a sports anachronism. It's easy today to see the tell-tale signs that Tebeau's histrionics on the field had

SEVEN. *Temple Cup Champs (1895–1896 seasons)* 193

morphed into serious manic episodes in the 1896 season. His pattern of wild behavior eventuated, after the Temple Cup series, into a disgraceful attack on a Cleveland sportswriter, as we shall see.

In a game umpired by Tim Keefe, in Boston on May 29, Tebeau spiked a baseball then threw it into the stands behind first base. Keefe ordered Tebeau to the bench and, when Tebeau issued a vile oath, ejected him from the game. The scene was not complete until the Cleveland manager lodged himself just inside the grandstand and refused to leave the park. Boston deducted $1.25, for the price of the ball, from Cleveland's take of the day's gate receipts. Later, Frank Robison defended Tebeau, claiming the offensive ball was an old one tossed from the Boston bench, as Boston was in the habit of making the visiting team hit a punky ball.[58] On June 19, one week before the Louisville riot, Patsy Tebeau became enraged in the seventh inning of a game against Chicago when Tom Lynch reversed his call at first base, calling Dandelion Pfeffer safe on a pickoff play. Tebeau's reaction was immediate:

"Why wasn't he out?"

"Because you blocked him," came back Lynch, and the brawl was on.

"Somebody ought to knock your block off," spit Pat.

"Well, you can't do it."

"Can't I, though? Take off that protector and get off the field and see if I can't."

Lynch rejected Tebeau for kicking but Patsy refused to leave his post at first base, so the umpire quit the field, instead. Chicago reserve catcher Con Daily and Cy Young alternated calling the rest of the game.[59]

There are further indications that the manager was in danger of losing control of himself and his team. In a July 28 game with Cincinnati, Tebeau, in a fit of rage, demanded that Cy Young switch positions with him—it was Patsy's nonce appearance on the mound—then he deliberately surrendered the game-winning hit. Only two days earlier, in the same series, Kid Childs tackled Eddie Burke, who was rubbing it in by stealing a base in the eighth inning of a 10 to 1 drubbing of the Spiders. Their ensuing fight cleared both benches and the stands.[60] And before a game on September 2, Tebeau had to fork over $5.25 before the notorious Spiders were allowed to dress on the Brooklyn grounds. It was reimbursement for the dressing room door he and his players had smashed with their bats on the last trip in.[61]

Inevitably, the manager's distractions and the president's war on the owners wore on the Spiders, who could gain no ground in the standings on the (equally rowdy) Orioles of Baltimore. On the eve of the Temple Cup series, Nick Young went on record to blame all the negative criticism in the press against Tebeau and team in wake of the Louisville incident, a blow compounded by the subsequent vote against Tebeau at the League meeting in Pittsburgh, for Cleveland's failure to win the pennant.[62] Reed Browning, too, figures that "the overall effect of the ensuing turmoil—a police presence wherever they played, hotels reluctant to house them, umpires disinclined to be fair to players who had slugged one of their own—hurt the team's play."[63] After the Giants badly outplayed the Spiders in Cleveland, *The Sporting News* observed, on the front page of its July 18 edition, that:

> A spirit of listlessness has taken possession of the Temple Cup holders and the club's troubles with the League is the cause of it. The players appreciate the loyalty of President Robison to his manager but the more practical members of the team have figured it out that he will lose in the long run and that the League will not allow the Cleveland Club to count its victories in which Tebeau has been a factor during his suspension.

The Spiders were judged to be no longer "playing the snappy aggressive article of ball which has made the team almost invincible at home and abroad." One wonders if the loyal, hard-playing Ed McKean counted himself among the team's "more practical members."

As things turned out, the Spiders were in no shape to defend their Temple Cup against the Orioles.[64] The team managed to survive yet another in a series of hardships, including a train wreck and extended 20-hour ride to Baltimore, and checked in at the Carrollton Hotel, on October 1, where Ned Hanlon was staying. Good and early next morning, Tebeau showed up in the Baltimore manager's room to ask his permission for Cleveland to practice at Union Park that afternoon. The entire final week of the Spiders' regular-season schedule of games had been rained out, so his team had worked out and staged exhibitions to try to keep in something like game shape. Friday's opening game of the postseason match up would be the first time they'd played for keeps since the previous Saturday. Ned Hanlon told Tebeau "no."

On October 2, Wizard Hoffer kept the Spiders spellbound all day, winning the first game of the fall classic easily, 7 to 1.[65] Cy Young, complaining before the game of the ill effects of his recent inactivity, was victimized for 14 base hits, three apiece by Jennings and Robinson. He'd won three games against Baltimore in the Temple Cup series just one year ago, beating Hoffer in the finale. Hoffer's spell had some kind of evil twist to it, at least as far as the Spiders' chances to keep the Temple Cup in Cleveland were concerned. The very first batter Young faced in the game, leadoff hitter John McGraw, hit a pitch back through the box and off his wrist. Young finished the game but his hand kept him from pitching again in the series. The Spiders also lost the services of Patsy Tebeau in the first game, after he wrenched his back on a swing that netted an easy fly ball to Joe Kelley in left.

SEVEN. *Temple Cup Champs (1895–1896 seasons)* 195

Just who managed the team in Tebeau's absence is unclear. Tebeau retired to groundskeeper Murphy's cottage beyond the outfield, where he submitted to an exam by a physician, after which he sat in torture on the hard Cleveland bench, wrapped up in his long coat, to witness the painful loss. He thereupon returned to the Carrollton Hotel with his team and took to his bed. On the advice of a second physician, Tebeau stayed away from the second game entirely. For game three, and apparently the next game in Cleveland, he sat in the grandstand beside the famous thespian DeWolf Hopper, a disenchanted Baltimore crank. Surely, the duties of interim field manager were assumed by either McKean or Zimmer, both of them experienced captains. In the same game, John McGraw, still weak from typhoid, fainted and had to be replaced at third base, but the Baltimore star returned to play in game two.

McKean solved Hoffer for one of Cleveland's two extra-base hits, a triple all the way to the center field fence in the third inning; back in the first, he'd coaxed the first of Hoffer's four walks on the day. On both occasions, McKean was stranded at third. His throwing error in the fourth figured not in the scoring.

In game two, Hanlon countered with Joe Corbett, a September addition from the Tri-State League, whose previous claim to fame was being the kid brother of heavyweight champ Jim Corbett. For the start, Hanlon passed over Arlie Pond, George Hemming, Sadie McMahon, and the only Orioles pitcher to win a Temple Cup game the previous year, Duke Esper. In short, the manager instinctively went with the 20-year-old instead of covering himself by relying on those pitchers who had combined for 56 wins in the past year. His gamble paid off: Baltimore won big, 7 to 2, over Tebeau's uninspired choice for his starter, Bobby Wallace, but 22 years old himself. McKean, on the first play of the game, made a dazzling stop of a McGraw grounder but threw wildly to first, once more, to help put Wallace in a 4 to 0 hole before the Spiders came to bat. He was charged with a second error in the fourth, misplaying another ground ball off McGraw's bat. On offense, McKean did beat Corbett for two hits, both dumped into his off field, a run-scoring double down the left field line in the third and a single to left in the seventh. After two hours of play, umpire Bob Emslie called the game for darkness, and so the official scoring reverted back to the last full inning of play—or else two more Baltimore runs would have been added to the final score.

Down two games in the best-of-seven format, the Spiders had to play game three, on October 5, in the hostile environs of Union Park.

With Dent Young unavailable and 17-game winner Zeke Wilson sick, Tebeau gave George Cuppy the ball. Tebeau had been quoted as declaring that Cuppy made Cleveland a favorite to repeat as Temple Cup champions, if he could go; he'd split to the bone the pinky finger on his pitching hand in a recent game in Cincinnati. His whole arm still hurt.⁶⁶ Nig Cuppy put in the heroic effort of the series, persevering through all nine innings and setting the Orioles batters down 1–2–3 in the last frame. Tebeau's words for the reporters were proving to be prophetic: Cuppy *was* the Spiders' only hope in this Temple Cup, and he would start the last game in Baltimore and the next game in Cleveland. But Bill Hoffer, pitching on two days' rest, allowed only one Cleveland hit after the fifth inning in his 6 to 2 victory. McKean wasn't much of a factor in the contest after the first inning, when he grounded toward first base and lost a race to the bag to Dirty Jack Doyle. However, he did pull off a nice catch-and-throw for the last out in the second inning, on a bounder over Cuppy's head. And his single with one out in the third advanced Burkett from first to third, where he would score on a Childs' groundout. Then in the ninth, with no one on base, McKean ventured to hit a five-run homer and fanned for the second Cleveland out, attempting too much or just venting steam.

It was back home to Cleveland, at long last, for the fourth game of the Temple Cup, to be contested before a disappointing crowd of 2,000 fans, on October 8. Wounded hero Nig Cuppy kept the Orioles sluggers off balance and the game scoreless through six innings, before Joe Kelley scored the winning run on an error by Chief Zimmer. Baltimore would pile up five runs in the seventh and eighth innings, while Joe Corbett was blanking Cleveland and making a reputation for himself. Facing a sweep by the Orioles, the Spiders reportedly played this game with ginger. McKean, the second batter in the game, lined a single to center and promptly stole second base. And in the bottom of the first, he made a fine play on McGraw's slow grounder. But Cleveland threatened to score only twice, in the fifth and the eighth innings. Bobby Wallace, pinch-hitting for Cuppy in the ninth, grounded out to first baseman Jack Doyle, and it was over.

There was a resounding finality to this postseason, like a bronze door slamming on a tomb. William Temple retired his trophy after the next Cup series, citing poor attendance and ambivalence among contesting teams. As it turned out, the Spiders did drink for a second time from Temple's Cup. At the Hollenden House bar, at 7 o'clock in the evening of October 9, the Robisons, Harry Vonderhorst, and their players assembled and drank until midnight in honor of the historic Baltimore victory. And Cleveland returned the trophy, somewhat worse for wear, to Baltimore's possession.⁶⁷ Nig Cuppy, in 1899, recalled "the impromptu game of football [they] played with the Temple Cup" that night. "It was the end, and a little wine would not hurt. That was Mr. Robison's hint to us when we met around the board." The good-intentioned owner meant, of course, the end of the trying

SEVEN. *Temple Cup Champs (1895–1896 seasons)* 197

season, although it sounds ominous to our ears. The "little wine" was served generously during the meal, as "the waiters sailed through the dining room with goblets, schooners, bottles, gondolas of wine." As Cuppy remembered it:

> After the spread, we were invited to another sail on "Lake Champagne," as Tebeau called the wine orgy. The marine scene took place at the bar. The Temple Cup, which had a capacity of 15 quarts [Baltimore sports writer Albert Mott reckoned it held a good 17 quarts[68]], was loaded and discharged till Heinie Reitz broke up the party by corkscrewing up to the bar, grabbing the trophy of baseball war, sticking his head into the silver maw and flip-flopping on the floor. The Temple Cup flagon immediately did service as a football. After Reitz was rescued from drowning in the silvery well, Doyle, acting as fullback for the party, toed the cup to Tebeau, and up and down the line it went till it was rescued by the barkeeper.[69]

The affair bore little resemblance to the comparatively sedate Elks Club celebration in Cleveland one year before; indeed, the boozy scenario degenerated into a Mad Hatter's tea party. What floral arrangements for the occasion may have been made, if any, history has failed to record.

Even though the playoffs had become foremost a matter of an extra paycheck for the jaundiced Baltimores, winners of the last three pennants, and doubtless a motivating factor for the Spiders, the 1896 Temple Cup games were a financial wash. The Baltimore columnist for *The Sporting News*, on October 10, made a joke of the Orioles' materialism, writing: "It is said that ... when McGraw took a fainting spell in the first Temple Cup game, and a doctor was called to prescribe for him, that Mugsy said before the doctor touched him: 'Remember, we get 10 per cent of the gross for letting you attend me.'" Sensing a disaster in the making before the third game, Ned Hanlon ordered ticket prices halved back to their regular season cost—to no appreciable affect at the gate. For the Baltimore players their share of the profits for four games was $200 apiece, down from the $800 cut in 1894 and from $600 in 1895. Actually, the club had to kick in the last $5 to make it an even $200. By comparison, Baltimore's exhibition games during the season, in Newark, Scranton, Wilkesbarre, and Cantonsville, plus a benefit for the rebuilding of Ford's Theater, had easily netted each Oriole over $70. Players on the losing Cleveland team were compensated $117 for their trouble.[70]

The week following the Temple Cup rout, Patsy Tebeau, Ed McKean, and those Spiders who had been arrested after the June 26 riot were excused from the unfinished business in Louisville. Their day in the Louisville police court never happened; Dr. Stucky, chief witness for the prosecution, had reconsidered his original position that would have banned the rowdies from the

League. Instead, sometime before October 14, he wrote the judge asking for the case to be settled; he now believed the Cleveland players had simply acted in the heat of competition.[71] From Cleveland, McKean duly paid his court costs of $11. It took the National League office another week to officially announce that their case against Tebeau had been dropped.[72] By then, it didn't especially matter, for the fatal blow to the viability of the Cleveland franchise was landed in the evening of October 13. This time, two leading members of the riotous Spiders would lose in the court of public opinion in their own hometown.

That night, Pat Tebeau and Jack O'Connor had been drinking in the Kennard House cafe when Elmer E. Pasco happened by.[73] A well-known Cleveland scribe, Pasco would retire as the sports editor of the *Press*, after a long career. According to the account in *The Sporting News* of October 17, the situation got hot when "Tebeau accused Pasco of having written a story about a quarrel [the September eye-blackening altercation] between him and McAleer. Pasco denied it and finally called Tebeau a liar. Tebeau knocked Pasco down and, it is said, kicked him." At this point, the bartender separated the two, only to have O'Connor jump the journalist and leave "the marks of one of his heels on his face." Although Pasco refused to swear out warrants for the arrests of the tag-team, his injuries were severe: "Pasco was unconscious when pulled away from the infuriated ball players. He was delirious all night and will probably be laid up for some days. His face was beaten almost to a jelly."[74] The Cleveland correspondent to *Sporting Life*, on October 24, published the opinion that the inexcusable affair "shows Tebeau up in a true light. In almost every other city in the country he has been denounced as a ruffian. Here at home [in Cleveland] we have fought his battles, claiming that he was merely aggressive, because of his great desire to win, but 'off the field he was always a gentleman.' That statement can never again be shoved down the throat of the public. Hence it is just as well to retract it now as any time."

The assault on Elmer Pasco was understood at once to be a turning point in the city's relationship with its team: "The affair is bound to hurt base ball in Cleveland." Such opprobrium would move another famous Cleveland sportswriter, Ed Bang, to reason that "Baltimore became a minor league town in point of attendance, and it took years and years for the Cleveland Club to induce the fans of the Forest City to forget the methods of Tebeau, McKean, and the rest of the bunch."[75] Attendance at Spiders home games did, in fact, fall off precipitously in 1897, from 152,000 fans down to 115,250.[76] Prior to the 1896 season, Frank Robison himself had recognized the negative ramifications of rowdy play, holding that "the people of Cleveland demand decency in their public amusements and base ball must be kept up to a high plane in order to make it as popular and profitable as it should be."[77] Unlike McKean, Oliver Tebeau was (to borrow the Irish expression) "a coat-trailer" off the field, especially when he'd been drinking. In the final analysis, the blood-stirring brand of baseball he demanded from his players on the field may very well have been his own chip-on-the-shoulder assault on the world, not just his managing style.

Eight
Home on the Road
(1897–1899)

> Baseball and malaria keep coming back.—attributed to Gene Mauch

Cleveland baseball in 1897 was center stage for the rise and fall of Louis Sockalexis, although the road show attracted many more paying fans than did League Park, which came in last in the League in home attendance. Cranks in the other 11 National League cities were wild to experience for themselves the frissons from this latest version of the Buffalo Bill Wild West Show, a diversion replete with its Native American rookie and the familiar cast of Spiders villains, all on one ticket. For a season, the unpopular Hibernian Spiders tried to reinvent themselves, in lieu of rebuilding a prematurely old team, as the Cleveland Indians; in the process, both the ball club and the phenom outfielder lost their identities.[1]

Ed McKean remembered Sockalexis, shortly after his teammate's premature death, in the fall of 1913: "Old Sox was a wonder when he joined us in '97. His coming to our club was one of the greatest sensations of the time. I can't recall any ball player of recent years, with the exception of Joe Jackson, who attracted as much universal attention on his arrival as old Sox…He was a remarkable hitter, a man of remarkable speed, and a fair outfielder." Fans and newspaper writers treated Sockalexis as a kind of fairy tale character cum anthropological specimen, a cigar store dummy come to life as the perfect ball player. "Why, he attracted so much attention that when we went East many of the big Eastern papers took pictures of him in every possible position. Some even photographed his legs, ankles and feet," in what we might see as a racist enactment of Thomas Eakins' photographs of the body in motion, "to demonstrate perfect muscles for running purposes. But poor old Sox was a wild bird"—Cleveland signed him after Notre Dame College dismissed him for drunken behavior—"one of those of which you'd say now I have him and now

EIGHT. *Home on the Road (1897–1899)* 201

I haven't," wistfully recollected McKean.[2] No one but Jackie Robinson could have held up to the public scrutiny and the choruses of war whoops from the stands in every city he played in. A state away in the city of Philadelphia, Larry Lajoie was having a breakout season in his first full campaign; following his record tenure in Cleveland, the club would be renamed the Indians for the second time around.

The 1896 season for Cleveland had been a brief interlude separating glory and outright collapse. In the official portrait taken at the National League owners meeting, in Baltimore on February 27, 1897, Frank Robison poses beside Ned Hanlon, who stands beside Chris von der Ahe; it is a tableau of From Where the Cleveland club had come (the 1895 Temple Cup victory) and

The nineteenth-century equivalent of a media circus, the addition of Chief Sockalexis to the Spiders bought Pat Tebeau's ticket for two more years in Cleveland (College of the Holy Cross Archives and Special Collections).

For Whence it was bound (transferred to St. Louis for 1899). A month later, Brooklyn would offer $100,000—the biggest bid ever made by a baseball club—to the Cleveland franchise, for the rights to Ed McKean and the rest of its best players.[3] The money must have been tempting. The Spiders president had just lost $4,000 on his farm team alone, in an innovative but largely failed attempt to restock his aging Cleveland roster.[4] Frank Robison had entrusted the Inter-State League Fort Wayne Farmers (note the functional nickname) to George Tebeau's management for 1896. Although "nearly a full nine of the Cleveland reserves [played] with that club," including Lou Criger, later Cy Young's personal catcher in the American League, and hurlers Cy Swaim and Jack Powell, only Powell would play a significant part on the 1897 Indians. Robison was heavily invested in Fort Wayne, Indiana, owning "the entire system of electric railways" that ran in the city.[5] Transforming Bobby Wallace from pitcher to third baseman was the year's big personnel success, but neither he nor Criger would develop in Cleveland or the National League. Frank Robison had no time to wait on his colts if he was going to field a competitive nine who would attract fans to League Park. Of interest here are the two lists Charles Mears printed naming the veteran players from 1887 and 1892 who were still in the League. By Mears' calculation, of the 80 men who played 10 years before, three were still Cleveland Indians (Tebeau, McKean, and McGarr); of the 54 men who were in the National League five years previously, Cleveland had seven on its current roster (Childs, Zimmer, Burkett, O'Connor, McAleer, Cuppy, and Young).[6] In short, Cleveland was a club past its prime. Robison had remained loyal to a fault to Cleveland, banking on the untapped revenue that Sunday baseball would bring in. He was obliged to underwrite the club with his own fortune.

While Cleveland stood pat, the League was rapidly changing. A new rule that came out of that winter meeting kept the Indians' baseline coachers so quiet that, by June, Father Chadwick passed right over Cleveland and Patsy Tebeau in his editorializing against the "rowdy tactics" of Pittsburgh that "will injure baseball"! Tebeau must have gotten a chuckle when he read Chadwick had advocated throwing manager Pat Donovan out of the National League.[7] The following March, baseball's owners adopted John Brush's anti-kicking rule specifically designed to eradicate abusive language from the game.[8] Of course, Volcano Tebeau could never be permanently stopped. The dormant one erupted the following year, on July 21, 1898, throwing a bat at a heckling fan in Baltimore.[9]

Now that an officially censored Tebeau seemed less and less to inspire his team on the field, the manager had lost control of his players in the dressing room, as well. The dilemma became, moreover, a question of the team's self-identity: neither Spider nor Indian, Kid Childs dubbed the club The Quitters and by mid-season he and his partner Ed McKean were no longer on speaking terms.[10] Jesse Burkett did talk; too much. The star was so jealous of Sockalexis, a player he'd given batting tips at Holy Cross, he spoke of his outfield mate only in the most racist language. Princeton Charlie Reilly told the press that "Jesse Burkett and Sockalexis are about as popular with each other as a pair of rival tenors in the same opera company," quoting The Crab as yelling out "He's a Jonah. I haven't hit over .100 since he joined the team," while coaching.[11] It was Tebeau's closest friend on the team, Jack O'Connor, who had befriended Sockalexis on the handball court even before the season began; unfortunately, that also meant the two made drinking buddies.[12] Well into the season, Earl Wagner reported that O'Connor was also joshing Sockalexis from the coachers' box whenever the rookie came to bat.[13] Once larger than life, Patsy Tebeau had become an anomaly, the manager who grew unable to account for his own actions; and Chief Sockalexis, the 25-year-old savior of the franchise, was proving himself at least as self-destructive as his manager. Before season's end, there was a line of disgruntled players—headed by McKean, Childs, Burkett, Zimmer, Cuppy, Blake, and O'Connor—who wanted to be traded out of Cleveland.[14]

The very fact that Ed McKean had quarreled with Tebeau is a measure of how far the manager's stock had fallen. McKean's final disenchantment with Tebeau and his bullying ways had its origins late in the season when the shortstop asked his manager for a game off because of sickness. Tebeau "gruffly" insisted that McKean get a physician's excuse. The thin-skinned McKean, never a shirker, carried his indignation into that offseason: "It's true I was told to get a certificate, and I felt hurt. I suppose Tebeau may have been right, but when a man has played nearly 1500 games and missed but 20 I think his word should be enough. Anyway, I want to play somewhere else next year."[15]

There was no lack of suitors for McKean's services; Pittsburgh sportswriters, in September, had McKean going to Philadelphia for Ed Delahanty, and George Davis returned to Cleveland before Christmas to try once again to induce McKean to play in New York.[16] Yet, the slugging shortstop continued to figure in Cleveland's plans, as he always had, especially on offense. The stubborn Tebeau's game strategy was not, he explained, to run like the Orioles. Instead, "I hold [Burkett] on first. That keeps the first baseman up and gives McKean a chance to smash one out to right."[17] Ed McKean suffered his way through his only bad individual season as a regular shortstop in 1897, his batting average slipping 65 points from the year before. Both the Spiders and Tebeau's vision of the game were badly in need of an overhaul. His team had scored 70 fewer runs than the season before. Only two teams in the National League stole fewer bases than Cleveland. McKean was slowing (he struggled to count 15 steals this year), although he wasn't the only star losing his edge on the field. Cap Anson, in his 22nd and last season as a player, pressed himself into service as a catcher, in a May 8 date in Cleveland. After doubling, "McKean drew a throw in the first inning that touched the clouds and caused the Chicagos to give Anse the merry ha ha."[18] A few weeks later, on June 18 against Baltimore, Anson would become the first major league player to reach the 3,000 hits milestone, but in his day a record lifetime achievement was largely ignored in favor of current effectiveness. Indians pitching had fallen off, as well, for 1897—team ERA slipped from first all the way down to fourth in the League—and Cleveland finished in fifth place, winning 69 games and losing 62. Cy Young did mark two career milestones during the lost season: on May 24, he passed Silver King and Jack Stivetts on the all-time list with his 200th win, and, on September 18, it took him an hour and a half to toss his first no-hitter.

The crusade in Cleveland against playing ball on Sundays was waged this year by local God-on-my-side Protestant ministers, who formed an association (which at least spared the Catholic McKean the moral dilemma). The most radical among them, the Reverend B.G. Newton, stood opposed not only to playing games on the Sabbath but also to professional baseball itself:

> If anybody should be sent to the penitentiary for interfering with the happiness of others, and adding to their cares and burdens as every evil doer does, we know of none who have over and over again deserved the penalty so much as the professionals who have prostituted innocent games and pastimes and forced decent men, hard working, persevering, and self-respecting, to abstain from amusements, innocent, harmless, commendable, because they do not want to be associated with worthless vagabonds, the blood suckers of society. Almost everything that we have to say against base ball is to be charged to the credit of these mountebanks, the professional players.... The professionals are paid by the thousand, which come from the hard earnings of the already over-burdened workingman. These professional players are no earthly good to the society of the state...They are engaged in no useful occupation, hence do not contribute to build up the commonwealth.... Every professional player is a living appeal for all men to cease work and court play.[19]

This was the strident rhetoric of what the Robisons were up against if they were ever to make professional baseball pay in the city.

Mistakenly confident that he had a deal with Mayor McKisson, Frank Robison picked Sunday, May 16, for his test case game in Cleveland.[20] Before the gates had to be closed that morning well before the first pitch, 9,500 fans thronged into League Park, leaving anywhere between 5,000 to 20,000 more fans outside. After Zeke Wilson retired the Senators in the first inning, policemen halted the game. Police Captain English, flanked by the deflated Frank Robison and a buoyant reporter from the *Cleveland Leader*, the newspaper that had served as the house organ for the ministers' association, took turns at home plate addressing the disappointed fans. The owner promised to take his case to the Ohio Supreme Court. But Robison saved his most vitriolic words for an impromptu press conference, held afterwards at the Hollenden House. First thing Monday morning, the arrested players, including Ed McKean and accompanied by umpire Tim Hurst and attorneys Judge George B. Solders and Harry C. Mason, appeared in Judge Fiedler's police court. A week later, halfway across the country in St. Louis, Frank and Stanley Robison checked into the Southern Hotel for negotiations with Chris von der Ahe and Earl Wagner about the prospect of relocating the Cleveland club in the Gateway City.

At length, on July 9, Court of Common Pleas Judge Walter C. Ong, ruling from Tiffin, Ohio, found statute 7032a, prohibiting baseball playing on Sunday, to be unconstitutional, declaring: "Custom has opposed the law." As a result of the judge's decision, Cleveland played its first legal Sunday game on a soggy field on July 11. The game started two hours late due to the rain, and only about 1,500 stuck it out to witness the landmark contest. McKean was on base all afternoon, with three base hits and a walk, in another Jack Powell win. The umpire was Hank O'Day. Monday, as he watched Dent Young lose to Boston, Patsy Tebeau reached the boiling point with his outfield of a sulking Burkett and a hobbling Sockalexis. After The Chief made two errors to let in six unearned runs, Tebeau yelled out to his right fielder, and anyone else who was within earshot, that he was going to equip him with a pair of boxing gloves. Attendance picked up a bit as the season progressed, in large part because of the Sunday dates added to the schedule—15,000 attended the July 25 Sunday game, the biggest crowd in Cleveland baseball history. McKean had two hits, but the fans were disappointed to see their hero Cy Young lose the game, with two outs in the 10th inning, in relief.

Back at the start of the season, when every club in the League had its reasons to be optimistic about its chances for the pennant, things shaped up as the year of Chief Sockalexis. For the team's first intra-squad game at Hot Springs, in mid–March, even Pat Tebeau got into the spirit of things, dividing the squads into the veteran Indians and rookie Papooses.[21] Louis Sockalexis wasn't even with the team yet; he'd worked out at the Cleveland Athletic Club, where he was often interrupted to pose for publicity photographs, before joining Tebeau's crew late, at the end of March, on its post-camp barnstorming tour through Columbus, Dayton, Indianapolis, Fort Wayne, Grand Rapids, and Toledo.[22] Just before the regular-season opener, the Indians lost twice to the Grand Rapids Bobolinks, Nig Cuppy starting one of the games, though the fans hardly noticed. At home or away, the cranks had eyes only for Louis Francis Sockalexis, who appeared to be major-league-ready at the bat but awkward in the outfield.[23]

On April 22, Cleveland opened in Louisville, the site of the fan riot a mere 10 months before. It was a hot ticket. Some 11,000 turned out to cheer and jeer Sockalexis and the notorious Clevelands. They were rewarded by the spectacle of McKean and Sockalexis, batting third and cleanup in the lineup, being held without a hit, and Cy Young losing to the Colonels. The Indians most resembled the riotous Spiders of recent vintage in the next game, two days later, when Sandy McDermott tossed Crab Burkett in the first inning, for calling the umpire a "robber" who was stealing the game from his team, and ejected Jack O'Connor in the ninth. Cuppy took the loss.[24]

Cleveland fans who were counting on the Young-Cuppy one-two punch to come around could content themselves meantimes with the team's hitting.

In the early going, it looked like Mac and Sox would make a famous slugging duo. On consecutive days in April, the teammates took turns belting longest-in-the-history-of-Sportsman's Park home runs to halt Cleveland's losing streak at five games. On April 29, McKean's round-tripper off Duke Esper carried over the right field fence and into Chute Lake.[25] The contest ended in a 6 to 6 tie, but it was nearly the Tribe's sixth loss without a win—Young gave up the tying runs in the ninth inning only to be saved by darkness. The day after was Sockalexis' turn. His mammoth homer to dead center field outdistanced McKean's cannon shot. As if to outdo even himself, the rookie also saved the day with an eighth-inning catch to make the Indians winners for the first time in 1897. The following game, Sox tripled with the bases loaded—it was one of his four hits off Red Donahue—and pilfered two bases.

In the Indians' much-anticipated home opener, on May 3, McKean hit from the second slot in a revised lineup, behind Burkett and ahead of man-of-the-hour Sockalexis. With stars Cupid Childs and Jimmy McAleer disabled, Patsy Tebeau was McKean's partner at second, Harry Blake taking charge in center field and Peach Pie O'Connor in Tebeau's place at first base. Ed McKean recorded the Indians' first hit, stolen base (two on the day), and run of 1897 in League Park. As it turned out, he'd also saved his first two-hit game of the season for the pleasure of the Cleveland fans. In the following days, Jim McAleer's chronic problem with charley horses had become so severe that he returned to Youngstown for treatment.[26] Soon Lou Criger supplanted the other Chief, Charlie Zimmer, behind the plate and Tebeau was forced to start an unraveling string of unknown rookie pitchers. The pattern of substitutions continued to trouble the team throughout the summer. Even Bull McKean had to miss a July 8 home game against the Senators, when he was called home to Grafton to be with his ailing father. Patsy Tebeau filled in at short and made the featured fielding play of Cy Young's win.[27]

On Memorial Day, 17,000 cranks grabbed up seats and claimed standing room to get a view of Chief Sockalexis. McKean stood tall against lefty Harley Payne for three hits, but Dent Young bowed to Brooklyn. By the first week of June, their arms were sore enough to keep both Young and Cuppy back in Cleveland while the Indians travelled to Washington, although they caught up with the team in Baltimore. After McKean was dropped to seventh in the batting order, he enjoyed his first real hitting tear for the season, during a homestand late in June. On June 21, McKean made three hits off Louisville slowballer Bert Cunningham. He also made three errors in Cy Young's ninth loss (against just six wins), and Cleveland missed the chance to even their record at .500. The following afternoon, Ginger Pappalau lost for Cleveland, in spite of three more hits by McKean and Lou Criger's feat of throwing out

EIGHT. *Home on the Road (1897–1899)*

six Colonels on the bases. McKean singled four times, on June 23, for Jack Powell's debut and victory. In Young's June 28 win over Pittsburgh, McKean recorded two more hits. And on June 30, McKean collected three base hits off left-hander Jesse Tannehill; Powell's win brought Cleveland's record to 27–27.

The club's fortunes permanently turned when Chief Sockalexis' personal Fourth of July celebration climaxed in his drunken leap from the second story window of a Cleveland brothel. He made the attempt to hide the injury and play on his broken right foot, but he'd never be the same player again.[28] A month later, President Robison was forced to discipline his self-destructing right fielder:

> I have received indisputable evidence to-day that he had been intoxicated two nights this week. I have to-day fined him $25 for his first offense of several weeks ago, $50 for his second offense, and $100 for the third, and have suspended him without pay until he shall get me a certificate from our club physician that he is in perfect condition to play ball ... I think I can truthfully say that I have done everything I could for Sockalexis, and he has repayed me, and the Cleveland Club, by the basest ingratitude. I have waited as long as I could.[29]

The Indians still had a doubleheader in Pittsburgh to play after Sockalexis' leap. In the seventh inning of game one, it was Ed McKean who drove in Burkett with the winning run off Frank Killen. The talented southpaw was twice a 30-game winner and won 29 another season. In the afternoon loss, the bases were loaded in the sixth when Jesse Burkett let a ball off the bat of Jim Donnelly skip between his legs. The Crab declined to go after the baseball. In the time it took McKean to hustle all the way into the outfield to retrieve the ball, all four Pirates runners had scored. It seems Burkett was one Indian who wasn't buying into the concept of the rehabilitated Hibernians. The recalcitrant Burkett's worst day was in Louisville, on August 4, when his team dropped a doubleheader. Cleveland had to forfeit the morning game, after Burkett called ump Chicken Wolf a vile name while kicking a called strike, and Patsy Tebeau refused to pinch-hit for the ejected batter. In the ninth inning of the second game, Burkett swore at Wolf again, and again he was ejected by the umpire who had turned sensitive since his own wild days as a Louisville Colonel. This time, Burkett refused to leave first base, so Wolf ordered two cops to escort him from the field. Jesse Burkett played emotionally out of control all season, unlike Tebeau, who conspicuously remained above the fray for the most part, being fined or ejected much less frequently these days.

McKean was on a midseason roll at the marble, especially before the home crowds. On July 18, when Jack Powell defeated Brooklyn in Cleveland's second legal Sunday game, McKean tripled in a sudden thunder storm. He counted two more hits off Arlie Pond, in a July 19 loss to visiting Baltimore, and three hits on July 20, as Cy Young turned back the Orioles. After a rained-out date, McKean realized another two-hit day, on July 22, in Frankie Wilson's win over Philadelphia. McKean had recorded four straight multi-hit games during the homestand that began with the July 25 Sunday game, as we have seen.

The longtime shortstop was as tough and wily as ever. Charles Mears remarked that "Ed. McKean is about as white a ball player as ever lived and is probably the most popular man on the Cleveland team with many of the club patrons, but occasionally he turns a trick and when he does it is worth the while." At a July 23 game in Philadelphia, the sportswriter was treated to a vintage ploy out of the Hibernian playbook: "Wallace made a wild throw that looked like a round trip for the batter, [Duff] Cooley. Mac saw how things were going and when Cooley came by gave that individual the leg. Cooley went sprawling ten feet from third and finally reached the bag safely. He made a kick to Umpire Emslie, who had not seen the affair, and Mac, grinning like a full fledged comedian got away with the trick."[30]

Meanwhile, the Chiefless Indians were fading fast in the standings, and the errors were piling up for McKean. It was his miscue in Chicago, on August 8, that negated a Cleveland rally and lost the game after Jack Powell had gotten two outs in the ninth. The fifth-place Indians had become irrelevant in the pennant race with a record of 45–43. Perhaps the low point, for McKean and the Indians, came in a 12 to 1 drubbing by Pawtucket in an exhibition staged in Providence, Rhode Island, on August 29. McKean couldn't have helped remembering the bad old days he spent in that city, in 1886, at the sputtering start of his career.

One of Patsy Tebeau's selective outbursts resulted in a forfeit of the second game of a September 8 doubleheader in Washington, handing the Senators the sweep. Cleveland had already dropped the morning contest, and was trailing, 6 to 2, in the fifth inning of game two, when Tebeau ordered McKean to let Roger Bresnahan, the home team's starter, hit him with a pitch. Bresnahan's second throw, a slow curve ball, struck McKean but umpire William Carpenter called him back from first base—it seems he'd overheard the manager's instructions. Tebeau, in a fit that seemed a throwback to the Hibernian Spiders, called his Indians off the field, and Cy Young lost his 19th. In some respects, this was a rather unique series of games: Dent Young hit cleanup and played first base (he made three errors) the day after Hall of Fame backstop Bresnahan twirled.

After that, the Indians got healthy—Childs and Sockalexis returned to the lineup—and mounted a too-little-too-late winning run for the pennant in September. In Cleveland, on Sunday, September 12, McKean got the scoring started by tripling in the first inning off the Browns' Billy Hart, following Burkett's leadoff double and preceding triples by Childs and Wallace. Cleveland rolled to a 15 to 4 win. Then on September 18, in the first game of a twin bill at League Park, Cy Young threw his first career no-hitter, the first by a Cleveland pitcher since One Arm Daily's gem 14 years before. Young's fielders were nothing special on his special day, though. McKean made a throwing error, and third baseman Bobby Wallace was charged with two more miscues on ground balls. The no-hitter was preserved only by an extraordinary measure: Wallace sent a note to official scorer Davis Hawley explaining that a play made close by his bad throw was his error and not a base hit. The game featured a number of other noteworthy oddities: Ira Belden, from the Euclid Beach Amusement Park team, played right field in place of Sockalexis that historic afternoon; it was the fastest game played in Cleveland all year; and, after the doubleheader, Nick Young canned John O. Kelly, the umpire for both games. On Sunday, September 28, Sport McCallister's first big league win made it 12 consecutive victories for Cleveland, vaulting them 10 games over .500 but still mired in fifth place. The season ended for the Spiders with a third-straight loss in Pittsburgh on October 2. Before the team broke up, it played an exhibition in Canton, Ohio, the following Sunday afternoon, No-Hit Young and the regular Cleveland lineup beating Doc Reisling and a local team, 9 to 2. In the aftermath of the lost season, a disgruntled McKean commented provocatively to the press that "Cleveland fans are as cold as Andy Freedman's eyes upon encountering John T. Brush," and he reiterated his desire to be traded before spring training.[31]

For the first time since his injury-shortened season of 1892, Ed McKean had failed to drive in his usual 100-plus runs, score 100 runs himself, or slug over .400. He came in below 600 plate appearances for the first time in four years, also collecting 50 fewer base hits than he had the previous season and 30 fewer RBIs. Even though Mac's 14 triples were 10th most in the League, his performance for 1897 signals the beginning of his decline as an elite player. He went five months between his two home runs for the year—on April 29 and September 4—and did not homer in League Park. His substandard range at short had seriously handicapped the team. One constant, and it persisted over McKean's whole career, was an abiding superstition of his. No one in Cleveland had ever seen McKean throw the ball back to the pitcher before a batter's turn. According to Charles Mears, "When the ball is being thrown around the diamond he always finds some one other than the box man to take it off his hands."[32]

No one was much in the mood for baseball on the afternoon of the Indians' home opener, on April 29, 1898. The men of the Fifth Regiment had departed Cleveland that morning, bound for President McKinley's war in Cuba; the game drew an underwhelming 2,000 fans.[33]

Frank DeHass Robison, a friend of William McKinley's, was engaged in his own little war with the President's handler, Mark Hanna, over the revenue derived from fans riding their consolidated streetcar line out to League Park. The overall result of the squabble was to make it even more difficult for fans to attend games.[34] Then, in late in April, the Ohio Supreme Court gave Robison more bad news: its ruling on the *State v. Powell* case overturned the Cleveland's court decision that had declared, for a time, the city's prohibition of Sunday ballplaying to be unconstitutional.[35] Among the remedies Robison dreamed up were a plan to build, in partnership with St. Louis horse racing promoter H.H. Dargan, a combination race track and ball park (no doubt inspired by Chris von der Ahe's dual obsessions), where Sunday games could be played legally.[36] As if in sympathy with their owner's darkening mood, the Indians wore heavy dark overcoats that spring instead of sweaters; and, on April 30, Tebeau had to be called away from an extra-inning game in St. Louis to be at his wife's bedside while she was operated on in their Cleveland home.[37] As it turned out, in June, the team managed to play three Sunday games at a hastily thrown together pavilion in Euclid Beach Park, outside of Cleveland in Collinwood, which took a week to construct. At the amusement park, Cleveland hosted Pittsburgh on June 12 and 19, attracting a total of 9,000 fans—in spite of a rain-delayed first game and player arrests in the eighth inning of the second game—but a contest versus the Giants that was scheduled for June 26 had to be cancelled when Mayor Hall of Collinwood betrayed the Spiders brass by promising he'd have the players arrested on site by 25 cops.[38]

On the heels of the failure in Collinwood, Frank Robison knew he'd lost his fight with the ministers' association and gave up further experiments for raising revenue to keep the club in Cleveland. The Indians were two dozen games over .500, and in possession of second place, when Frank Robison deemed it would be more profitable, starting in August, to play most of Cleveland's remaining home schedule on the road at "neutral" sites like Chicago and Cincinnati (where the umpires and cranks had never been neutral), Rochester, New York, Philadelphia, Weehawken, New Jersey, and St. Louis (where fans flocked to see the team that rumors had moving to their city). Robison figured rightly that the club would draw several times better for away games, and its share of the gates would turn a profit, even after accounting for transportation and hotels. With an assist to Cleveland, the Chicago club led the League in attendance and set franchise records, in their first season without their biggest drawing card, Cap Anson.[39] Cleveland came in dead last in National League attendance.

EIGHT. *Home on the Road (1897–1899)* 211

Naturally, no man's efforts to keep major league baseball in Cleveland while playing at home on the road could be successful in the long run. By the end of the expanded 154-game schedule, nobody was calling his team the Cleveland Indians any more, and in 1898 most cranks and scribes and referred to them variously as the Wanderers, the Vagrants, the Outcasts, the Tramps, the Pothunters, and the Nomads. The team without a city became the team without a name.[40] Last year's headliner Chief Sockalexis rode Patsy Tebeau's bench until his release, right after the one-year anniversary of his Fourth of July escapade. Somehow, Cleveland found its way through the wilderness to a winning season, although 21 games out of first place. The fifth-place finish was undoubtedly Pat Tebeau's greatest job as a manager. It was Ed McKean's last hurrah in the majors.

McKean performed like the unofficial National League Comeback Player of the Year for 1898. He rebounded nicely from his previous season's batting figures, if only by sheer perseverance. For his last full season, the final one in a Cleveland uniform, he willed himself to come to the plate 674 times, fourth most in the League, and play in 151 games, the most in his career. He ranked fourth in the League in home runs (nine) and ninth in runs batted in (94). McKean's hands and arm were surer than ever—his career-best fielding percentage ranked him third among all shortstops—although his range was now below average, and Tebeau had begun to spot him occasionally at second and first base to keep his bat in the lineup. Bull McKean still possessed the strength and mentality of a middle linebacker and the leadership qualities of an infantry non-com. He could still drink the Mickey Mantles of his era under the table at midnight (there were many contenders), and hit like Mantle in the afternoon (much rarer). No comeback was in the cards for Louis Sockalexis, who went AWOL and missed the train when his teammates pulled out of Cleveland for their Hot Springs training camp.[41] After Sox sat on bench for the first two games of season, he was asked to hit leadoff when Tebeau put him back in the lineup. Elmer Bates, friend to all players, claimed the only reason Sockalexis got the unexpected start in right field was because Harry Blake, the regular, had been called back to Elkhart, Indiana, where his mother-in-law was dying.[42]

The team in 1898 never did utilize its impressive roster of talent: at the catcher's position alone, for example, were Zimmer, Criger, O'Connor, and Ossee Schreckengost. Second-year man Jack Powell wound up with five shutouts, tying him for National League honors. Furthermore, the Wanderers pitching staff actually paced the League with 142 complete games, and, for the second season in a row, issued the fewest bases on balls (309). Part of the trouble was that, more and more, Pat Tebeau was being required to manage from the bench, where he was never successful. He'd long held that "signaling from the bench is very much minor league."⁴³ Also, the National League's Brush Rule prohibiting kicking, now in its second year, had effectively defanged Tebeau and, in turn, wrought a change in the team, from riotous Spiders to quietus Tribe.

In a game in middle of June, umpire Charley Cushman and Kid Childs found themselves in the familiar territory of debating a call. What was disconcertingly alien to Childs, and to McKean, who had wedged himself in between the arbiter and the second baseman, was the Cleveland manager's reaction: "'Go to the bench,' said Captain Tebeau to Childs...The player obeyed orders. 'Now come out and play!' sang out Patsy and Childs resumed his position on the field, and the Cleveland players [this writer assumed] enjoyed the captain's byplay, which saved his second baseman being put out of the game by the umpire."⁴⁴ At least early in the season, it was said that even "Burkett has a deep reverential regard for the Brush resolution and the improvement in Jesse's manner on a base decision is most marked." In a game in May, Hank O'Day called the runner safe at first and turned his head to the South, his method of turning down a protestor kick in the old days. Burkett started on a run for O'Day, the blood mounting to his face and neck in earnest protest against the so-called "robbery." Jess had not gone ten feet before McAllister, Wallace and Childs held out warning hands, calling a halt.⁴⁵

The Spiders' efforts to observe the zero-tolerance rule was not without its lighter moments. The *Cleveland Plain Dealer* reported from spring training that "the players have learned new vocabularies to be used instead of the old familiar language that would not look well in print":

> Jack O'Connor has a little speech that he says will fix the umpires...Removing his cap with a Chesterfieldian air and bowing low, Jack begins something like this: "Pardon the intrusion, my dear Mr. Umpire, but you do not agree with me that your decision is a slight injustice? I have no desire to question your ability or fairness, but merely suggest that under some misapprehension you have inadvertently wronged us in a slight degree." Said O'Connor: "A fellow can learn to get just as much satisfaction out of that as in calling him a _____ _____ robber or a _ _ _ _ _ _ _ _ _, and it will be a heap cheaper, too." Sockalexis says he has [it] the best of all other players under the new rule. "I'll cuss the umpire in Penobscot," says the Indian, "and if they call me, I'll say I was telling them they are just right and that you fellows are dead wrong in kicking." Jesse Burkett is taking lessons from Sockalexis in the latter's native tongue and can already say "hickehowgo," (robber), "kanylanyee" (green lobster), and several adjectives that fit in quite nicely.⁴⁶

For the season opener at Cincinnati, on April 15, Mayor William Howard Taft threw out the ceremonial first ball. Jimmy McAleer must have been paying attention: at his request, in 1912, then President Taft tossed out the opening day ball in Washington, and established the tradition. Burkett's three hits, including a double and a triple, were the only features of the Cleveland effort. Ed McKean committed an error and went 0-for-3 against Theo Breitenstein, who would no-hit the Pirates exactly seven days later. Sockalexis did not play.[47] The Indians dropped two of three games in the Cincinnati series, including a 12 to 1 shellacking in the get-away game, then rallied to take the next five contests, in St. Louis and Louisville, all low-scoring, closely played games. McKean had to wait for his first base hit of 1898 until Cleveland's fourth game of the season, a 10 to 5 April 20 win in St. Louis. He'd also committed three errors in the three previous games. McKean's second and third hits came on a muddy field, on April 22, against the Browns' Wee Willie Sudhoff. Wrote Elmer Bates: "Eddie McKean's second hit of the season," a rattling double, "sent three runs skipping across the rubber. Batting in runs is an old trick of the Grafton boy. Last year they refused to go safe for the big short stop, but this season he is again splitting the boards on the right field fence."[48]

McKean quickly followed up with another two-hit game in St. Louis on April 24. Then, two days later in Louisville, McKean collected three hits and scored twice to help Powell beat Lou Mahaffey, 9 to 8, in a thrilling ninth-inning come-from-behind victory. (Mahaffey threw a complete game for his only major league appearance.) Starting with a win over the Browns in Cleveland's home opener, April 29, the team won 10 of the next 12 games, as the Indians' bats came to life. In their three-game series sweep of the Browns, the Indians scored 31 runs. Hosting Louisville, in the afternoon game of a May 7 twin bill, Cleveland enjoyed what would be its biggest romp of the whole season, punishing Colonels pitchers for 14 runs. By mid–May, Elmer Bates judged that "McKean is setting a pace at the bat that threatens to make him a formidable rival of both Burkett and Wallace for the position of champion batter on the local team."[49]

Just when Charles Mears happily reported that Tebeau and Childs were finally hitting the ball with regularity, McKean had to be held out of the lineup with a fever, missing a doubleheader at home against the Phillies. Tebeau filled in at short and Cleveland took both games.[50] Cleveland was winning ball games—their record was 36–24 to start July—even while the under-the-weather McKean slumped at the plate, falling to 54th in the League in batting average.[51] In late June, the Chicago correspondent to *Sporting Life* had estimated: "Down at short, Long and Dahlen, ranking about even up with one another, are far ahead of honest, heavy bulky McKean, but fat Edward [still] gets into the general team play in corking style."[52] Presently, McKean reclaimed his authority at the plate. Bates had taken note that, after 32 home games, no Indian had managed to hit a home run in League Park yet.[53] Ed McKean rectified that shortcoming in a hurry, victimizing the eventual pennant-winning Boston Beaneaters for two-run home runs on three consecutive days.[54]

On Thursday, June 30, McKean drove one of Welsh-born Fred Klobedanz's fastballs all the way to the fence and legged out an inside-the-park home run. On Friday, in the July 1 win at home over Boston, McKean had four hits in his four at-bats against Parsons Lewis and Duke Klobedanz, adding a sacrifice fly and a stolen base. His big blow off Klobedanz sailed high over the right field fence. The left-handed Klobedanz had led the League in winning percentage the season before, and Lewis would turn the trick this season. In the Saturday, July 2, game, McKean enjoyed another big day against Boston and Cleveland swept the series. This time, he touched up Ted Lewis for a double and a ninth-inning homer. As it turned out, the homer was McKean's last in League Park in a Cleveland uniform. The moment would not have seemed special to McKean as he routinely circled the bases, if he believed there would be more home games in Cleveland. Of course, he *had* heard those rumors about the Robisons transferring the team to St. Louis...

Cleveland split this year's July Fourth doubleheader with visiting Chicago. In the morning game, McKean continued his firecracker at-bats by going 2-for-4 and a double off rookie Walt Woods, and in the second game, he doubled in four times up. On July 5, McKean extended his hitting streak with a single off Henry Clarke. Clarke eventually won the game against his former team, in his only pitching appearance of the year for the Orphans. When play resumed in Chicago, on July 6, McKean hit out of the cleanup position, going 2-for-3 and doubling, against 20-game-winner Nixey Callahan. The following day, back in Cleveland against St. Louis, McKean went 2-for-5, with another double, off 29-game-loser Brewery Jack Taylor. In Philadelphia, on July 13, McKean capped off his streak with a ninth-inning homer off Red Donahue. He had already doubled and singled twice in the victory.

Cleveland's record stood 15 games over .500 before Frank Robison's decision rendered irrelevant McKean's latest offensive success and removed the team from contention. The Cleveland Wanderers, as the team soon came to be called throughout baseball, played but twice at League Park from the July 9 game until the final home date on August 26. And then, from August 27 to October 15, the team played its next 45 games away from home. The 50-day tour to end the season marked the third longest string of away games in Cleveland baseball history (the longest in duration since the 1884 Blues), and ranks with two of the 1899 Spiders' extended road trips.[55] It was considered newsworthy when the team *was* in Cleveland:

> The Cleveland Wanderers spent a couple of hours in this city last night [September 3] on their way to Cincinnati. They expected to arrive at noon yesterday and

EIGHT. *Home on the Road (1897–1899)* 215

have a chance to take a look at their former homes, but they missed connections and were only in the city a short time, as they were obliged to start for the Reds' stamping grounds at 8:30.

The players are not in as high spirits as a team that has been playing such excellent ball is wont to be. The strain of their long wanderings is telling on them and they are rapidly becoming tired of their lot....

The men feel that they have no prospects of playing except to hostile audiences and that is not encouraging. As one player put it, "It is hard enough to endure the rooting of the other fellows' fans half the time, but when we have no relief from it and are kept jumping around and changing climates and board continually it's a wonder we have not struck the slide long ago...."

Excepting in the brief stay in Cleveland recently they had not had a chance to bat a dozen balls in practice in a month. "The little work we get before the game amounts to nothing," one said, "What we want is good hard morning practice occasionally and when we are traveling we can't get it. Our batting has been poor and that is the reason for it."[56]

Cy Young's biographer notes: "Initially the players had hoped to demonstrate their professionalism by shrugging off the inconvenience of homelessness, but the absence of supportive crowds, the constant confrontation with home-team umpiring, and the lack of familiarity with playing grounds finally took a toll on morale. Their offensive power dissolved, and the team finished ninth in team batting averages."[57] On August 11, Cleveland's record had stood at 59–36–3; it is a credit to Tebeau and his players that the team "came home" with a respectable 81 wins, 68 losses, and seven ties. The big number of tie games is probably another indication of the "home-team umpiring."

A month into the marathon road test, the team narrowly averted a tragic crack up in Philadelphia. McKean and his teammates were returning to their hotel from the Baker Bowl around 7 o'clock at night, on August 8, when their horse-drawn bus stopped at Broad and Hamilton streets to allow a train to pass:

> When the engine was almost across the wide street the bus driver, thinking the track was clear, started his horses. He failed to see a second engine following the first until there was a warning cry from a pedestrian. It was then, apparently, too late to either go forward or back, and the vehicle came to a standstill directly in the middle of the track. Cuppy, who was on the front seat with the driver, grasped the rail of the seat and prepared to jump for his life. One and all proceeded to make a dash for the rear door and there was a wild scramble for safety. Eyewitnesses to the scene declare Childs and Blake never touched the rear steps. Burkett squeezed through a window and leaped to the ground. Other players were trying to do likewise when the driver whipped up his horses and cleared the track.[58]

While he was still enjoying home cooking, back at the beginning of August, Ed McKean's .320 batting average ranked 19th best in the League. He was 15th in extra-base hits, with 17 doubles, a triple, and four homers.[59] A month later, he was hitting .299, only 28th in batting average.⁶⁰ McKean finished the season 15 points below .300, tagging on to his totals just six more doubles and a home run. In addition to the exhaustion McKean suffered from unrelieved months of road games and hotel living, time had conspired to erode his skills. At 29 years old, he was not the elite shortstop he had been for more than a decade, and he knew it. In a later era, Ernie Banks at a similar point in his career would be moved over to first base, Cal Ripken to third. A switch to designated hitter would no doubt have extended McKean's usefulness to a team. However, this was 19th-century baseball and, after 12 years as Cleveland's shortstop, Ed McKean played his final home game in League Park on August 26. Batting fifth in the order that afternoon against the Giants, he was held hitless in five tries against Jouett Meekin. It was a game the Wanderers were never in. Following the 8 to 1 loss, McKean's team clung by a spike to fourth place.

His last round-tripper for the season, in the first inning of a September 22 contest in Philadelphia, was the only run preventing Wiley Piatt from shutting out Cleveland for his third time this year. McKean had also played the spoiler earlier in Baltimore, where his home run was the only run in a Cleveland loss to Al Maul.⁶¹ Maul had been a member of the Rochester Maroons; suddenly, for McKean, 1886 was a long time ago. Ironically, one of Robison's neutral sites provided a homecoming of sorts for McKean, when he came back to play at Rochester's newly rebuilt Culver Field, on August 27 and 29. All told, McKean's nine home runs in 1898 amassed 17 RBIs.

What turned out to be Ed McKean's final appearance in a Cleveland uniform occurred in, of all places, Louisville on October 15, the last scheduled Wanderers game of the year and, due to rainouts, the last National League game played in 1898.⁶² McKean was one of the few veterans in the lineup, with unknowns behind the plate (Ossee Schreckengost), in right field (Emmet Heidrick), in center (Fred Frank), at third base (Jimmy Burke), and pitching (Frank Bates). Batting second, McKean went 0-for-4 against Canadian-born Bill Magee. The first baseman for the Colonels that day, a big kid named Honus Wagner, had three hits and a double.

Although the team was rarely to be found in Cleveland during the season, McKean was putting down deep roots in the city. He had become a father for the first time, with the birth of Edward J. McKean, Jr., in June 1898.⁶³ Soon, the young family moved out of the apartment at 242 Oregon Street (renamed Rockwell Avenue in 1906) and built the house on Jay Street, in the Ohio City district. Belle made an income as a seamstress and a launderer, and the homestead always had one or two female boarders.⁶⁴ Citizen McKean was also at work expanding his public role in West Cleveland. It was during this period

EIGHT. *Home on the Road (1897–1899)* 217

that he was campaign manager for his business partner Charles M. Creighton's unsuccessful run for city council. McKean's candidate lost by 130 votes running as a Democrat in a heavily Republican district.[65] In March 1901, Ed McKean was the Democratic nominee, for the same council seat from Ward 41, and he lost by 156 votes.[66] Undeterred, Bull McKean ran again, in November 1905, and won. Sportswriters had been calling him Alderman McKean for years by then.[67]

With two weeks left to play in the 1898 season, John T. Brush, operating at the very pinnacle of his power, directed the National League to strip Chris von der Ahe of his ownership of the Browns, effective at the turn of October, and award the St. Louis franchise to the Robison family.[68] They were to transfer the choice Cleveland players from the 1898 roster to St. Louis for the upcoming season. In the era of syndicate baseball, it was legal for the Robisons to own and operate two teams, the new St. Louis Perfectos and what was left of the Cleveland Spiders. Every Cleveland regular, excepting stalwarts McKean, Zimmer, and McAleer, at once allowed their contracts to be transferred to the Gateway City. (Baltimore made a comparable transit of players that year, sending Keeler, Jennings, and Joe Kelley to Brooklyn, along with Ned Hanlon. But at least John McGraw was allowed to stay on in Baltimore, unlike the dislocated McKean.) Next season, the National League Cleveland Misfits would set the all-time record for futility, winning 20 and losing 134 games, 101 of the losses on the road and safely distanced from irate Cleveland fans. No Cleveland pitcher would win more than four games; no regular player would hit better than .286; the offense scored 529 runs. John Clements, the aging lefty, would be one of the seven solutions the Misfits would try at catcher. Robert Henry Lochhead, McKean's replacement at short, registered a .261 slugging average in 148 games.

St. Louis became to McKean little more than a sickbed in a rented room. His body was wracked by waves of fevers, chills, sweats, and rigor-shakes. For interminable stretches at a time, he had nothing to distract himself from thoughts about his wife and year-old son, half the continent away, or worries about his diminishing career and uncomprehending fans.[69]

Ed McKean was struck down by recurring bouts of malaria and stuck in the Imperial Hotel, just about the only two things he still had in common with his estranged partner, Kid Childs.[70] Years of alcohol abuse and overweight were conspiring with the lingering effects of an illness he'd no doubt contracted from a mosquito bite in spring training with—he could hardly wrap his mind around it—the St. Louis Perfectos. The exiled Clevelander was staring down a premature retirement in June of his unlucky 13th season. Even the new uniform they assigned him was an indignity. (The picture of old Eddie McKean stuffed into the Perfectos outfit, with its garish red-striped stockings and red-trimmed shirts, was turn-of-the-century baseball's equivalent to the spectacle of Boog Powell nearing the end of his playing days inside the blood-clot-red Indians togs of 1974.)

He'd fought to stay in Cleveland with the reformulated Spiders. He'd been among the last players to refuse a transfer. He'd purchased a resort in the city, a month before spring training, rechristened it The Short Stop Inn, and fully intended to make a headquarters for Cleveland sporting men.[71] Ed McKean may even have held out hopes of being appointed the playing-manager at Cleveland, a deal like the one McGraw landed in Baltimore. As it turned out, McKean didn't leave Cleveland as much as the team ran out on him, and he reluctantly followed it to Missouri. More like, "to the Imperial" than "to Sportsman's Park," he reckoned. Whereas St. Louis was a homecoming for Patsy Tebeau and Jack O'Connor, Cleveland and Cleveland baseball had been essential to McKean's identity. Indeed, McKean and Burkett had signed contracts *to play for Cleveland*, on March 9, five days before the Browns went up for auction.[72] At the time, McKean was reported to be "entirely satisfied with the terms offered if he is to play in Cleveland, where he has a home and where his business is well established. If, however, the team is to be transferred to St. Louis the big short-stop will ask for considerable more money."[73] The shortstop had been one of eight on the roster to settle for the League cap salary of $2,400, agreeing to a contract "without any qualifying clause" after being assured by Tebeau himself that the team would remain in Cleveland.[74] The day after McKean signed, March 10, Jimmy McAleer retired as an active player.[75] Another of McKean's teammates from the Youngstowns, Ed Cartwright, had preceded McAleer into retirement from the game. These days, Jumbo was a master iron molder and supervisor of workers in a Minneapolis rolling mill.[76]

During the first week of March, Tebeau was busy arranging to take 19 Cleveland Indians, including the newly inked McKean, to training camp in Hot Springs. *Sporting Life* reported business as usual for the Cleveland team—"Tebeau insists that he has received no intimation of any kind that the Indians are to be transferred to St. Louis"—and, for emphasis, the manager dramatically added, "I have just ordered 20 new uniforms, and the word Cleveland will be printed across the breast of every one of the shirts."[77] The March 18 *Sporting News* still had McKean, and Chief Zimmer, in those Cleveland uniforms, forming "the nucleus of a splendid team there, supplemented by the men who would be transferred from St. Louis." For a time in this unraveling tale of two baseball cities, where McKean would play continued to be a matter for speculation. After the winter meeting, it was the *Washington Evening Star*'s educated guess that he would be left in Cleveland, since he was "one of the

EIGHT. *Home on the Road (1897–1899)* 219

best players in baseball today, and Tebeau is too wise a general to disrupt an organization that plays like well-oiled machinery as a result of years of constant playing together."[78] No less informed an observer than Ned Hanlon presumed McKean would play for Cleveland, and Bobby Wallace would be the St. Louis shortstop; his statement, in the April 1 *Sporting News*, looks like an April Fool's joke on McKean a dozen decades after the fact.

On March 29, E.J. McKean was officially reassigned from the Cleveland active roster to St. Louis. Recent business decisions had predetermined McKean's baseball fate. In St. Louis on March 14, the Browns franchise along with properties of Sportsman's Park were sold at a public auction for $33,000, thus divesting Chris von der Ahe of the team he'd built. The scene was a memorable one:

> The sale attracted the largest crowd that ever gathered at the Court House door at a public auction. The steps, portico and corridor were crowded and the overflow made the sidewalks impassable... The character of jests indicated that the crowd was made up in the main of base ball cranks and not capitalists intent on investment. When there was an interruption in the reading of the notice of sale, there were cries of "Play ball," "Get in the game," "Put 'em over the plate," and other phrases familiar to the followers of the game.

Ed McKean and the Cleveland players were rooming, at the very hour of the sale, at nearby Lindell Hotel, en route with Tebeau to spring training.[79] Although local millionaire merchant Edward Becker bought the controlling interest in the St. Louis Base Ball Company, he wasn't a baseball man and didn't fancy running a club; so, he completed a deal, on March 20, that gave Frank Robison 49 percent of the company's shares in return for his team of players, the Cleveland Wanderers nee Spiders.[80]

Who could really blame the Robisons for giving up on trying to make a go of pro baseball in Cleveland? They couldn't sell the Spiders—the League turned down the only offer, from businessmen in Detroit—so the brothers, legal owners of two teams now, patched together a Cleveland team from the St. Louis roster and renamed the old Cleveland team the St. Louis Perfectos. In St. Louis, the owners would have no Sabbatarian movement to face down, and the city's fans were hungry for a return to the glory years of the 1880s: von der Ahe's Browns had managed to win only 68 games in the last two years combined. Von der Ahe had spent all of his million-dollar fortune on the franchise and his race track. At the mogul's trial, it was the testimony of Al Spink, his old business partner, that proved to be critical in the verdict against him. Spink testified that the former owner had let the city down, and the court ordered the humiliating public auction. There was one bad moment before the sale, at the National League winter meeting in New York, when Frank Robison and von der Ahe had to be restrained from coming to blows. Frank Robison did not attend the auction.[81] Later, "Paying their respects to the ruined owner, the new owners, Edward C. Beckser and Frank DeHass Robison, sent their very first complimentary tickets to Von der Ahe. He was too proud to accept it."[82]

The story of the Robison era had a sunny dawning after the dark storm. The Perfectos seemed to have been the only team in the League blessed with good weather, and the players readily worked themselves into playing condition in Hot Springs. The St. Louis pilot divided his roster into Tebeau's Tigers and Burkett's Brigadiers for the first intra-squad scrimmage.[83] The St. Louis columnist who was working for von der Ahe's sworn enemy Spink, welcomed the incoming regime by invoking extravagant terms of matrimony and resurrection. "Base ball has been resurrected in St. Louis," he pontificated, "and Tebeau and his team of championship caliber will represent it in the next National League race. This desirable change has been anticipated for months and its consummation completes the happiness of the local enthusiasts, who have been loyal to the game in the darkest days at Sportman's park...Tebeau's team is strong in all departments and figures on form to finish one, two, three in the pennant race."[84]

Ned Hanlon, in the same issue, predicted the pennant for St. Louis. In general, expectations were heady for the Perfectos in their debut season, as they were widely viewed as a kind of all-star team. After the season was lost, the team's underachieving finish was to be blamed on the man who was absent, Ed McKean, without due consideration of his debilitating health.

> When the old Clevelands came to St. Louis last spring there was not a base ball writer or manager in the entire land who did not pick them to finish in the first four, and the majority of them were of the opinion that first or second place would be theirs...Inside of a month McKean showed that it was all off with him, and Tebeau himself says that he can trace seventeen defeats caused by big Ed's failure to field properly.[85]

Baseball historians have recently condemned Tebeau for remaining too loyal, too long to shortstop McKean when the likes of George Davis and Bobby Wallace were available, but the manager's support was brutally withdrawn after the Perfectos disappointed in 1899.[86] "Tebeau attributes St. Louis' downfall to Ed McKean, whose collapse in Tebeau's opinion cost the Perfectos not less than 20 games."[87] Pretty damning words from an old comrade, considering an additional 17 wins that season would have comfortably ensconced St. Louis in second place and only a notch below preseason expectations. It would be more accurate to say the Perfectos "all-star" infield of McKean, Childs, Tebeau, and Wallace fell apart. Only third baseman Wallace performed as advertised, and Tebeau made the right move too late to make a difference in the season, benching McKean and shifting Wallace to short in a series in Philadelphia in

EIGHT. *Home on the Road (1897–1899)* 221

late August.[88] The *Indianapolis Star* remembered McKean as "gallant" in his acceptance of Tebeau's career-ending decision.[89]

But let's go back to the sunny start. Opening day for the Perfectos, April 15, against who else but the Spiders, attracted more than 16,000 fans to Sportsman's Park for what Reed Browning has aptly called "a game pitting the Robisons' A-team against their B-team."[90] Only one Cleveland player, right fielder and eighth-place batter George Bristow, had not ended the erstwhile season as a Brown; every man on the field for St. Louis had been a Spider six months before. The Spiders were no match for Cy Young, who breezed to a 10 to 1 victory. McKean, bating from the coveted third slot in Tebeau's lineup, went hitless. He was charged with an error but did turn a double play from short. "A cold windstorm handicapped the players ... after the first half of the fifth inning," provoking 10 errors from the teams, in all.[91] An enormous crowd of 18,000 came out the next afternoon—on a Sunday, which delighted Frank and Stanley Robison and confirmed the rightness of their recent decision-making—and got to admire Rhoddy Wallace's game-winning home run in Jack Powell's win.[92] (Another Sunday in St. Louis saw 26,000 turn out for a thrilling extra-inning victory over Cincinnati.) However, the mood was soon mitigated, as personal tragedy struck Frank Robison. Back in Cleveland, his oldest daughter died on April 27, so the Spiders home opener against Louisville needed to be rescheduled as part of a May Day doubleheader. Fewer than 500 League Park patrons paid to watch the ersatz Spiders renew their once blood rivalry with the Colonels. The *Cleveland Leader*, reflecting on the first week of baseball in Cleveland, wrote: "The crowds that have attended the game do not deserve that name—being simply stragglers."[93] One gate amounted to all of 125 customers. "Cleveland is a base ball cemetery," *The Sporting News* declared on May 6, and deadpanned the observation that second baseman Joe Quinn, the best player on the club, spent most of his time while in town visiting funeral parlors. Quinn worked as an undertaker off-seasons.

In St. Louis, the fans were hardest on Kid Childs, figuring him for their scapegoat, but nevertheless inconsolably disappointed in the Ed McKean they got in the bargain. The local *Sporting News* had little appreciation for its starting shortstop:

> McKean is exasperating. He takes his time and gets his man, but he calculates so nicely and makes the plays at first so close, that the nerves of the average crank give way every time the great shortstop handles a grounder. There is no apprehension when a fly falls in his territory for when "Bull" bellows: "It's mine," everyone is satisfied that he will deliver the goods.[94]

The same week in April, Charlie Zimmer was granted his release by the Perfectos so he could play for his hometown Exiles. McKean must have envied him. And yet, the once-feared slugger did show flashes of his former self, and the time-tested combination of McKean and Childs could still, on occasion, click. On April 22, McKean doubled across Childs with the winning run against Pittsburgh's tough Sam Leever, the Ohio school master. The hit came in the fifth inning of a come-from-behind, rain-shortened contest.[95] Tebeau persisted in batting McKean third in the lineup, and the Perfectos had won all five of their games at home, well on their way to taking nine of the first 10 in Sportsman's Park.

When Ed McKean made his return to Cleveland on May 9 as a Perfecto, the hometown Spiders were a miserable 3–15. The starting pitchers for the afternoon must have reminded some among the 1,500 in attendance of better days for Cleveland, and the brilliant duel between Cy Young and Jack Stivetts in the 1892 "world's series." Now Stivetts was attempting to resurrect his pitching career on a staff featuring Harry Colliflower and Crazy Schmit.

The St. Louis Perfectos club of 1899 was Ed McKean's final outpost in the majors. On paper, the roster seemed like an all-star team, but it finished in fifth place. (Top row left to right) Zeke Wilson, Charlie Zimmer; (third row) Jack Powell, George Cuppy, Frank Bates, Jack O'Connor, Lou Criger; (second row) Emmet Heidrick, Ossee Schreckengost, Oliver Tebeau, Jesse Burkett, Bobby Wallace, Ed McKean; (front) Cy Young, Cupid Childs, Jake Stenzel, Harry Blake, Bert Cowboy Jones (Library of Congress).

EIGHT. *Home on the Road (1897–1899)* 223

This day, Young and Stivetts kept the score tied, 1 to 1, until the eighth inning—McKean's triple was the lone extra-base hit by either team—the Perfectos prevailing in the end, 8 to 1. McKean saved his best slugging performances for his games against Cleveland this season, including the last three home runs of his career. His dramatic solo home run against Kid Carsey, with none out in the 10th inning, decided a May 12 contest in League Park (Cleveland's ninth consecutive loss at the time). It was the fourth time in McKean's career he had touched up Carsey for a round-tripper, and the last home run he hit as a shortstop. The previous game, he'd rapped out four hits in five at-bats. He continued his hot hand into the first game of the next series, on May 13 in Cincinnati, with a double and a single, but Dent Young lost.[96]

Then the season turned into a struggle for Mac just to stay on the field.

Time and again, he made the heroic effort to return to the team from his sickbed. *The Sporting News* took a wait-and-see position on June 3. "McKean resumed his position at shortstop in the afternoon game of Decoration Day and the big fellow showed no trace of the nervousness which he manifested for several days before his lay-off. He will have a chance to recover confidence in himself while on the [upcoming road] trip and will, it is hoped, find favor with the local fans on his return to [Cleveland's] League Park." But another writer in the same week's newspaper took a darker approach to remind, yet again, that "McKean is highly sensitive to criticism and ... takes a roasting to heart and becomes morose. His work is affected by it. The applause which a brilliant bit of fielding or of batting earns for him is only a reminder of the displeasure that has been vented on him" of late in St. Louis, the city of his growing discontent. His cause wasn't helped any, either, by the style of journalism of his day. The *Washington Post* charged that McKean these days could not cover as much ground as paraplegic Charlie Bennett, a tasteless and twice-cruel jibe.[97]

Second baseman Ed McKean ambushed Spiders pitcher Creed Napoleon Bates for a solo home run on July 6, with St. Louis behind in the seventh inning of an eventual Perfectos home win. That same day, back in Frank Bates' hometown of Cleveland, Stanley Robison announced the Spiders would not play in the city after the first of July; gate receipts for the 50-cent tickets, he claimed, were averaging the grand sum of $25 a game. In the three games against the Spiders over the two following days in St. Louis, Ed McKean enjoyed his last hurrah as a headlining slugger. On July 7, as the Perfectos swept the Spiders in a doubleheader, McKean hit safely six times, singling four times in the afternoon game off Ohio-born James Ulysses Hughey, although he did make one error playing second base. The twirler they called Coldwater Jim for his nerve in the box was good enough to lose 30 games in 1899. (A lesser man would have lacked the starts; he remains the last pitcher in a season to lose that many.) Two days later, on July 9, McKean hit the final home run of his career, a two-run blast off Crazy Schmidt, with St. Louis behind in the eighth inning. A Sunday throng of 11,300 looked on.

Apparently Schmidt hadn't consulted his book on how to pitch to McKean. Frederick M. Schmidt, a.k.a. Germany, was a prototype for the off-kilter left-handed pitcher soon to be canonized by Rube Waddell. Although he never won much at the big league level, stories circulated about Schmidt were legendary, many of them concerning the notebook. "When he was pitching in the big league he kept an account of the weakness at-bat of his opponents, setting them down in a small book, which he always carried with him on the diamond," *The Sporting News* told the story. "One day, when he had the Chicagos as opponents..., Anson came to the bat. 'Crazy' Schmidt looked at the big first baseman, then went down into his pocket, and, taking out his book, read 'Anson, base on balls.'"[98] Hugh Jennings offered this anecdotal portrait, in 1902:

> One time his teammates in Baltimore decided to have some fun with Schmidty. They were on Chesapeake Bay. They took his suitcase and hung it over the back of the boat so it would just be touched by the waves. In the morning it was learned that the suitcase had been lost. The rope had broken and the case had dropped into the water. Schmidt was frantic when he learned of it. His notebook was inside it. He wanted the bay dragged for it and was almost willing to jump overboard and dive himself. He couldn't remember what any batter wanted. He went right down from that time on. He never was any good after he lost his little book that he had spent years compiling.[99]

On another occasion, during Crazy Schmit's days in the Southern Association with Macon in 1892, a local citizen had him arrested, claiming that the pitcher had thrown a brick at him. Schmidt, acting as his own attorney (of course), pleaded innocence cum arrogance: "Your Honor, sir, that the man now lives is sufficient evidence that I, who have such splendid control, did not throw a brick at him."[100] After his fling in the major leagues, Schmidt went from keeping book on hitters to publishing an instruction book on the game; he is listed as the publisher, in Chicago, of an early edition of John McGraw's *How to Play Ball*. The book's subtitle, *Humor, Jokes and Statistics of Base Ball Players*, sounds like a book Crazy Schmit should have written himself.

It was in June, their team languishing in third place, when the fans grew tired of waiting for their Perfectos to round into championship form. Even then, some loyalists predicted fewer errors from the keystone partnership of McKean and Childs as summer weather came to the city on the Mississippi. *Sporting Life* speculated on its front page that "the long, wet, cold spell here

EIGHT. *Home on the Road (1897–1899)*   225

some two weeks ago seemed to have an awful [lingering] effect ... and as a result Burkett, then McKean, Childs and Criger all were forced to retire from the game [an 11 to 2 June 3 loss in Washington] in the order mentioned."[101] McKean's statistics are misleading—at middle of May, he ranked as the League's second-best shortstop for fielding average (.953), behind only Herman Long, and he was hitting a strong .315[102]—but his arm was weak, and his legs were crippled by charley horses. Eventually, the mental part of his game abandoned him, too. On May 21, he disgraced himself in front of the home crowd by failing to cover second base on a steal by George Davis, prompting Lou Criger to throw the ball into center field. The miscue opened up a four-error first inning in the late game of a Sunday doubleheader against the Giants.[103] Another McKean error, this one in the 10th inning after playing shortstop miserably all day, let in the Orioles' winning run in a June 1 game. Afterwards, the *Sporting News* columnist eulogized a McKean who "has lost his speed and ... does not hit as of old, and worse than all he seems to have 'quit on himself.'"[104] Under the unrelieved pressure of the transfer, the old Cleveland warriors were fighting themselves in St. Louis. It took only until early June for a frustrated Patsy Tebeau and a diminished Cupid Childs to break out in a public shouting match. During a pregame practice, "Tebeau ordered him to the bench and declared that he would show him how to play second himself" in front of the other players and fans who arrived early for a show before the show.[105]

Scrambling now, Tebeau made plans to use McKean at first base, a less demanding position in the infield, explaining that "his batting is needed and as soon as he gets his eye on the ball and gets accustomed to his new position, he will become a popular idol. His arm is not strong enough for a shortstop, and he is no longer to cover ground as he did two or three seasons ago."[106]

This alteration also meant that Tebeau would be his own utilityman and manage the team from the bench, where he was much less effective. The move was temporarily shelved when McKean was confined to his bed with a recurrence of malaria.[107] But when McKean returned to the team as the new first baseman, the experiment seemed to be working with mixed results: "Childs and McKean were under a cloud when the Perfectos picked up their bats and luggage and started East," *The Sporting News* duly reported on June 24. "Several times the spectators had gone at them vigorously and it really looked as if they were marked for a season's guying and roasting. Cupid was given the glad hand in true St. Louis style and McKean's reception was almost as warm." Both played good ball, McKean making several fine plays at first on badly thrown balls...." However, in a four-team Sunday doubleheader on June 25, with 10,000 St. Louis cranks looking on, Ed McKean went hitless and made two glaring errors at first base—glaring because they were the home team's only miscues of game two, and the lowly Spiders were the competition—in a long day when the Perfectos dropped both games. Finally, Tebeau benched McKean in favor of himself at first base.[108]

McKean was held out of action until coming back to play second base for Childs, and bat sixth, on July 2. It was in that game that he hit his last career home run, a drive into the right field bleachers at Sportsman's Park. At the time when he was still 24th in extra-base hits in the National League, both McKean and *The Sporting News* were writing the prologue for his imminent farewell from St. Louis:

> Big Ed's bat was for years a big factor in the Spiders' success...He is not any too well satisfied in St. Louis and would welcome a chance to go to Cleveland, but there is little prospect of his wishes being gratified. McKean is of the opinion that the Robisons should have left him and Childs in the Forest City and retained Quinn and Cross in St. Louis. "That pair of players are popular here, and Childs and I had our friends in Cleveland. This would have given both teams a better pull with the public and helped the patronage. I am not kicking, however, and am confident to stay or go where my employers can use me to the best advantage."[109]

Earlier in the month, Elmer Bates had lobbied to have McKean returned to Cleveland for a much-needed drawing card. "No one man that could be brought to Cleveland would attract more people within the gates than McKean," Bates reasoned. "He has a most extensive acquaintance throughout the city, and all his acquaintances are his friends and supporters. With Eddie at short the home team would be assured of at least 500 people per game." The friendly writer did, however, concede: "There is probably little chance of him coming here now that he is being tried at first. Tebeau has been anxious to direct the game from the bench for some time, and with a topnotch batter to send to first in his place will probably direct the work of his team from the side lines."[110]

Regardless of Tebeau's tweaks to the Perfectos starting lineup, the team didn't win. In Brooklyn, on July 11, at the onset of an eastern trip, McKean filled in at his old position when Tebeau sent regular shortstop Wallace to man third. Beside Bobby Wallace, who "played brilliantly ... some of his stops ... thrilling in dash and execution," *The Sporting News* reported that "McKean made a horrible mess of playing short," in the 11 to 10 loss, "and dissipated the hope of his admirers that he would regain his old form. His speed has deserted him and no one realizes his defects more than the once great shortstop."[111] In Boston, on July 18, Pat Tebeau restored the banished Childs to second base, and McKean to short, but did so only after Wallace had injured his back.[112]

The previous week, McKean had ended a game in Washington attempting to tie the score from third base at the head of a double steal with Tebeau.[113] This brings to mind the picture of the daredevil young Ed McKean dancing off third in his Youngstown days, 15 years gone.

McKean was at shortstop for the series in Brooklyn when the Perfectos dropped three of four games. A St. Louis scribe wrote an impassioned appreciation that turned out to be more like a final testament: "Ed had some awful bad balls to handle Thursday, and out of three chances made two errors, doing nothing with the bat. Some of the crazy know-nothing fans were unkind, and made life almost unbearable for the great short stop, and that night he begged Manager Tebeau to leave him out of the game for a while." Mike Donlin, one of the Perfectos' left-handed pitchers, was at short the next day. In the same August 5 edition of *Sporting Life*, Elmer Bates toasted his idol with a glass half full:

> Yesterday morning, I was at the Park and indulged in a little practice with McKean, Jack Crooks, "Scrappy Bill" Joyce, Lacy Crawford and one or two others, and of all the stops and one-handed pick-ups I ever saw, big Ed made the most remarkable. I am willing to stake anything on Mac's ball playing, and I hope Tebeau does not make the mistake of letting him go. He has been full of malaria and badly out of condition all spring and summer, but seems to be rounding to in good shape.

However, the end was not long in coming. McKean's last major league hit came in Boston, on July 20. He batted fourth in the lineup that day, going 1-for-4 off Vic Willis, and played an errorless shortstop. Cy Young got the win, 3 to 2. In St. Louis on July 27, sixth-spot batter McKean hit for the collar against Doc McJames, the last big league pitcher he would ever face. The box score for his final game shows one putout and two errors for the shortstop, in an otherwise forgettable 12 to 3 blowout at the hands of Brooklyn.

The Sporting News published its last word on Perfecto McKean on July 30: "McKean declares that he will rest for the balance of the season and start 1900 with a National League club. Big Ed is personally popular with the fans and it is their wish that all his hopes will be realized. He will not go to a minor league club, as he has a paying business in Cleveland." He and Charles Creighton had opened a saloon, at the corner of St. Clair and Seneca Streets, in January 1899.[114] The business was ironically located at the site of the first church building, dating back to 1829, inside the city limits. Instead of waiting for the inevitable, Ed McKean asked for, and was granted, his unconditional release by St. Louis, on August 7.[115] His last team photographs with the Perfectos show the elder statesman sporting a mustache and styling his ball cap into a kind of slouch hat. At the age of 30, the athlete had assumed the superannuated appearance of a man older than his years.

On September 2, *Sporting Life* reported that he turned down an offer to play shortstop for Chicago, but McKean, still in the throes of malarial attacks, was in no condition to respond.

For the first time since his release by Nashville, in the spring of 1885, McKean was out of baseball. Back in Cleveland, businessman McKean couldn't watch the Spiders play if he'd a mind to; by that point in the season, the hometown Clevelands were no longer scheduling games for League Park. It's clear that McKean still thought of himself as a baseball player—he didn't retire for another decade. Instead, like some ghost of lore whose death is so sudden that he lingers among the living for a term, he haunted the minor league outposts in town after town, descending gradually the circles of dim baseball afterlife, from Class A all the way to Class D.

"He was as steady and nervy a fielder as there was, and one of the game's brainiest players," John Phillips wrote in his late paean to McKean's ballplaying. "Earlier in his career, he was one of the timeliest and best hitters in the game."[116] Even in his abbreviated last season in the majors, Ed McKean had continued to produce at the plate, driving in a highly respectable 40 runs in 67 games. But his fielding had become a great embarrassment to him and an object of fan derision. Mac's life turned out to be short by modern standards, yet it might be said that he lived too long; long enough to see his legend airbrushed from Cleveland popular memory to be replaced by the image of a player gone to seed. If he bothered to follow the fortunes of the Perfectos, he may have found some degree of solace in the way the club was being run. For 1900, Frank and Stanley Robison followed up on their bad business decisions of 1899 with a classically wrong-minded bit of team engineering, uprooting an aging John McGraw from the East to play under the management of his eternal rival Patsy Tebeau!

It had all the appearances of a good business decision in the short run, unless you were the ruined Chris von der Ahe. The Robisons had stopped underwriting, with their own fortunes, baseball in Cleveland. As a result, the siblings realized a profit of $40,000 in their first season in St. Louis, their Perfectos attracting 100,000 more fans to Sportsman's Park than the Browns had been able to draw over the last two years combined.[117] On the other hand, the Cleveland Spiders suffered through the worst season in baseball history, and then disbanded. When Jim McAleer helped to bring a brand new American League franchise to Cleveland, that club had little to do with Ed McKean or the track record of the riotous Spiders. The story took one last twist, in August of 1899: upon McKean's return to Cleveland, a syndicate of businessmen proposing to hire him to manage the Cleveland franchise if the Robisons could be induced to sell, held days of conferences on the matter.[118]

EIGHT. *Home on the Road (1897–1899)* 229

On October 28, Elmer Bates found McKean umpiring a Sunday game between two amateur clubs at Scenic Park, in Rocky River, 10 minutes from the former player's home. The event had attracted 4,800 baseball fans, reigniting McKean's enthusiasm. "I have not one word of fault to find with Frank De Hass or Stanley Robison," he assured the reporter. "They are liberal, high-minded gentlemen, but the fact remains that the people here in Cleveland will not go out to see a club that is owned and controlled by them play ball. It isn't a revolt against base ball: it is a revolt against conditions." He had grown tired of enduring the whispers around baseball about Cleveland's inability to support a major league team. McKean called, that bucolic day in the sun, for the formation of a new league to compete against the National League monopoly for 1900.[119] In December, Bates revealed that McKean, who was "one of the heavier stockholders" in the newly opened Businessmen's Athletic Club, had been approached by city fathers "to open a book to receive subscriptions" toward bringing an American Association club to Cleveland.[120] The next time Bates caught up with McKean in Cleveland, just before Christmas, he was informed that the shortstop "has cut out wrestling in favor of hand ball this winter."[121] He didn't stay out of the sport entirely, though, as *Sporting Life* on December 31 reported that McKean had settled for managing the career of wrestler Tom Jenkins.

The first two years of the twentieth century saw Ed McKean variously employed in and about Cleveland. He maintained his partnership in a local saloon and tended bar himself when he wasn't on the road with Tom Jenkins or refereeing professional boxing matches.[122] McKean was behind the bar one night in the last week of August 1900, when he "stopped a race riot in Cleveland and saved a negro from serious injury," according to *Sporting Life*.[123] McKean had been a boxing referee since February 15, 1898, when he officiated the Eddie Connolly–Tim Kearns fight in Cleveland. He refereed at least seven more bouts, around the city and also in Akron, Canton, and Massillon.[124] *Sporting Life* quipped, after the Joseph Burns–Jerry Smith match of January 6, 1900: "Ed McKean found that fight followers can hoot and howl louder than base ball fans. 'Mc' recently gave a decision to the man that 99 per cent of the crowd thought had been whipped. The hisses he received made him imagine a Goose Trust [wildlife preserve] had been organized."[125]

McKean's major league ergon was finished, although he had never officially retired as a baseball player, and indications are that he harbored hopes of a comeback after regaining his health. If his legs and arm were no longer shortstop caliber, his mind and his bat were sound and valuable. Chances for McKean's return received a boost, now that he was no longer a liability for St. Louis, from Patsy Tebeau, who gift-wrapped a ready-made excuse for the shortstop's poor fielding in 1899: "Tebeau declares that Childs and McKean were shy on ground-balls last season because of accidents from bad bounding balls during practice at the [Hot] Springs." Pebbled gullies had formed from rainfall on the infield, according to the manager's defense of his players' defense.[126]

In spring 1900, McKean aimed to make the roster of the Cleveland Lakeshores, a team in the first year of operation of the minor-league American League. The previous season in the Western League, the franchise had operated out of Grand Rapids by owner Tom Loftus and manager George Tebeau, both old McKean acquaintances. For 1900, the Grand Rapids club was transferred to Cleveland, and, by March, new owners Charles Somers and John Kilfoyl had brought back Jimmy McAleer to manage the team and play a little outfield. McAleer gave McKean permission to work out on the field at League Park, the scene of their glory days with the Spiders, but that was as close as McKean came to playing for the Cleveland Lakeshores. Instead, his friend and the club decided to go into the season with Charley Buelow at shortstop. In the weeks before the McAleer hiring, Elmer Bates had loudly banged the drum, instead, for two other ex–Spiders: "Either Eddie McKean or Charlie Zimmer would be acceptable to the people of Cleveland as captain [playing-manager] of the new team. Both players are immensely popular here and both understand the game from A to Z."[127] McKean suffered another humiliation when his old Baltimore nemesis Bill Hoffer made the Lakeshores pitching staff. When the Cleveland club was part of the upstart major-league American League for 1901, it dusted off the old nickname to call itself the Cleveland Blues. Ed McKean must have felt ostracized by those in charge in the front office. The mutual parting of the ways was to last the remainder of his life.

Although the creation of the Lakeshores put an end to the local attempt to resurrect the old American Association in Cleveland, McKean didn't abandon his attempts to get back into baseball in some capacity. Well into the 1900 season, the rumor circulated that McKean "has been practicing hard in Cleveland, and doubtless will get back in the game in that city."[128] Beginning in July, *Sporting Life* kept readers updated on McKean's progress, writing that he "says he will join New York as soon as he has worked off a little more flesh,"[129] and he was still training hard to get down to playing weight, apparently in response to a fresh contract offer by the Giants.[130] *Sporting Life* continued to be friendly toward the old shortstop. In its pages, in December, W.A. Calhoun ventured the opinion that Ed McKean and other 19th-century greats "could practice a week on the old rules...[and] make monkeys of any team of League stars under the same."[131] Another time, McKean was remembered as "the strongest player in the business" before Ossee Schreckengost appeared on the scene.[132]

Eight. Home on the Road (1897–1899)

Ed McKean remained a standard of comparison for many, even during the great caesura of 1899 to 1901.

McKean learned, in early February 1901, that W.C. Bryan was organizing a minor league team in Washington, and he wrote to him at once requesting a job, indicating "that he will be back to his old playing weight, 170 pounds, by the time the season opens," according to *Sporting Life*. Bryan, who had briefly managed McKean at Nashville 16 years before, said he'd play McKean at first base.[133] The team, along with many of Will Bryan's machinations, never materialized. Instead, Washington joined Cleveland that season, as charter members of the major-league version of Ban Johnson's repackaged American League.

Ed McKean finally got his call to return to baseball, early in 1902.

1895 Temple Cup: October 7, Game Four

"Let's fight til six, and then have dinner," said Tweedledum.

If anything, Baltimore cranks had grown increasingly hostile to the Spiders—a team that mirrored their own—over the seasons. Of course, Baltimore's Union Park had the reputation for being a tough road venue, firmly established by McKean's rookie year. The August 20, 1887, issue of *The Sporting News*, for example, printed a sketch called "Two Pistols Please" on the matter. It went, in full:

> "I'll take two of those largest revolvers you showed me yesterday," said a young man with false tooth in a Washington avenue gun store yesterday.
> "Self-acting?" asked the clerk.
> "If you please; and just throw in three boxes of cartridges."
> "Any thing else?"
> "Keep hand grenades?"
> "Yes; how many do you want?"
> "Half a gross of the largest size."
> "What else?"
> "A steel breast-plate, if you have it, and you might toss in a small hand-axe."
> "Must be going to hurt somebody, eh?"
> "Not necessarily. And while you are about it just wrap up a repeating rifle with a gross of explosive bullets."
> "Going after [king of the con men Tom] O'Brien?"
> "No, no. Got any torpedoes?"
> "Don't keep 'em. What are you going to do with all this truck?"
> "I've just hired out as an umpire in Baltimore," said the young man with false teeth, "and I want to prepare myself for some close games."

In Baltimore, McKean and the Spiders played game four in the eerie penumbra of their total eclipse on the field. The contest, the only Cleveland loss during the series, was already decided by the second inning, when Baltimore scored the first run off Nig Cuppy, who got the start apparently without consideration of what the cold weather might do to his injured thumb. A fresh Duke Esper, making his first start in this Temple Cup, shut out Cleveland, allowing but two Spiders to venture as far as second base all day. No Spider enjoyed a memorable day on the field. Oddly enough, his team's one loss in the series was also the only game in which McKean went errorless. Coming into the game, the head-to-head matchup between elite shortstops McKean and Hugh Jennings was in Cleveland's favor. Although both men already had four base hits in the three games played in League Park, McKean was the superior performer with the glove, ranging far in the infield to collect 28 chances to Jennings' 21. In this game, Jennings caught up with his rival, for the time being—he put together three hits in four at-bats, doubled and stole a base, fielded four chances flawlessly, and participated in the second double play of the whole Cup competition so far.[1] One wonders if McKean was trying too hard to pull a pitch into the right field swamp that was created by nearby Brady's Run?

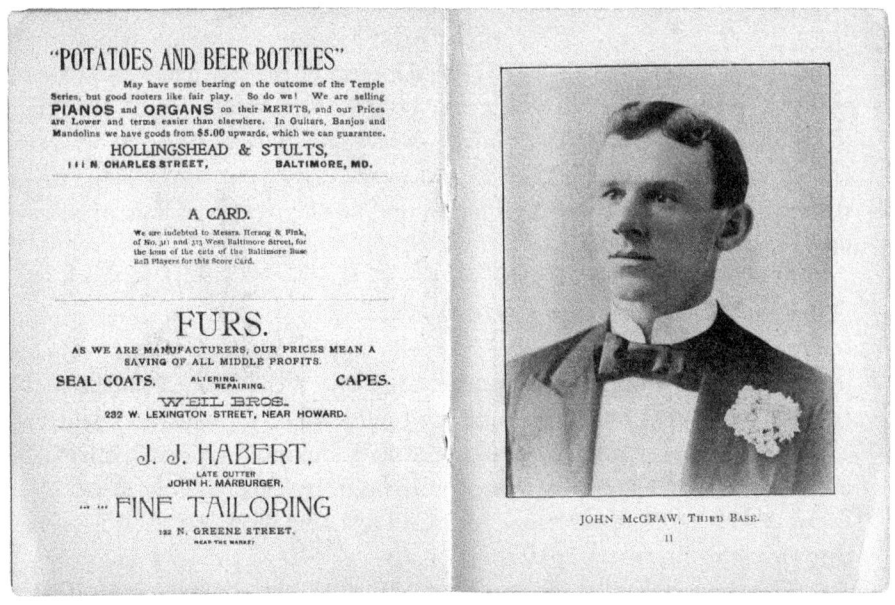

Pages from a souvenir program, printed at Baltimore's Union Park, for the fourth game of the 1895 Temple Cup. The ad for a local business, advocating "fair play" over "'POTATOES AND BEER BOTTLES,'" appears opposite a portrait of a guileless-looking John McGraw (Robert Edward Auctions).

But what is most remembered about that dark day in baseball lore is the hot reception the Orioles crowd gave the Spiders. Enraged Baltimore cranks rioted, mobilized by the accounts they'd read in the local papers about the abuse their Orioles and scribes had suffered at the hands of the Cleveland fans, and fueled by journalistic images of their favorites, McGraw, Kelley and Robinson, being pelted by debris.

Baltimore cranks were a frustrated bunch. They had rooted their team on to another National League pennant, only to stand by while the Orioles dropped seven Temple Cup games in a row, dating back two years and counting. And the thinking fans among them, upset by Ned Hanlon's choices of starting pitchers in the three losses in Cleveland, were clamoring for the well-rested lefty Charles Esper, whose assortment of curveballs had been effective against Cleveland's left-handed hitters during regular play. (Duke Esper would be finished by 1898, winning 101 and losing 100 in his career; perhaps his most memorable pitch was the one he threw to Roger Connor for his 100th home run.) After the third game, *The Sporting News* observed of Baltimore, "The local rooters have been very much disgusted with the bad judgment shown by the management [while] in Cleveland in refusing to put Esper in the box against the Spiders, and to-day's game fully justified them. Esper is the only Oriole pitcher who has shown any skill against the Forest City team." Worse, "The young America of the city had been stirred up by the reports of the bad treatment to which the champions had been subjected in Cleveland, and determined" on revenge.[2] No citizen was foolhardy enough to challenge the likes of Ed McKean or Jack O'Connor to a fair fight—their revenge would occur according to the classic precepts of mob psychology.

Outside Baltimore's Carrollton Hotel, before game four, police were obliged to push back a crowd so the Spiders could board the team omnibus to Union Park. The vehicle became a slow-moving target for a rain of hand-launched missiles; humiliated players had to lay on the floor of the bus and cover themselves as best they could with duffle bags, bat bags, and fielder's gloves. At this point, assorted items in the malicious mob's grocery-list arsenal included, depending on what source you read, rotten apples, eggs, dirt clods, sticks, peanuts, balls of paper, and rocks. All accounts agree that potatoes were thrown at the Hibernian Spiders.

The potatoes landed, each one a racial slur, a backhanded slap at the Irish Orioles, as well. In retrospect, the attack worked much like the centerpiece at the post–Cup banquet in Cleveland did, signifying the cultural defeat of both clubs in the course of a few days. At the time, the Baltimore *American* invited its readers to shrug it off in a bit of verse:

> Temple Cup,
> 'Ninety-four.
> Didn't get it—
> Awful bore.
> Cup again,
> 'Ninety-five.
> *Potatoes flew—*
> *We survive.*[3]

Game time was a respite from fans behaving badly. Ticket-holders were relieved of their bushels of eggs at the gate, and inside the ball park club president Von Der Horst, John McGraw, Joe Kelley, and Boileryard Clarke took turns imploring the stands to keep the peace. The umpires on the field, Tim Keefe and rough-and-ready Tim Hurst, were a formidable force for maintaining order through the two-hour contest.

In the words of Albert Mott, the Baltimore correspondent for *Sporting Life*, "The men [Spiders] were somewhat cowed" from the bus ride to the park; as a result, "the Cleveland club, while it played good, scientific ball, did not put up the aggressive game that it usually does when there is an entire absence of fear as to consequences." Mott claimed the Spiders "were frightened" by a few boys, who threw "missiles" at them on their route to Union Park, among the otherwise pacific host of 7,000 to 10,000 in the stands and outside the park. In his view, the only distraction originating from the bleachers during the game was a lonesome cowbell.[4] Less biased witnesses reported fanatics before the game throwing waves of fruit, paper balls, peanuts, eggs, bricks and rocks. It has been established that other spectators showered the visitors from the stands with bits of brick in Cleveland's half of the first inning, until Patsy Tebeau turned hisses into cheers in the next inning by stepping out of the batter's box and tipping his cap to the crowd. Of course, game time was only the calm eye of the storm; the distracted Spiders had to play nine innings knowing the way they came in the park would be the way they would leave. As Jerry Lansche puts it, "The only thing the police feared more than a Baltimore loss was a Baltimore victory."[5]

Following their defeat, Cleveland players and writers exited the park by a different door, but the crowd caught on. Before long, the 10 policemen in charge of protecting them were overwhelmed by a mob of 1,500 surrounding the team omnibus. When the rioters ran out of fruit and eggs, they threw fresh volleys of bottles, rocks, sticks, bricks, pieces of metal, and eventually the players' own bags of clothes and bats. It took McKean and his mates a terrifying five minutes to make the 15-foot walk to the bus. It was another dicey 10 minutes before the police could push the frenzied mob aside enough to hazard the re-boarding. Even though the attackers had exhausted their ammunition, the moment turned increasingly anxious as someone held the harnessed horses (already spooked by the flying debris), while another one tried to unhitch the team and strand the players. Remarkably, only one rock seems to have struck its mark before the Clevelanders fled down Huntington Avenue at top speed. The three rioters arrested by the beleaguered cops were fined $9 apiece that same evening by Justice Murray, down at Central Police Station, and given a lecture.[6]

In the aftermath, newspapers across the country roundly condemned the unsportsmanlike conduct of the roughs in both cities, and in Baltimore writers called openly for an end to Temple Cup play. Writing the day following the fan riot, the Baltimore correspondent to *The Sporting News* declared:

> There will be no more Temple Cup contests. This seems to be the impression among the prominent base ball men here from other cities and the local patrons of the game. While John M. Ward and other authorities on base ball, who have been attending the Temple Cup series here, are not openly expressing any opinions on the matter at the present time, it is obvious that they as well as the base ball writers who have witnessed the games in Cleveland and Baltimore, are convinced that the bitterness shown and ugly demonstrations made in both cities will have a damaging effect on the national game.

The writer went on to quote the Baltimore *American*'s assertion that:

> We hope for the sake of base ball and the reputations of cities that this will be the last year of the Temple Cup series. The events in Cleveland and the proceedings that followed the opening game here illustrate the bad effects of a contest which is really little more than a money-making opportunity for the players of the two clubs...The natural climax of the playing is the winning of the championship, and to add a second competition is to discount and confuse the whole fight.[7]

The embarrassment was real, but all the talk was premature. Come next fall, the Baltimore Orioles would contest the Cup one last time before William Chase Temple retired his hardware.

This night, the Orioles cranks were sensing a three-game sweep in the making that would send the series back to Cleveland for a deciding seventh game. In the safety of a hotel room inside the Carrollton, Jesse Burkett was displaying a keepsake from his recent cross-town trip, an 18-ounce piece of slag thrown into the bus. Cupid Childs, the single casualty, nursed a bump on the head.

Downstairs, in the lobby, Patsy Tebeau had already regained his composure, if he ever lost it, and was consenting to a postgame interview. "One swallow don't make a summer, and we'll get the cup yet," he famously quips. As an afterthought he added, buoyed by the confidence of his own remark: "Young will pitch tomorrow, and we think the trophy will come our way, of course."[8]

Nine

The Hero of Rochester Revisited (seasons of 1902, 1905–1906)

> There are no second acts in American lives.—F. Scott Fitzgerald

The calendar had turned to March and the Rochester board of directors, under the leadership of acting general manager William T. Callahan, still hadn't hired a manager for the 1902 Bronchos. The front office had been left in disarray in the wake of manager Al Buckenberger's return to the major leagues with Boston, after he'd brought to Rochester two Eastern League championships and a second-place finish in three seasons. The names of Joe Quinn and Hal O'Hagan had topped the owners' short list back in January.[1]

Joseph J. Quinn, born in Sydney, Australia, began his career as a standout defensive infielder in 1884. He'd played against McKean's Spiders as Boston's starting second baseman in the 1892 "world's series" and, with Baltimore in 1896, he hit safely in five of the six Temple Cup games. A Cleveland Spider in 1899, Joe Quinn led National League second basemen in fielding percentage. He came recommended as the loyal company man, putting together two standout seasons playing for Chris von der Ahe and then Frank Robison, while taking his lumps managing their horror-show teams, the 1895 St. Louis Browns and the 1899 Cleveland Misfits. It turned out that Quinn chose to go instead to Des Moines, where he was the player-manager for 1902. Patrick Henry O'Hagan was touted in the Rochester newspapers as a baseball man "schooled" by Buckenberger, having played on all three of the beloved manager's Bronchos teams. The owners did bring him back during the 1902 season to captain manager McKean's club and fill in for him at first base. After McKean's resignation, O'Hagan was promoted to playing-manager.

February brought rumors that Rochester's search had narrowed to two

NINE. *The Hero of Rochester Revisited (1902, 1905–1906)*

other candidates for the position, Joe Bean and Count Campau.[2] Playing for Rochester the season before, Bean had been the best shortstop in the league, a distinction Ed McKean had earned 15 years earlier. Unlike his predecessor, Bean could never parlay his success in a career; his only time in the big leagues would be two months with the 1902 Giants. Charles Columbus Campau once led two leagues in homers in one season, starring in 1890 for International League Detroit and St. Louis of the American Association. The Count was a regular outfielder on Al Buckenberger's 1899 and 1900 teams and held on in the minor leagues for two more seasons. At the start of 1902, Campau caught on with Binghamton in the New York State League; his intention to sign with Rochester made the headlines in late April, but he wound up leaving Rochester shy a middle infielder when he jumped to the Giants, joining Bean.[3] Rochester learned late that The Count was not to be counted on. Or counted out—by season's end, the Charles Capmau had wound up with the third-best batting average in the Eastern League, as the shortstop of the Providence Grays.

Finally, on April 16, a week before the Bronchos' opening exhibition game, Will Callahan hired McKean.[4] It had been Callahan who brought the unknown Eddie McKean to Will Bryan at Nashville, and he was gratified to at length reacquire his services. McKean arrived in Rochester with all of two days in which to meet his players at Culver Grounds and prepare for the first exhibition. As it turned out, Mary MacLane wasn't the only one in 1902 who made a Devil's bargain.

The *Rochester Democrat and Chronicle* wrote admiringly, on April 15, about McKean's initial practice: "Manager McKean handled the willow for a considerable time. It's true the balls pitched to him were not particularly puzzling, yet the mere demonstration that he could line them away out to the pennant pole with seemingly little effort is most encouraging." F. Scott Fitzgerald would famously remark that Americans are never granted a second act, but Rochester must have seemed the place for resurrecting a career, with smiles all around the ball park that day and even club president Callahan reportedly "beaming." When McKean originally came to the Flour City, Frank Bancroft had plucked the no-name kid from the rubble of the Providence Grays franchise because his Maroons badly needed a shortstop. Now "the famous shortstop" was returning after his struggle with malaria to see if he could manage a team and still play on the field. Callahan would have further associated Ed McKean with the memorable International League pennant race of 1886. A long-time Rochester baseball figure, Will Callahan had himself played infield for various Rochester minor-league teams and pitched for the Bronchos in 1890, the year his 15 wild pitches tied a record held by many.

Naturally, Rochester baseball had changed in McKean's absence. Culver

Park, newly constructed when the 17-year-old first arrived in town, was now a relic; the club's affiliation switched long ago from the International League to the Eastern League; and the Rochester Maroons had become the Bronchos. It may have struck Ed McKean, when he entered the batter's box to take those practice swings, that the most startling change was the design for home plate; before 1902, through all of McKean's previous seasons, home plate had been a square, like any base.

Over the last number of seasons, locals had taken to calling the team The Champions, but the Rochester team McKean inherited had lost six star players to the National League from last year's championship club.[5] Not a single career .300 hitter was to be found on his roster.[6] McKean had landed himself in the middle of an austerity program following two years of overspending that had brought Rochester a pennant in 1901. The rookie skipper was up against the likes of Toronto's brain trust (president Ed Mack and manager Ed Barrow) in one series and Buffalo's (president-manager George Stallings) the next. McKean didn't precisely fit the bill for his new job, either. Rochester had wanted a manager who could fill the club's need for a second baseman; McKean was not among the leading candidates largely because he was beyond his days as a middle infielder. He hadn't played at any position since the aborted 1899 campaign. Then, there was the concern over his playing shape: working out with Tom Jenkins, McKean reportedly weighed "not over 200 at present" in March.[7]

Going into the season, McKean and the Bronchos were banking on the left-handed bat of Jack Hayden. An all-round athlete good enough to quarterback the Canton football team, Hayden had played in the Philadelphia A's outfield for part of 1901. He was bright, too; the year after Zane Grey's graduation from the University of Pennsylvania, Hayden began studies toward what became his own degree from that school of dentistry. Unfortunately, Jack Hayden proved to be mostly a distraction during the 1902 season and a threat to McKean's leadership. When his young left fielder was among five players who still hadn't reported to camp by the third week of April, McKean had to have reflected upon his own year of indecision, 1890, when he jumped and flopped teams as a young talent.[8] But McKean was the manager now, and his best hitter was scuttling the team's chances to compete. The depleted and underpaid Bronchos roster was to remain unsettled all season. Joe Bean declined to re-sign with the club for the low salary that Rochester offered, and his replacement at short, Lee Demontreville, brother of the big-league shortstop and a future major leaguer himself, jumped McKean's team only to return in July to play second base. McKean could thank the baseball gods for Harry Blake, the former Spider, who was steady in center field and at the plate for the Bronchos all season. Soon enough, the clutch-hitting star of Cleveland's

NINE. *The Hero of Rochester Revisited (1902, 1905–1906)* 241

Temple Cup would be out of baseball altogether, and working as a butcher. Ironically, Jack Hayden, manager McKean's problem child, turned out to be a manager himself, with the minor league Louisville Colonels from 1912 to 1915.

Ready for prime time or not, the Rochester Bronchos staged their first exhibition game on April 15, against George Weidman's independent team.[9] Since being run out of the National League as a result of the Cleveland-Louisville riot of 1896, Stump Weidman had umpired in the minors and managed the Rochester Brownies, the precursor to the Bronchos. The Rochester native would be dead from throat cancer by 1905. Ed McKean slugged a double and a home run in six at-bats, scored three times, and stole two bases—one on a double steal he'd called for. McKean's homer came in the seventh inning, when his rocket to "extreme right" rolled in "cold mud" for an inside-the-parker. He also acquitted himself well at first base. Rochester's other hitting star for the practice game was a pitcher known as Herky Jerky. Elmer Horton, from Hamilton, Ohio, went 12–18 in 31 starts for the Bronchos, and managed in the New York State League before and after his stint with Rochester. The following afternoon, in another training game, this one against the University of Rochester club, McKean batted himself cleanup and settled in at first base, a local paper applauding McKean's "all-around play."

Ultimately, though, the Bronchos played their exhibition schedule like the haphazardly concocted team they were, picking up a few more games in Rochester and then touring New York State League cities. On April 18, Rochester was shut out on three hits—McKean was 0-for-3—at the hands of two Binghamton pitchers in a miserable road game that attracted only 200 bystanders. McKean's team salvaged one win in the three-game series before moving on to Schenectady, where they lost to the Dorphians on April 22. That afternoon, Rochester kept the score even until the eighth inning—but the final score was 10 to 2. McKean, playing this contest at second base, still had no errors in the preseason. The next day, Schenectady turned back Rochester again, this time, 8 to 3; McKean, playing short, made his first error and went hitless to boot. Rochester did not lose on April 24—the game was called a tie on account of high wind—although McKean made another error and no hits. The Bronchos were granted a second reprieve when their exhibitions in Johnstown were cancelled due to muddy conditions on the playing field. The way home to Rochester and the start of the championship season went through Utica, where they were easily beaten, 7 to 3, on April 26. There, McKean did emerge from his doldrums to go 2-for-4, with a double, but he made two more errors at shortstop. Just 48 hours before his team's season opener, and his own managerial debut, McKean was in Cleveland to secure the services of a middle infielder in the aftermath of Joe Bean's jump to the

Giants. He did sign somebody named Andrus from the Ohio State League, a player he knew from the Cleveland sandlots, who never saw action for Rochester. After a dismal exhibition season, the Bronchos were the surprise of the Eastern League with their fast start out of the gates, taking advantage of a schedule which had them play mostly at home early on.

Ed McKean made it back to Rochester for opening day, May 1, 1902, to bat fifth and man first base. A fine crowd of 2,500 cheered the hoisting of the 1901 Eastern League pennant beyond the Culver Park outfield, at the culmination of elaborate pregame ceremonies. Two hours before, a parade of carriages had carried, from city hall to the ballpark, Eastern League president P.T. Powers, ex–Rochester president George W. Sweeney, Montreal club president Sheher, umpire Thomas B. Kelley of Brockton, and former manager Al Buckenberger, who had come back for the occasion.[10] Manager McKean chalked up his first career victory as pitcher Dan McFarlan and the Bronchos persevered over the Royals on that gala day. First baseman McKean worked his second walk off Montreal starter Holly Souders, after two Bronchos had singled in the ninth inning, and came around to score the winning run on Harry Blake's base hit. Rochester won the next day on the strength of McKean's base running and three hits and made it three in a row over Montreal, becoming the league's only undefeated team in the early going, on May 3. McKean made two hits in four times up and added a stolen base on a nifty double steal in the 9 to 7 win. But, when Ed Barrow's Toronto Maple Leafs came to town, the Rochester team's patchwork defense was exposed. McKean made one of his team's six errors (his first of the regular season), when he threw a good yard over the head of his shortstop, Ike Francis, and allowed two Toronto runners to score in the 5 to 1 defeat.

Following a rainout, Rochester turned the tables on Toronto, winning 3 to 1 against former Baltimore and Temple Cup star twirler Duke Esper on May 7. This time, the Bronchos were guilty of nary an error in a contest highlighted by what the *Rochester Democrat and Chronicle* deemed "a great play between McFarland and McKean." Rochester finally lost a road game, playing on May 8 to make up for the rained-out game, 6 to 2 in Toronto. McKean's double was the Bronchos' only extra-base hit that afternoon; he also singled. In his May 9 return to Providence, the scene of some of the worst games from his early career, McKean led his charges to a thrilling 6 to 5 win before 2,000 in the Rocky Point Park stands, Providence's Sunday-only ball park. The big first baseman had a hit and a sacrifice, and he scored a key run when Rochester rallied with four runs in the tenth inning. The extra-inning victory enabled the Bronchos to reclaim first place, by percentage points.

Rochester was quick to relinquish its lead in the standings to Buffalo.

NINE. *The Hero of Rochester Revisited (1902, 1905–1906)* 243

On May 12, in a 5 to 4 loss in Worcester, Ed McKean's finest hitting exhibition for the whole season—he rapped out a home run and a double in four trips to the plate—was wasted. Undaunted as always, McKean continued his hot hitting the next day versus the Worcester Hustlers, finishing up 3-for-5, with a double. A May 14 win pushed the Bronchos back into first place for a time. Worcester happened to be the hometown of Jesse Burkett's wife, and the former Spider would in a few years own and manage the Worcester team. Joe Delahanty was the Hustlers' regular second baseman in the 1902 season, and its best pitcher was Cy Falkenberg, who would one day make his name with Cleveland. Back home in the friendly environs of Culver Park, McKean enjoyed a 3-for-4 game at-bat, including a double, when Rochester hosted the Newark Sailors on May 16. After the game, the 9-and-5 Bronchos were once again atop the league standings.

Wayward Jack Hayden was manager McKean's problem child on the 1902 Rochester Bronchos. Within 10 years, Hayden jumped through careers as major league baseball player, dentist, and football quarterback to manage his own team, the Louisville Colonels (Library of Congress).

The first hint of trouble came in an article appearing in *The Sporting News*, on May 17, in which the *Rochester Democrat and Chronicle* was quoted: "McKean shows a disposition to fight for everything. He jaws at the umpire and when told to shut up he says 'No, I won't shut up,' and the ex-member of the famous old Cleveland Spiders, which won one-half of the double championship season of 1892, keeps right on until he has had his say out." Warned *The Sporting News*: "The umpire'll get him before long." Indeed, retribution was not long in coming. The June 7 issue of *The Sporting News* reported approvingly that "the directors of the Eastern League have begun a crusade against rowdyism." Managers Stallings of Buffalo and Barrow of Toronto had already been fined $50 each for assaulting umpires, and "a special police officer is to be employed at each park to remove from the grounds any player or players who use profane or indecent language." Conspicuous in its absence was any mention in the newspaper of Rochester's McKean, whose managerial style was modeled after Patsy Tebeau's burn-the-boats attack.

McKean's overachieving Bronchos drew 3,300 fans for a May 18 game at Culver Park to cheer on their team, which stood alone in first place with a record of 11–5. McKean had hit safely in every game save two, the season opener and the May 5 loss to Toronto. As rain and bad weather interrupted the schedule (May 19 was the day when every Eastern League game had to be called for rain), the Bronchos' surprisingly good start to 1902 turned into heavy going. May 21, on a wet field in Jersey City, Rochester scored six times in the ninth, but still lost to the Skeeters, 14 to 10. McKean racked up two more hits, and scored twice, against the team with the nickname that could only remind him of the origin of his troubles with malaria. The series against Jersey City was a reunion for McKean, since Cupid Childs, who had regained his strength after his own bouts with malaria, was at second base for the Skeeters. Childs had also resumed his batting stroke—he hit .290 in 33 games—and his kicking habit, as well. A week later, in a game in Utica, Childs was so discombobulated when an umpire named Johnson called a runner safe to rule out his double play, he struck the ump and "went into a clinch" that had to be broken up by players from both sides.[11]

Toronto celebrated Victoria Day, on May 23, by hosting Rochester for a doubleheader as part of the festivities for the late queen's 83rd birthday. McKean managed only one base hit in seven at-bats, and the Bronchos lost two close ones, 5 to 4 then 4 to 3. Meanwhile, Buffalo won both ends of its doubleheader to relieve Rochester of its claim on first place. That week, the Bisons kept right on winning while Rochester was helpless to improve in the standings, idled as they were by rain and wet fields in Montreal. And when the northern sun deigned to make an appearance and the Bronchos finally got back on the field, the team mustered only a split in a May 30 doubleheader in Montreal. The Bronchos lost by a run in the ninth inning that morning, in a game in which McKean, on base after singling in the first inning, was thrown out easily at the plate on a recovered wild pitch. The last day of May was Rochester's final one atop the Eastern League standings, on the strength of a shutout over Montreal by Herky Jerky Horton. McKean, who suffered through an 0-for-3 game at-bat, had already dropped himself to sixth in the order. His club's thin roster afforded the manager few lineup options beyond local talent. Lately, McKean was trying out the University of Rochester's John Dillon behind the plate. Dillon eventually appeared in 58 games for the Bronchos that year, and recorded two extra base hits.

Entering June, Rochester was still in second place when they returned home after surviving three weeks—15 straight games—on the road, going 8 and 7. *The Sporting News* remained a fan of the Bronchos' playing-manager. "McKean's case proves that a player's work is not always impaired by a long absence from the diamond. Besides hitting in great form, the veteran is playing a splendid game at first. Then, too, he is exhibiting a marked capacity for management. Everything considered, Rochester was most fortunate in securing the services of the veteran."[12] "McKean is getting good results out of the material at his command and deserves great credit."[13] It was if *The Sporting News* writers were getting their information on a time delay. In fact, by the first week of June, Ed McKean's extra-base power had abandoned him, and the team had fallen into third place, mere percentage points above fourth-place Providence. McKean was starting to feel the pressure. In a lopsided June 4 loss in Toronto, the team's third straight defeat, McKean protested the game on the basis of umpire Snyder's calls. The day following, Rochester slipped down into fourth place, after losing in Buffalo; McKean's two errors made it three for the slumping first baseman in two games. His team lost again to Buffalo, on June 6; the fading Bronchos loaded the bases three times but failed to score after the Bisons turned double plays.

When Rochester's 18–16 record made them a fifth-place team by the middle of June, Ed McKean reached his boiling point. It happened when his team was playing at home in a June 14 twin bill that it split with Toronto. In the 5 to 1 win that morning, when Jack Hayden failed to score from third on a teammate's grounder, the manager "didn't hesitate to criticize the left fielder most forcibly." After the blowup, McKean returned his mind to the game at hand (the local paper noted that a feature of the afternoon loss was Ed McKean's bare-handed catch of a high-and-wide throw from his second baseman); the disaffected Hayden reacted to his public dressing-down by quitting the team.

McKean responded by calling off an exhibition game with Schenectady, which had been scheduled for June 15, to travel with his team, minus leadoff hitter Hayden, directly to Montreal to prepare for their next game. Forced into yet another doubleheader because of rainouts, Rochester dropped both games in Montreal on June 16, by a disconcerting combined score of 16 to 6, to sink below .500 for the first time. McKean could summon up but one hit in eight at-bats; worse, he was responsible for three errors that day. Apparently, news of the Bronchos' recent demise was slow to reach Baltimore readers, who remembered the great McKean from the Temple Cup battles. The *Baltimore Morning Herald* for June 18 credited McKean with "making a marked success as manager of the Rochester Eastern League team." Two weeks earlier, the newspaper had written, at the very time of his hitting slump, McKean "is hitting the sphere as hard as ever. 'Grandpa' is now working at bag No. 1, and doing quite nicely."[14] But Grandpa had no remedies to offer his boys as Rochester plummeted from first place to fifth in three weeks during June. *The Sporting News* cited Hayden's desertion, "dumb coaching" on McKean's part, and undisciplined base running as reasons for the precipitous downturn.[15] Two weeks later, *The Sporting News* correspondent Sweeney pointed to the Fourth of July home game as the low point to date in the Rochester season.[16]

When the Bronchos record bottomed out at 24–28, Ed McKean took himself out of the lineup for July 6, choosing to play pitcher Dan McFarlan in his stead. John Dillon and Elmer Horton were tried at first base in subsequent games, as McKean was in and out of the lineup, with no good result. By now, the freefall in the standings had taken Rochester down to sixth place, barely above seventh. While Buffalo was commanding huge crowds (a record 18,000 attended Olympic Park for a Memorial Day doubleheader against Toronto, featuring two teams in the heat of the pennant race plus the artistry of Duke Esper), the fans in Rochester were staying away from Culver Park. "That Rochester fans are not evincing much interest in the team is evidenced by the attendance at the afternoon game [on] Independence Day," observed *The Sporting News*. "With no counter attraction and an ideal day for ball playing, only 3,500 witnessed the game ... after the highest type of minor league ball for three years the fans do not relish the in-and-out article which they have been served with the past month."[17] Still, the press held fast behind the Bronchos manager, maintaining: "Little blame can be attached to McKean, as he is, doubtless, getting the best work possible out of the material he has charge of."[18]

The Bronchos did mount one brave rally, for McKean and fans, around the end of July. In the glow of a 5 to 4 win at home in extra innings over the team ahead of them in the standings, Providence, and their despised shortstop Joe Bean, the Rochester "deserter," the *Democrat and Chronicle* wrote, on July 30, that "the Rochester forces were finally marshaled by McKean and led to a glorious victory." McKean's two base hits, a sacrifice, and a walk offset his error in the infield, and Hayden, the other jumper, was back in the Rochester outfield to make a circus catch. Next day, the home team Bronchos drew a good house of 2,826 and survived 11 innings to win 9 to 8 over the Grays. One of the momentarily reprieved playing-manager's three hits was a double, pulled on a rope into right field.

Rochester started play in the dog days of August by beating up on Newark, the doormat of the league, but did not improve in the standings. And McKean was a rumor at first base. He would be finished with the Bronchos, both as player and manager, by the middle of the month; however, the old warhorse made sure to depart at his best. At Providence, on August 11, McKean singled

NINE. *The Hero of Rochester Revisited (1902, 1905–1906)*   247

and doubled. In an August 13 game in Worcester, the beleaguered manager, in a gesture of good sportsmanship, allowed the Hustlers to substitute a runner for their catcher, Pat Crisham, who found he could not play through an injury. (Crisham had spent the 1900 season with the Cleveland Lakeshores.) Player McKean also doubled in the Worcester game. His Bronchos fell short in the ninth inning in Providence the following afternoon, losing 6 to 4, but McKean played a clean first base and singled and doubled. On August 16, in his last game with Rochester, Ed McKean ripped two doubles in four at-bats out of the number six hole in the order, scored a run, and added a sacrifice. However, the game was Rochester's third straight loss in Providence. Afterward, McKean did not return with the team to Rochester, deciding it was best to tenure his resignation rather than be fired. The reason he cited was business in Cleveland that he had to personally attend to. His record with Rochester amounted to 44 victories against 53 defeats. Fan-favorite Hal O'Hagan took over as manager, on August 18. In his debut game as the Bronchos playing-manager, in Jersey City's West Side Park, O'Hagan pulled off an unassisted triple play at first base. It would be the one memorable event of his time as manager of the Bronchos.[19]

After McKean's exit, the fans of Rochester gave up on the team. When Jersey City shut out the Bronchos, on September 18, an intimate gathering of 47 (including the ushers) looked on from the Culver Park stands.[20] Hal O'Hagan's team finished the season at 57–76, seventh of eight Eastern League clubs in the standings. McKean's replacement wasn't an upgrade at first base, either. In 38 games for Rochester, the Prince Hal of the minor leagues recorded one extra-base hit.

Returning to active status after a two-year hiatus, Ed McKean had, at the very least, proved he could still hit. His .314 batting average ranked 13th best in the league. He and the enigmatic Jack Hayden were Rochester's only .300 hitters. McKean appeared in 78 games, logging 92 hits in 293 at-bats and scoring 31 runs.[21] Official league statistics for players appearing in less than 100 games that season are incomplete, but a hand-count from newspaper box scores credits him with at least 12 doubles and a home run. McKean's fielding statistics were less impressive. In 77 games at first base, he was charged with 20 errors, for a fielding percentage of .976. His record indicates 763 putouts and 42 assists.[22]

Ed McKean's whereabouts can very often be ascertained from a perusal of the sports pages of northern Ohio newspapers. The *Elyria Chronicle Telegram* of May 11, 1903, tells us that McKean was playing first base on an Elks Club team from Elyria organized by Billy Smith. The team's first game was scheduled for May 17, against the Sandusky Elks.

And we can glean from the Canton *Repository* that McKean operated the independent Canton Marines for 1904.[23] Semipro baseball, directed by the National Association of Independent Base Ball Clubs, was operating viable developmental teams like the Canton one across the country. He apparently formed a partnership with William L. Delaney, who had been a Spiders teammate for the last six months of the 1890 season. Delaney had previously managed Canton teams, in the Tri-State, Inter-State, and Ohio-Michigan leagues, on and off from 1887 through 1895. Bill Delaney managed the team for McKean and filled in at second base. McKean's Marines were talented. The pitching staff featured Samuel Smith, the younger brother of Pirates catcher Harry Smith, and curveballing Buck Ehman; shortstop Henry Maag also played for the Canton Athletic Club, the same organization that fielded the football Bulldogs; and first baseman Bert Biery, who, like Maag, would graduate to the minor leagues.[24]

The Marines played an ambitious schedule of games against touring teams like the Nebraska Indians, the Cuban All-Stars, in addition to teams around Ohio's Western Reserve region.[25] Canton's Mahaffey Park, also home field for the Bulldogs, could handle crowds of 5,000 to 6,000. While McKean was associated with Canton, the Cleveland Naps played two "home" games on Sunday in Mahaffey Park, on May 10 versus Detroit and June 21 against Boston; another Sunday, July 24, the Brooklyn Dodgers beat the Canton Marines 5 to 2, in an exhibition in Canton.[26]

In early July, McKean flirted with playing again in the minor leagues. *Sporting Life*, for July 9, 1904, reported that Toronto of the Eastern League had signed him to a contract. The Maple Leafs were in next-to-last place at the time, with a record of 29–35, and badly in need of help. However, Toronto finished last that season without McKean. It turned out that Ed McKean did resuming his playing career, catching on with Colorado Springs of the Western League to start the 1905 season.

McKean gave to the minor leagues his last five playing years, a period of peregrinations across the baseball map which has been left unvisited by historians. Between the ages of 33 and 39, he saw action with 10 teams in eight cities and small towns, never once finishing a season with the team he'd started with. In one two-year span, between 1905 and 1906, he was a member of five different teams. McKean's minor-league odyssey never brought him back to the majors, if that was ever a goal. Perhaps it was enough for the ball player, at this stage of his career, simply to swing the bat in competition and drink with teammates afterwards, as the summer sun slowly set in places like Colorado Springs, Little Rock, Dayton, and Bay City. In McKean's era, any number of former major leaguers were extending their playing days in the expanding

Nine. The Hero of Rochester Revisited (1902, 1905–1906)

minor-league system, but his multiple-team years (twice his clubs were transferred; other times, he was released) destabilized the regular migrations of the baseball season, spring to summer to fall to offseason, that had ordered McKean's life since adolescence.

The Colorado Springs Millionaires represented for McKean a second chance, both to manage his own team and to play shortstop at the Class A level, one step below the majors. Ira Belden, who was an outfielder for the Denver team at the time, joked about the wild, if not Wild West, conditions he remembered at Boulevard Park during McKean's tenure in Colorado.

> The hottest time I ever had on a ball field was in Colorado Springs. A ball was batted out into my field and fell into a nest of hornets. As I reached for it, one of the disturbed tribe struck me under the eye, and I went down. When I got up I was running for the club house and doing a better sprint than you ever saw me do after a ball. Some of the other players ran over to get that ball I was running away from, and—say, you should have seen them start for the fence when the hornets got after them.[27]

Hiram Rogers had named the team in consideration of the town's recent history during the gold rush of the previous decade. Colorado Springs had become known as The City of Millionaires with 35 of the 100 wealthiest men in the country making their fortunes in the Cripple Creek mining fields nearby.[28] City of Millionaires was an apt nickname for the boomtown but not for the team. The Millionaires, alas, were broke.

It was April Fool's Day when Ed McKean signed to play shortstop for Colorado Springs.[29] General manager Jack Tanner and team president Thomas F. Burns had been reluctant to make McKean their manager; his dual appointment as playing-manager came as a backup measure. The hometown *Gazette* obviously didn't care to know much about the new old shortstop from the east, either:

> Much is expected of Ed McKean, and should Burns fail to land Gatins, he will probably captain [i.e., manage] the Millionaires this season. Last season McKean ran an independent team of his own in Canton, Ohio, and the year before [sic] was manager of the Rochester, N.Y., team of the Eastern League. He is about 35 years of age [sic] and is married, although Mrs. McKean does not accompany him. McKean has an enviable record with the stick and during the nine years [sic] that he played in the National League he never fell below the .300 mark [sic]. He is a "lefty" with the wagon-tongue. McKean plays at short and the first bag but will probably play short for the local bunch.[30]

Johnstown, Pennsylvania, native Frank Gatins played short for the Eastern League Newark Sailors that season, creating the opening for McKean.

As had been the case with his hiring by Rochester three years previously,

McKean was handed the job of playing-manager for Colorado Springs late into spring training, when the sports pages were reporting the competition—George Tebeau's Denver Grizzlies, especially, and the Des Moines Underwriters, Omaha Rourkes, Sioux City Packers, and St. Joseph Saints—already rounding into form in exhibition games. Some who knew Ed McKean from the old days were openly skeptical about his chances to play again, much less at short as the Millionaires were projecting. The *Youngstown Vindicator*, of April 4, 1905, yawned condescendingly: "Old Ed McKean is back in the game. He is to play for Colorado Springs. He is as big as an elephant."

McKean's arrival would have been especially welcomed by Harry Blake, a second-year veteran of the team, who'd played for Jimmy Ryan the year before in Colorado Springs; also, Tom Delahanty, who played a few games at third base beside McKean on the 1896 Spiders, was to be McKean's double-play partner. George Tebeau, of late one of the Western League's magnates and the owner of the Denver Grizzlies, had preceded him in Colorado by years. The Millionaires had assembled a team of veterans for 1905 to complement McKean, Blake, and Delahanty. Pop Schriver, the longtime catcher now at first base, was McKean's age; batterymate Archie Stimmel's nickname was Lumbago. Catcher Tom Messitt, at 30, was the youngest of the experienced hands. On the other hand, at least three players on McKean's roster were 19 or under. One of the younger ones, a 21-year-old infielder called Dutch Knabe, later fashioned a solid major league career. The front office hadn't found a replacement for Bunk Congalton, the Western League's best hitter, when he graduated to the Cleveland Naps.

Age and experience of its players notwithstanding, the club's unsurmountable problem was revenue. Although Colorado Springs charged fans an exorbitant 65 cents to enter the park, nothing could overcome the city's small market. Colorado Springs, with only 21,085 residents, was by far the smallest venue in the Western League; rivals Denver, St. Joseph, and Omaha all drew paying fans from populations over 100,000. In fact, in all of professional baseball, only three towns—Shreveport and Memphis in the Southern League, and Amsterdam in the New York State League—were less populated than was Colorado Springs in 1905. The second-least-populous town in the Western League, Sioux City, was also finding it difficult to compete on the field and at the box office. And yet, Colorado Springs paid out $14,000 in player salaries, the same amount expended by four established teams in the league. Denver's payroll was only $1,000 more than the figure Colorado Springs was saddled with.[31]

McKean and his Millionaires rang in the 1905 season in Omaha, on April 26, with league president O'Neill in attendance.[32] By June 1, the team was in

NINE. *The Hero of Rochester Revisited (1902, 1905–1906)* 251

last place, with a dismal 10–24 record.³³ The year's one priceless play came for Millionaires fans in the fourth inning of a May 8 game at Boulevard Park, when third baseman Otto Knabe threw to Tom Delahanty to pull off a triple play, but the home team lost as usual that day, this time 7 to 5 to the St. Joseph's Saints. McKean's double, off former Canton Marines pitcher Elwood Eyler, was the only extra-base hit for Colorado Springs.³⁴ Through the month of May, the Millionaires regularly featured its keystone combination, second baseman Delahanty and shortstop McKean, batting second and third.

At the same time Colorado Springs was losing two games to every one win, owners of Class A ball clubs, at war with the major leagues over raids on minor-league rosters and unfair signing practices, were meeting in New York to form an alliance. *The Sporting News* warned ominously of "the apparently hopeless condition of Colorado Springs" in the race for the pennant, although "the efforts Burns is making to put together a band of ball players indicates that he intends to figure in the outcome." "Colorado Springs has been losing in interest and attendance and the coffers of the Millionaires will suffer unless there is an immediate and marked improvement," the paper underscored a week later. "The summer season is just commencing and the tourist is the man that makes the crowds at the Springs."³⁵ From a modern-day perspective, it seems a dubious enterprise for the small-market team to have to count on tourists for its financial life. *The Sporting News* was quick to make George Tebeau the scapegoat for the failure in Colorado.³⁶ Prior to the season, the paper was railing against what it termed the "Blight of Tebeauism," meaning his "hoggishness" in signing all the good players and owning multiple teams. Owners Burns and Tebeau had been at loggerheads for the last five years, ever since the Colorado Springs silver financier had bought out White Wings' half-interest in the old Western League Pueblo club and brought it back to his town, bragging that he'd booted Tebeau out of the Western League.³⁷ At length, Tebeau lost his American Association Kansas City club but bought his way back into the Western League—and into Burns' gunsights—with Denver.

It is evident, however, that it was Burns who was culpable for having spent so much of his fortune (not to mention attention) trying to outmaneuver Tebeau that "at the close of the last race [for the 1904 pennant], he ... sold his stars and signed a cheap team, which has been a consistent tail-ender." The end results would be that Ed McKean fell victim to Burns' cutbacks and vengeance; *The Sporting News* had its designated villain in Tebeau, who it sneeringly identified as "Chairman of the National Board of Arbitration, Representative of the Western League on the Governing Board of the Association of Class A Base Ball Leagues, Louisville-Kansas magnate, Half-Owner of the Denver Club and Ball Players' Friend, etc."³⁸; and the newspaper made the unlikely Jack Tanner its wounded hero. "In spite of the heroic efforts that are now being made by the club-owners and President 'Tip' O'Neill, of the Western League, to hold the circuit intact," *The Sporting News* informed its readership on July 8, "Jack Tanner, who recently completed a month's sentence as [general] manager for the Colorado Springs team, does not believe that the 'administration entity' of the league will last over another season." Tanner had authored an open letter for the *Denver News*, in it specifying that "baseball angel" Thomas Burns had spent $40,000 of his personal fortune to keep a team in Colorado Springs over the last season and a half before he got out, selling the club to a syndicate of local businessmen.[39] In any event, President O'Neill re-relocated the club to Pueblo, from hence it had come, and organized in that city a stock company worth $30,000. He acted swiftly, reducing monthly salary costs to $1,000, releasing players (including Ed McKean), and trotting out Tanner, who had no previous baseball experience beyond his front-office desk, to manage the team on the field.[40]

The cut-rate team under McKean started bad and never panned out. The Millionaires struggled to 22 wins against 48 losses before he was fired as a manager, and released as a player, after their July 13 game. McKean was not in the lineup that afternoon. Forty-eight hours later, the Colorado Springs Millionaires became the Pueblo Indians.[41] Jack Tanner steered the Indians to a next-to-last finish, with a record of 52–92 on the season (30–44 in Pueblo). As for Ed McKean, his batting record for Colorado Springs was as dismal as the won-loss record. The midwestern slugger never seemed to adjust to playing baseball a mile above sea level. He appeared in just 22 games, officially batting 94 times. Among his 18 hits, McKean counted but three extra-base hits (all doubles), eking out a batting average of .191 for his efforts. He slugged .223.

In wake of the great disappointment of Colorado, McKean returned to Ohio—to play baseball! Demonstrating the exceptional athlete's short memory for failure, he rebounded quickly by agreeing to terms with, but never playing for, the Evansville club in the Class B Central League.[42] The playing-manager of the Evansville River Rats, Jimmy Ryan, was the man McKean had succeeded at Colorado Springs, and Cap Anson's old center fielder had subsequently settled in to make good in Indiana. (Ryan wouldn't lose interest in acquiring McKean and finally landed his man the following season.) McKean did wind up playing in the Central League in 1905, filling a void at second base for the Springfield, Ohio, team. Springfield's manager, Jack Hendricks, was so eager to part ways with Bill Cooley, his team captain and a fielding star at second base, that he sold him to not one but two teams, South Bend *and* Fort Wayne.[43]

Mac was no babe when he joined the Babes for a game at Grand Rapids, sending home a 19-year-old Springfield town boy, Frank Donahue, who'd been filling in manfully at second.[44] The team's best pitcher was 20 years old and fresh from Wabash College: Kickapoo Ed Summers was destined to win 24 games as a rookie, in 1908, for Hugh Jennings and the pennant-winning Detroit Tigers. For the final two months of the season, shortstop Champ Osteen, a veteran at 28 years old, was brought in to partner with McKean on a much-improved Babes double-play combination.

McKean was at least seven years the Springfield manager's senior. Jack Hendricks was in his first full-time season as a playing-manager. After taking degrees from Butler and Northwestern, he'd practiced law in Chicago for the previous 15 years, keeping baseball as a sideline. Hereafter, he would make baseball his career, managing in the minors and majors for 24 years. Hendricks is best remembered at the helm of the Cincinnati Reds teams of the 1920s, at the time of Frank Bancroft's tenure as business manager. Branch Rickey had given Hendricks his start, signing him to a two-year contract to manage the Cardinals in 1918, but before Hendricks could return from office duties in France during World War I, Rickey had replaced him with himself.[45] It was natural for John Hendricks to surround himself at Springfield with college players, including Osteen (Erskine College), Bill Friel (Niagara University), and Gene Curtis (West Virginia University). For McKean, the clubhouse environment must have seemed as rarified as the nearby campus of Wittenberg College (or, in another way, his high-altitude baseball experience in the Rocky Mountains), but Hendricks settled matters by making McKean his captain.

As it turned out, college boy John Hendricks and the Babes proved to be something of a throwback to the glory days of Patsy Tebeau and the Spiders. In mid-August, at home in Hilltop Park, the manager and his catcher tag-teamed umpire Cy Rigler over a call at the plate in a close game, resulting in players and fans swarming the field.[46] McKean may have found added consolation in joining a team whose regular catcher, Owen Dennis Ignatius Shannan, was in possession of the most lyrical Irish name in all the Central League. As an added attraction, McKean would have been amused to compete against a team from Canton, which had joined the league soon after his own year with the independent entry in that eastern Ohio city. All in all, Springfield was a good fit for McKean after the Colorado Springs debacle. Springfield, Ohio, at the turn of the century, was a railway hub, which would have reminded McKean of his hometown, and his father Martin would easily have identified the city as home to International Harvester, the manufacturer of Champion farm machinery. Just that spring, the baseball world might have briefly taken note of Springfield favorite son Dick Harley, a 30-year-old rookie who pitched nine games with the Boston Beaneaters. Surely, the whole world was sitting up to notice Springfield's Lillian Gish, who was dancing in New York City on a bill with Sarah Bernhardt.

It was McKean's decision to leave a losing team in Colorado to join a last-place Springfield team.[47] They were struggling at 12–27 on June 10, and, a week after his addition to the lineup, the Babes were still floundering at 22–38. But then, the season began to improve for Springfield. Entering play in August, the team rose as high as sixth place for the first time all year, improving its overall record to 44–52. The high-water mark came on September 2, when the team had clawed its way to a game below .500, having won 63 and lost 64. Ed McKean had had a most-valuable-player effect on the Babes. During his three months with the team, Springfield played at a 41–26 clip, and the owners realized a profit for the year.

In a season that ended on a positive note, the ancient fielder provided fans some highlight moments along the way. McKean won a July 7 game over Evansville with "a lucky home run" off Charles McCafferty. What the reporter meant by luck is unclear, although it's hard to picture McKean at this stage of his career legging out an inside-the-park homer.[48] McCafferty's whole season was one of mixed fortune: he won 20, and he lost 20. In Springfield, on July 24, McKean launched two doubles and Sidney Merryman, the club's 20-game winner, shut out South Bend.[49] Somehow, McKean had rediscovered his power stroke in 1905, getting lucky at least seven more times in 1905. He and Jimmy Ryan tied for the league lead in home runs with eight, McKean's biggest number since 1898.[50] McKean's .273 batting average (84 hits in 307 at-bats) was good for 10th among batters appearing in as many as his 83 games.[51] It was the best average on the Springfield team in that year of the pitcher in the Central League, when eight pitchers won at least 20 games. All this, even though McKean had had to battle through "a leg so sore he [could] scarcely walk," in August.[52] (For the record, Bill Cooley, the player McKean replaced on the Babes, finished ninth among league hitters, with a .275 average. Both Cooley and Mac came in well behind Paddy Livingston, the Cleveland, Ohio, catcher, who enjoyed his best year, hitting .312 for champion Wheeling.) After the season, *Sporting Life* named E.J. McKean one of its "stars" at second base for the Central League.[53]

When the news that McKean had been elected to a seat on Cleveland's city council reached Springfield, John Hendricks "fear[ed] that the big fellow will retire, and bemoans the loss of his star." The manager admitted that "McKean has slowed up but little in fielding, but can hit a ball right on the nose," but added, "I was told that Ed was hard to handle and a bad man for a team. I found him a gentleman, a fine fellow and a veteran who could show the youngsters a lot of things."[54] Ed McKean was one of 11 players Springfield placed on their reserve list for the upcoming season.[55]

NINE. *The Hero of Rochester Revisited (1902, 1905–1906)*

Alderman McKean did return to baseball in the spring of 1906—but it was in response to Chief Zimmer's call to help with the Southern Association team in Little Rock, where the old catcher had purchased a block of stock and appointed himself playing-manager.[56] Mac would rejoin his longtime comrade in arms and, for a time, do battle against the inevitabilities of aging. His interlude in Little Rock, McKean's second crack at the Southern Association (originally called the Southern League) after an absence of 21 years, turned out to be nearly as brief as his stay in Nashville. These would be the last games McKean would play as high as Class A level. This time, he had figured in the thinking of the front office from the very inception of the team— McKean had agreed to a contract with Little Rock the middle of February[57]—although as late as February 3, he was one of three applicants still in the mix for the job of managing the Akron Rubbernecks team in the Class C Ohio-Pennsylvania League.[58] (That job went to Walter R. East, who went on to play for Little Rock and Nashville two years down the road.) In January, the *Daily True American* had gotten word in Milwaukee that McKean and Amos Rusie were lined up to manage teams in the Wisconsin State League for 1906.[59]

The thought of playing a summer campaign in Little Rock was a novel one; McKean's previous experience with Arkansas was as a place to go for spring training. Little Rock wouldn't come into the consciousness of Cleveland baseball fans until after 1908, the season 20-year-old Tris Speaker led the Southern Association hitters in average, runs scored, and doubles, and outfielder putouts and assists. McKean did recognize plenty of familiar faces on Southern Association teams; most carried a veteran from the National League about McKean's age who was trying to hold on to his career. Pitcher Ted Breitenstein would win 21 games for the New Orleans Pelicans; Red Ehret had caught on with the Montgomery Senators; Farmer Vaughan, the old catcher, was the Birmingham Barons manager; Erve Beck, who had been the original second baseman for the American League Cleveland Blues, performed for the Nashville Volunteers; and Bobby Gilks, now 41 years old, was a Shreveport Pirates outfielder. A season before, Chief Zimmer had managed the Philadelphia Phillies to a disappointing seventh-place finish and played his last games in the majors. For 1904, the Spiders alumnus had been a National League umpire. Now, charged with making a team in Little Rock, he was quick to bring in McKean to join himself and veterans Frank Killen (who was trying a comeback that spring), Klondike Douglass, Jackrabbit Gilbert, King Brady, Doc Carney, Ed Hickey from Cleveland, and minor-league journeyman Pat Meaney.[60] It was a spring roster laden with players in the autumn of their years.

When March 18 came around, McKean was one of four Little Rock Indians to report early for training camp.[61] He painfully worked his way into shape in the exhibition season, and even contributed a couple of significant base hits along the way. His was the only hit, a scratch single at that, to break up Pirates rookie lefty Eddie Karger's no-hit bid after five innings, on the last day of March. The cleanup hitters for the two squads that game in Hot Springs were Honus Wagner and Ed McKean; Charlie Zimmer was one of the two umpires.[62] Two weeks later, "Chief Zimmer's Indians, headed by that ancient Alderman, McKean," shut out the St. Louis Cardinals at Little Rock's Travelers Field. The correspondent for *Sporting Life* noted it was St. Louis who made the season's first kick, against the umpire in that contest, sore from two consecutive losses to the Indians.[63] The first Indians win came on March 27, in a game when they were outhit by the major league team, 10 to 4, but took the game on a wet field by a run, 3 to 2. The managers had to come up with umpires before they could play the second game; Chief Zimmer chose teenaged outfielder Beals Becker, while St. Louis manager John McCloskey chose second baseman Pug Bennett. Becker's decisions preempted any chances the Cardinals had of winning that day.[64] David Beals Becker later played in three World Series but was known to be so sensitive to hometown heckling that he played best on the road. Due to March weather conditions in Little Rock, described as "raw and chilly and the grounds wet and unsafe for any of the boys to let themselves out to any great extent," the team got in only eight exhibition games, with "very little practice of value."[65]

When the regular season arrived, the Indians turned out to be so underprepared that the great Chief Zimmer's team didn't have an experienced catcher to put behind the plate, his own arm being bum.[66] The Indians were losers of 14 of their first 16 games, 19 of their first 22, and already a cinch to finish in the basement.[67] By the end of May, Little Rock occupied last place in the league, with a record of 10 wins against 30 defeats. The team's lone all-star was first baseman Klondike Douglass.[68] Box scores show Zimmer trying unsuccessfully to find a spot in his order for his second baseman's bat—he hit McKean third in April, fifth in May, fourth then back to fifth in June.[69] There was nowhere on the field to hide his over-the-hill glove. Batting in the third spot, McKean had three hits in his first two games, as Little Rock split their home series with New Orleans. The contests were exciting, both decided in the eighth inning, and encouraged the home fans to expect more of the same. *The Sporting News*, on April 21, reported: "Ed McKean is landing on the ball in his old-time form." But he also made an error at second in his first game as an Indian, and two more over the next half a dozen games.

McKean enjoyed one of his best days in a Little Rock uniform, doubling

NINE. *The Hero of Rochester Revisited (1902, 1905–1906)* 257

Chief Zimmer, despite his nickname, was not a Native American. A leader on a decade of hard-drinking, quick-fisted, foul-mouthed Spiders teams, he was quiet, slow to anger, and never known to take a drink. A non-smoker, he endorsed and sold his own brand of cigars. Although he remained loyal to the National League during the Brotherhood player revolt, and caught a record number of games that season, he later worked with John Ward to organize a players' union (Library of Congress).

and singling twice, in a 2 to 1 loss to Memphis, on May 7. The Egyptians pitcher that day was southpaw spitball artist Glenn Liebhardt, whose 35 wins set an all-time Southern Association record that season before his call up to join a Cleveland Naps staff anchored by Addie Joss.[70] After a miscue in a May 14 game, McKean halted a three-game error streak and immediately went on a 7-for-14 hitting tear, beginning with a 3-for-4 performance against Birmingham, on May 22. It was a rare Little Rock victory.

With the Indians' record worsening (11–34), Zimmer was forced to jettison more starting players from his original 14-man roster; this included the hard task of telling Mac that he was being released.[71] On May 28, McKean went 0-for-4 with an error in his last game for Little Rock, against Montgomery. According to *The Sporting News*, "E.J. McKean was released because he did not cover enough ground, though he was batting well. Age has not dimmed his batting eye."[72] McKean did average a hit per game as a Little Rock Indian. In 140 at-bats over those 35 games, however, he slugged an irrelevant .314 on the basis of seven doubles and a triple to go with 27 singles. His production amounted to 44 total bases.

He washed ashore at Evansville, the Indiana city situated downriver from Louisville and Cincinnati on the old National League baseball circuit he knew so well. The Evansville River Rats, losers of 11 of their last 14 games and 21–28 overall, fell into last place in the Central League standings on the day they signed McKean.[73] The inheritor of second base did not pay immediate dividends. Jimmy Ryan inserted McKean into the second spot in his batting order for his debut, two days after his last appearance for Little Rock, in a June 11 home game at Bosse Field—with the result that McKean was held by O.B. Scott without a hit in six at-bats, as Evansville lost to Wheeling, 4-to-3.[74] He went hitless over his first 11 plate appearances for Evansville, although the team did begin to play better with him at second, reaching the .500 plateau at the start of July (31 up and 31 down) for the first time all year.

Ed McKean had finally caught up with the man he'd succeeded as manager at Colorado Springs, making it to Evansville on his second try. Ryan had coveted McKean's bat—the River Rats badly needed a hitter besides his capable self—at least since he'd tentatively signed Mac only to lose him to Springfield last year. Jimmy Ryan, like McKean, grew up Catholic; he launched his career at Boston College and Holy Cross and developed into the superstar leadoff man for the famous Chicago Colts teams. In the 1888 season, Pony Ryan led the National League in hits, doubles, home runs, total bases, and stolen bases. Also like the young McKean, Ryan was an all-round athlete. On July 28 against Detroit, he was the winning pitcher in a game in which he hit for the cycle; his 22 career leadoff homers were the record till Eddie Yost finally broke it in 1959; he remains third all-time in assists by an outfielder. Jimmy Ryan was a truly heroic character—while Chicago's West Side Grounds was ablaze, on August 5, 1894, he and Walt Wilmot hacked through a barbed wire fence to let 1,600 fans escape the burning grandstand onto the field. Evansville's playing-manager had led the Central League in batting for the season before

NINE. *The Hero of Rochester Revisited (1902, 1905–1906)* 259

McKean's arrival. McKean would have been pleased to know that Frank Cross, the youngest of Cleveland's three baseball-playing brothers, had played that season for Ryan's River Rats.

And yet, Ed McKean never settled in as a River Rat. It seems he'd been brought in by a manager who was already falling out of favor with the front office, and Mac was gone again in a month, like a rental bat. Club president John Walker and the Evansville ownership undertook a selloff, starting with the sale of pitcher Jim Freeman, the best overall player in the Central League, to the Chicago White Sox. Eventually, the directors axed Jimmy Ryan in favor of left fielder Tom Letcher, the pride of Bryan, Ohio, charging that "Ryan's actions on the field have been strenuous as regard to patrons and players. In many instances when criticized openly at a game he would become angry and would make rude comments." Jimmy Ryan told *Sporting Life* another version of the breakup: he'd left Evansville to get out of the way of a $20,000 damage suit brought against the club by Charles Erdman, a traveling salesman from Louisville, whom Ryan had rousted from the grandstand.[75] At any rate, McKean fell victim to the same administrative housecleaning, during a period when he probably should have been on the sick list. According to *The Sporting News*, "McKean has been suffering in the past few weeks from sores on his arm as a result of playing."[76] McKean followed upon his manager's dismissal with his own letter of resignation from the club, on August 8, announcing his intention to return to his neglected business interests in Cleveland.[77] Twenty-two-year-old Charlie French, hailing from Indianapolis, succeeded McKean at second for the River Rats; the mid–July pickup hit .175 for the season.

McKean probably didn't mind putting Evansville behind him. Due to the overbearing presence of Jimmy Ryan, he'd had to suppress his instincts as a natural-born team leader, a loss both for him and the team. McKean probably had something else in mind if he read what *Sporting Life* reported, on July 21, as a positive development: "The Evansville bench is credited with being the best behaved outfit in the Central. Not once have they been fined or any member benched this season. This is perhaps due to the management of Jimmy Ryan who, it cannot be denied, is the cock of the walk with that bunch." In short, on Jim Ryan's team, only the manager was allowed to kick and vent. The actual statistical tale of Ed McKean's month with Evansville is obscure, since President Dr. Frank C. Carson's official Central League averages combine his performance in Evansville with his performance in Dayton. Perhaps that is best after all, for Dayton, the team that claims him next, is a happier story for Ed McKean.

When Ed McKean came to play in Dayton, Ohio, so few had witnessed man's first airplane flights that even around the Wright brothers' hometown nobody much believed in the historical feat. Not many Daytonians had witnessed a home game at Fairview Park that year, either. In 1906, the Dayton team was even less stable than the Wrights' early gliders—the front office had experimented with four managers by the time McKean was given the pilot's job. Even then, ownership acted indecisively. McKean was originally signed as a player, and the popular Tom McKinley was allowed to continue to manage and play on the team through the last week of July. Second baseman and manager-elect McKean had to stand by as Vet fans stopped a game to present the outgoing manager with a $65 watch in his presence.[78] When McKean was finally appointed, he became the last and most successful of Dayton's five managers on the year.[79]

Since the Fourth of July, sixth-place Dayton had been the team trailing Evansville in the standings; when McKean replaced McKinley, Dayton was struggling with a record of 46 and 56. In a late–August surge overseen by McKean, the Vets passed by Evansville to finish the season in the first division, in fourth place, ahead of both Wheeling and Evansville. Dayton came in at a respectable 78–71 and, even though the team had dropped its last five games, management rewarded McKean by extending a contract that would bring him back for 1907. *The Spalding Guide* wrote that the Vets manager "had them going at a pace that might have made them pennant contenders with the season a month longer."[80] Instead, Joseph Ganzel's Wolverines took the pennant home to Grand Rapids for 1906. Joe Ganzel had played in the minors with New Castle and Youngstown, a decade after McKean was a member of the Youngstowns. His brother John Ganzel enjoyed a notable major league career, starting in 1898.

Still, it was with Dayton that McKean can be said to have most influenced the early development of future big leaguers of considerable note. Pepper-pot shortstop Donie Bush learned to play short beside Ed McKean. Third baseman Jimmy Austin and center fielder Dode Paskert, the latter a fellow Clevelander, both enjoyed long careers in the majors. And Bob Bescher, a speedster out of Wittenberg College, would graduate from McKean's Vets to lead the National League in stolen bases four straight seasons. McKean made himself a key part of the team by leading his charges, regardless of their position, by his example on the field of play. When he had to pull himself out of the lineup for a few games in September, "suffering with several boils," the *Dayton Journal* lamented: "The absence of Manager McKean was badly felt, the Vets putting up only a second division article of ball without him." McKean's temporary replacement at second base played the infield with mixed results:

> Paskert's ambition to shine as an infielder was dampened yesterday when he tried the second base job—not with any huge success. The outfielder tried to take an assist with one hand and, naturally, dropped the ball. This one-hand style of play

will probably become popular when they put handles on the ball, but until then the average player will satisfy himself with using two. In fact, six hands would not be too many sometimes."[81]

The following season, Paskert began a 15-year career in the National League—as an outfielder. McKean's boils were probably caused by the malaria that continued to infect his blood stream; a scratch incurred during a game could turn into a painful eruption on the infielder's arms or legs. Regardless, McKean's passion for the game remained undiminished.

On occasion, that passion could result in displays of the showmanship he'd learned from the master, Patsy Tebeau. In the middle of a September 6 blowout in Springfield, a contest the Vets would eventually lose, 12 to 3, "Dayton made a farce of [the] game when Umpire Alloway started in to give the locals the best of everything that came along. Monte Wood, pitching for Dayton, time after time put the ball over the plate, only to have Alloway declare it a ball, and after standing this treatment for a short time, Manager Ed McKean decided to give the fans a royal farce, if that was what they wanted to see." McKean was determined to make former Grand Rapids' pitcher Arthur Alloway's transition from player to umpire as uncomfortable as possible. "He jerked his infield into the outfield positions and placed his gardeners on the bases, sending in Richardson, a first baseman, to pitch."[82] McKean had been frustrated since the third inning, having made a costly error in front of Jack Hendricks and his old team. His antics may have had a serious intent, as well, for McKean was pulling out the stops to motivate, Tebeau style, his fourth-place team to better its mediocre 67–64 record.

The case of Brickyard Kennedy affords special insight into McKean's style as a manager, and his disciplinary code. Winner of 187 National League games, mostly with Brooklyn in the 1890s, Bill Kennedy had gravitated to Dayton to be nearer to his native Bellaire, Ohio, for the last years of his pitching career.[83] The trouble began when the *Dayton Journal*'s South Bend correspondent wrote that Kennedy was intoxicated when he pitched all nine innings of a 2 to 0 loss to the Greens on August 16. The reporter alleged: "In the first inning Kennedy spent most of his time swearing at Alloway and doing everything possible to get the umpire to take him out of the game, but McKean and [South Bend's playing-manager Angus] Grant were both in favor of Kennedy remaining in and Alloway did not put him out on this account. McKean said Kennedy knew that it was his turn to pitch and that he was the only pitcher in condition." The twirler, however, required the manager's constant attention during the contest: "McKean had to call Kennedy down several times [while] Kennedy spent most of his time laughing at the players and doing all sorts of ridiculous things in the infield. He was effective because of the wonderful fielding of

McKean, Bush, Austin, [center fielder] Decker and [first baseman] Richardson. McKean made several sensational stops." In answer to reporter questions, "McKean stated after the game that he would fine Kennedy $10 for the affair."[84] Ed McKean's follow-up, in the classic manager's mode of protecting his player and his player's dignity, deftly put an end to the clamor next day, and demonstrated a touch of the Cleveland politician in the process. "Manager McKean denies that pitcher Perk Kennedy was in other than a natural condition Thursday and had several kinds of complimentary remarks to offer the *Journal*'s South Bend correspondent, who, in his story of that game, alleged that 'Brickyard' was not exactly driving the water wagon."[85] Next summer, McKean's vexing relationship with his errant pitcher would divide the clubhouse.

McKean had been underwhelming in his July 30 debut with the Vets, a 4 to 0 loss in Springfield witnessed by 637 souls. Hitting cleanup behind first baseman Tom McKinley (who, remained as the team's lame duck manager), McKean went 0-for-4 and contributed an error.[86] On August 1, Dayton lost again, this time on the occasion of the opening of the new Liberality Park on Wheeling Island. McKean's double—his first hit for his new team, and the only time a Veteran reached second base that afternoon—was rewarded with a derisive note in next day's *Dayton Journal*: "Only big Ed McKean and his 200 avoirdupois [weight] succeeded in the trot to second."

Ed McKean's delayed first game as manager turned out to be a 4 to 0 victory in Grand Rapids, on August 9. The win brought the record for the sixth-place Vets up to 46 and 54. McKean went 1-for-4, batting third in his own lineup.

Brickyard Kennedy, twice a 20-game winner for Ned Hanlon's championship teams in Brooklyn, walked out on manager McKean and the Dayton Vets during the 1907 season (**Huggins and Scott Auctions**).

With the victory against a top Central League team, the *Dayton Journal* eased up a bit on its treatment of McKean, and started to forget about Tom McKinley, reflecting that "Manager McKean is raising a little dust on his own account. In all events, he got the proper kind of start." The team came back to reality the next afternoon, shut out by Grand Rapids, 5 to 0.

McKean saved his first outstanding performance for an August 13 away game. He managed Dayton's 10 to 0 whitewashing of South Bend, his work in the infield with Donie Bush rated "star work," and he made his one hit in the game count, driving in three runs with a two-run single and a sacrifice fly. The win marked the turning point in McKean's season and the fate of the team, as the Vets went on to sweep the road series. McKean added three more hits in five at-bats, and drove in two runs, in another win the following day. When the Vets took both games of an August 15 doubleheader, the playing-manager produced three more RBIs in the first game and doubled in game two, while remaining error-free at second. Central League cranks were starting to notice Dayton, as the final game in the South Bend series attracted 4,280, the highest attendance figure in the league at that point in the season.

Finally, it came time for the new-look Veterans to come home and perform before their Dayton supporters. There, in the morning game of a doubleheader on August 21, McKean stroked three hits in his four at-bats and scored two runs. The most veteran of Vets even stole two bases off former Dayton catcher Tom Hawkins, in a convincing 9 to 5 win over Grand Rapids. Brickyard Kennedy repaid McKean's earlier defense of his conduct by hurling a brilliant shutout in the afternoon game. McKean went hitless, but his fielding behind Kennedy helped Dayton's single run to stand up for the win. "Ed McKean pulled off some sensational stunts around the middle of the diamond," the *Journal* oohed. By mid–September, he'd made believers of the newspapers; the *Journal*'s sportswriter had even taken to affectionately calling the team McKean's Old Soldiers instead of the Veterans. It was one of McKean's biggest victories in Dayton. The dyed-in-the-wool Ohio Democrat could have anticipated friendlier treatment in James M. Cox's evening paper, the *Daily News*, than in the pages of Dayton's Republican morning paper. Cox was later Governor of Ohio, and the nominee for President of the United States in 1920.

In the end, the team had too much ground to make up in too few games. But McKean had silenced his critics, especially concerning his fielding ability at age 37, and his motivational skills were the admiration of the league. He still hit the ball with authority: his 134 total bases included 15 doubles and six home runs, although he failed to record a triple. His .287 batting average, in 97 games and 373 at-bats with Evansville and Dayton combined, was 12th best in the league. He scored 45 runs on the strength of 107 hits and 33 walks. To top it all off, he swiped 16 bases for the team. While McKean ranked the fifth-best second baseman in terms of fielding percentage (.936, with 25 errors in 388 total chances), his range was continuing to decrease (as his 245 putouts and 118 assists indicate).[87] His playing record, had he been a dozen years younger, would describe a promising baseball prospect.

Ten

A Pennant for Springfield (1907–1908 seasons)

> I now wish to hear from the man, who, more than any other, has helped to win the pennant for this city.
> —Springfield playing-manager Jack Hendricks, 1907

McKean figured he'd found a baseball home with Dayton, who sent him the early Christmas present of a contract to manage the Vets for the upcoming year. That same month of December 1906, *Sporting Life* dished that McKean was "somewhat overweight but still ... able to get around some."[1] It would be the only period in Ed McKean's ascendant minor league career that he enjoyed the continuity of spring training with the same team he'd finished the previous season with. Peace of mind was worth something; to be sure, in 1907 there was little money to be made by a player in the Central League. With one hand, Dr. Carson gave himself a $500 raise to a salary of $1,500, with the unanimous consent of the league directors; he hired four umpires for $175 a month; and, with his other hand's tight fist, he set a salary cap for players that boiled down to $1,800 per team for monthly payrolls. Of course, McKean's stipend for managing would increase his monthly take-home to a modest figure somewhat above his players' paltry $128 apiece.[2] A grateful ownership did move to grant McKean the power to sign players for the team over the off-season.[3]

Rotten weather kept the Veterans off the practice fields for most of April, and McKean's gaggle of young players never seemed to grow into a team. Pre-season forecasts, mostly based on last year's strong finish, proved overly optimistic ("Dayton, depending in a large measure on the hitting ability of the team, will be in the running in spite of the bad weather," *The Sporting News* predicted on April 27), since the team's hitting mostly meant McKean, when he connected, and the pitching staff was mediocre at best. Worse, the playing-manager and his hitters never really got in synch; too often in the coming months, when McKean hit well, the rest of the Vets slumped at the plate. About two weeks into the season, and his team maintaining a .500 record, McKean gave his boys a boost while feeding the friendly papers a good quote. "At Dayton," one reporter faithfully wrote, "McKean is so well satisfied with his club he claims the pennant."[4] The manager's bromide presented a kernel of truth wrapped up inside the unknowable. This *was* the year he'd win the Central League; but his winning team would *not* be the Vets.

The fact remained that this year's Dayton club was badly assembled. The offense relied too heavily on a soon-to-be 38-year-old McKean, uncontestably the Vets' most reliable hitter; 21-year-old left fielder Bob Grogan was a distant next best, averaging .263 on the year. Starting first baseman and reserve catcher Bill Richardson, who was a .301 hitter over a long minor league career, disappointed with his .246 batting average and generously spaced 99 base hits. Outfielder Shawnee Bill Bailey suffered through his career-worst year, nursing a .236 average; future major league center fielder Bob Bescher couldn't build on his good 1906 season with the team; Scott Walker, the regular shortstop, averaged .236 at the plate; and Cleveland native Steve Evans hit .226, exhibiting few signs of the outstanding big league right fielder he would make.[5] Malachi Jedediah Kittridge, last seen as a member of the Cleveland Naps, was the only Veteran with significant experience in the majors besides McKean, but he didn't provide much stability behind the plate in his 18 games for Dayton. Kittridge had had one of the three Chicago hits in Cy Young's debut game with the Spiders.

On opening day, McKean started himself at second base and hit second, but the following day he settled into the cleanup spot where he would remain for most Dayton games. Unfortunately, he couldn't hit everywhere in the batting order. Although they met with some success, the Vets proved they were an offensively challenged team in an early homestand.[6] They were shut out, 1 to 0, by Canton on May 8, in a game in which McKean once again showed his trust in Brickyard Kennedy, asking his wayward pitcher to umpire in place of an ill Frank Killen. The following day, it was Canton twirler Curtis Bales who shut out the Vets, this time by 2 to 0. And, on May 11, Terre Haute scored the only run in its whitewashing of Dayton. The one good offensive showing by McKean and the Veterans came on May 10, when he slashed out three hits in four at-bats and swiped a base. The team piled on 14 runs against Canton, and 20-year-old sensation Rube Marquard, the Central League's best pitcher, had to be brought in to mop up for the Chinamen. The win brought Dayton's record to 6–7 in the early going. Two days later, Dayton evened its record in a home win against Terre Haute, the Vets scoring all their runs in the fifth

TEN. *A Pennant for Springfield (1907–1908 seasons)*

inning, in a rally started by Bob Grogan, with Brickyard Kennedy pitching effectively. McKean's bat was quiet, as he took a comfortable 0-for-3 collar.

The team had fallen into a precarious pattern: when Dayton was scoring at all, all the runs came in one inning. If home fans were late getting to the park on May 13, they missed out on the excitement—the Vets won the game in their first at-bats and held on for the rest of the game, defeating Frank Cross' Hottentots, 5 to 1. McKean's contribution was limited to a hit in four trips to the plate, but he belted two doubles in four at-bats the following day to help his team sustain its modest winning streak. This 3 to 2 victory over Terre Haute was secured by Steve Evans' clutch ninth-inning triple. Dayton got past Punch Knoll's River Rats in another low-scoring contest, 2 to 1, when it was Evansville's turn to come into town, on May 15. McKean welcomed pitcher Bill Pearson with a pair of doubles and a single in three at-bats.

It took Dayton 10 innings to beat Evansville, 4 to 3, on May 17, in a game marred by the Vets' kicking and their fanatics' abuse of umpire Jack Grimm, who had to be escorted from the field past the menacing crowd. After what the June 1 *Sporting Life* described as Grimm's "strenuous time with several Dayton players," the umpire turned in his resignation to Dr. Carson. Two Ed McKeans figured in this game: there was the old Spider McKean, who'd retained venom sufficient to drum a bad ump out of the league, and also an innovative McKean, who used a pinch-hitter for his pitcher in the 10th inning. His Veterans scrambled into third place, on May 18, a game above .500 at 10 and 9. McKean had lately come to experiment with himself driving in runs from the fifth spot in the order, but no amount of tinkering would prevent what was the imminent team collapse. McKean doubled and singled in Herm Malloy's shutout win over the Hottentots of Terre Haute, on May 19. Twenty-two-year-old Malloy won a team-best 18 times for the Vets this season. Dad McKean took himself out of the lineup for a week of games, beginning on May 21. His replacement at second base was Arch Bern, a pickup from the McKeesport Tubers of the Pennsylvania-Ohio-Maryland League. Managing from the bench, he watched the team fall into fifth place (15–16); back in the lineup for the May 28 game, he went 2-for-4, with a double.[7]

If the Vets under McKean hadn't hit much, their pitching turned out to be surprisingly effective early; McKean had coaxed the overachieving team into second place in early June before half of his pitching rotation walked out. After that, even the team's nickname (the Veterans were named after the town's National Military Home and were known as the Old Soldiers until 1903) provided easy target practice for any disaffected crank or newspaperman, as McKean, a veteran of the baseball wars, was overnight considered too old for baseball. Predictably, President George A. Wolf and franchise reversed to the unstable ways that had led to five managers only the season before. This year's annual crisis was precipitated by McKean's wrenched back, which took his much-needed bat out of the everyday lineup, and was made the stuff of melodrama by the mutiny of two of his starting pitchers.[8] A year after defending Brickyard Kennedy for pitching under the influence, manager McKean suspended him indefinitely "for failure to keep in condition." Kennedy's friend on the staff, Ray Luther Hale, soon joined him in a "sympathy strike."[9]

Bill Kennedy had won five of six decisions in his 10 outings for McKean, and Hale had been the outstanding pitcher on the 1906 version of the Vets. Kennedy, a regular clubhouse lawyer, played by his own rule book. Over the seasons, his inflated persona and legendary antics grew too big to be contained within a single nickname. As a result, William Park Kennedy was variously known as Pert, in the Dayton papers (less a lively echo of his middle name than a recognition of his impertinence), or Roaring Bill (from his disconcerting habit of conducting conversations at the top of his lungs), but most often Brickyard (for his unyieldingness to hitters). Even at the height of his success, he'd gone his own way. When he was winning twin championships for the Brooklyn Bridegrooms, Ned Hanlon was forced to discipline his ace for supplementing his income by pitching for local semipro teams.[10] Kennedy had taken the ball for the last time as a major leaguer in game five of the 1903 World Series, against Boston and Cy Young, on his 36th birthday four years before. These days, Bill Kennedy was roaring at the sun setting on his career, a man apart more than a teammate.

He could be sure that McKean needed him more than Kennedy needed the Vets; he could simply choose to go home and wait out the situation, or latch on with the next team. In this manner, the Kennedy coeval divided the clubhouse into factions, the pro–McKean and the anti–McKean, and strolled away with Hale in tow. Dayton had originally signed Roy Hale from Southern League Montgomery right after McKean's arrival, and he had been nearly invincible down the stretch in 1906, victorious in 12 of 14 starts.[11] Presently, Kennedy and Hale jumped the Dayton club to await results from their homes in nearby Bellaire and Dowagiac, Michigan.[12] The name of Hale's village comes from the Potawotomi word for fishing waters, which affords us an image of the pitcher's activity during his retreat.

Doc Carson was only too happy to be called in to straighten out affairs a trifle at Dayton." The meddlesome league president had spread it around that he'd be pleased to buy any team in his league that was failing in the ledgers. Carson urged the franchise to lash McKean to the helm of the damned ship, denying "the rumor that Dad McKean would be replaced by Pop Schriver as manager of the Dayton team," and claiming instead that "McKean has now overcome his run of hard luck." Before Carson left town, he even engineered the loans of two replacement pitchers from South Bend to Dayton.[13] A club run by the league, not to mention by two rebel pitchers, was more than Edward McKean could suffer, and ownership's public show of a lack of confidence in McKean to solve internal problems proved to be fatal. By the time fans read, in their copies of the June 22 *Sporting Life*, that Dayton management was denying any plans to "depose" the manager, McKean had asked for, and been granted, his release. The contract of Steve Evans, whose nickname was Prankster, was soon sold off, sobering the Vets clubhouse at the expense of a big league talent. Within days, Charles W. Bippus, president of the East Liverpool club of the Pennsylvania-Ohio-Maryland League, announced the purchase of Brickyard Kennedy.[14]

After indeterminate weeks of being in and out of the lineup, McKean performed well in his last games for Dayton, batting fifth and manning second base, starting on the Fourth of July. He played both ends of the holiday doubleheader against first-place Springfield. By going 2-for-7 in the second game, he earned the renewed interest of Jack Hendricks, even though the Vets lost the two away games by a combined score of 17 to 10. McKean followed up, the next afternoon, with three singles in four at-bats—the 3 to 2 victory counting for his last win with the Vets, as well as his last career game as a manager.

It was still the first week of July when sixth-place Dayton, a game below .500 (33–34), parted ways with McKean and made first baseman Bill Richardson the interim manager.[15] The club drifted for a time, sticking with Richardson after it couldn't come to terms with Tommy Corcoran or St. Paul Saints outfielder Joe Sugden, only to make the switch to Malachi Kittredge for a while![16] To his credit, Corcoran had sized up the mess and declined the job. He decided instead on a Uniontown, Pennsylvania, team in a lesser league (the P-O-M) for rest of the current season, where he joined ex–Cleveland Nap Alex Pearson, and later managed in New Bedford, Massachusetts, nearer to his Connecticut home. Tommy Corcoran had recently retired from an 18-year career as one of the better fielding shortstops in the National League. Before the 140-game Central League schedule exhausted itself, Dayton called in Pop Schriver from his wanderings up and down the minor league circuits, which included an interlude with McKean in Colorado Springs, and made him its eighth manager in two years. Schriver's main claim to fame dated back to a stunt it turns out he didn't pull off 17 years earlier. The man celebrated for catching a ball dropped from the Washington Monument later confessed that he'd lost his nerve on the second attempt.[17]

McKean wasn't out of a baseball job for long. Jack Hendricks jumped at the chance to reacquire McKean's savvy and slugging for the pennant stretch, understanding that he could be the difference-maker for Springfield. He'd wanted badly to re-sign the second baseman going into the 1906 campaign, when the two got as far as agreeing in principle on a contract before Hendricks lost McKean to Jimmy Ryan. Springfield could easily afford to rent McKean's bat for a couple of months this summer. Hendricks had it worked out so that, in effect, its best ball players paid their own salaries plus a tidy profit for the ownership; his trick was to showcase a player, sell his reserve rights to a big league club, and play him in Springfield most of the season.[18] Besides, Babes owner Claude H. Varnell, a prosperous insurance broker based in Wheeling, had deep pockets to complement an abiding trust in Hendricks' judgment. The partners had met in Chicago, 15 years before. Upon graduating together from the same high school, C.H. Varnell became the general manager for the Illinois Cycling Club's indoor and outdoor baseball clubs, and Johnny Hendricks was his star player, hitting the home run off Ironman Joe McGinnity that decided the state amateur championship game, 4 to 3. The Babes' lanky first baseman Guy Dickey played first base for the ICC team that year, too. Ever since Varnell purchased the Springfield franchise on Hendricks' advice, on June 22, 1906, Hendricks, Varnell, and Dickey had been the team within the team.[19]

Springfield would be McKean's last hurrah as a ball player. In proud defiance of the old adage and his own failing body, and setting aside his bad experience in Rochester five years before, Ed McKean did have his second act, leading Springfield to the Central League flag in his second stint with the Babes. McKean hadn't known the excitement of a pennant race since 1896, the last season the Spiders were in contention, and he was reinvigorated at the prospect of playing meaningful game after game. Indeed, life in the Central League fast lane offered much to McKean, even a renewal of his old war with Arlie Latham, of all people, hired by Dr. Carson to umpire starting in August.[20] It's rich to picture McKean strolling up to the plate and saying a few choice words of greeting to the freshest ump on earth. If McKean harbored any reservations about coming back to Springfield, it was due to the poor condition of its infield. When he was the Dayton manager, he'd vociferously complained that "these are the worst grounds in the circuit, and that he is very thankful he does not have to play here all season," after losing a game on a sloppy Snyder Field.[21]

McKean's injection into the lineup proved to be just the tonic a good Springfield team needed to become an outstanding one. Jack Hendricks had already assembled a talented bunch. This championship season, James Champion Osteen had his career year in Springfield, home to the famous Champion farm machinery. Champ Osteen took the batting title and led the league in

TEN. *A Pennant for Springfield (1907–1908 seasons)* 271

steals. Manager Hendricks pushed all the right buttons in 1907. When Osteen had been McKean's teammate in 1905, he'd played third base; now, with McKean installed at second base, Hendricks moved Osteen to short, creating a dynamic left-handed-slugging keystone combination reminiscent of the hey days of Childs and McKean. Although Osteen failed to hit or catch the ball during brief trials in the majors, before and following 1907, he is remembered to this day as Joe Jackson's idol, the pioneer who led the way to the big leagues for fellow South Carolina textile-league players. Harry Corns, at 32 the old man on the staff, won 18 games and chipped in with a .282 batting average. He was a .299 hitter in over 600 career minor league games, as an outfielder and pitcher. Joe Collins was one of the more dependable hitters for Springfield. In the Little Rock outfield, he played beside Tris Speaker in the immortal's breakout season of 1908. Perhaps the most intriguing talent on the Babes roster was 21-year-old left fielder Sheldon Aldenburg Lejeune, who once threw a baseball 134 yards in a skills competition and won the long-distance throwing title at Cincinnati's Field Day this September.[22]

McKean felt strangely at home playing the infield behind the team's best battery, two Irish boys, Matthew Muldowney and Billy Kelly. Muldowney was another of Hendricks' reclamation projects; he went 18–5 for the championship Babes, after losing 23 games with a Sharon, Ohio, team the year before. The boy the fans naturally called King Kelly later caught for two seasons with the Pittsburgh Pirates. Overall, the Babes cultivated a distinctly Hibernian look, as third baseman Frank Donahue, a Boston Red Sox prospect and the third Donahue brother to play professional ball (Jiggs Donahuue was a star with the White Sox), held down the hot corner, and Ted McGraw served as the utility infielder. Sometimes, Jack Hendricks even managed like a later-day Tebeau (or, if you like, a more recent-day McKean), when he was suspended for 10 days, starting May 17, for his row in Wheeling with an ump by the name of Hewellyn; it was already the second time Dr. Carson had to discipline the Springfield manager that season.[23] Like Tebeau late in his career, Hendricks was playing fewer games, choosing instead to manage from the bench. But Hendricks added a wrinkle that never occurred to Patsy: he directed his players through a megaphone.[24]

Hendricks plugged McKean right into the coveted third slot in his lineup, ahead of Champ Osteen, who had led the team in hitting all season. McKean debuted with this year's Babes—who were neck-and-neck with Wheeling at the time—in South Bend on July 13, contributing a single in the morning game and a double in the afternoon. Over the next eight games, however, Hendricks' hit man scraped out only four singles in 31 at-bats, and made matters worse by committing two errors. When McKean did not have immediate success with his new team, he heard and read the inevitable grumbles from the Springfield writers and cranks. The Springfield *Gazette*, on July 18, complained: "McKean failed to get a single again yesterday and had another error chalked up against him. If 'Dad' could only start his hitting, the errors could be looked over." In the same column, the writer sniped, "Manager Richardson of Dayton has started the 'Dad' McKean stunt of umpire baiting, and was put out of the game yesterday," then warned, "If he keeps that kind of work up, he too may follow the tin can bordered route of his predecessor." The local press didn't share Jack Hendricks' high estimates of their newest player and his recent meanderings through the Central League. Then Ed McKean went on the last great charge of his playing career.[25]

It began with McKean's three hits in the first game of a July 23 doubleheader, followed up by a triple in the second game, and didn't let up all the way through a decisive August 3 win, 13 to 7, at Evansville, in which he went 3-for-5 (and had a hand in two double plays). By the time it was over, McKean had amassed 20 base hits in 57 at-bats, for a .351 batting average, under the pressure of a pennant race with Wheeling. In the 15-game tear, he belted four triples and a double. "Dad" even stole four bases and played an errorless second base. During this span of games, Springfield put Wheeling behind them in the standings for good. As of August 3, the top three teams in the league were Springfield (57–33), Canton (47–39), and Wheeling (49–41). The Babes ran away with the pennant. On the final day of the season, September 15, Springfield's record went into the books as 87 wins against only 49 setbacks; Wheeling came in a distant second, at 77–57.

McKean was Springfield's MVP for the second half. When he was called back to Cleveland, where his son was ill, as when Hendricks rested him after the first-place finish was assured, the Babes played listlessly—and home games drew as few as 200 onlookers.[26] When he was in the lineup, he tirelessly led at-bat and in the field. The August 17 Springfield *Gazette* wrote admiringly: "'Dad' McKean played a nice game yesterday. In the first game [of a series against Wheeling] he took care of 10 chances in errorless style. He also rapped out three hits out of five times at-bat. 'Dad' is playing nice ball these days, and his heavy stick work has done not a little towards winning the pennant." McKean also took part in the two double plays of that game.

Match-ups against the Stogies were important since the Babes finished only 9–9 against Wheeling, while blowing away the league's other six teams.[27] The bare-handed infielder of old was once more drawing raves for his fielding: "Dad McKean is establishing a record in those one-handed spears of his. He repeated the trick again yesterday [on August 23, in South Bend]. He took Maloney's liner on the meat hand in the fifth, and [his former player Donie

TEN. *A Pennant for Springfield (1907–1908 seasons)* 273

Bush, thinking that it was going safe, turned second. Dad threw to Dickey and Bush was caught so far off that he made no attempt to get back to station one."[28] A Springfield writer's appreciation for McKean's work, accomplished the previous day against the Greens, unknowingly echoed McAleer's appreciation from yesteryear: "Dad McKean can always be relied upon to do something with the stock when a hit is needed. He scored Corns yesterday with a clean hit for the first run of the game. No wonder Manager Hendricks hands McKean a large share of the credit for winning the pennant for the Babes." McKean had also contributed one of Springfield's two sacrifice hits of the game.[29] His triple against Evansville, on September 5, was considered in Springfield to have been "about as long a drive as has been seen on the home grounds."[30] McKean's performance made Johnny Hendricks look like a baseball genius. McKean's dazzling pace with Springfield drove up his final Central League average to almost .300. His combined totals, between Dayton and Springfield, were 108 games played, 422 at-bats, 124 hits, with 16 doubles and nine triples, and a .294 batting average. He slugged .374 while amassing 158 total bases.

The banquet for the champions took place at Springfield's grand Arcade

At the Arcade Hotel, Springfield, Ohio, precisely a dozen years after Cleveland's Temple Cup victory and the subsequent Elks lodge fete of October 1895, Ed McKean was toasted, in the hotel banquet room, as the man who brought the Central League pennant of 1907 to Springfield (Library of Congress).

Hotel, on the evening of September 16. Taking over for toastmaster W.R. Burnett, who was called away to a meeting, Jack Hendricks sounded like the trained lawyer he was in real life, when he talked about McKean. "I now wish to hear from the man, who, more than any other, has helped to win the pennant for this city," he began. "When Dayton saw fit to let him go we gladly signed him, and the fact that we have won the pennant shows how wisely we acted in the matter." In his magnanimous tribute, reported the local paper, "Hendricks then announced that in recognition of McKean's services he is at liberty to leave the club next season in case he secured a better position."[31] Was the Babes manager already measuring McKean for a big league uniform in 1908? Hendricks later took the precaution of listing him on the reserve list for Springfield.[32] What McKean said that evening went unrecorded. The fete in Springfield came fully 12 years after the Temple Cup banquet in Cleveland. McKean might just as well have celebrated the simple fact that he was still playing baseball at a skilled level after so long.

The 1907 Central League Campion Springfield Babes: 1. Ed McKean, 2. Matthew Muldowney, 3. Joseph Collins, 4. Guy Dickey, 5. Harry Corns, 6. Del Hallman, 7. Harry Hammond, 8. Leroy Clark, 9. Sheldon Lejeune, 10. Claude H. Varnell, 11. Jack Hendricks, 12. Boyd Chambers, 13. Frank Donahue, 14. Champ Osteen, 15. Billy Kelly, 16. Anthony Fremer (author's collection).

TEN. *A Pennant for Springfield (1907–1908 seasons)* 275

It is thrilling to read the microfilmed box scores of McKean's inspired hitting, great day after great day, during the streak that made time stand still for the prematurely middle-aged man, and for the author in the library a dozen decades after the fact. And yet, there was always the awareness that this once-great athlete's body had betrayed him. It's easy to discern from the team photo that McKean was suddenly past being a physically intimidating player. A number of his Springfield teammates, including his manager, look tougher. And Springfield's new plaid uniform didn't help; inspired by Brooklyn's togs, it looked unflattering on the rapidly aging McKean, only accentuating his bloated physique.[33] Comparing the 1905 Springfield team photo, taken by the Staples studio of South Bend, with the shot of the 1907 team, we see McKean's appearance underwent a dramatic change during these years. McKean, in 1905, confidently kneels in the front row, second from right, looking strong and dark haired, a big man but not out of shape. His granite countenance is the same one we remember from pictures made in 1899 and earlier.

After the season, McKean was loath to leave Springfield. Instead, he decided to capitalize on his newfound status among the locals, going into business with his best friend on the team. He and young King Kelly opened "a booze bazaar" in town, the celebrity McKean ensconced as "head bartender," like Pete Rose at a Las Vegas autograph table. "Many base ball tales likely will go down with the suds in King's place this Winter," predicted *Sporting Life*.[34] In the end, the club left him at the bar, when Claude Varnell relocated the franchise in Fort Wayne for the coming season.

Ed McKean wanted to manage again, no doubt recognizing that his fabled playing skills were fading. After all, his old mate Jesse Burkett had turned a profit in 1907, when the Worcester Busters he owned and managed took the New England League pennant. *Sporting Life*, on November 30, 1907, spread the rumor that he would manage the new Central League team to be located in Fort Wayne, which would mean sending Jack Hendricks to Grand Rapids. At Christmastime, the *Youngstown Vindicator* handed on the gossip that McKean "is said to be the choice of East Liverpool directors for the management of next season's base ball club," where Brickyard Kennedy had wound up a few months earlier.[35] We know that he was a finalist, in a busy December for McKean, for the managerial opening in Akron. His chances looked good, since the Akron club was reporting only two applicants, McKean and Percy Stetler, the manager of the previous season's Steubenville entry in the Pennsylvania-Ohio-Maryland League with East Liverpool. At length, he lost out to a third candidate, 26-year-old John Brackenridge, who would manage the Akron Champs and win 16 games pitching for them in the upcoming season. The Akron job would have situated McKean closer to his family and elderly father for the summer months.[36]

There were real incentives urging McKean to re-sign with Hendricks and Varnell for another year.[37] Hendricks had brought back Champ Osteen to play shortstop, after having sold him to the Chicago White Sox for a spring trial, so McKean and Osteen could pick up where they left off in September.[38] He'd detested fielding balls on the old Springfield infield; Fort Wayne was to play its home games on a newly constructed grounds, with a welcoming name (League Park, as in Cleveland), where the groundskeeper was an Irishman named Donovan. Claude Varnell was planning a state-of-the-art clubhouse for Fort Wayne, which featured baths, dressing rooms, and lounges, practically luxury accommodations considering that players had to dress at the hotel before coming to the old park.[39] Moreover, Fort Wayne was a real baseball town, with a tradition that intermingled with McKean's Cleveland roots. On May 4, 1871, the National Association played the first professional game in Fort Wayne, as the local team hosted the Cleveland Forest Citys. The city's former park, Hamilton Field, was popularly celebrated as The Grand Duchess, although the locals reserved the nickname for the elaborate Victorian grandstands only.[40] All the while, Dr. Carson was talking big-league-style improvements for the Central League. His modernistic dream was "to provide every team in the league with a private [electric] trolley car to be used through the season. Each club could have a car that would care for sixteen players, with dining equipment and berths, which could be used in all trips over the circuit." "All but two cities," Grand Rapids and Wheeling, "in the league can be reached by trolley," he added, in an attempt to sound more practical.[41]

Ultimately failing to find a team to manage, McKean decided about the Ides of March that he'd return as a player, as the second baseman on Jack Hendricks' club.[42] McKean was held out of Fort Wayne's spring training debut, against the Toledo Mud Hens on April 4, in this way saving his first appearance as a Billiken for an exhibition game played, three days later, against the Boston Americans. In the mist, Eddie Cicotte's knuckleball flummoxed Fort Wayne batters, keeping the Billikens off the scoreboard and returning McKean, the cleanup hitter, to the bench three times without a hit.[43] However, a tuned-up McKean was ready to hit from the third slot in Hendricks' lineup (Champ Osteen was fourth) for the regular-season opener, in Wheeling on April 23. "Big Ed McKean played an all around star game," one of the Fort Wayne newspapers put it. "A two base hit in the fourth cleared the bases and a sacrifice hit in the eighth brought in another run." Mac seems to have played his trademark all-out game in the Billikens infield that day. "Although he had one error chalked up against him he played a great fielding game and made some of the prettiest plays that have ever been witnessed on the local diamond," McKean's newfound admirer gushed.[44] The following afternoon, Fort Wayne smoked

TEN. *A Pennant for Springfield (1907–1908 seasons)* 277

the Stogies, 6 to 1, McKean contributing a double and a single but making another error.[45] Fort Wayne swept the three-game series from Wheeling, their nemesis from the previous year, and won their next three games handily before returning home to a brand new ball park and eager baseball fanatics who hadn't had a pro team to cheer for several years.

The transferred Springfield Babes had been renamed the Fort Wayne Billikens after an elfin charm doll (the pet rock of a by-gone era) popularly marketed by Florence Pretz in 1908. The hometown press sometimes called them the Shamrocks.[46] And, indeed, the season did open like one big smile for the new club—until, in the early morning of May 3. On the eve of the 37th anniversary of the town's hosting of the first major league game, and just hours before the scheduled home opener, disaster struck. It came with little warning. Afterward, the instantly luckless Billikens seemed never to recover.

"Fire! For God's sake, if you value your lives, get out!" the night clerk cried door to door above the gong he banged, his alarm to awaken guests, for as long as he could stand the smoke.

The blaze that started sometime around 3:15 on that Sunday morning quickly destroyed the New Aveline Hotel, killing a dozen guests from smoke inhalation in windowless interior rooms, or from desperate jumps from fifth-story windows. Several survivors tiptoed along the narrow ledges on the sixth floor until they could leap to safety onto the rooftops of adjacent buildings. Jack Hendricks made a harrowing escape, lowering his wife and five-year-old son Jon three floors down an obstacle course of a fire escape; the only belongings he took with him were the pants he'd managed to throw on, and his cache of 17 diamonds (probably stashed beneath his pillow). Claude Varnell abandoned his fifth-floor rooms and marched barefoot, a coat over his pajamas, directly to the *Journal-Gazette* offices to telegraph his wife and sit for an interview. He'd just "lost all of his personal belongings, valued at several thousand dollars," to the flames.[47] "I never expected to see Hendricks or his people again," Varnell told the newspaper, while the landmark hotel was burning to the ground.[48]

The owner's statement is unspeakably vulgar if he meant John Hendricks' family members, and not the Billikens players, including McKean. Although McKean's name does not appear on the lists of those injured in the conflagration (and Ralph Hopkins, the heroic night clerk, added to the mystery when he left behind the register to burn with the front desk), it is reasonable to place Ed McKean in the doomed hotel on the eve of the ball game. The New Aveline was the kind of house where he would choose to board, a popular stopover for traveling salesmen, nurses, and members of the working class of his day (a wrestler was among the casualties) and made, as well, a convenient residence for Claude Varnell and the Hendricks family. Its well-stocked bar offered a convivial corner to hash out the fine points of the Central League games.

Wherever McKean went to bed that night, it is certain that he rose a changed man. Among the citizens of Fort Wayne, he mourned the tragic deaths of the innocents. It would be only natural if matters of life and death crowded out the ballplayer's thoughts of games to be played; little Jon Hendricks' narrow escape would have made him think in a different way about Ed Junior (10 years old now) and Robert (seven), who were growing up in Cleveland in their father's absences. Belle was a month pregnant with their third son, Martin. In Fort Wayne, McKean was neither here nor there, like a runner when he takes a daring lead while leaning back toward first. Even its river, the Maumee, leading back over the border into Ohio and Lake Erie, seemed to call him back to Cleveland. For the rest of the schedule, the team and its supporters waited in vain for their Cheshire cat season to solidify.

If McKean's bat wasn't incinerated in the hotel inferno, he certainly hit like he was missing something essential, something like his desire to play. The team who had come back to Fort Wayne undefeated lost for the first time on May 5, the rescheduled home opener. McKean played well, ignoring the cold wind blowing off the flat Indiana corn fields. One of his two base hits off Joseph Jaeger drove home a run in the third inning, but the Billikens disappointed, losing to the Stogies by the lopsided score of 9 to 4. After a 4–3 week, post-traumatic Fort Wayne had stumbled into second place behind Grand Rapids[49]; the Billikens were to occupy seventh place by the middle of June, the team's record trending to 22 wins against 27 losses. Before finally "winning" on June 15, Fort Wayne had dropped 15 games in a row, but even then, there wasn't much cause to celebrate. "On that day," wrote *Sporting Life* on July 4, "it finally won a game on forfeit because pitcher Moore of South Bend, in the sixth inning hurled umpire Arundel to the ground and pummeled him severely before [being] pulled off." Eugene Moore was fined $15 afterward in the municipal court of Fort Wayne,[50] and Chauncey Arundel was destined to be fired by Dr. Carson.[51] Ed McKean wasn't around to celebrate the elusive win.

Fort Wayne had no need for the services of a .200-hitter, who was pushing 40, during their tailspin toward the basement, and, to make life even more miserable for the club owners, they were suffering serious losses in income due to bad weather since the home opener.[52] By August, things had gotten so bad for the team that Hendricks launched a road trip by leaving four of his players behind in Fort Wayne with instructions for them to get in shape.[53] So, with the team in sixth place and half a dozen games under .500 (15–21), Hendricks unloaded Ed McKean's contract, giving him his release about the day of his

Ten. A Pennant for Springfield (1907–1908 seasons)

39th birthday. In all the newspaper notices of McKean's demise, he was still referred to as "the famous veteran shortstop Ed McKean," although he hadn't played at short for years and his so-called fame was already a thoughtless epithet. The *Youngstown Vindicator* on June 15 ran a front-page article, under the headline "Grand Old Player Is Now Too Slow For Central City," stating flat out that "McKean has lost his batting eye. He has played ball for over 20 years and although he has not been so fast on the infield for the past few years he was carried because he could hit the ball. This year he has completely lost everything." On June 21, the *Washington Herald* categorically assumed McKean "will retire."

It was the reasonable conclusion to draw, considering McKean's age and his awful post–May 3 performance for Fort Wayne. Appearing in 34 games, the offensive star of 1907 produced only 22 hits and scored 13 runs. His batting average of .169 was 76 points below the average Central League hitter in 1908. McKean's fielding statistics read somewhat better on the page than the second baseman looked on the diamond (he was charged with just eight errors; his .954 fielding average was sixth best in the league), but he was limited to 109 putouts and 49 assists. McKean was essentially a stationary fielder for Fort Wayne.

When a fabled warrior falls on the field, to paraphrase Anne Carson, he rarely gets up again. McKean confounded the sports pundits, and may very well have surprised himself, by his continuing desire to play baseball. Right after *Sporting Life* printed news of his dismissal from Fort Wayne, in its June 20 issue, Ed McKean became the second baseman for the Bay City Reds (probably newspaper shorthand for Redbirds or Cardinals). A pessimist would call McKean a man of exceptional hubris who had fallen and kept on falling, until he hit bottom with a last-place team in the lowest level of the minors. More positively, the justly proud McKean refused to live with the Fort Wayne termination; he would play out the rest of the season, and retire from the game on his own terms. It would be his call this time, not by Hendricks or, as had been the case in 1899, Tebeau. Lacking McKean's letters to his wife from Fort Wayne and Bay City, we may never understand his reasons and his state of mind. (McKean also had time to return to Cleveland, where he and Belle could have decided what was left of his baseball future.) Within the span of half a baseball season, McKean had suffered the confusing dislocation of his ball club from an Ohio town which had embraced him to an Indiana city where he nearly lost his life. By going up to Michigan, the long-time National League headliner was willingly submitting himself to the humiliation of hanging on, with a team of players half his age, in a baseball backwater that was miles further removed from home.

Decision made, it would have been a simple matter for McKean to request a position with Bay City. He could have written to Dad Clarkson, a pitcher for half a dozen big league seasons and currently a Bay City Reds board member. His famous brother John Clarkson (McKean's teammate on the 1892 Spiders playoff team) had preceded him in Michigan, running a cigar emporium in downtown Bay City for a decade following his retirement from the National League, in 1895. John Clarkson had capped off his minor league apprenticeship pitching for the Saginaw Old Golds, in the glory days of the Northwestern League of the mid–1880s, when the likes of Dave Foutz and Hank O'Day were heroes in rival Bay City. In March 1908, his plans to manage the Bay City team, and serve as vice president of the Southern Michigan League, were dashed when failing mental health necessitated his hospitalization and the subsequent return to his parents' home, in Cambridge, Massachusetts, where he died.[54] The spring after McKean's late summer in Bay City, a newly constructed ball field was dedicated in the name of the beloved John Clarkson. With its seating capacity of 4,000, Clarkson Park was the biggest venue in the league.[55] It is also possible that Hall of Fame boxer Kid Lavigne recommended his acquaintance McKean to the club owners, or sang the praises of his off-the-track native city in the ballplayer's ear over a drink or two. In any case, Ed McKean's signing was clearly not a matter of money, for him or the Reds: the top player salary for a full Southern Michigan season was capped at $1,000.[56]

So, why did Ed McKean choose Bay City? It could be speculated that McKean was caught up in an instinctive flight back to the northlands out of which his father had emerged over 40 years before. There was also the practical consideration. Catching on with Bay City, although the town was located about 60 miles farther away from Cleveland than Fort Wayne, meant a welcome respite for him from the hardships of team travel. *The Spalding Guide for 1907* tells us what McKean might have considered in his decision: "It is believed that the South Michigan has the most compact eight-city circuit in organized ball. There are six jumps of less than forty-two miles each. From the extreme northeastern town, Bay City, to the extreme southwestern stand, Kalamazoo, the trip by rail can be made inside one hundred and fifty miles."[57]

Further, the young ownership was welcoming. Into the vacuum created by the demise of John Clarkson, M.E. Taylor had stepped forward to manage the Bay City entry. That the samaritan volunteer was not a baseball man (*Sporting Life*, on February 8, 1908, portrayed Taylor as the only manager in the league who was "not actively engaged in the game") became a moot point when he fell ill and resigned. An overhaul of the front office made George H. Crawford president, Lorina N. Crawford secretary-treasurer, and outfielder

TEN. *A Pennant for Springfield (1907–1908 seasons)*

Clyde McNutt vice president. The Crawfords were a dynamic couple, still in their twenties when they directed the franchise. Both husband and wife were naturalized citizens (he was born in Scotland and immigrated in 1899; she was born in Canada to Scottish parents), a fact that may have made them more appealing to McKean.[58] Mrs. Crawford held the distinction of being "the only baseball woman" in the country at that time; that is to say, the only woman in charge of running a professional baseball team.[59] She valued a veteran presence on her teams; next season, she brought in the old catcher Fritz Buelow. If she followed through on Dad Clarkson's suggestion to add Ed McKean to the roster, Mrs. Crawford's idea may have been to tweak fan interest in a weak team with the novelty of one of John Clarkson's old teammates. Thirty-year-old vice president Clyde McNutt, last season's team captain, would also manage. The Ohio-born McNutt turned out to be a bargain, leading off and playing center field in all

John Clarkson, the legend of Bay City, Michigan, won his 300th game in 1892 as a Cleveland Spider (*The Sporting News*/Mears Auctions).

but one of Bay City's 128 games. He had been a manager before, with Saginaw in 1906 and, before that, with the Henderson, Kentucky, Blue Birds.[60] Manager McNutt respectfully made McKean his number three hitter.

The Bay City that McKean knew was a lonely outpost for a fading star to end his career, but a low-pressure place for kid players to be nurtured, or weeded out. McKean just missed playing on the 1907 team with Ed Pinnance, the first Native American to pitch in the major leagues. And he was gone before the arrival of the two best prospects on the 1909 team, Leonard (King) Cole, the Chicago Cubs pitching phenom in waiting and model for Ring Lardner's Alibi Ike stories, and future Federal League slugger Dutch Zwilling. Two of McKean's teammates on the Reds were named by *The Sporting News* among the "rising young players" considered to be "ready for faster company," first baseman Cliff Webster and catcher Patrick Newcombe, although only pitcher Pecks Daly made it to the majors.[61] In a way, McKean had come full circle in his baseball life. One of the pitchers that Southern Michigan season was the kid brother of Lou Criger, the man who had caught Cy Young in Cleveland and Boston. Elmer Criger finished his rookie season with the Jackson Convicts about the time McKean was making his exit.[62]

Two Bay City doubleheaders against runaway pennant-winner Saginaw, one early in the season and one later, may suffice to illustrate McKean's service with the Reds. The Fourth of July twin bill in Saginaw was the most visible early test of what he brought to the Bay City lineup. Ed McKean was the team's best hitter, but his best didn't keep his team from dropping both games, 6 to 2 and 5 to 0, to the delight of the 2,200 in attendance. Cleanup hitter McKean's double drove in both of the Reds runs in the seventh inning that morning; they were shut out the rest of the day. He also had one of Bay City's two hits off Cummings in the afternoon game. Making his debut, Cummings pitched a shutout and made three hits of his own. It so happened that the other Bay City base hit was by their pitcher, Clements. Oddly enough, neither rookie pitcher's Christian name was recorded in the newspapers; neither pitcher's record is to be found in the baseball encyclopedias. McKean was batting against untamed pitching in Class D-level ball, as he had in his old American Association days, when local boys were often signed for the day.[63] Another doubleheader with the Saginaw Wa-Was, in early August, proved to be Ed McKean's swan song.

The Reds entered play that month having won five of six closely contested games. McKean was again hitting from the third slot these days, and still making such contact good with the ball that, when he struck out against Flint's George Weeder in an August 2 game, the newspaper found it newsworthy: "Something happened in the last part of the first [inning] that has not occurred on the home lot before this year. That phenomenal occurrence was the fanning of Dad McKean." With two outs in the ninth inning, though, McKean drove in a run, with a signature hit to right, and was on first base when the game ended. That 5 to 4 loss to the Vehicles put the brakes on the Reds three-game win streak, after Bay City had gotten itself up off the floor and swept a home series against Battle Creek. Bay City won again the next day, on August 3, the first game of a series against Lansing. The *Bay City Times* called the 3 to 1 victory a "lucky" one, since the Senators outhit the home team but self-destructed by way of bases on balls and wild pitches. McKean managed to contribute to the Reds' cause even though he went without a hit, coaxing one of those walks, in the sixth, and scoring the winning run. A luckier Senators team shut out the Reds, on August 4, McKean still hitless and making an error. Lansing took the series by winning the August 5 game decisively, 7 to 1. McKean continued his undistinguished play, going 1-for-4 at the plate, and he watched the mem-

TEN. A Pennant for Springfield (1907–1908 seasons)

orable play of the game from the bench. The triple play came after Bay City had loaded the bases, with nobody out, in the second inning. The next Reds batter Tom "Lovett knocked a little one to [pitcher Timothy] Hogan, who tossed the ball to [his catcher Bill] Harris and forced [Guy] Blair out. From Harris the ball went to [C.A.] Nipple on first, where Tommy was caught on the run. [Lou] Bensley, trying to save something from the wreck, attempted to steal the plate, but a rapid return of the ball to Harris proved too much for Bens and he was touched out."

Bay City got an unlikely complete game win, on August 6, when a high school recruit who went as Dutch Mueller scattered 10 hits against the Kalamazoo White Sox (sometimes called the Celery Pickers). Ed McKean's second-inning double, described in the newspaper as the longest hit of the contest, drove in the third run in the 4–3 victory. But, on the following day, Kalamazoo's George Sage shut out Bay City and kept McKean off the bases. Bay City's best efforts could make them no better than a .500 team; they'd already lost too many games to contend.

The last two games of Ed McKean's once-fabled career passed without ceremony on a day when the last-place Reds split a doubleheader with the first-place Wa-Was in Saginaw. Home for the Wa-Was was Recreation Park, located at the foot of the Johnson Street Bridge, across the Saginaw River from today's downtown.[64] Bay City had won two of four games coming in, and McKean felt the kind of temporary relief a bad small-town team gets on the road. In the morning game, on August 10, Bay City ambushed the home team, scoring four runs in the first inning off Irwin Gough on its way to a 12 to 4 decision over the Cleveland Naps pitching prospect.[65] McKean scored three runs, and one of his two base hits went for a double, which was the last extra-base hit of his career. McKean also made one of his team's five fielding errors, but he was the pivot man on the game's only double play. The afternoon game, a lopsided 17 to 0 reckoning by the far superior Wa-Was, was mercifully called by umpire O'Toole after seven frames. McKean went 0-for-3 against another green Southern Michigan League pitcher, Roy Green, who had just turned 21 two days before. Roy James Green would finish this season with a record of 9 wins and 3 losses in 14 games, and retire a seasoned veteran of 117 wins in the minors. Although he was twice a 21-game winner, the high mark in his pitching career amounted to three appearances at the level of Class A. Green made a living after retirement from baseball as a machine operator in Saginaw. The last man to throw a pitch to Ed McKean died on January 15, 1975.[66]

In the end, it may well have been an artist who nudged Ed McKean into leaving the team and retiring from baseball. The August 10 *Bay City Times* printed a caricature of an exaggeratedly overweight "McKean At Work." The staff artist hadn't especially taken the care to be accurate, as his clownish McKean, so fat he obscures the tiny catcher lost somewhere behind the plate, bats *right-handed*. In truth, McKean had not been singled out for abuse— tasteless caricatures of home team players were a regular feature of the country's sports pages—but if this player got his hands on a copy of the *Times* (and it was likely he did, on a travel day), the bad joke would have come as a blow to the perpetually thin-skinned one, a knockout blow at his age. For McKean, the game had ceased to be fun. He called it quits, after a playing career of 21 seasons, on August 12. The team was en route to Battle Creek, but McKean informed Clyde McNutt of his decision and got off the train at Jackson. He'd retired, in the wake of the cartoon, within 48 hours after the 17-run defeat.

When Ed McKean made his last out, nobody, perhaps not even the batter himself, took much note of the old man with the perfect swing on the forgettable team. Maybe a guy and his gal in the stands were falling in love or breaking up when it happened; or some man was thinking of his supper; or the sportswriter was probably too busy praying the game summary he'd drafted would hold up at the end of a game that had been decided early. Afterwards, no one thought to write the eulogy for the passing of Ed McKean's momentous playing career. The league president at the time, Joe S. Jackson of the *Detroit Free Press*, wrote nothing on the occasion. Instead of a tribute, on August 13, the *Bay City Times* printed a dismissal under the headline "Dad McKean Quit":

> A telegram from Clyde McNutt ... dated Battle Creek yesterday, conveys the information that "Dad" McKean, second baseman jumped the Bay City team at Jackson on the way to the pure food city. McKean's offense is not very serious, however, as he was not under contract with the local management, merely coming here to play as long as he desired.

It was unfair, of course, to charge McKean with jumping, when his contract with Mrs. Crawford stipulated all along that he was free to decide when he'd had enough.[67] Anyhow, this matter of "jumping" was nothing so dire as the contract mess he'd navigated in 1890, a baseball life ago. Piling on, the writer's pun on "serious" slams McKean for his diminished production as an offensive player, when, in fact, McKean's final record with Bay City looks tantalizingly good on paper, over a century later.

He led the team in batting, and his .289 average was ninth highest in the league, for players with at least his 194 at-bats. However, careful scrutiny reveals that McKean failed to continue his mysterious hitting pattern, since 1905, of redeeming a miserable first half by a strong performance at season's finish. While McKean was a .306 hitter over his first 35 games for Bay City (sixth best in the league), he fell off badly in his last 13 games, managing just 13 hits, two of them doubles, in 50 at-bats (a .260 average), and scoring only three

Ten. A Pennant for Springfield (1907–1908 seasons)

runs. Overall, McKean appeared in 48 games as a Red, garnering 194 at-bats and scoring 21 times. Among his 56 hits, 13 went for extra bases, all doubles. He did not steal a base. Even more out of character for McKean than the power outage were his two sacrifice hits, his signature as a team player going all the way back to the Cleveland Blues. His .937 fielding average (15 errors) ranked him ninth best among second basemen in the eight-team league. He was credited with 109 putouts and 115 assists.[68] Bay City came in last in the league, winning 48 and losing 78; at McKean's departure, its record stood at 34–48. The year following, John Clarkson Park was ready for the throng of visitors returning to Bay City for Old Home Week, part of the town's semi-centennial celebration which kicked off on July 4, 1909. There is one final irony to contemplate. For 1910, two seasons after Ed McKean's arrival from the Fort Wayne Billikens, the Bay City baseball team would have a new nickname—that's right, the Billikens.

Group photograph from Ed McKean's last appearance on the League Park filed, August 14, 1909: (Standing left to right) Sam Wise, Larry Twitchell, manager Owens, Charlie Zimmer, Joe Battin; (seated) McKean, Pete Hotaling, George Strief, Joe Archer; (ground) Chief Goodman, Bert Buttons Briggs. McKean played the whole game at short, as the old-timers beat an all-star team of Cleveland amateurs.

Now the train was taking him back to his city and his family, returning him to the everyday existence after years of summers as an absentee father and seasonal businessman. On the long ride, McKean had abundant time to reimagine himself as a year-round father and full-time citizen of Cleveland. He rode past Detroit, where in another month Donie Bush would join Hugh Jennings and Ty Cobb to play an updated version of the old Spiders' hell-bent game. The day Bush had reported to McKean in Dayton, he was "so green he didn't know how to put on a uniform," and teammate Tommy Smith recalled (for the July 16, 1909 *Tacoma Times*) having to show him in the locker room how to keep up his stirrups. Outside of Toledo, inside Ohio now, did he picture Cleveland's latest pitching star Addie Joss, the former Mud Hen, sizing him up beside Cy Young? With the cities behind him, the view outside his coach resembled what his father saw coming down from Wisconsin to Grafton. Here was a preponderance of flat space and empty time for McKean to think these thoughts. And then again, he may have slept like a dead man, succumbing to the molar grinding of the tracks, like Odysseus, returning home asleep.

Much of McKean's work over the final decade of his life was accomplished in the service of M.J. Hinkel and, so that the retired ballplayer's world might retain something of the seasonal order of baseball, Hinkel's amateur baseball teams. Of course, such employment was a happy way for McKean, now in his forties, to combine his considerable experience in tavern-keeping with his even greater expertise as a baseball man. McKean would have met his future employer through their mutual interest in boxing, as Matt Hinkel was among many things a professional boxing promoter and referee.[69] The partnership was blessed with early success; Hinkel's Base Ball Club was Cleveland City Champs for 1910 and, two years later, McKean was still proudly using the club's letterhead for a letter to Grafton.[70] McKean joined Local 108 of the Hotel and Restaurant Employees and Bar Tenders International Union, in January 1909, and remained an active member, working for Hinkel, until his death.[71] The M.J. Hinkel Company is remembered in Cleveland as the local wholesale distributor for the Old J.H. Cutter Kentucky whiskies. Matt Hinkel (1867–1936) is sometimes remembered for his involvement, years after Ed McKean's death, in one of the infamous bootleg schemes during Prohibition.[72]

The good name of Ed McKean was regularly invoked in the Cleveland Naps' initial plans to stage an old-timers exhibition at League Park. Ed Bang, who had been 15 years old when the Cleveland Spiders captured the Temple Cup, reports a Naps/Spiders alumni game in the offing, and lists McKean prominently among the veterans (Tebeau, Childs, Wallace, Young, Zimmer,

TEN. *A Pennant for Springfield (1907–1908 seasons)* 287

O'Connor, and Burkett) who had apparently "signified their willingness to play."⁷³ Earlier, in January, the *San Antonio Light* had circulated the rumor that "there is a movement on foot [*sic*] to arrange a series of games between the old Clevelands and the present-day Naps. Many of the old guard are still alive, some of them actively engaged in baseball."⁷⁴ Nothing concrete ever came of these plans involving the Cleveland club; the 15th anniversary of the Temple Cup championship came and went. By the time McKean did return to League Park to play in an exhibition game, on August 14, 1909, the event had been reduced to a few Spiders and old-timers from the area challenging an all-star team of Cleveland amateurs. McKean played the whole game at shortstop and, one last time, shared the thrill of a victory with his teammates. It was to be

Johnny Kilbane, featherweight champion of the world, was the McKeans' neighbor in West Cleveland (Library of Congress).

"McKean's last appearance on the diamond."⁷⁵ Afterward, he took off the vintage Spiders uniform and folded it like a flag.

The day he left the National League, in 1899, he grew four years younger, dropping the ruse of the 1864 birth date. At the so-called "reunion" game, McKean appeared to have aged two decades in two years. The Ed McKean in the team photograph is barely recognizable as the man who peers steadily ahead in the Springfield team picture from only two years before. The broad McKean forehead and high cheekbones have been disfigured by a bloated face. His unfocused eyes are turned toward some remote object, while the other players look at the camera. The old man wears a puzzled expression, as if wondering at the change in himself. The athlete's body has morphed unexpectedly, as well, reverting to the plebian features of a farmer having sold his land and moved into town. Limp hands seem useless in his lap. Seated below his senior, Sam Wise, McKean would be taken instead for the elder. On the other hand, reports indicate that, as long as McKean could play baseball, he preferred the hard-nosed variety. Henry P. Edwards, who worked in the American League office during World War II, remembered last seeing McKean play in a charity game in 1907: "After about two innings, he tossed his glove away and played bare-handed, saying he could not get used to playing with a glove."[76] While the Cleveland front office had been making overtures to bring in all of "the old guard ... still alive," the number of old Spiders family was shrinking. Frank DeHass Robison passed away in early October 1908. His daughter, Helene Hathaway Britton (1879–1950), would inherit the St. Louis Cardinals franchise in three more years, after the death of Stanley Robison, her uncle. Frank Robison's stars Ed McKean and Charles Zimmer were the only two Spiders in attendance at his Cleveland funeral.[77]

The death of Martin McKean, in November 1911, pretty much closed the Grafton chapter in Ed McKean's life. As late as 1896, he'd continued to vote in Grafton, and Lorain County newspapers noted his frequent visits.[78] Now that both of his parents were gone, the identity of Ed McKean the Clevelander became firmly established. He seemed from the start to have always been part of Cleveland, even though today's "born in Cleveland" epithet is inaccurate. Ed McKean was a living, working, story-telling landmark in his Ohio City neighborhood more than a decade before the West Side Market was established. In 1912, from the upstairs windows at the rear of his house, he could watch the Market's landmark tower under construction.

Citizen McKean had special cause to celebrate the occasion of one of Cleveland's biggest St. Patrick's Day parades, on March 17, 1912, in honor of Johnny Kilbane's world featherweight championship. McKean had been the referee in the controversial Kilbane versus Biz Mackey fight of March 29, 1909. That night, Kilbane claimed a foul after being floored by his opponent, but the ring-side physician found no evidence of a low blow, and Ed McKean made an unpopular decision, ruling it a technical knock-out.[79] Both Kilbane and McKean were highly visible figures in the community. Kilbane, in his retirement from boxing, served a term in the Ohio senate and ran a gym for kids in McKean's neighborhood. Later, he worked in city hall with Ed McKean's son Robert, as Clerk of Courts for Cleveland, until his death in 1957. Ed McKean also maintained his interest in developing baseball players in the area. The September 28, 1911, *Sandusky Star-Journal* carried a story about the All Professionals, an amateur team from Cleveland managed by McKean, playing one

TEN. A Pennant for Springfield (1907–1908 seasons)

of its games at Sandusky. McKean was touring with a good barnstorming team he'd pieced together from major league signees like Pete Johns of Akron, and two Cleveland boys, Silent Bill Hopke and Ed Havel. Hopke and Havel presented unusual resumes, having lately played in the New York State and Negro leagues. On McKean's recommendation in the spring of 1911, Tom O'Brien, who was managing the Duluth White Sox of the Minnesota-Wisconsin League at the time, picked up third baseman Emil Leber, a lad from Cleveland.[80]

This was the period when some enterprising journalist, the likes of Elmer Bates or Charles W. Mears, could have played McKean's Boswell. He was always good for a quote. The garrulous old baseballist was sometimes interviewed by the newspapers, McKean behind his bar and holding forth on baseball past and present, but there was no demand for such a book.[81] On the other hand, his old friend Bates might have been a stranger to McKean of late; a year after McKean's death, Bates' activities in GOP politics made him a delegate to the convention that nominated for President Warren G. Harding, the former owner of the Marion, Ohio, baseball team. Tempting as it might be to see Ed McKean as the victim of one last defining cultural stereotype—that of the loquacious Irish saloon-keeper dispensing "the creature" (whiskey)—he seems to have been happy at his trade and appreciated by his employer and colleagues. McKean may have found fulfillment in his work in the community. He always was a team player.

McKean's name would occasionally surface in the papers. Ed Bang announced prematurely, in *Sporting Life*, that a Cleveland team in the Columbia League would compete for fans with the Naps. The rogue league's president, John Powers, did award a franchise to Matt Hinkel, who, in turn, made McKean the team's manager. The partnership pledged to have $10,000 in the bank to get things started at the opening of the season. McKean and Hinkel subsequently went into negotiations with Fredrick Ingersoll, owner of Luna Park, an amusement facility out on East 110th Street (about six miles from Public Square), concerning the erection of a 20,000-seat baseball stadium.[82] Nothing ever came of the new league, and Ingersoll claimed bankruptcy on his Cleveland developments in 1908.

Ed McKean began seeing Dr. Ralph A. Scherz, a physician with an office on Lorain Avenue, on July 14, 1919, complaining of severe abdominal pain, most severe after eating, and blood in his vomit. McKean had probably left untreated what turned out to be a gastric ulcer, and continued drinking would have kept the ulcer from healing. A month later, on August 16, Dr. Scherz was called to the Jay Street residence when McKean's ulcer had burst, sending his patient into shock as he hemorrhaged uncontrollably.[83] The physician specified

The grave of Edward McKean, Calvary Cemetery, Cleveland (courtesy Tom Kryss).

the cause of death, filling out State of Ohio Bureau of Vital Statistics certificate of death number 47354, as "Gastric Ulcer due to alcoholism." Edward John McKean passed away at home, at 6 o'clock in the evening of August 16, 1919. It was an offday on the Indians calendar, while the Yankees came to Cleveland.

His funeral mass was performed at St. Patrick's Catholic Church on Bridge Avenue, at 9 o'clock in the morning of August 19.[84] McKean would have heard the cathedral's chime of 11 bells daily from his house. He was buried the same day in Calvary Cemetery. McKean must have attended the funeral of Ed Delahanty and, more recently, that of Oliver Tebeau, friends who were already at rest in the cemetery.[85]

Tebeau was interred in these sacred grounds even though he'd ended his own life, one morning before opening time in his St. Louis pub, after his wife left the marriage.[86] Patsy's ghost must have kicked until the Umpire let him in. Clarence Childs had died of Bright's disease in a Baltimore hospital 17 years after the Spiders' great Temple Cup victory in his native city. Ed McKean's widow never remarried. Belle McKean raised their children—Edward J. (1898–1968), Robert D. (1901–1975), Martin J. (1908–1961), and Marie M. (1912–1988)—in the homestead, before retreating to the suburbs, at the Sunset Country Club allotment in Sheffield Lake, in October 1926.[87] She died on September 23, 1952. Her funeral mass was performed in the same church as her husband's funeral had been 33 years before, but her remains were not interred beside his.[88]

TEN. *A Pennant for Springfield (1907–1908 seasons)*

Ed McKean's grave at Calvary can still be found, located a short distance down the wooded hill from his two mates' plots. (He might have hit a baseball and let it roll that far.) Past his grass-level marker, beyond the crushed gravel drive, a weedy railroad track makes an occasional quotation from Grafton in its runs.

1895 Temple Cup: October 8, Final Game

> Long has paled that sunny sky:
> Echoes fade and memories die:
> Autumn frosts have slain July.
> —On the last page of *Through the Looking-Glass*

While more than 1,500 Spiders fans sat transfixed in Cleveland's Music Hall, watching little ballplayer figures in a play-by-play reenactment of telegraphed updates, game five in Baltimore was sparsely attended, the Orioles' fans fearing another riot. The sight of only 4,100 supporters in the stands may have contributed to Baltimore's uninspired, petty play.[1] Until the seventh inning, when Dent Young crossed the plate with the first run of the game, the afternoon was enlivened mostly by Jesse Burkett's chagrin, to open the Cleveland half of the third inning, upon falling for Scoops Carey's hidden-ball trick after he'd bunted himself to first.[2]

Indeed, a cool-headed Patsy Tebeau went out of his way to avoid the customary fight and ejection, or the extraordinary replay of the riot, in the bottom of that seventh inning. First, Tim Hurst's blown call had cost the home team a base hit. Then, with an Oriole in scoring position and the game on the line, Bill Hoffer grounded routinely to McKean who threw on to first. Mac's throw had Hoffer beat. But first baseman Tebeau, for reasons of his own, caught the ball with his foot off the bag and, as Hoffer crossed the base, neatly tripped him with his leg, correctly calculating that Hurst could not clearly see the play. Hoffer had arrived at the park mad about losing game two, and the two opponents had a history; earlier, the pitcher had accused the playing-manager of "giving him the leg" whenever he ran the bases. As quick as the out call issued from Hurst's mouth, Hoffer sprang upon Tebeau, throwing him to the ground. Pat

"K is for Keeler, / As fresh as green paint, / The fastest and mostest / To hit where they ain't" is a stanza from the Ogden Nash poem "Line-Up for Yesterday," published in the January 1949 issue of *SPORT Magazine* in honor of Willie Keeler (Mears Auctions).

Tebeau coolly refused to accommodate the irate pitcher, with the championship only a few outs away.

Tim Hurst would reflect on the postseason series: "They are the hardest of all [games] to umpire; it is hard enough to officiate in a regular League game, but when the receipts are to go to the players the poor umpire has more

Scorecard, in a Baltimore program, from the deciding game of the 1895 Temple Cup (Robert Edward Auctions).

than his share of trouble."[3] As it turned out, Oliver Tebeau enjoyed a great day in the sun; as the game played out, it was his single to right field which scored Kid Childs with the winning run in the seventh. On the other side of the field, an all-but-defeated Baltimore team was paying more attention to trying to provoke Tebeau into a mistake than it was to playing—they committed five errors on the afternoon. In the eighth inning, third baseman McGraw got into the act, viciously tagging Tebeau in the mouth as he slid into third to the loud approval of the stands. And still Tebeau did not fight.

Baltimore's last chance was granted by the series' best pitcher and best infielder. Cy Young had held the Orioles at bay until he tired in the ninth and, with two outs, walked McGraw and Keeler before hitting Jennings with a pitch. He'd suddenly loaded the bases, and the potential winning run strode to the plate in the form of Joe Kelley. Left fielder Kelley had misplayed Childs' can-of-corn fly ball, allowing Young to score and opening up Cleveland's big three-run seventh inning. Now, in one at-bat, Kelley damned near put his goat's horns on Ed McKean. Just a year before, on September 3, Joe Kelley had gone 9-for-9 in a doubleheader. His prowess at the bat made him so vain that he took a mirror with him to the outfield. Young composed himself and succeeded in inducing Kelley, a feared right-handed pull hitter, to send a routine grounder out to short. But McKean booted the ball, John McGraw scored, and the bases were still full of Birds.

There is some disagreement about the fielding play. John Phillips calls it "a hot shot" that went for a scratch hit. Cy Young's biographer, also sympathetic to McKean in this case, judges Joe Kelley's ball was "a sharp hit that McKean could only knock down," keeping it in the infield and saving a second run.[4] Every source, from game day on, agrees in calling it a "boot," but the box scores never charged McKean with an error for his effort. What's clear is, McKean was feeling the pressure. He had failed at the plate with runners on in the seventh inning, right before Childs hit the fateful ball out to Kelley, and his only hit in the game came back in the third, a single to left that went for nothing. Before this play, he'd fielded five chances without a miscue. The extra out brought to the plate Steve Brodie, who had driven in 134 runs that season for Baltimore. McKean and the Cleveland infielders set themselves for the pitch, as Young was already into his windup.

According to Reed Browning, Cy Young "did not raise his left leg high; his stride was closer to a big step than a kick, and today we would probably call it a slide step." Then, "when his left leg was raised, he briefly pivoted away from the plate on his right leg, turning some of his back toward the batter ... to hide his ball and glove." And "after releasing the ball he did not fling his right arm far across his body, preferring to get his raised right foot back down to the ground and so to plant himself to be able to deal with any batted ball."[5]

After Young delivered, Brodie tapped a weak one-hopper back to him. Tebeau had Cy Young's toss in his glove at first base, and—it seemed irrationally abrupt—the battle was over and won. And then silence. The crowing achievement of Ed McKean's baseball life was met with silence. "There was not a shout for the Temple cup winners," the *Cleveland Plain Dealer* reported, "while the crowd filed out of the grounds like a funeral procession." After the final out, fans by the hundreds did rush the Cleveland omnibus; however, this day a phalanx of Baltimore's finest routinely escorted the team to safety.[6]

On the inhospitable field of a city far away, Patsy Tebeau's Hibernian Spiders had claimed the first championship in Cleveland's considerable baseball history. *The Sporting News* of October 12 was unequivocal: "No one will deny now that Oliver Tebeau ranks with Hanlon and Anson as a base ball general and leader. His able management of the Spiders merits the success he has achieved. His only fault is a proneness to dirty ball playing and a disposition to resort to unwarranted methods to gain a victory. Pat's loyalty to his club is responsible for this." And the *Spalding Guide for 1896* had "McKean leading [Cleveland] in the infield with phenomenal work."[7]

For his third postseason, McKean batted an even .300. Mac reached base nine times in 23 plate appearances, on the strength of six hits, including a double and a triple, and three walks. The slugger led Cleveland in playoff RBIs in 1895, as he had in 1892; he would tie for the club lead in 1896. Ed McKean retired with 11 RBIs in 15 career postseason games, and a batting average of .361. Among his 22 career hits were two doubles and two triples. Opposing pitchers walked McKean five times. He seemed constantly to be on base. On defense, to recall the words of Charles W. Mears:

He was everywhere, getting everything.

Appendix A
Ed McKean's Major League Career Batting Record

Sources: Lee Sinin, *Complete Baseball Encyclopedia*, 2013; www.baseball-reference.com.

Year/Team	G	AB	R	H	2B	3B	HR	RBI	BB	SO	SB	BA	SLG	OBA	OPS	TB	XBH
1887 Blues	132	539	97	154	16	13	2	54	60	32	76	.286	.375	.358	.733	202	31
1888 Blues	131	548	94	164	21	15	6	68	28	30	52	.299	.425	.340	.765	233	42
1889 Spiders	123	500	88	159	22	8	5	75	42	25	35	.318	.424	.375	.799	213	35
1890 Spiders	136	530	95	157	15	14	7	61	87	25	23	.296	.417	.401	.818	221	36
1891 Spiders	*141*	603	115	170	13	12	6	69	64	19	14	.282	.373	.352	.651	225	31
1892 Spiders	129	531	76	139	14	10	0	93	49	28	19	.262	.326	.325	.651	173	24
1893 Spiders	125	545	103	169	29	24	4	133	50	14	16	.310	.473	.372	.846	258	57
1894 Spiders	130	554	116	198	30	15	8	128	49	12	33	.357	.509	.412	.921	282	53
1895 Spiders	131	565	131	193	32	17	8	119	46	25	13	.342	.501	.397	.898	283	57
1896 Spiders	133	571	100	193	29	12	7	112	45	9	13	.338	.468	.388	.856	267	48
1897 Indians	125	523	83	143	21	14	2	78	40	14	15	.273	.379	.330	.708	198	37
1898 Spiders	151	604	89	172	23	1	9	94	56	18	11	.285	.371	.346	.717	224	33
1899 Perfectos	67	277	40	72	7	3	3	40	20	4	4	.260	.339	.310	.649	94	13
13-Year Total	1655	6894	1227	2084	272	158	67	1124	636	257	323	.302	.417	.365	.781	2873	497

Appendix B

Ed McKean's Year-by-Year Offensive Rankings

Sources: David Nemec, *The Great Encyclopedia of 19th-Century Major League Baseball*; www.baseball-reference.com.

		Among League SS	*On Team*	
1887 AA				
Cleveland				
132	G	5th	1st	
539	AB	3rd	1st	
154	H	4th	1st	
97	R	5th	3rd	
16	2B	5th	4th	
13	3B	7th	9th	
2	HR	4th	3rd	
54	RBI	7th	3rd	
60	BB	4th	1st	
76	SB	2nd	2nd	*Fifth-most stolen bases by a rookie in history.*
.286	BA	5th	2nd	*Averaged .357 according to 1887 scoring rules.*
.375	SLG	4th	3rd	
1888 AA				
Cleveland				
131	G	6th	1st	*Only 78 games at shortstop.*
548	AB	1st	1st	
164	H	1st	1st	*Third-most hits in AA.*
94	R	1st	1st	
21	2B	1st	1st	
15	3B	1st	1st	*Second-most triples in AA.*
6	HR	1st	1st	
68	RBI	1st	1st	

28	BB	3rd	4th
52	SB	1st	3rd
.299	BA	1st	1st
.425	SLG	1st	1st

1889 NL
Cleveland

123	G	2nd	3rd
500	AB	2nd	4th
159	H	2nd	1st
88	R	2nd	2nd
22	2B	2nd	1st
8	3B	1st	3rd
5	HR	2nd	2nd
75	RBI	2nd	3rd
42	BB	1st	4th
35	SB	3rd	2nd
.318	BA	2nd	1st
.424	SLG	2nd	1st

1890 NL
Cleveland

136	G	2nd	1st	
530	AB	2nd	2nd	
157	H	2nd	1st	*.401 on-base percentage.*
95	R	2nd	2nd	
15	2B	4th	3rd	
14	3B	2nd	1st	
7	HR	2nd	1st	
61	RBI	3rd	2nd	
87	BB	1st	1st	*Second-most walks in NL.*
23	SB	6th	1st	
.296	BA	2nd	1st	
.417	SLG	2nd	1st	

1891 NL
Cleveland

141	G	1st	1st	
603	AB	1st	1st	*First NL player to bat 600 times in a season.*
170	H	1st	1st	*Second-most hits in NL.*
115	R	2nd	2nd	
13	2B	3rd	7th	
12	3B	1st	2nd	
6	HR	2nd	1st	
69	RBI	2nd	4th	
64	BB	2nd	3rd	
14	SB	7th	7th	
.282	BA	1st	2nd	
.373	SLG	2nd	3rd	

1892 NL
Cleveland

129	G	9th	6th	
531	AB	9th	7th	
139	H	6th	6th	
76	R	6th	6th	
14	2B	7th	5th	
10	3B	3rd	6th	
0	HR	12th	8th	
93	RBI	1st	1st	*Tops NL clutch hitting index.*
49	BB	3rd	6th	
19	SB	9th	4th	
.262	BA	6th	4th	
.326	SLG	7th	7th	

1893 NL
Cleveland

125	G	5th	1st	
545	AB	2nd	1st	
169	H	1st	3rd	
103	R	4th	4th	
29	2B	1st	2nd	
24	3B	1st	1st	*Third best in NL.*
4	HR	4th	2nd	
133	RBI	1st	1st	*Career-best 1.06 RBI per game.*
50	BB	7th	4th	
16	SB	7th	8th	
.310	BA	3rd	5th	
.473	SLG	1st	3rd	*Third on clutch hitting index.*

1894 NL
Cleveland

130	G	1st	1st	
554	AB	2nd	1st	
198	H	1st	1st	*Career best.*
116	R	5th	3rd	
30	2B	3rd	1st	
15	3B	3rd	1st	
8	HR	4th	1st	
128	RBI	1st	1st	*Fifth most in NL.*
49	BB	3rd	3rd	
33	SB	2nd	1st	
.357	BA	1st	2nd	*Career high.*
.509	SLG	2nd	1st	*Career best.*

1895 NL
Cleveland

131	G	1st	1st	
565	AB	1st	1st	*Led NL in at bats.*

193	H	2nd	2nd	
131	R	2nd	2nd	*Career best.*
32	2B	2nd	1st	*Career best.*
17	3B	1st	1st	
8	HR	2nd	1st	
119	RBI	2nd	1st	*Fourth best in NL.*
45	BB	3rd	4th	
12	SB	11th	6th	
.342	BA	2nd	2nd	
.501	SLG	2nd	2nd	*284 total bases.*

1896 NL
Cleveland

133	G	1st	1st	
571	AB	1st	2nd	
193	H	2nd	2nd	
100	R	4th	3rd	
29	2B	2nd	1st	
12	3B	2nd	2nd	
7	HR	3rd	1st	
112	RBI	2nd	1st	*Fourth best in NL.*
45	BB	4th	5th	
13	SB	11th	7th	
.338	BA	5th	3rd	
.468	SLG	3rd	2nd	

1897 NL
Cleveland

125	G	4th	3rd	
523	AB	2nd	1st	
143	H	6th	4th	
83	R	5th	4th	
21	2B	5th	4th	
14	3B	1st	2nd	
2	HR	7th	3rd	
78	RBI	4th	2nd	
40	BB	5th	4th	
15	SB	6th	6th	
.273	BA	10th	7th	
.379	SLG	8th	6th	

1898 NL
Cleveland

151	G	2nd	2nd	*Career high.*
604	AB	2nd	2nd	
172	H	2nd	3rd	
89	R	4th	2nd	
23	2B	4th	2nd	
1	3B	9th	7th	
9	HR	1st	1st	*Fourth most in NL.*

94	RBI	2nd	2nd
56	BB	4th	1st
11	SB	8th	3rd
.285	BA	5th	3rd
.371	SLG	5th	2nd

1899 NL

St. Louis

67	G	13th	11th	*Only 42 games at shortstop.*
277	AB	13th	9th	
72	H	13th	9th	
40	R	13th	9th	
7	2B	12th	11th	
3	3B	8th	10th	
3	HR	4th	5th	
40	RBI	12th	9th	
20	BB	11th	7th	
4	SB	13th	13th	
.260	BA	11th	8th	
.339	SLG	9th	8th	

Appendix C

Lines from a Poem Attributed by Elmer Bates to Ed McKean (Sporting Life, September 26, 1891)

"The Season's Over; or, The Short Stop's Reverie"

The sun shone bright in the ball field,
And all nature seemed so gay,
When a batter, who a bat could wield,
Stepped forth like a baleful bay;
And smashed the ball with power immense,
And it came down fast and sweet;
Some thought 'twas going through the fence,
But I got there with both feet.

That night when we went to our suppers
My steak and tea were cold,
The girl turned on her uppers
And said I was bad and bold,
It was her fellow who made the smash,
And she wasn' going to see
Warm tea, and bread and steak and hash
Fed to a brute like me.

Chapter Notes

Preface

1. Left-handed-hitting shortstops were commonplace in the Deadball Era. Besides McKean, a partial list would include Sam Wise, Herman Long, Jack Rowe, Doc Irwin, Candy Nelson, Frank Shugart, and Monte Ward. George Davis was a switch-hitter but, of course, mostly hit from the left due to the preponderance of right-handed pitchers. Furthermore, David Nemec lists, on page 345 of *The Great Encyclopedia of 19th-Century Major League Baseball* (New York: Donald I. Fine, 1997), half a dozen shortstops who *threw* left-handed: Jimmy Hallinan, Billy Redmond, Bill McClellan, Jimmy Macullar, Jack Leary, and Bill Hulen. (The sinister catcher was not unknown, either. John Clements, Sy Sutcliffe, and Sam Trot, three of the century's most serviceable catchers, threw the ball left-handed. Clements had already become the first man to play 1,000 games behind the plate when the Cleveland Spiders brought him in for four games in 1899.)

2. Bob Seltzer, "'Mr. Pension' Works at City Hall," Cleveland *Press*, June 26, 1964. Clipping in the McKean player file at the National Baseball Hall of Fame.

3. John Phillips, *The Spiders: Who Was Who* (Cabin John, MD: Capital, 1988). It's edifying to note that Jerold Casway, when he was writing his biography of Ed Delahanty, was able to contact a Smith family, descendants of Jim Delahanty, still living in Ed McKean's home town of Grafton, Ohio. Ed McKean's friendship with the Delahantys goes back to his earliest days in Cleveland—and all the way up to the present.

4. Phillips, in *The Spiders: Who Was Who* (Cabin John, MD: Capital, 1991 revised ed.), furnishes the following itemized comparison:

	McKean	Boudreau
Seasons in Cleveland	12	13
Games w/ Cleveland teams	1687	1560
Lifetime BA	.302	.295
Top BA	.357	.355
HRs w/ Cleveland teams	66	63
Hits w/ Cleveland teams	2011	1706
Runs w/ Cleveland teams	1187	823
RBIs w/ Cleveland teams	1030	740

5. David Nemec, *Major League Baseball Profiles, 1871–1900*, Volume 2 (Lincoln: University of Nebraska Press, 2011), p. 95.

6. David Nemec, *The Beer and Whisky League* (New York: Lyons & Burford, 1994), p. 139.

7. Bill James, *Whatever Happened to the Hall of Fame?* (New York: Fireside, 1995), p. 177. By James' standard, the average Hall of Famer earns 50 points; he awards Ed McKean 48.

8. Frederick Taylor, *The Runmakers: A New Way to Rate Baseball Players* (Baltimore: Johns Hopkins University Press, 2011), pp. 151, 149.

9. David Nemec and Dave Zeman, *The Baseball Rookies Encyclopedia* (Washington: Brassey's, 2004), p. 115.

10. Bill Felber, ed., *Inventing Baseball* (Phoenix: SABR, 2013), pp. 211–213, 214–216, 241–243, 254–256. The designated games are Boston at Cleveland, October 2, 1889, New York at Cleveland, October 5, 1889, Washington at Cleveland, May 16, 1897; the playoff series between Boston and Cleveland, October 17–24, 1892, counts as a game.

11. Luke Salisbury, *The Cleveland Indian: The Legend of King Saturday* (Seattle: Black Heron Press, 2007) and Bill Bildner/Loren

Long, *Blastin' the Blues* (New York: Simon and Schuster Books for Young Readers, 2011).

12. David L. Fleitz, *The Irish in Baseball* (Jefferson, NC: McFarland), p. 71.

13. Phillips, *Who Was Who* (1991), and Nemec, *Profiles*, p. 95. Both authors cite an April 4, 1894, article in the Cleveland *Leader*.

14. Elmer Bates perpetrated an innocent hoax, as an expression of his endearment for McKean and also for the entertainment of his readers. Bates' fun demonstrates how very different the sports page of McKean's day was from today, where a running joke like theirs would be considerd unprofessional or misleading. I confess, my original impulse was to search for the book of verse authored by Ed McKean that Bates goes on about. I was not alone in my gullibility. Bates laughs about having years earlier planted a similar tall tale, the one about George Cuppy "building" a 17-story tavern in his hometown of Logansport, which caused actual building contractors to hound the pitcher for a year (Cleveland *Press*, November 17, 1906. Clipping in the George Cuppy player file, National Baseball Hall of Fame.) Like the contractors, I wished the story to be true—one of my original interests in writing about McKean was to recover the lost poems of the Spiders poet. In his September 26, 1891, column, Bates prints 16 lines from "advanced proofs" of a poem, entitled "The Season's Over, or The Shortstop's Reverie," from a book authored by McKean and recently sold "to an Eastern syndicate." (See Appendix C for the text of the poem.) He presents himself as having read the book-length manuscript: "The [whole] poem would fill about 146 columns of The Sporting Life [that amounts to one entire issue], and is, of course, too long to publish, although its merits[—]its clever conceits; its Lowellian style; its crisp epigrammatical climaxes[—]entitles it to the publicity which The Sporting Life columns alone can give it." Over the next three years, Bates mentions the shortstop's activity in composing and apparently publishing poems in at least 13 columns for *Sporting Life* (four references in 1891, eight in 1892, and two in 1893). Throughout, Bates' language tends to blur the distinction between imaginary poem and book-length poem, a clue that what he says may be pulling his reader's leg. However, sometimes Bates' attention to specifics can be convincing; when McKean injures his finger in a gun accident, in April, 1892, Bates writes: "During his long rest McKean has about finished his poem on 'Some Grounders That We Have Stopped.'" Other times, Bates presents his reader an obvious send up of the player's country origins in terms of George B. Foster's best-selling expose from 1850, "New York by Gaslight," announcing that "McKean has begun a new poem entitled 'Grafton by Gaslight.' At least one reporter passed along Bates' non-story. The October 3, 1891, *The Sporting News* observes: "Mac goes for everything that comes to short and is now going for poetry!" I personally thank David Nemec for setting me straight. "McKean was a man of many interests," he broke it to me in his July 30, 2012, email, "but poetry?"

Prelude

1. The account of the Elks Club banquet is drawn from the following sources: *Spalding's Official Base Ball Guide*, 1896, pp. 58–59; Cleveland *Press*, October 13, 1895; *Sporting Life*, October 19, 1895; *The Sporting News*, October 19, 1895; Reed Browning, *Cy Young* (Amherst: University of Massachusetts Press, 2000), pp. 56–57; David Nemec, *Encyclopedia of 19th-Century*, pp. 540, 543; and James M. Egan, *Base Ball on the Western Reserve* (Jefferson, NC: McFarland, 2008), p. 242. Party-goer Nig Cuppy recollected, years afterward, a champagne-fueled bacchanal climaxing in an impromptu game of drop-kick with the Temple Cup. The event, if it's not an embellishment, must have occurred a year later, in 1896, when Cleveland returned the Cup to Baltimore in that city. For Cuppy's anecdote, see John Phillips, ed., *Uncle Nick's Baseball Party* (Cabin John, MD: Capital, 1991), p. 81.

2. "The difference between Tweedledum and Tweedledee" was a favorite trope among newspaper writers of the period. They employed it, in columns on baseball, cycling and shooting, to mean there was really no difference or choice (see, e.g., *Sporting Life*, December 14, 1895, June 9, 1886, June 1, 1887, August 8, 1888, March 18, 1893, February 16, 1895, and January 4, 1896). Some postmodern literary critics of the scene in Book 4 of *Through the Looking-Glass* have suggested that the novelist's intention was specular—to make a mirror image of Dee beside himself, not the fat twins so memorably drawn by the book's illustrator, John Tenniels. To briefly employ Lewis Carroll's logic, if Ed McKean is a mirror to the nineteenth-century game,

then we must be vigilant not to sometimes take the reverse image (i.e., McKean as a right-handed batter, or McKean as a 100-error shortstop, or McKean as slow afoot) for the reality.

3. *Sporting Life*, March 23, 1895.
4. Cleveland *Leader*, May 2, 1891.
5. *The Sporting News*, March 17, 1886.
6. Egan, *Western Reserve*, p. 202.
7. Clarence Childs' personal background is drawn heavily from Jimmy Keenan's "Cupid Childs," SABR BioProject.
8. Stolen-base figures were inflated for the 1887 season, when a runner taking an extra base was officially credited with a steal.
9. *Sporting Life*, July 25, 1891.
10. *Sporting Life*, November 29, 1890.
11. New York *Tribune*, February 26, 1922.
12. Jerrold Casway, *Ed Delahanty in the Emerald Age of Baseball* (South Bend: University of Notre Dame Press, 2004), p. 33.
13. Ring Lardner, *Some Champions* (New York: Scribners, 1976), p. 21.
14. *Sporting Life*, October 12, 1895.
15. *Sporting Life*, September 28, 1895.
16. Browning, *Cy Young*, p. 10.
17. *The Sporting News*, April 15, 1899.
18. *Sporting Life*, December 26, 1896.
19. Bill Burgess, www.baseballguru.com.
20. Nemec, *Beer and Whisky League*, p. 134.
21. *Sporting Life*, October 19, 1895.
22. *Spalding's Official Base Ball Guide*, 1896, p. 58, probably written by attendee John B. Foster.
23. Kate Greenaway's 1884 *The Language of Flowers* was a standard.
24. Oysterville was an epithet for the city of Baltimore commonly used in period newspapers.
25. Borrowing of Casway's term from *Ed Delahanty in the Emerald Age of Baseball*.
26. Charles C. Alexander, *John McGraw* (New York: Viking, 1988), p. 47.

Chapter One

1. Warner Berthoff, *Hart Crane: A Reintroduction* (Minneapolis: University of Minnesota Press, 1989), p. 39.
2. Doris P. Wildenheim, ed., *Grafton Ohio: Our Heritage Trail* (Grafton, OH: Grafton Village History Association, 2008), pp. 31–32.
3. www.villageofgrafton.org.
4. Wildenheim, *Grafton*, p. 46.

5. Walter B. Rideout, *Sherwood Anderson: A Writer in America*, vol. 1. (Madison: University of Wisconsin Press, 2006), p. 155.
6. This narrative of McKean family geneaology, including details of the emigration and immigration of Martin McKean, his marriage to Margaret Moran, and Ed McKean's birth, is a careful reconstruction of history. Official records, some handwritten and dating back two centuries, and family lore can be conflicting or unavailable. Take one example: handwritten documentation of the marriage is ambiguous. The first entry on page 10 of "The Cuyahoga County Record of Marriage," Volume 11, clearly shows "1864," and not 1863, for the date of the nuptial vows. However, all of the entries that follow on the page are for weddings in August, September, and October of 1863. Because it is unlikely that a record for 1864 would appear out of chronological order on a page for 1863 notices and, since the McKean entry is the only one on this page that wasn't signed by one of two justices, it seems likely that, in order to legally record the Wisconsin birth of their first child, the couple took the trouble to register their marriage at the Cuyahoga County courthouse in Cleveland. In an era when government and church maintained separate if not discrete files for marriages and births, it was commonplace for a Catholic ceremony to be documented with the state at the applicants' convenience. I've made every attempt to make my account accurate, in the realization that it may prove to be only the first stage in recovering Ed McKean's family history. I have relied on the following additional sources: records for St. Mary's Catholic Cemetery, Grafton, Ohio; "U.S. Census of Ohio Deaths, 1908–1953"; Lorain County deed for March 27, 1866; Lorain County Common Pleas Court case 23520, *Robert McKean vs. M.B. McKean*, July 20, 1926; U.S. Census reports for the years 1840, 1850, 1860, 1870, 1880, 1890, 1900, 1910, and 1920; obituaries for Martin McKean published in the Elyria *Republican*, November 17, 1910, and the Elyria *Evening Telegram*, November 14 and November 16, 1910; obituary for Edward J. McKean in the Cleveland *Plain Dealer*, August 17, 1919; Ohio death certificate of Edward J. McKean, file number 47354; obituary for Belle Moran McKean in the Cleveland *Press*, September 25, 1952; and information provided graciously at Midview Public Library, Grafton, Ohio. Also, I have had the advantages of communications and visits with

Thomas M. McKean and family, and descendants of the baseball player's son Martin, as well as phone conversations with Doris Wildenheim, Grafton village historian.

7. Wildenheim, *Grafton*, p. 68.
8. Wildenheim, *Grafton*, p. 239.
9. Phillips, *Who Was Who* (1991), Nemec, *Profiles*, p. 95, and Cleveland *Leader*, May 3, 1894.
10. See U.S. Bureau of Education, *Report of the Commissioner of Education for the Year 1886-87* (Washington: Government Printing Office, 1888).
11. Phillips, *Who Was Who* (1991) and Nemec, *Profiles*, p. 95.
12. Thomas A. Jackson, *Ireland Her Own: An Outline History of the Irish Struggle*, Desmond Greaves, ed. (New York: International Publishers, 1970), p. 234.
13. Quoted in Jackson, *Ireland*, p. 244.
14. John O'Beirne Ranelagh, *A Short History of Ireland*. Cambridge: Cambridge University Press, 1983), p. 111.
15. Michael C. O'Laughlin, *The Book of Irish Families, Great & Small*. 3rd ed. (Kansas City: Irish Geneaological Foundation, 2002), p. 121.
16. See Cornelius McKean, compiler, *McKean Geneaologies: From the Early Settlement of McKeans, or McKeens in America to the Present Time, 1902* (Charleston, SC: BiblioLife, 2009), passim.
17. www.ancestry.com, posted October 22, 2000.
18. www.usarchives.org.
19. www.Wisconsinhistoricalsociety.org.
20. Lorain County deed, dated March 27, 1866. In Wildenheim, *Grafton*, p. 27, on the vintage map of Eaton Township printed there, we can see the McKean lot (number 63) was cut across its lower section by the CCC railroad track to the Eaton quarry. Over these rails, workers brought the sandstone for constructing Immaculate Conception Church, the center of McKean family life.
21. *Sporting Life*, December 28, 1895.
22. E.g., *Sporting Life*, November 26, 1910.
23. Thomas Gallagher, *Paddy's Lament, Ireland 1846-1847: Prelude to Hatred*. (San Diego: Harcourt Brace, 1982), p. 290.
24. Wildenheim, *Grafton*, p. 70.
25. Egan, *Western Reserve*, p. 5.
26. Cited in Harvey Frommer, *Primitive Baseball* (New York: Atheneum, 1988), p. 10.
27. Richard L. McBane, *A Fine-Looking Lot of Ball-Tossers: The Remarkable Akrons of 1881* (Jefferson, NC: McFarland, 2005), p. 14; the citation, from the original article in the Cleveland *Leader*, is quoted in the Akron *Sunday Gazette*, April 27, 1879.
28. McBane, *Ball-Tossers*, pp. 22–23.
29. *Sporting Life*, July 21, 1886.
30. www.FamilyTreeMaker.com.
31. Alexander William Gillman, compiler, *Searches into the History of the Gillman or Gilman Family* (London: Elliott Stock), 1895.
32. Elyria *Republican*, December 27, 1883, and *Sporting Life*, April 27, 1887.
33. *Sporting Life*, April 27, 1887.
34. www.thedeadballera.com; also, the Elyria city directories for 1943, 1945, the Elyria *Republican*, August 11, 1892, and the *Cleveland City Directory* for 1892.
35. *The Official Gazette of the United States Patent Office*, vol. 279 (Washington: Government Printing Office, 1920), p. lvii.
36. Material for the history of Youngstown baseball was generously furnished by Robert Ault, reference librarian at Youngstown State University, in his email of July 31, 2012.
37. There exists hearsay evidence that Eddie McKean played for Youngstown as early as 1882. Reporters from McKean's playing days take for granted that 1882 was his rookie season, making him teammates with Cartwright and McAleer for three years. Also, John Phillips (who has no doubt accounted for every Cleveland newspaper article concerning the Spiders) always dates McKean's service with the Youngstown team from 1882. I believe Eddie McKean was too young to have played pro ball that early, and I am aware of no evidencial box score confirming the earlier date.
38. New Castle *News*, February 27, 1884.
39. New Castle *News*, April 4, 1884.
40. Harry Casey, "The Story of Baseball," *Baseball Magazine*, March 1912, 27.
41. McBane, *Ball-Tossers*, pp. 126–127, and *Sporting Life*, February 20, 1884.
42. McBane, *Ball-Tossers*, pp. 126–128; *Sporting Life*, February 20, 1884 and April 9, 1923. According to the October 28, 1885, *Sporting Life*, the UA promised the Oil and Iron League contract protection providing its teams would go along with their refusal to recognize the National Agreement, (especially its reserve clause) or a players' union.
43. Pittsburgh *Commercial Gazette*, April 6, 1884.
44. *Sporting Life*, October 21, 1885.

45. New Castle *News*, April 6, 1884, and *Sporting Life*, May 18, 1887.
46. Egan, *Western Reserve*, p. 159.
47. Pittsburgh *Commercial Gazette*, May 9, 1884.
48. Bill James, *The New Bill James Historical Baseball Abstract* (New York: Free Press, 2001), p. 764.
49. *Sporting* Life, January 23, 1897.
50. Robert Tiemann and Mark Rucker, eds., *Nineteenth Century Stars* (Kansas City: SABR, 1989), p. 84.
51. "Descendants of Owen McAleer," www.FamilyTreeMaker.genealogy.com.
52. See, e.g., *Sporting Life*, August 10, 1895.
53. New Castle *News*, May 11, 1884.
54. New Castle *News*, May 31, 1884.
55. *The Sporting News*, September 1, 1894.
56. *Sporting Life*, March 30, 1895.
57. *Sporting Life*, August 7, 1897.
58. Nemec, *Profiles*, p. 461.
59. Phillips, *Who Was Who* (1988).
60. *Sporting Life*, August 14, 1909.
61. New Castle *Daily News*, July 8, 1885.
62. New Castle *News*, July 5, 1884.
63. *New York Times*, March 14, 1915.
64. *Sporting Life*, August 14, 1909, and January 13, 1912.
65. New Castle *News*, July 6, 1884.
66. New Castle *News*, June 23, 1884.
67. New Castle *News*, July 25 and 30, 1884. (It provides some historical perspective to know that Tubby Spencer, McAleer's backup catcher on Browns teams, was born in 1884 in Oil City.)
68. New Castle *News*, July 8, 1884.

Chapter Two

1. Wildenheim, *Grafton*, p. 28. Around the time of Ed McKean's death, his son Robert suffered a nervous breakdown, withdrew from St. Ignatius High School on doctor's orders, and went to work for the Pennsylvania Railroad. Those six years as a yard clerk and dispatcher were healing for the young man who, over time, became senior cashier for the city of Cleveland. (Seltzer, "Mr. Pension.") Another son, Martin J., worked on the railroad as a tender of switches in his thirties.
2. Bill O'Neal, *The Southern League* (Austin: Eakin Press, 1994), pp. 38–39, 282. According to O'Neal, Grantland Rice, the first sports editor of the Nashville *Tennessean*, renamed the ball grounds Sulphur Dell so he could make rhymes for his baseball poems.
3. O'Neal, *Southern League*, p. 2.
4. O'Neal, *Southern League*, p. 2.
5. The starting lineup for that May 4, 1885, game was printed in the Nashville *Daily American*.
6. Milwaukee *Journal*, October 16, 1884.
7. *Sporting Life*, February 9, 1901.
8. *Sporting Life*, May 27, 1885.
9. Nemec, *Profiles*, p. 331.
10. *Sporting Life*, May 6, 1885.
11. Don Thompson, "Sam Thompson," SABR BioProject.
12. Bill Traughber, "Looking Back: The 1885 Nashville Americans, Part I," www.nashvillesoundsbaseball.com, May 11, 2006.
13. *Sporting Life*, April 15 and 29, 1885.
14. *Sporting Life*, April 22, 1885.
15. Paul Dickson, *The Dickson Baseball Dictionary*, 3rd ed. (New York: Norton, 2009), pp. 181–182. Dickson believes the term was originally applied to the Chicago teams of the 1870s, and the less derogatory term than "skunk" remained in use during McKean's career.
16. *Sporting Life*, April 22 and 29, 1885.
17. *Sporting Life*, June 3, 1885.
18. *Sporting Life*, October 22, 1892.
19. *Sporting Life*, June 17, 1885.
20. Nemec, *Profiles*, p. 356.
21. Nemec, *Profiles*, p. 461.
22. Nemec, *Profiles*, p. 347.
23. *Sporting Life*, May 20, 1893.
24. *Sporting Life*, January 20, 1886.
25. *Sporting Life*, February 24, 1886, and March 24, 1886.
26. *Sporting Life*, April 27, 1895.
27. All games for Providence are from *Sporting Life*, May 12 and 26, June 2 and 9, and July 7, 1886.
28. Nemec, *Profiles*, p. 14.
29. Edward Achorn, *Fifty-Nine in '84* (New York: Smithsonian Books, 2010), p. 50.
30. Rochester *Democrat and Chronicle*, June 9 and 11, 1886.
31. *The Sporting News*, August 2, 1886.
32. *Sporting Life*, June 30, 1886.
33. *The Sporting News*, August 9, 1886.
34. *The Sporting News*, August 9, 1886.
35. *The Sporting News*, June 28, 1886.
36. *The Sporting News*, August 2, 1886.
37. *The Sporting News*, September 6, 1886.
38. Unless otherwise noted, all games for Rochester are from the Rochester *Democrat and Chronicle*, June 9 through September 25, 1886.

39. *Sporting Life*, September 22, 1886.
40. *The Sporting News*, September 27, 1886.
41. *The Sporting News*, April 30, 1887.
42. *The Sporting News*, October 11, 1886.
43. *Sporting Life*, October 6, 1886.

1895 Temple Cup: October 1

1. John Phillips, *The 1895 Cleveland Spiders, Temple Cup Champions* (Cabin John, MD: Capital, 1990).
2. Browning, *Cy Young*, p. 234.
3. Much in this paragraph owes to Nemec, *Encyclopedia of 19th-Century*, pp. 536–537.
4. Bill Felber, *A Game of Brawl* (Lincoln: University of Nebraska Press, 2007), pp. 21–22.
5. Fleitz, *Irish*, pp. 87–88.
6. *Sporting Life*, September 28, 1895.
7. *The Sporting News*, Sepembert 21, 1895.
8. Frommer, *Primitive*, p. 71.
9. *The Sporting News*, August 24, 1895.
10. *Sporting Life*, October 5, 1895.
11. *The Sporting News*, August 24, 1895.
12. *The Sporting News*, August 31, 1895.
13. *The Sporting News*, September 7, 1895.
14. *Sporting Life*, July 7, 1894.
15. Egan, *Western Reserve*, pp. 222–223, and *The Sporting News*, April 14, 1894.
16. *Sporting Life*, September 28, 1895.
17. *Sporting Life*, August 16, 1913.
18. Robert Tiemann and Pete Palmer, "Major League Attendance," in *Total Baseball V*, ed. John Thorn, et al (New York: Viking, 1997), p. 102.
19. Nemec, *Encyclopedia of 19th-Century*, p. 403.
20. Franklin Lewis, *The Cleveland Indians* (New York: G.P. Putnam's Sons, 1949), p. 25.
21. Fleitz, *Irish*, p. 75.
22. Charley Rosen, *The Emerald Diamond: How the Irish Transformed America's Greatest Pastime* (New York: Harper, 2012), p. 108.
23. *The Sporting News*, August 17, 1895.
24. Henry Childs Merwin, "The Irish in American Life," *Atlantic Monthly*, March 1896, pp. 289–291.
25. McBane, *Ball-Tossers*, p. 97.
26. Phillips, *Uncle Nick's*, p. 91.
27. Fleitz, *Irish*, p. 65.
28. Phillips, *Who Was Who* (1988).
29. Rich Blevins, ed., *Addie Joss on Baseball* (Jefferson, NC: McFarland, 2012), pp. 1–2, 4.
30. Fleitz, *Irish*, pp. 65–70.
31. Fred Stein, *And the Skipper Bats Cleanup* (Jefferson, NC: McFarland, 2002), p. 55.
32. *Sporting Life*, December 19, 1896.
33. I quote the first two of four stanzas, clipping dating from February 1897, Charles W. Mears Baseball Scrapbooks, volume 42b, Cleveland Public Library.

Chapter Three

1. Pittsburgh *Press*, September 7, 1919.
2. This brief history of the shortstop comes from Dickson, *Dictionary*, p. 772, unless otherwise noted.
3. Tiemann and Rucker, *Stars*, p. 67.
4. Ross Barnes finished his career at short, but he was a second baseman for his remarkable power-hitting seasons a decade before McKean arrived in the majors.
5. While I was writing this chapter, Bill Dahlen made the ballot of the Hall of Fame's Veterans Committee. I felt confirmed in my belief that Ed McKean should have preceded him.
6. *Sporting Life*, February 2, 1887.
7. *Sporting Life*, September 14, 1887. When it came time for Chief Zimmer to sign his contract with the Blues, he initially confused S.D.W. Cleveland and the Cleveland club represented by Jimmy Williams.
8. *Sporting Life*, February 9, 1887.
9. *Sporting Life*, February 16, 1887.
10. Nemec, *Beer and Whisky*, pp. 133–134.
11. Nemec, *Beer and Whisky*, p. 21.
12. *Sporting Life*, February 16, 1887.
13. *Sporting Life*, April 13, 1887.
14. Material for the games during McKean's hitting streak are from *Sporting Life*, April 27 to May 25, 1887, and *The Sporting News*, May 7 to 28, 1887, unless otherwise noted.
15. *The Sporting News*, April 23, 1887.
16. Thorn, et al, eds., *Total Baseball V*, p. 1840.
17. Nemec, *Profiles*, pp. 288–289.
18. Egan, *Western Reserve*, p. 148.
19. *Sporting Life*, March 30, 1887.
20. *The Sporting News*, May 7, 1887.
21. The "Peter James Hotaling" entry in Tiemann and Rucker, *Stars*, p. 63, was written by Dan Hotaling, a descendent.
22. *Sporting Life*, May 18, 1887.

Notes—Chapter Four

23. *Sporting Life*, May 25, 1887.
24. *The Sporting News*, June 25, 1887.
25. *The Sporting News*, July 23, 1887.
26. In accordance with the rules of the day, he was credited with only 19 strikeouts when his catcher misplayed a third strike and the batter reached first.
27. Nemec, *Profiles*, pp. 226–227.
28. *The Sporting News*, September 24, 1887.
29. *The Sporting News*, September 17, 1887.
30. Batting statistics from Nemec and Zeman, *Rookies Encyclopedia*, p. 36. Fielding statistics from www.baseball-almanac.com, www.baseball-reference.com, and *The Sporting News*, October 17, 1887.
31. "Chief Zimmer" entry in David Pietrusza, et al, eds., *Baseball: The Biographical Encyclopedia* (Kingston, NY: Total/Sports Illustrated, 2000), p. 1279.
32. *The Sporting News*, September 17, 1887.
33. Philip Lowry, *Green Cathedrals* (New York: Walker, 2006), p. 70.
34. *Sporting Life*, March 28, 1888.
35. Egan, *Western Reserve*, pp. 155, 157, and *The Sporting News*, April 6, 1888.
36. *The Sporting News*, May 3, 1888.
37. Egan, *Western Reserve*, p. 156.
38. Nemec, *Beer and Whisky*, p. 149.
39. *The Sporting News*, June 16, 1888.
40. *The Sporting News*, June 13, 1888.
41. Thorn, et al, eds., *Total Baseball V*, p. 1844.
42. *The Sporting News*, June 2 and August 4, 1888.
43. *The Sporting News*, August 18, 1888.
44. *The Sporting News*, September 8, 1888.
45. I relied on Egan, *Western Reserve*, pp. 164–168, for my summaries of the Sunday games of 1888.
46. *The Sporting News*, September 22, 1888.
47. Nemec, *Beer and Whisky*, pp.161–162.
48. *Sporting Life*, October 31, 1888.

Chapter Four

1. *The Sporting News*, March 9, 1889.
2. *The Sporting News*, March 30, 1889.
3. *The Sporting News*, March 9, 1889.
4. Thorn, et al, eds., *Total Baseball V*, p. 1846.
5. Cited in Frommer, *Primitive*, p. 56.
6. Cleveland *Plain Dealer*, May 12, 1889, *Sporting Life*, May 18, 1889, and Egan, *Western Reserve*, pp. 173, 175.
7. I have not identified John O'Brien by his other nickname, used often by Cleveland sportswriters, to avoid confusing him with Darby O'Brien, the notorious Brooklyn outfielder.
8. *The Sporting News*, March 23 and 30, 1889.
9. Exhibition game descriptions are drawn from *The Sporting News*, March 23, 1889.
10. *The Sporting News*, April 27, 1889.
11. *The Sporting News*, May 18, 1889.
12. See John Phillips, *The Astonishing Cleveland Babes of 1889* (Cabin John, MD: Capital, 1994) for a game-by-game account of the Spiders season.
13. Unless otherwise noted, Phillips, *Babes of 1889*, is the source for the game accounts.
14. *The Sporting News*, May 11, 1889.
15. *The Sporting News*, July 20, 1889.
16. *Sporting Life*, March 19, 1892.
17. *Sporting Life*, March 19, 1892.
18. Obituary in *The Sporting News*, March 19, 1892.
19. *The Sporting News*, June 22, 1889.
20. *The Sporting News*, June 29, 1889. On the importance of the fire house as a social center for Irish-American males, see Casway, *Ed Delahanty*, p. 17.
21. *The Sporting News*, June 22, 1889.
22. *Sporting Life*, July 17, 1889.
23. *The Sporting News*, July 27, 1889.
24. *The Sporting News*, August 3, 1889.
25. Unattributed newspaper article in Phillips, *Babes of 1889*.
26. Unattributed newspaper article in Phillips, *Babes of 1889*.
27. *The Sporting News*, September 14, 1889.
28. Egan, *Western Reserve*, pp. 179–180.
29. Thorn, et al, eds., *Total Baseball V*, p. 102.
30. *Sporting Life*, July 4, 1891.
31. *The Sporting News*, October 18, 1889.
32. *The Sporting News*, April 26, 1890.
33. *The Sporting News*, April 12, 1890.
34. *Sporting Life*, November 27, 1889. *Spalding's Official Base Ball Guide*, 1890, p. 20, also listed McKean's base salaries for 1887 ($1,400), 1888 ($1,800), and 1889 ($2,000).
35. Egan, *Western Reserve*, p. 183.
36. Casway, *Ed Delahanty*, p. 46.
37. Robert P. Gelzheiser, *Labor and Capital in 19th Century Baseball* (Jefferson, NC: McFarland, 2006), pp. 119–120.
38. *The Sporting News*, February 8, 1890.
39. Gelzheizer, *Labor and Capital*, p. 141.
40. *Sporting Life*, February 19, 1890.
41. Separate articles in *Sporting Life*, February 26, 1890.

42. *Sporting Life*, January 8, 1890. Among other notable jumpers were Buck Ewing ("Floating on the Wind"), Jake Beckley ("They All Do It"), and Jack Glasscock ("'Tis Hard to Give the Hand Where the Heart Can Never Be").
43. *The Sporting News*, March 22, 1890.
44. *Sporting Life*, March 26, 1890. The same issue of *Sporting Life* informs its readers that attorney Russell, on behalf of the Cleveland Players' League club, filed a petition in common pleas court to enjoin McKean and Zimmer from playing with any other club.
45. Ethan M. Lewis, "'The Wildest Kind of Crank': The Story of Players' League Magnate Al Johnson," www.ethanlewis.com, 2007.
46. *The Sporting News*, April 11, 1891.
47. Separate articles in *The Sporting News*, March 22, 1890.
48. *The Sporting News*, March 8, 1890.
49. *The Sporting News*, April 19, 1890.
50. *The Sporting News*, April 19, 1890.
51. *The Sporting News*, April 26, 1890.
52. Egan, *Western Reserve*, p. 186.
53. *The Sporting News*, May 31, 1890.
54. *The Sporting News*, May 24, 1890.
55. *The Sporting News*, June 21, 1890.
56. Schmelz appointed Zimmer on July 12; see *Sporting Life*, July 19 and August 16, 1890.
57. *Sporting Life*, March 19, 1890.
58. *The Sporting News*, October 18, 1890.
59. www.lorain.lib.oh.us.
60. Browning, *Cy Young*, pp. 11–13.
61. *The Sporting News*, August 16, 1890.
62. *The Sporting News*, August 30, 1890.
63. *The Sporting News*, September 6, 1890.
64. *The Sporting News*, September 20, 1890.
65. *Sporting Life*, August 23, 1890.
66. www.baseball-reference.com.
67. Egan, *Western Reserve*, p. 192.
68. *The Sporting News*, October 4, 1890.

1895 Temple Cup: October 2

1. John Phillips, *The Fall Classics of the 1890s* (Cabin John, MD: Capital, 1989).
2. New York *Times*, September 3, 1895. Cuppy is affectionately called Slow Boy Cuppy in Cleveland *Critic and Amusement Gazette*, June 6, 1896.
3. Phillips, *The 1895 Spiders*.
4. Pittsburgh *Press*, October 3, 1895. The headline-writer enthused: "McKean Was the Bright Particular Star in the Argument—It Was One of the Most Royal Battles Ever Seen on the Diamond."
5. Originally in the Cleveland *World*; reprinted in both *The Sporting News*, October 12, 1895, and *Sporting Life*, October 26, 1895.
6. www.baseball-reference.com
7. Casway, *Ed Delahanty*, p. 121.
8. Phillips, *Uncle Nick's*, p. 36.
9. Pittsburgh *Press*, September 7, 1919.
10. *Sporting Life*, April 13, 1887.
11. "1800 shortstops," www.baseball.reference.com. Bid McPhee was probably the last barehanded infielder, holding out until he finally donned a glove when coming back from a hand injury in 1895.
12. Phillips, *Fall Classics*.
13. All statistics in the paragraph are from Nemec, *Encyclopedia of 19th-Century*.
14. Sources for the game recreations are Egan, *Western Reserve*, p. 235+, *The Sporting News*, October 5, 1895, and Phillips, *Fall Classics*.
15. Jerry Lansche, *Glory Fades Away: The Nineteenth-Century World Series Rediscovered* (Dallas: Taylor, 1991), p. 261.
16. *The Sporting News*, February 1, 1902.
17. Bryan Di Salvatore, *A Clever Base-Ballist: The Life and Times of John Montgomery Ward* (New York: Pantheon, 1999) p. 369+.
18. *Sporting Life*, November 24, 1894. "Zimmer's Base Ball Game," patented on February 7, 1893, and produced by McLoughlin Bros., is considered by collectors to be the best of its kind. Mark Cooper calls it "The Mona Lisa" of baseball board games in *Baseball Games, Home Versions of the National Pastime, 1860s-1960s*. The game matches two all-star teams of nine a side, featuring the likenesses of eight Cleveland Spiders, including the obscure pitcher George Davies, and W[illiam H.] Zimmer, a brother who had a brief career as a minor league catcher (*Sporting Life*, March 25, 1893). Ed McKean is conspicuously absent; Jack Glasscock and Germany Smith are Zimmer's shortstops. (Sources: www.huntauctions.com and www.robertedwardauctions.com.)
19. *Sporting Life*, May 16, 1896.

Chapter Five

1. *The Sporting News*, March 18, 1891.
2. *The Sporting News*, March 25, 1891.
3. *Sporting Life*, November 28, 1891.

Notes—Chapter Five

4. *Sporting Life*, August 8, 1891
5. *The Sporting News*, April 24, 1891.
6. *The Sporting News*, July 4 and 11, 1891.
7. *The Sporting News*, June 13, 1891.
8. Also, Burkett's OPS for both seasons was better than 1.000 (Sinins, *Complete Baseball Encyclopedia*, 2009).
9. David Jones, ed., *Deadball Stars of the American League* (Dulles, VA: SABR/Potomac, 2006), p. 485.
10. *Sporting Life*, September 24, 1891. Boston writer Tim Murnane was among those who argued early on that Tebeau's reputation as a manager who develops young talent was flawed; see *Sporting Life*, January 18, 1896.
11. Lowry, *Green Cathedrals*, p. 71.
12. Egan, *Western Reserve*, pp. 195–196.
13. *Sporting Life*, June 10, 1899.
14. *Sporting Life*, October 2, 1897.
15. *The Sporting News*, April 11, 1891.
16. *The Sporting News*, April 4 and 11, 1891.
17. *The Sporting News*, April 18, 1891.
18. *The Sporting News*, May 2, 1891.
19. Opening day details are from Egan, *Western Reserve*, pp. 195–199, and *Sporting Life*, May 9, 1891.
20. *The Sporting News*, March 18, 1891.
21. E.g., www.fultonhistory.com, and *Sporting Life*, May 6, 1891.
22. From a clipping forwarded to *The Sporting News* by Boston scribe Joe Quinn.
23. *Sporting Life*, May 30, 1891.
24. Phillips, *Uncle Nick's*, p. 79.
25. *The Sporting News*, June 13, 1891.
26. *Sporting Life*, July 25, 1891.
27. Phillips, *Who Was Who* (1991).
28. *Sporting Life*, June 6, 1891.
29. *Sporting Life*, June 13, 1891.
30. *The Sporting News*, June 27, 1891.
31. Egan, *Western Reserve*, p. 201.
32. *Sporting Life*, July 18, 1891.
33. *Sporting Life*, July 11, 1891.
34. *Sporting Life*, August 15, 1891.
35. Browning, *Cy Young*, pp. 18–19.
36. *Sporting Life*, September 26, 1891.
37. *The Sporting News*, August 1, 1891.
38. *The Sporting News*, August 15, 1891.
39. *The Sporting News*, August 22, 1891.
40. *The Sporting News*, August 22, 1891; also recalled in L.M. Sutter, *Arlie Latham* (Jefferson, NC: McFarland, 2012), p. 139.
41. *Sporting Life*, October 3, 1891.
42. *Sporting Life*, October 17, 1891.
43. *Sporting Life*, October 24, 1891.
44. *Sporting Life*, October 31 and November 28, 1891. According to Brian McKenna (www.baseballhistoryblog.com), in November, 1891, Al Lawson organized the team, which included Bill Alvord, Ed Seward, Joe Neale, and McKean from Cleveland, as well as John McGraw, Bill Dahlen, and the Browns' Billy Earle, who had toured with A.G. Spalding in 1888. Players met in New Orleans in late November and played exhibition games, funded by oyster magnate J.E. Hooper, against Lawson's Mobile, Alabama, teammates and local clubs. Billed as Hooper's All-American Base Ball Club, the barnstormers sailed out of Mobile on December 4, 1891. The team easily beat the 10-man Cuban teams and turned a profit.
45. *Sporting Life*, January 24, 1892, and www.baseballfever.com.
46. *Sporting Life*, November 21, 1891.
47. *Sporting Life*, December 19, 1891.
48. *Sporting Life*, January 30, 1892.
49. *Sporting Life*, March 26, 1892.
50. *The Sporting News*, February 27, 1892.
51. *The Sporting News*, March 5, 1892.
52. *The Sporting News*, April 9, 1892.
53. *The Sporting News*, March 12, 1892.
54. Egan, *Western Reserve*, p. 204, and *The Sporting News*, March 19, 1892.
55. *The Sporting News*, April 2 and 9, 1892.
56. Frank Graham and John McGraw, *McGraw of the Giants: An Informal Biography* (New York: G.P. Putnam's Sons, 1944), p. 9.
57. *The Sporting News*, April 23, 1892.
58. *Sporting Life*, April 16, 1892.
59. *The Sporting News*, May 7, 1892.
60. Personal emails from Thomas M. McKean, July 27 and 28, 2012.
61. *The Sporting News*, May 4, 1892.
62. *The Sporting News*, June 4, 1892.
63. *The Sporting News*, June 18, 1892.
64. *The Sporting News*, July 16, 1892.
65. *The Sporting News*, July 23, 1892.
66. Brian McKenna, "John Clarkson," SABR BioProject.
67. *Sporting Life*, September 24, 1892.
68. *The Sporting News*, August 6, 1892.
69. *The Sporting News*, August 27, 1892.
70. *The Sporting News*, August 20, 1892.
71. *The Sporting News*, September 17, 1892.
72. *The Sporting News*, October 8, 1892.
73. According to Browning's recount (Browning, *Cy Young*, pp. 28 and 235, n. 45), Young tied Bill Hutchison for most wins.
74. *The Sporting News*, October 8, 1892.
75. *Sporting Life*, December 17, 1892.

76. *Sporting Life*, December 10, 1892.
77. For my account of the 1892 "world's series," I drew heavily from Phillips, *Fall Classics*, Egan, *Western Reserve*, pp. 211–215, and Browning, *Cy Young*, pp. 26–28. Frank Williams suggests it would be more accurate to call the Cleveland-Boston playoff the original LCS; see his "The First League Championship Series, 1892," *Grandstand Baseball Annual* 5 (1989): 99–111.
78. *The Sporting News*, October 22, 1892.
79. Phillips, *Fall Classics*.
80. *The Sporting News*, October 16, 1892.
81. Browning, *Cy Young*, p. 27.
82. *The Sporting News*, October 22, 1892.
83. Phillips, *Fall Classics*.
84. Browning, *Cy Young*, p. 28.
85. *Sporting Life*, December 17, 1892.
86. *Sporting Life*, October 29, 1892.

Chapter Six

1. *The Sporting News*, March 25, 1893.
2. *Sporting Life*, February 18, 1893, and *The Sporting News*, March 25, 1893.
3. Egan, *Western Reserve*, p. 215.
4. *Sporting Life*, May 20, 1893.
5. *Sporting Life*, January 14, 1893. The game was probably Nig Cuppy's 7–6 win on September 23, 1892. Chances are, McKean was one of the base coaches, working with Tebeau on the play.
6. Nemec, *Profiles*, pp. 318–319.
7. *Sporting Life*, March 21, 1891, www.jockpost.com, www.futilityinfielder.com, and Egan, *Western Reserve*, p. 216.
8. *The Sporting News*, April 1, 1893.
9. *Sporting Life*, December 30, 1892.
10. *Sporting Life*, January 28, 1893, and www.prowrestlinghistory.com.
11. *Sporting Life*, February 4, 1893.
12. *Sporting Life*, February 11, 1893.
13. *Sporting Life*, March 4 and February 11, 1893.
14. *The Sporting News*, April 8, 1893.
15. *The Sporting News*, April 15, 1893.
16. Egan, *Western Reserve*, p. 215.
17. The source for the paragraph is Egan, *Western Reserve*, pp. 215–217.
18. The source for the game accounts is John Phillips, *Buck Ewing and the 1893 Cleveland Spiders* (Cabin John, MD: Capital, 1992), unless otherwise noted.
19. *The Sporting News*, May 13, 1893.
20. *Atlanta Constitution*, June 19, 1912.
21. *The Sporting News*, August 5, 1893.
22. *The Sporting News*, August 12, 1893.
23. Roy Kerr, *Buck Ewing* (Jefferson, NC: McFarland, 2012), p. 145.
24. *The Sporting News*, September 16, 1893.
25. *The Sporting News*, September 23, 1893.
26. *The Sporting News*, July 29, 1893.
27. *The Sporting News*, August 12, 1893.
28. Browning, *Cy Young*, p. 47.
29. *The Sporting News*, January 6, 1894.
30. *The Sporting News*, January 20, 1894.
31. *Sporting Life*, December 15, 1894.
32. *The Sporting News*, March 10, 1894. After the end of the season, Monte Ward was ready to concede, in a letter to Elmer Bates printed in *Sporting Life*, October 30, 1894: "With a short stop like McKean to help us out we would have won the pennant in a walk."
33. *Sporting Life*, March 24, 1894.
34. *The Sporting News*, February 25, 1894.
35. *The Sporting News*, February 17, March 24 and 31, 1894.
36. *The Sporting News*, January 27, 1894.
37. *The Sporting News*, February 10, 1894.
38. *The Sporting News*, March 17 and 24, 1894.
39. *The Sporting News*, March 24, 1894.
40. *The Sporting News*, April 14, 1894.
41. Phillips, *Who Was Who* (1991).
42. *Sporting Life*, October 30, 1894. Buck Ewing's board game was also a good seller.
43. *The Sporting News*, March 24, 1894.
44. *Sporting Life*, March 24, 1894.
45. *Sporting Life*, March 16, 1887.
46. *Sporting Life*, April 5, 1890.
47. *Sporting Life*, May 16, 1896.
48. A fuller version of Tebeau's pronouncement appears in Chapter Five of this book. Chadwick's response appeared in *The Sporting News*, February 10, 1894.
49. *The Sporting News*, February 10, 1894.
50. *The Sporting News*, April 7, 1894.
51. Egan, *Western Reserve*, pp. 222–223.
52. *The Sporting News*, April 14, 1894. The thespian umpire, Charles W. (Billy) Stage, was the star of the Cleveland Athletic Club. A world-class sprinter, he equaled the world record time for the 100-yard dash in 1893. The Painesville, Ohio, native interrupted his law studies to serve part of the 1894 season as one of Nick Young's seven umpires. (Peter Morris, "Billy Stage," SABR Bio-Project.)
53. Egan, *Western Reserve*, pp. 224–225.
54. *The Sporting News*, June 2, 1894.

55. *The Sporting News*, August 11, 1894.
56. *The Sporting News*, August 18, 1894.
57. *The Sporting News*, August 11, 1894. Refer to *Sporting Life*, August 11, 1894, which made the fine $50 apiece for Tebeau and O'Connor.
58. *The Sporting News*, August 18, 1894.
59. *The Sporting News*, May 12, 1894.
60. *The Sporting News*, June 30, 1894.
61. *The Sporting News*, July 28, 1894.
62. *The Sporting News*, August 18, 1894.
63. *The Sporting News*, September 8, 1894.
64. *Sporting Life*, August 4, 1894.
65. *Sporting Life*, September 1, 1894.
66. *Sporting Life*, September 8, 1894.
67. Egan, *Western Reserve*, p. 229.
68. *Sporting Life*, October 6 and 13, 1894.
69. *Sporting Life*, December 12, 1894.
70. *Sporting Life*, December 22, 1894.

1895 Temple Cup: October 3 and 5

1. *Sporting Life*, September 28, 1895.
2. Egan, *Western Reserve*, pp. 236–237.
3. Alexander, *McGraw*, p. 46.
4. Cleveland *Plain Dealer*, October 4, 1895.
5. Unnamed Baltimore newspaper, quoted in Cleveland *Plain Dealer*, October 5, 1895.
6. *Sporting Life*, October 12, 1895.
7. *Baseball Magazine*, September 1917, p. 535.
8. *The Sporting News*, October 26, 1895.
9. Phillips, *Fall Classics*.
10. Sources for the game summary are Egan, *Western Reserve*, pp. 236–237, and Phillips, *Fall Classics*.
11. Egan, *Western Reserve*, p. 238.
12. *The Sporting News*, October 12, 1895, Browning, *Cy Young*, p. 54, and Egan, *Western Reserve*, p. 237.
13. *The Sporting News*, Ocobert 12, 1895.
14. Cleveland *Plain Dealer*, October 6, 1895.
15. Phillips, *1895 Spiders*.

Chapter Seven

1. *The Sporting News*, March 9, 1895.
2. Phillips, *1895 Spiders*. Also named were Glasscock, McGraw and Boileryard Clarke of Baltimore, Jack Doyle, Jake Beckley, Tom Tucker and Hugh Duffy of Boston, Calliope Miller, and Farmer Vaughan. The committee's models for good behavior were Dave Foutz, Arthur Irwin, and, incredibly, Cap Anson and Arlie Latham. *1895 Spiders* is the source for game accounts from the 1895 regular season, unless otherwise noted.
3. *The Sporting News*, May 18, 1895.
4. *The Sporting News*, April 6, 1895.
5. *Sporting Life*, June 1, 1895.
6. Browning, *Cy Young*, p. 50+.
7. *Sporting Life*, April 27, 1895.
8. *Sporting Life*, April 27, 1895.
9. *Sporting Life*, May 4, 1895.
10. *The Sporting News*, May 18, 1895.
11. *The Sporting News*, May 11, 1895.
12. *The Sporting News*, September 14, 1895.
13. Browning, *Cy Young*, pp. 50–57.
14. *The Sporting News*, July 20, 1895.
15. Brian McKenna, "Pussy Tebeau," SABR BioProject.
16. *Sporting Life*, June 15, 1895.
17. *The Sporting News*, September 7, 1895.
18. *Sporting Life*, September 28, 1895.
19. *Sporting Life*, October 26, 1896.
20. *Sporting Life*, October 26 and November 16, 1895.
21. *The Sporting News*, October 19, 1895.
22. *Sporting Life*, January 18, 1896.
23. *Sporting Life*, May 18, 1895.
24. *Sporting Life*, January 4, 1896.
25. Scott Beeckman, *Ringside: A History of Professional Wrestling* (Westport, CT: Praeger, 2006), p. 45.
26. *Sporting Life*, March 20, 1897.
27. *Sporting Life*, January 2, 1897.
28. *Sporting Life*, August 7, 1897. McKean "defeated an unknown" challenger at a Marquette Club smoker on the evening of November 22, for example (*Sporting Life*, November 27, 1897).
29. www.ancestry.com, and U.S. Census Bureau, federal census for 1910 and 1920.
30. *The Sporting News*, September 21, 1895.
31. The source for the game account is Egan, *Western Reserve*, pp. 245–247, unless otherwise noted.
32. From Weidman's obituary in *Sporting Life*, March 8, 1905.
33. Quoted in John Phillips, *The Riotous 1896 Cleveland Spiders* (Cabin John, MD: Capital, 1997), pp. 92–93.
34. *The Sporting News*, July 4, 1896.
35. *The Sporting News*, June 27, 1896.
36. Egan, *Western Reserve*, p. 246.
37. Browning, *Cy Young*, pp. 60–61.
38. Phillips, *Riotous*, p. 48.
39. Nemec, *Encyclopedia of 19th-Century*, p. 562.

40. *Sporting Life*, April 7, 1906.
41. *Sporting Life*, May 16, 1896.
42. *The Sporting News*, September 19, 1896.
43. Umpire Bud Lally was a notorious "homer" for Cincinnati. For the same offense, Fred Clark struck him during an August 9 game, weeks after the Louisville riot.
44. *Sporting Life*, August 22, 1896.
45. *The Sporting News*, July 11, 1896.
46. *The Sporting News*, July 4, 1896.
47. *The Sporting News*, July 11, 1896.
48. Phillips, *Riotous*, p. 53, and Egan, *Western Reserve*, pp. 246–247.
49. These highlights were drawn from Phillips, *Riotous*, p. 43+, unless otherwise noted.
50. *Sporting Life*, June 6, 1896.
51. *The Sporting News*, July 4, 1896.
52. *The Sporting News*, May 16, 1896.
53. *The Sporting News*, July 11 and 18, 1896.
54. *The Sporting News*, July 4 and August 1, 1896.
55. *The Sporting News*, July 25, 1896.
56. *The Sporting News*, August 15, 1896.
57. *The Sporting News*, August 22, 1896.
58. Phillips, *Riotous*, p. 31.
59. *The Sporting News*, June 27, 1896.
60. Browning, *Cy Young*, pp. 62–63.
61. *The Sporting News*, September 3, 1896.
62. Phillips, *Riotous*, pp. 118–119.
63. Browning, *Cy Young*, p. 61.
64. Phillips, *Riotous*, p. 119.
65. The source for the Temple Cup games is Phillips, *Fall Classics*, unless otherwise noted.
66. *Sporting Life*, October 3, 1896.
67. Egan, *Western Reserve*, p. 257, and *The Sporting News*, October 17, 1896.
68. *Sporting Life*, November 28, 1896.
69. The Cuppy anecdote is in Phillips, *Uncle Nick's*, p. 81.
70. *The Sporting News*, October 17, 1896.
71. Egan, *Western Reserve*, p. 258.
72. *Sporting Life*, October 24, 1896.
73. *The Sporting News*, October 17, 1896, and *Sporting Life*, October 17, 1896; *Sporting Life*, October 24, 1896, cites the Cleveland *World* account.
74. *Sporting Life*, October 17, 1896.
75. *Sporting Life*, August 16, 1913.
76. Thorn, et al, eds., *Total Baseball V*, p. 102.
77. *The Sporting News*, January 4, 1896.

Chapter Eight

1. Tobacco cards of the era featured, in addition to baseball players, Buffalo Bill Cody and Annie Oakley. Frank Robison's publicity campaign to buck up attendance was aided by the Cleveland *Plain Dealer*'s renaming of the team (Egan, *Western Reserve*, p. 262); by the May 8, 1897, *The Sporting News*, Charles Mears was calling the club the Indians. The source for the games of the 1897 season is John Philips, *Chief Sockalexis and the 1897 Cleveland Indians* (Cabin John, MD: Capital, 1991), unless otherwise noted.
2. *Sporting Life*, January 10, 1914.
3. *Sporting Life*, March 20, 1897.
4. *Sporting Life*, October 17, 1896.
5. *The Sporting News*, May 23, 1896; *Progressive Men of Northern Ohio* (Cleveland: Plain Dealer), p. 174.
6. *The Sporting News*, April 17, 1897.
7. *The Sporting News*, June 1, 1897.
8. For an excerpt from Brush's "Special Instructions to Players" memorandum, see John Thorn, *Baseball in the Garden of Eden* (New York: Simon & Schuster, 2011), p. 247 and the note on p. 342.
9. Egan, *Western Reserve*, pp. 276–277.
10. Browning, *Cy Young*, pp. 69–70.
11. Phillips, *Uncle Nick's*, p. 78.
12. Egan, *Western Reserve*, p. 262.
13. Phillips, *Uncle Nick's*, p.78.
14. Browning, *Cy Young*, p. 70.
15. *Sporting Life*, November 6, 1897.
16. Pittsburgh *Press*, September 17, 1897; also, *Sporting Life*, December 18, 1897.
17. *Sporting Life*, February 6, 1897.
18. *The Sporting News*, May 15, 1897.
19. *The Sporting News*, April 10, 1897.
20. The sources for the paragraphs on Sunday baseball are Philips, *Sockalexis and 1897*, and Egan, *Western Reserve*, pp. 266–267.
21. *The Sporting News*, April 10, 1897.
22. Egan, *Western Reserve*, pp. 260–261.
23. *The Sporting News*, April 24, 1897.
24. The source for the game accounts in this section is Phillips, *Sockalexis and 1897*, unless otherwise noted.
25. Brian McDonald, *Indian Summer: The Tragic Story of Louis Francis Sockalexis, the First Native American in Major League Baseball* (Emmaus, PA: Rodale, 2003), p. 93.
26. *Sporting Life*, May 8, 1897.
27. *The Sporting News*, July 17, 1897.
28. From Tebeau's report of the Sockalexis incident, in Phillips, *Uncle Nick's*, p. 78; otherwise paraphrased from David Fleitz, "Louis Sockalexis," SABR BioProject.
29. *The Sporting News*, August 7, 1897.
30. *The Sporting News*, July 31, 1897.

Notes—Chapter Eight

31. Phillips, *Sockalexis and 1897*.
32. *The Sporting News*, July 31, 1897.
33. Egan, *Western Reserve*, p. 270.
34. Browning, *Cy Young*, p. 72.
35. *The Sporting News*, April 23, 1898.
36. *The Sporting News*, April 9, 1898.
37. *The Sporting News*, April 23 and May 7, 1898.
38. Egan, *Western Reserve*, pp. 273–276.
39. Nemec, *Encyclopedia of 19th-Century*, p. 606.
40. Egan, *Western Reserve*, p. 276.
41. Egan, *Western Reserve*, pp. 270–271.
42. *Sporting Life*, July 9, 1898.
43. The Tebeau quote dates from 1896, in Phillips, *Uncle Nick's*, p. 73.
44. *The Sporting News*, June 18, 1898.
45. *The Sporting News*, May 28, 1898.
46. *The Sporting News*, April 2, 1898, quoting the Cleveland *Plain Dealer*.
47. *Sporting Life*, April 23, 1898.
48. *Sporting Life*, April 30, 1898.
49. *Sporting Life*, May 14, 1898.
50. *The Sporting News*, May 21 and 28, 1898.
51. *The Sporting News*, June 11, 1898.
52. *Sporting Life*, June 25, 1898.
53. *Sporting Life*, July 9, 1898.
54. The source for the game accounts is *The Sporting News*, July 16, 1898.
55. Statistics are from www.sabr.org.
56. *The Sporting News*, September 10, 1898.
57. Browning, *Cy Young*, p. 73.
58. *The Sporting News*, August 13, 1898.
59. *The Sporting News*, August 6, 1898.
60. *The Sporting News*, September 3, 1898.
61. *Sporting Life*, October 1, 1898.
62. *Sporting Life*, October 22, 1898.
63. *Cleveland City Directory* for 1898, and U.S. Census Bureau, federal census for 1900.
64. US Census Bureau, federal census for 1900 and 1910.
65. *Sporting Life*, April 22, 1899.
66. *Sporting Life*, March 2, 1901, and Phillips, *Who Was Who* (1991).
67. E.g., *The Sporting News*, June 18, 1898.
68. Cleveland *Plain Dealer*, October 3, 1898.
69. McKean was first confined to his room with a confirmed attack of malaria on May 27, 1899, according to *Sporting Life*, June 3, 1899.
70. *Sporting Life*, April 29, 1899.
71. *Sporting Life*, February 11, 1899.
72. John Phillips, *The '99 Spiders* (Cabin John, MD: Capital, 1988).
73. *Sporting Life*, March 11, 1899.
74. *Sporting Life*, March 18, 1899.
75. Phillips, *'99 Spiders*.
76. *Sporting Life*, June 17, 1899.
77. *Sporting Life*, March 11 1899 (Cleveland, March 6 dateline).
78. Washington *Evening Star*, March 26, 1899.
79. *The Sporting News*, March 18, 1899.
80. Phillips, *'99 Spiders*, n.pag.
81. J. Thomas Hetrick, *Chris Von Der Ahe and the St. Louis Browns* (Lanham, MD: Scarecrow Press, 1999), p. 224.
82. Edward Achorn, *The Summer of Beer and Whiskey* (New York: Public Affairs, 2013), p. 258.
83. *The Sporting News*, April 8, 1899.
84. *The Sporting News*, April 1, 1899.
85. *Sporting Life*, November 11, 1899.
86. See, e.g., Nemec, *Encyclopedia of 19th-Century*, p. 584, and Fleitz, *Irish*, p. 78.
87. *Sporting Life*, August 19, 1899.
88. John A. Garraty, et al., eds. *American National Biography*, vol. 22 (New York: Oxford University Press, 1999), p. 527.
89. Indianapolis *Star*, March 24, 1912.
90. Browning, *Cy Young*, p. 76.
91. *The Sporting News*, April 22, 1899.
92. The game accounts are from Phillips, *'99 Spiders*, unless otherwise noted.
93. Cleveland *Leader*, May 5, 1899.
94. *The Sporting News*, April 29, 1899.
95. *Sporting Life*, April 29, 1899.
96. *Sporting Life*, May 20, 1899.
97. Washington *Post*, July 16, 1899.
98. *The Sporting News*, February 3, 1894.
99. Phillips, *Uncle Nick's*, pp. 23–24.
100. *The Sporting News*, February 3, 1894.
101. Front page of *Sporting Life*, June 10, 1899.
102. *The Sporting News*, May 13, 1899.
103. *The Sporting News*, May 27, 1899.
104. *The Sporting News*, May 27, 1899.
105. *The Sporting News*, June 10, 1899.
106. *The Sporting News*, June 10, 1899.
107. *Sporting Life*, June 17 and 24, 1899.
108. *The Sporting News*, July 1, 1899.
109. *The Sporting News*, July 9, 1899.
110. *Sporting Life*, June 17, 1899.
111. *The Sporting News*, July 23, 1899.
112. *The Sporting News*, July 23, 1899.
113. *The Sporting News*, July 16, 1899.
114. Sandusky *Star-Journal*, January 24, 1899, and *Cleveland City Directory* for 1899.
115. *Sporting Life*, August 12, 1899.
116. Phillips, *'99 Spiders*.
117. Browning, *Cy Young*, p. 79.

118. Sandusky *Star-Journal*, August 8, 1899.
119. *Sporting Life*, November 4, 1899.
120. *Sporting Life*, December 2, 1899.
121. *Sporting Life*, December 9, 1899.
122. *Sporting Life*, May 4, 1901.
123. *Sporting Life*, September 8, 1899.
124. www.BoxRec.com.
125. *Sporting Life*, January 20, 1900. According to www.BoxRec.com, some other matches refereed by McKean are Boston Kid Lavigne's in Massillon on November 21, 1899; Art Simms v. John Dennison, Loudon Campbell v. Denny Gallagher, and George Church v. Kid Robinson on a triple bill in Cleveland on October 23, 1899; Tipperary-born Dick Moore v. Billy Moore in Massillon on September 7, 1900; Galway-born James (Squirrel) Finnerty v. Art Simms in Canton on December 6, 1900, and the same day, Joseph Burns v. Jem Smith in Massillon; Art Simms v. Jack Hamilton in Akron on June 7, 1901. In January 1907, McKean counted off the 10 seconds when Cy Flynn of Buffalo KO'd Billy Butler in 12 rounds in Erie, Pennsylvania (Elyria *Daily Reporter*, January 17, 1907).
126. *Sporting Life*, March 10, 1900.
127. *Sporting Life*, February 17, 1900.
128. *Sporting Life*, June 23, 1900.
129. *Sporting Life*, July 14, 1900.
130. *Sporting Life*, July 28, 1900, and January 12 1901.
131. *Sporting Life*, December 15, 1900.
132. *Sporting Life*, November 17, 1900.
133. *Sporting Life*, February 9, 1901.

1895 Temple Cup: October 7

1. Unless otherwise noted, the sources for this chapter were Alexander, *McGraw*, pp. 46–47, and Egan, *Western Reserve*, pp. 239–240, on the pre- and post-game rioting; Phillips, *Fall Classics*, Phillips, *1895 Spiders*, and Browning, *Cy Young*, p. 55, for the game account.
2. *The Sporting News*, October 12, 1895.
3. Reprinted in *The Sporting News*, October 19, 1895; italics added.
4. *Sporting Life*, October 12, 1895.
5. Lansche, *Glory Fades*, p. 266.
6. *The Sporting News*, October 12, 1895, makes the fine $25, perhaps the sum for all three detained players.
7. *The Sporting News*, October 12, 1895.
8. Lansche, *Glory Fades*, p. 267.

Chapter Nine

1. *The Sporting News*, January 25, 1902.
2. *The Sporting News*, February 8, 1902.
3. Rochester *Democrat and Chronicle*, April 24 and 29, 1902.
4. *The Sporting News*, April 12, 1902.
5. *The Sporting News*, January 4, 1902
6. *The Sporting News*, April 26, 1902.
7. *Sporting Life*, March 15, 1902.
8. *The Sporting News*, April 26, 1902.
9. The source for Rochester game accounts is Rochester *Democrat and Chronicle*, April 15 to August 17, 1902, unless otherwise noted.
10. *Sporting Life*, May 10, 1902.
11. *The Sporting News*, August 2, 1902.
12. *The Sporting News*, June 7, 1902.
13. *The Sporting News*, June 14, 1902.
14. Baltimore *Morning Herald*, June 6, 1902.
15. *The Sporting News*, June 28, 1902.
16. *The Sporting News*, July 12, 1902.
17. *The Sporting News*, May 31, 1902.
18. *The Sporting News*, July 12, 1902.
19. *The Sporting News*, August 30, 1902, called it "the first unassisted triple play ever made on a professional ball field." The New York *Times*, August 24, 1902, had earlier confirmed it as the second in baseball history.
20. Rochester *Democrat and Chronicle*, September 19, 1902.
21. *Spalding's Official Base Ball Guide*, 1902, p. 170.
22. *Reach's Official American League Base Ball Guide*, 1902, p. 175.
23. Canton *Repository*, March through August, 1904.
24. *Sporting Life*, July 16, 1904 and January 2, 1904.
25. Canton *Repository*, April 17, 1904.
26. *Sporting Life*, July 30, 1904.
27. *Sporting Life*, September 16, 1905. The Cleveland-born Belden had played in eight games with the Spiders in 1897, his only time in the majors. His stats are intriguing, at least redactively: two triples, four runs batted in, and two assists from the outfield. Twelve seasons of his long minor league career were spent with Denver teams.
28. Elizabeth Wallace, *Colorado Springs* (Chicago: Arcadia, 2003), p. 71.
29. *Reach's Offical American League Base Ball Guide*, 1905, p. 134.
30. As quoted in *The Sporting News*, April 8, 1905.
31. *The Sporting News*, April 29, 1905.

32. *The Sporting News*, April 29, 1905.
33. *The Sporting News*, June 3, 1905.
34. *Sporting Life*, May 27, 1905.
35. *The Sporting News*, June 10 and 17, 1905.
36. *The Sporting News*, June 24, 1905.
37. *The Sporting News*, December 10, 1904. Consider that George Tebeau's headstone, recently erected in Wheat Ridge, Colorado's Crown Hill Cemetery, recognizes him as the "father of Colorado baseball," who "brought organized baseball to the west" (www.thedeadballera.com).
38. *The Sporting News*, June 24, 1905.
39. *The Sporting News*, July 8, 1905.
40. *The Sporting News*, July 29, 1905.
41. *Sporting Life*, August 5, 1905.
42. *Sporting Life*, June 17, 1905.
43. *The Sporting News*, June 24, 1905.
44. *Sporting Life*, June 24, 1905.
45. Lee Allen, *The Cincinnati Reds* (New York; G.P, Putnam's Sons, 1948), pp. 169–170.
46. *The Sporting News*, August 26, 1905.
47. Team records are according to *The Sporting News*, June 17 to September 30, 1905.
48. *Sporting Life*, July 19, 1905.
49. Fort Wayne *News*, July 25, 1905.
50. *The Sporting News*, September 2, 1905.
51. *The Sporting News*, September 30, 1905.
52. Fort Wayne *News*, August 17, 1905.
53. *Sporting Life*, September 16, 1905.
54. *Sporting Life*, December 16, 1905.
55. *The Sporting News*, October 7, 1905
56. *The Sporting News*, March 31, 1906.
57. *Sporting Life*, February 17, 1906.
58. *Sporting Life*, February 3, 1906.
59. Milwaukee *Daily True American*, January 4, 1906.
60. *The Sporting News*, March 31, 1906.
61. *The Sporting News*, March 24, 1906.
62. Pittsburgh *Press*, April 1, 1906.
63. *Sporting Life*, April 14, 1906.
64. *The Sporting News*, March 31, 1906.
65. *The Sporting News*, April 7, 1906.
66. This year, *The Sporting News* referred to the team as the Indians, in honor of Zimmer and McKean, not as the Travelers.
67. *Sporting Life*, May 12 and 19, 1906.
68. O'Neal, *Southern League*, p. 25.
69. *Sporting Life*, April 28, May 12, June 2 and 9, 1906.
70. *The Sporting News*, May 21, 1906.
71. *Sporting Life*, June 16, 1906.
72. *The Sporting News*, June 23, 1906.
73. *Sporting Life*, June 16, 1906.
74. *The Sporting News*, June 23, 1906.
75. *Sporting Life*, August 11, 1906.
76. *The Sporting News*, August 4, 1906.
77. *Sporting Life*, August 11, 1906.
78. *The Sporting News*, August 3, 1906.
79. *Sporting Life*, July 14 and August 11, 1906.
80. *Spalding's Official Base Ball Guide*, 1907, p. 333.
81. Dayton *Journal*, September 21, 1906.
82. Dayton *Journal*, September 8, 1906.
83. Coincidentally, Sol White, the Negro League baseball player and author, was born in Bellaire, Ohio, a year after Kennedy.
84. Dayton *Journal*, August 17, 1906.
85. Dayton *Journal*, August 18, 1906.
86. The source for the Vets game accounts is Dayton *Journal*, July 31 to August 22, 1906.
87. Statistics are according to *Sporting Life*, December 15, 1906.

Chapter Ten

1. *Sporting Life*, December 15, 1906.
2. *The Sporting News,* March 30, 1907.
3. Fort Wayne *News*, January 8, 1907.
4. *Sporting Life*, May 11, 1907.
5. Steve Evans was buried in Calvary Cemetery, Cleveland, where McKean is interred.
6. The source for the game accounts in this paragraph is *Sporting Life*, May 25, 1907.
7. *Sporting Life*, June 1, 1907.
8. *Sporting Life*, June 8, 1907.
9. *Sporting Life*, June 15, 1907, and Elyria *Evening Telegram*, July 9, 1907.
10. Nemec, *Profiles*, p. 51.
11. *Sporting Life*, August 4, 1906.
12. *Sporting Life*, August 31, 1907.
13. *The Sporting News*, June 22, 1907.
14. *Sporting Life*, June 29, 1907.
15. *Sporting Life*, July 20, 1907.
16. *Sporting Life*, August 17, 1907, and *The Sporting News*, August 29, 1907.
17. The stunt dates from August 25, 1890, as reported in the Washington *Post*, August 26, 1890; the catcher recanted in *Sporting Life*, June 12, 1897.
18. *The Sporting News*, July 28, 1907.
19. Fort Wayne *Journal-Gazette*, December 29, 1907.
20. *Sporting Life*, August 17, 1907.
21. Springfield *Gazette*, June 1, 1907.
22. *Sporting Life*, August 17, 1907, Spring-

field *Gazette*, September 9, 1907, and *The Sporting News*, September 19, 1907.

23. *Sporting Life*, May 18 and June 1, 1907.

24. *Sporting Life*, October 5, 1907.

25. The game accounts and team standings are according to the Springfield *Gazette*, July 24 through August 4, 1907, and *The Sporting News*, July 28 through August 11, 1907.

26. Springfield *Gazette*, September 9, 1907.

27. *The Sporting News*, September 26, 1907.

28. Springfield *Gazette*, August 23, 1907.

29. Springfield *Gazette*, August 29, 1907.

30. Springfield *Gazette*, September 6, 1907.

31. Springfield *Gazette*, September 17, 1907.

32. *Sporting Life*, October 12, 1907.

33. *Sporting Life*, June 29, 1907.

34. *Sporting Life*, October 5, 1907.

35. Youngstown *Vindicator*, December 26, 1907.

36. Youngstown *Vindicator*, December 4, 1907, and June 15, 1908.

37. *Sporting Life*, March 14, 1908.

38. Fort Wayne *News*, April 15, 1908.

39. Fort Wayne *Journal-Gazette*, April 4, 1908.

40. Robert D. Parker, "Batter Up: Fort Worth's Baseball History" *Old Fort News*, Summer, 1967.

41. *Sporting Life*, April 4, 1908.

42. *Sporting Life*, March 14, 1908.

43. Fort Wayne *Journal-Gazette*, April 4 and 8, 1908.

44. Fort Wayne *News*, April 24, 1908.

45. Fort Wayne *Journal-Gazette*, April 25, 1908.

46. Fort Wayne *News*, April 18, 1908.

47. Los Angeles *Times*, May 4, 1908.

48. Fort Wayne *Journal-Gazette*, May 4, 1908.

49. *Sporting Life*, May 23, 1908.

50. *Sporting Life*, July 4, 1908.

51. *Sporting Life*, June 27 and July 4, 1908.

52. *Sporting Life*, May 30, 1908.

53. *Sporting Life*, August 8, 1908.

54. Brian McKenna, "John Clarkson," SABR BioProject.

55. Paul Jablonski, "Early History of Baseball in Bay City," Bay City *Times*, February 28, 1937, and Bay City *Tribune*, May 18, 1909.

56. *Sporting Life*, August 22, 1908.

57. *Spalding's Official Base Ball Guide*, 1907, p. 209.

58. US Census Bureau, federal census for 1930.

59. The April 18, 1908, *Sporting Life* story ran under the headline "Woman Runs Ball Club." McKean also knew baseball's second woman executive, Frank Robison's daughter Helene Hathaway Britton, who ran the St. Louis Cardinals.

60. Fort Wayne *News*, February 12, 1906.

61. *Sporting Life*, August 29, 1908.

62. Lou Criger would also manage Boyne City, in the Michigan State League, in 1911.

63. The source for game accounts is Bay City *Times*, July 5, and August 3 to August 11, 1908, unless otherwise noted.

64. Personal email from Chris Applin, Saginaw Public Library, April 18, 2013.

65. *Sporting Life*, August 22, 1908.

66. www.ancestry.com.

67. Bay City *Times*, August 13, 1908.

68. *Sporting Life*, October 24, 1908.

69. Sandusky *Star*, December 27, 1898.

70. The letterhead names E.R. Carney as team manager. Ed McKean's March 3, 1912, letter, written in pencil, in possession of Tom McKean. A vintage collage of Hinkel's 1910 city champs, with player photos encircling the likenesses of the owner and his manager and coach, does not include a photograph of McKean (eBay item, sold June 16, 2013, by oldfloodstore, Yulee, FL).

71. Obituary in Cleveland *Plain Dealer*, August 17, 1919, and p. 43 in *The Mixer and Server*, the union house organ.

72. William A. Cook, *King of the Bootleggers: A Biography of George Remus* (Jefferson, NC: McFarland, 2008), p. 110. Matt Hinkel was an inveterate sportsman. In addition to his baseball club, Hinkel All-Stars football teams competed by 1905 with regional powers Canton and Massillon (C. Robert Barnett, "Reviews," *Journal of Sports History* (Spring 2002): 145–146).

73. *Sporting Life*, September 19, 1908.

74. San Antonio *Light*, January 8 1908.

75. Cleveland *Plain Dealer*, August 17, 1919.

76. January 20, 1942, letter to Robert D. McKean, in the McKean player file, National Baseball Hall of Fame.

77. *Sporting Life*, October 10, 1908.

78. *Sporting Life*, October 31, 1896.

79. www.BoxRec.com.

80. Fort Wayne *Journal-Gazette*, May 10, 1911.

81. *The Day Book* (Chicago), February 6, 1913, Washington *Times*, December 25, 1911,

Spokane *Press*, December 27, 1910, and Washington *Herald*, December 31, 1911.

82. *Sporting Life*, February 3, 1912, and Galveston *Daily News*, February 13, 1912.

83. See, e.g., W.R. Felix, Jr. and L.H. Stahlgren, "Death by Undiagnosed Perforated Peptic Ulcer: Analysis of 31 Cases," *Annals of Surgery* (March 1973): 344–351.

84. Cleveland Public Library necrology file, reel 053.

85. In *Ed Delahanty*, Casway writes, on p. 282, that John McGraw was the only baseball player at the burial site. McGraw was the one pallbearer representing the national game; it is unthinkable that McKean would not have taken his place among the family friends, either there or at the wake held at Delahanty's parents' home, or at the funeral at the Church of the Immaculate Conception in Cleveland. (*Sporting Life*, July 18, 1903.)

86. Newspaper clipping in the Oliver Tebeau player file, National Baseball Hall of Fame.

87. Records of the Lorain County, Ohio, Common Pleas Court.

88. Cleveland *Press*, September 25, 1952.

2. The sources for this game account are Phillips, *The 1895 Spiders*, and Egan, *Western Reserve*, pp. 240–242, unless otherwise noted.

3. *Sporting Life*, October 12. 1895. *Spadling's Official Base Ball Guide*, 1896, p. 58, indicates gate receipts for the 1895 Temple Cup series exceeded $15,000. It also breaks down the figure: $10,056 brought in by the three Cleveland games, and $4,600 brought in by the two games in Baltimore; the four umpires cost $420; $152 went to grounds expenses. The result was net receipts of $14,752. Sixteen Cleveland regulars made $528.33 each. (Bobby Wallace, Phil Knell, Zeke Wilson and Eddie O'Mears were all granted shares although they didn't appear in the series.) Each Baltimore regular pocketed $316. (Lansche, *Glory Fades*, p. 269+.)

4. Browning, *Cy Young*, p. 56.

5. Browning, *Cy Young*, p. 37.

6. Cleveland *Plain Dealer*, October 9, 1895.

7. *Spalding's Official Base Ball Guide*, 1896, p. 58.

1895 Temple Cup: October 8

1. *The Sporting News*, October 12, 1895, estimates the crowd at 9,000.

Bibliography

Books and Articles

Achorn, Edward. *Fifty-Nine in '84.* New York: Smithsonian Press, 2010.

———. *The Summer of Beer and Whiskey.* New York: Public Affairs, 2013.

Akin, William E. "Bare Hands and Kid Gloves: The Best Fielders, 1880–1899." *Baseball Research Journal* 10 (1981): 60–65.

———. "Edward John McKean." In *Nineteenth Century Stars*, edited by Robert L. Tiemann and Mark Rucker, 88. Kansas City: SABR, 1989.

Alexander, Charles C. *John McGraw.* New York: Viking, 1988.

Allen, Lee. *The Cincinnati Reds.* New York: G.P. Putnam's Sons, 1948.

Anson, Adrian. *A Ball Player's Career.* Chicago: Era, 1900.

Barnett, C. Robert. "Reviews." *Journal of Sports History* (Spring 2002): 145–146.

Barry, Dan. *Bottom of the 33rd.* New York: Harper, 2011.

Beeckman, Scott. *Ringside: A History of Professional Wrestling.* Westport, CT: Praeger, 2006.

Berthoff, Warner. *Hart Crane: A Reintroduction.* Minneapolis: University of Minnesota Press, 1989.

Bielewicz, Paul. "A Look at Rochester's Ballparks." www.milb.com.

Blake, Mike. *The Minor Leagues.* New York: Wynwood, 1991.

Browning, Reed. *Cy Young.* Amherst: University of Massachusetts Press, 2000.

Caillault, Jean-Pierre, ed. *The Complete New York Clipper Baseball Biographies.* Jefferson, NC: McFarland, 2009.

Callahan, Nelson J., and William F. Hickey. *Irish Americans and Their Communities of Cleveland.* Cleveland: Cleveland State University Press, 1978.

Carlyle, Thomas. *On Heroes, Hero-Worship and the Heroic in History.* Lincoln: University of Nebraska Press, 1966.

Carroll, Lewis. *The Complete Works.* New York: Barnes & Noble, 1994.

Casey, Harr. "The Story of Baseball, Part II." *Baseball Magazine*, March 1912, 21–28.

Casway, Jerrold. *Ed Delahanty in the Emerald Age of Baseball.* South Bend: University of Notre Dame Press, 2004.

Cleveland City Directory. 1886–1920.

Cook, William A. *King of the Bootleggers: A Biography of George Remus.* Jefferson, NC: McFarland, 2008.

Cooper, Mark. *Baseball Games, Home Versions of the National Pastime, 1860s-1960s.* Atglen, PA: Shiffer, 1995.

"Descendants of Owen McAleer." www.FamilyTreemaker.genealogy.com.

DeValeria, Dennis, and Jeanne Burke DeValeria. *Honus Wagner.* Pittsburgh: University of Pittsburgh Press, 1998.

Dickson, Paul. *The Dickson Baseball Dictionary.* 3d ed. New York: Norton, 2009.

Di Salvatore, Bryan. *A Clever Base-Ballist: The Life and Times of John Montgomery Ward.* New York: Pantheon, 1999.

Egan, James M. *Base Ball on the Western Reserve: The Early Game in Cleveland and Northeast Ohio.* Jefferson, NC: McFarland, 2008.

"1800 Shortstops." www.baseball-reference.com.
Felber, Bill, ed. *Inventing Baseball: The 100 Greatest Games of the Nineteenth Century*. Phoenix: SABR, 2013.
Felix, W.R., Jr., and L.H. Stahlgren. "Death by Undiagnosed Perforated Peptic Ulcer." *Annals of Surgery* (March 1973): 344–351.
Filiche, Peter. *Professional Baseball Franchises from the Abbeyville Athletics to the Zanesville Indians*. New York: Facts on File, 1993.
Fleitz, David L. *The Irish in Baseball*. Jefferson, NC: McFarland, 2009.
_____. "Louis Sockalexis." SABR BioProject.
Frommer, Henry. *Primitive Baseball*. New York: Atheneum, 1988.
Gallagher, Thomas. *Paddy's Lament*. San Diego: Harcourt Brace, 1982.
Garraty, John A., et al, eds. *American National Biography*. Vol. 22. New York: Oxford University Press, 1999.
Gelzheiser, Robert P. *Labor and Capital in 19th Century Baseball*. Jefferson, NC: McFarland, 2006.
Gillman, Alexander, compiler. *Searches into the History of the Gillman or Gilman Family*. London: Elliott Stock, 1895.
Gloag, John. *Victorian Taste*. New York: Barnes & Noble, 1972.
Gramling, Chad. *Baseball in Fort Wayne*. Charleston, SC: Arcadia, 2007.
Hetrick, J. Thomas. *Chris Von Der Ahe and the St. Louis Browns*. Lanham, MD: Scarecrow Press, 1999.
_____. *The Misfits*. Jefferson, NC: McFarland, 1991.
Husman, John R. *Baseball in Toledo*. Charleston, SC: Arcadia, 2003.
Jablonski, Paul. "Early History of Baseball in Bay City." Bay City *Times*, February 28, 1937.
Jackson, Thomas A. *Ireland Her Own: An Outline of the Irish Struggle*. Edited by C. Desmond Greaves. New York: International Publishers, 1970.
James, Bill. *The Bill James Guide to Baseball Managers*. New York: Scribner, 1997.
_____. *The New Bill James Historical Baseball Abstract*. New York: Free Press, 2001.
James, Bill, and Rob Neyer. *The Neyer/James Guide to Pitchers*. New York: Fireside, 2004.
Jones, David, ed. *Deadball Stars of the American League*. Dulles, VA: SABR/Potomac, 2006.
Keenan, Jimmy. "Cupid Childs." SABR BioProject.
Kerr, Roy. *Buck Ewing*. Jefferson, NC: McFarland, 2012.
Lamb, William F. "George Davis." *The National Pastime* 17 (1997): 3–8.
_____. "Mr. and Mrs. George Davis: Living in Sin and Thereafter." *The Inside Game* 13 (2013): 13–16.
Lansche, Jerry. *Glory Fades Away: The Nineteenth-Century World Series Rediscovered*. Dallas: Taylor, 1991.
Lardner, Ring. *Some Champions*. New York: Scribners, 1976.
Lewis, Ethan M. "'The Wildest Kind of Crank': The Story of Players' League Magnate Al Johnson." www.ethanlewis.com., 2007.
Lewis, Franklin. *The Cleveland Indians*. New York: G.P. Putnam's Sons, 1949.
Lowry, Philip J. *Green Cathedrals*. New York: Walker, 2006.
Macht, Norman L. *Connie Mack and the Early Years of Baseball*. Lincoln: University of Nebraska Press, 2007.
Masur, Louis. *Autumn Glory: Baseball's First World Series*. New York: Hill and Wang, 2003.
McBane, Richard L. *A Fine-Looking Lot of Ball-Tossers: The Remarkable Akrons of 1881*. Jefferson, NC: McFarland, 2005.
McDonald, Brian. *Indian Summer: The Tragic Story of Louis Sockalexis, the First Native American in Major League Baseball*. Emmaus, PA: Rodale, 2003.
McKean, Cornelius, compiler. *McKean Genealogies: From the Early Settlement of McKeans, or McKeens in America to the Present Time, 1902*. Charleston, SC: BiblioLife, 2009.
McKenna, Brian. "John Clarkson." SABR BioProject.
_____. "Pussy Tebeau." SABR BioProject.
Merwin, Henry Childs. "The Irish in American Life." *Atlantic Monthly*, March 1896, 289–291.

Miller, Jay, Joe Gonsowski, and Richard Masson. *The Photographic Baseball Cards of Goodwin & Company (1886–1890)*. Santa Monica: privately printed, 2008.

Morris, Peter. "Billy Stage." SABR BioProject.

Nemec, David. *The Beer and Whisky League*. New York: Lyons & Burford, 1994.

_____. *The Great Encyclopedia of 19th-Century Major League Baseball*. New York: Donald L. Fine, 1997.

_____. *Major League Baseball Profiles, 1871–1900*. Vol. 2. Lincoln: University of Nebraska Press, 2011.

_____. "McKean, Edwin John." In *Major League Baseball Profiles, 1871–1900*. Vol. 2, 95–96. Lincoln: University of Nebraska Press, 2011.

Nemec, David, and Dave Zeman. *The Baseball Rookies Encyclopedia*. Washington: Brassey's, 2004.

Nichols, J.B. *History of Lorain County*. Oberlin: privately published, 1924.

Okkonen, Marc. *Minor League Baseball Towns of Michigan, Adrian to Ypsilanti*. Grand Rapids: Dickinson Press, 1997.

O'Laughlin, Michael C. *The Book of Irish Families, Great & Small*. 3rd ed. Kansas City: Irish Geneaological Foundation, 2002.

O'Neal, Bill. *The Southern League*. Austin: Eakin Press, 1994.

Parker, Robert D. "Batter Up: Fort Wayne's Baseball History." *Old Fort News*, Summer 1967.

Perry, Thomas K. *Textile League Baseball*. Jefferson, NC: McFarland, 2004.

Phillips, John. *The Astonishing Cleveland Babes of 1889*. Cabin John, MD: Capital, 1994.

_____. *Buck Ewing and the 1893 Cleveland Spiders*. Cabin John, MD: Capital, 1992.

_____. *Chief Sockalexis and the 1897 Cleveland Indians*. Cabin John, MD: Capital, 1991.

_____. *The 1895 Cleveland Spiders*. Cabin John, MD: Capital, 1990.

_____. *The Fall Classics of the 1890s*. Cabin John, MD: Capital, 1989.

_____. *The '99 Spiders*. Cabin John, MD: Capital, 1988.

_____. *The Riotous 1896 Cleveland Spiders*. Cabin John, MD: Capital, 1997.

_____. *The Spiders: Who Was Who*. Cabin John, MD: Capital, 1988.

_____. *The Spiders: Who Was Who*. Revised ed. Cabin John, MD: Capital, 1991.

_____. "Temple Cup Series Epilogue." *Grandstand Baseball Annual* 11 (1995): 131–132.

_____, ed. *Uncle Nick's Birthday Party*. Cabin John, MD: Capital, 1991.

Pietrusza, David, Matthew Silverman and Michael Geshman, eds. *Baseball: The Biographical Encyclopedia*. New York: Total Sports/Sports Illustrated, 2000.

Porter, David, ed. *The Biographical Dictionary of American Sports*. Westport, CT: Greenwood, 1987.

Progressive Men of Northern Ohio. Cleveland: Plain Dealer, 1906.

Ranelagh, John O'Beirne. *A Short History of Ireland*. Cambridge: Cambridge University Press, 1983.

Reach's Official Base Ball Guide. 1887, 1902, 1905.

Rideout, Walter B. *Sherwood Anderson: A Writer in America*. Vol. 1. Madison: University of Wisconsin Press, 2006.

Ritter, Lawrence. *The Glory of Their Times*. Enlarged ed. New York: Harper, 2010.

Rombach, Jerry. "Add Ed McKean to List of Lorain County Big Leaguers." *Elyria Chronicle-Telegram*, January 26, 1984.

Rosen, Charley. *The Emerald Diamond: How the Irish Transformed America's Greatest Pastime*. New York: Harper, 2012.

Samelson, Ken, and Richard Topp, eds. *The Baseball Encyclopedia*. New York: Macmillan, 1993.

Schiff, Andrew J. *"The Father of Baseball": A Biography of Henry Chadwick*. Jefferson, NC: McFarland, 2008.

Seltzer, Bob. "'Mr. Pension' Works at City Hall." *Cleveland Press*, June 26, 1964.

Seymour, Harold, and Dorothy Seymour Mills. *Baseball: The Golden Age*. New York: Oxford University Press, 1971.

Sheridan, J.B. "Hitting 'Em Out When Hit Means Run and Game." *Ogden Standard*, magazine section, May 11, 1918.

Simon, Tom, ed. *Deadball Stars of the National League*. Cleveland: SABR, 2004.
Sinin, Lee. *Complete Baseball Encyclopedia*. Version 13.0. 2013. DVD.
Spalding's Official Base Ball Guide. 1890, 1896, 1902, 1907.
Spatz, Lyle, ed. *The SABR List & Record Book*. New York: Scribner, 2007.
Stein, Fred. *And the Skipper Bats Cleanup: A History of the Baseball Player-Manager*. Jefferson, NC: McFarland, 2002.
Sutter, L.M. *Arlie Latham*. Jefferson, NC: McFarland, 2012.
Thorn, John. *Baseball in the Garden of Eden*. New York: Simon & Schuster, 2011.
Thorn, John, Pete Palmer and Michael Gershman, eds. *Total Baseball VII: The Official Encyclopedia of Major League Baseball*. Kingston, NY: Total Sports, 2001.
Thorn, John, Pete Palmer, Michael Gershman and David Pietrusza, eds. *Total Baseball V: The Official Encyclopedia of Major League Baseball*. New York: Viking, 1997.
Tiemann, Robert L., and Mark Rucker, eds. *Nineteenth Century Stars*. Kansas City: SABR, 1989.
Traughber, Bill. "Looking Back: The 1885 Nashville Americans, Part I." www.nashvillesoundsbaseball.com, May 11, 2006.
U.S. Bureau of Education. *Report of the Commissioner of Education for the Year 1886–87*. Washington: GPO, 1888.
U.S. Census Bureau. Federal census 1840–1970.
U.S. Patent Office. *The Official Gazette of the United States Patent Office*. Vol. 279. Washington: GPO, 1920.
Waldo, Ronald T. *Fred Clarke*. Jefferson, NC: McFarland, 2011.
Wallace, Elizabeth. *Colorado Springs*. Chicago: Arcadia, 2003.
Weisberger, Bernard A. *When Chicago Ruled Baseball*. New York: Harper, 2006.
Wildenheim, Doris, ed. *Grafton, Ohio: Our Heritage Trail*. Grafton, OH: Grafton Village History Association, 2008.
Williams, Frank J. "Temple Cup Series Thoughts." *Grandstand Baseball Annual* 11 (1995): 129–130.
Worth, Richard. *Baseball Team Names: A Worldwide Dictionary, 1869–2011*. Jefferson, NC: McFarland, 2013.
Ziff, Larzer. *The American 1890s*. New York: Viking, 1966.

Libraries and Collections

Alice and Jack Wirt Public Library, Bay City, MI
Bay County Historical Society, Bay City, MI
Carnegie Library, Pittsburgh, PA
Charles W. Mears Baseball Collection, Cleveland Public Library, Cleveland, OH
Cleveland *Press* Collection, Michael Schwartz Library, Cleveland State University, Cleveland, OH
Cuyahoga County Courthouse Records, Cleveland, OH
Doris P. Wildenheim Collection, Midway Public Library, Grafton, OH
Giamatti Research Center, National Baseball Hall of Fame, Cooperstown, NY
Hillman Library Special Collections, University of Pittsburgh, Pittsburgh, PA
Hoyt Public Library, Saginaw, MI
John McGraw Collection, St. Bonaventure University Archives, St. Bonaventure, NY
Kent State University Library, Kent, OH
Lake County Historical Society, Painsville, OH
Lorain County Courthouse Records, Elyria, OH
Lorain County Historical Society, Elyria, OH
Maag Library, Youngstown State University, Youngstown, OH
Mahoning Valley Historical Society, Youngstown, OH
Michael T. McGreevey Collection, Boston Public Library, Boston, MA
Medina County District Library, Medina, OH
Millstein Library, University of Pittsburgh at Greensburg, Greensburg, PA

Bibliography

New Castle Public Library, New Castle, PA
Oberlin College Library, Oberlin, OH
Ohio Historical Society, Columbus, OH
Ralph Lin Weber papers, Toledo Lucas County Public Library, Toledo, OH
Rochester Baseball Historical Society, Rochester, NY
Rochester Red Wings Baseball Club Archives, Rochester, NY
Rush Rees Library, University of Rochester, Rochester, NY
Rutherford B. Hayes Presidential Center, Fremont, OH
Western Reserve Historical Society, Cleveland, OH
Youngstown State University Library, Youngstown, OH

Newspapers

Akron Sunday Gazette
Atlanta Constitution
Baltimore Morning Herald
Baseball Magazine
Bay City Times
Bay City Tribune
Brooklyn Eagle
Canton (Ohio) Repository
Chicago Daily News
Chicago Suburbanite Economist
Cleveland Critic and Amusement Gazette
Cleveland Leader
Cleveland Plain Dealer
Cleveland Press
Cleveland Recorder
Cleveland Town Topics
Colorado Springs Gazette
The Day Book
Dayton Daily News
Dayton Journal
Denver News
Detroit Free Press
Elyria Chronicle Telegram
Elyria Daily Reporter
Elyria Evening Telegram
Elyria Republican
Fort Wayne News
Fort Wayne Journal-Gazette
Galveston Daily News
Indianapolis Star
Lake County Republican Herald
Lorain County Reporter
Los Angeles Times
Louisville Courier-Journal
Milwaukee Daily True American
Milwaukee Journal
Nashville Daily American
New Castle Daily News
New Castle News
New York Clipper
New York Times
New York Tribune
Ogden Standard
Oil City (Pennsylvania) Derrick
Painsville Telegraph
Pittsburgh Commercial Gazette
Pittsburgh Press
Rochester Democrat and Chronicle
Rochester Union and Advertiser
San Antonio Light
Sandusky Star
Sandusky Star-Journal
Spokane Press
Sporting Life
Springfield (Ohio) Gazette
The Sporting News
Tacoma Times
Utica Morning Herald
Utica Post-Express
Utica Sunday Herald
Washington Evening Star
Washington Herald
Washington Post
Washington Times
Youngstown News Register
Youngstown Vindicator

Selected Internet Sites

www.ancestry.com
www.andrewclem.com/Baseball/League Park.html
www.baseball-almanac.com
www.baseballfever.com
www.baseballguru.com
www.baseballhistoryblog.com.
www.baseballlibrary.com
www.baseball-reference.com
www.baseball-statistics.com
www.bchsmuseum.org (Bay County Historical Museum, Bay City, MI)
www.BoxRec.com

http://chroniclingamerica.loc.gov (Chronicling America, Library of Congress)
www.clevelandmemory.org (Cleveland Memory Project, Cleveland State University, Cleveland, OH)
http://cplorg.cdmhost.com (History of Baseball, Digital Gallery, Cleveland Public Library, Cleveland, OH)
www.thedeadballera.com
http://eagle.brooklynpubliclibrary.org
www.ech.case.edu (*Encyclopedia of Cleveland History*, Case Western Reserve University, Cleveland, OH)
www.ethanlewis.com
www.familysearch.com
www.FamilyTreeMaker.com
www.fultonhistory.com
www.futilityinfielder.com
www.huntauctions.com
www.jockpost.com
http://loc.gov/pictures (Library of Congress)
www.lorain.lib.oh.us
www.milb.com (Minor League Baseball)
www.myancestory.com
www.nashvillesoundsbaseball.com
www.ohiohistory.org (Ohio Historical Society, Columbus, OH)
www.oldtimefamilybaseball.com
www.ootpdevelopment.com (Out Of The Park Baseball)
www.paperofrecord.com
www.prowrestlinghistory.com
www.retrosheet.org
www.rochesterbaseballhistory.org
www.sabr.org
www.sabr.org/BioProject
http://thisgameofgames.blogspot.com/
www.usarchives.org
www.villageofgrafton.org
www.Wisconsinhistoricalsociety.org

Index

Abell, Ferdinand A. 191
Achilles 128
Adams, Dr. Daniel L. 71
Adelbert College (team) 131
Akron, Ohio 27, 30, 45, 155, 158, 229, 289
Akron (team) 97
Akron Akrons 27, 28, 67, 74, 153
Akron Champs 275
Akron Rubbernecks 255
Akron Summits 147
Albany (National Association minor league) 59
Albany (team) 120
Alberts, Gus 86
Alexander, Charles C. 167
Alexandria, Egypt 3
Alibi Ike 281
All Professionals (Cleveland) 288–289
Allen, Myron 81, 82
Allentown Kelly's Killers 139
Alliance (team) 76
Alloway, Arthur 261
Altoona Mountain Citys 30
Alvord, Billy 151
American Association (major league) 3, 4, 9, 13, 26–27, 30, 43, 46, 47, 72–74, 76, 77, 78, 79, 80, 82, 83, 86, 87, 98, 113, 119, 143, 150, 159, 186, 191, 239, 251, 282
American League 17–18, 33, 64, 121, 166, 174, 201, 228, 230, 231, 288, 255
Amsterdam, New York 250
Anderson, Sherwood 19, 20, 38
Andrews, Ed 27, 67
Andrus, _____ 241–242
Anson, Cap 36, 40, 41, 56, 69, 91, 106, 107, 109, 129, 136, 148, 159, 188, 203, 210, 224, 252, 296
Anthony, Susan B. 50
Arbitration Committee 73–74
Arcade Hotel, Springfield, Ohio 273–274
Ardner, Joe 90, 106, 285
Argyllshire, Scotland 23
Arkansas 255
Arthurian legends 12

Arundel, Chauncey 278
Arundel, Harry 27
Associated Press 52
Athletic Park, Indianapolis 91
Atlanta Atlantas 116
Atlanta Crackers 174
Atlanta Windjammers 147
Auburn Yankees 44
Augusta Browns 40
Austin, Jimmy 260, 261–262
Australia 23
Averill, Earl 121

Bailey, Bill 266
Bakely, Jersey 32–33, 46, 51, 52, 55, 84, 86, 87, 90, 91, 92–93, 101, 119, 163
Baker, Kirtley 153–154
Baker, Norm 39
Baker Bowl, Philadelphia 210, 215
Baldwin, Kid 147
Bales, Curtis 266
Ball, _____ 51
Baltimore, Maryland 9, 10, 12, 16, 17, 63, 64, 65, 70, 81, 158, 167–168, 194, 197, 201, 234, 235, 236, 245–246, 290, 293, 296
Baltimore Central Police Station 236
Baltimore Orioles (American Association) 39, 81, 86, 87
Baltimore Orioles (National League) 17, 41, 56–70, 103, 111, 114, 115, 117, 134, 137, 153, 154–155, 164, 166–173, 177–178, 179, 182, 183, 189, 193–197, 203, 206, 208, 216, 217, 218, 224, 225, 232–237, 238, 242, 293–295
Bancroft, Frank 43–55, 239, 253
Bang, Ed 64–66, 198, 286, 289
Bangor, Maine 182
Banks, Ernie 216
Baptists 16
Barrett, _____ 76
Barrow, Ed 240, 242, 243
Bates, Elmer 5, 7, 12, 14, 15, 24, 33, 43, 59, 69, 118, 130–131, 142–143, 146–147, 155, 156–157, 168, 180, 182, 187–188, 211, 213, 226, 227, 229, 230, 289, 305

Bates, Frank 216, 222, 223
Battin, Joe 45, 285
Battle Creek, Michigan 284
Battle Creek Crickets 282
Bay City, Michigan 248, 279, 280, 281, 285
Bay City Billikens 285
Bay City Reds 279–285
Bay Citys 280
Bean, Joe 238–239, 240, 241, 246
Beard, Ollie 40, 109
Beatin, Eb 88, 90, 91, 95, 96, 97, 100, 102, 103, 104, 107, 108, 109, 119
Beck, Erve 255
Becker, Beals 256
Becker, Edward C. 191, 219–220
Beckley, Jake 161
Belden, Ira 209, 249
Bellaire, Ohio 261, 268
Bennett, Charlie 121, 138, 140, 142, 223
Bennett, Pug 256
Bennett Park, Detroit 140
Bensley, Lou 283
Berea, Ohio 168
Bern, Arch 267
Bernhardt, Sarah 254
Bescher, Bob 260, 266
Betts, William 173, 190–191
Beyerle's Park, Cleveland 87
Biery, Bert 248
Bildner, Bill 4
Billiken doll 277
Binghamton Bingoes 239, 241
Binghamton Crickets 50, 53
BioProject (SABR) 40
Bippus, Charles W. 269
Birmingham (team) 42
Birmingham Barons 255, 257
Black, William 173
Black River in Ohio 19, 20
Blair, Guy 283
Blake, Harry 115, 116, 156, 172, 174, 176, 177, 178, 180, 187, 190, 203, 206, 211, 215, 222, 240, 242, 250
Bliss, Robert 13
Boggs, Wade 9
Bonner, Frank 58
Bosse Field, Evansville, Indiana 258
Boston, Massachusetts 23, 141
Boston Beaneaters 13, 32, 46, 49, 54, 56, 59, 89, 92, 95, 96, 97, 109–110, 124–125, 126, 127, 134, 135, 136, 138–143, 149, 152, 155, 157, 162, 176, 177, 179, 188, 189, 193, 205, 213–214, 226, 227, 238
Boston College 258
Boston Red Caps (National Association) 71–72
Boston Red Sox (American League) 33, 150, 248, 253, 271, 276, 282
Boston Reds (American Association) 150
Boston Reds (Players' League) 110
Boston Reds (Union Association) 46, 82

Boswell, James 289
Boudreau, Lou 1, 3, 172, 307n4
Boulevard Park, Colorado Springs 249, 251
Bowerman, Frank 64
Boxing Hall of Fame, International 280
Boyd, Frank 147
Brackenridge, John 275
Brady, King 255
Brady's Run, Baltimore 234
Bratenhal, Ohio 144
Breitenstein, Ted 163, 213, 255
Bresnahan, Roger 208
Brian Boru 16
Bridgeport Giants 45
Briggs, Bert (Buttons) 285
Bristow, George 221
Britton, Helene Hathaway (Robison) 288
Broad Street and Hamilton Street, Philadelphia 215
Brockton, Massachusetts 242
Brodie, Steve 59, 63, 112, 114, 116, 153, 169, 296
Brooklyn Atlantics 71
Brooklyn Bridegrooms (Trolley Dodgers) (Dodgers) (National League) 9, 56, 62, 126, 150, 164, 178, 189, 193, 201, 206, 217, 226, 227, 248, 261, 268, 275
Brooklyn Trolley Dodgers (American Association) 79, 81, 85, 86
Brotherhood Park, Cleveland 99, 100, 110
Brouthers, Dan 51, 58
Browning, Pete 7, 12, 78, 99, 129
Browning, Reed 170, 186, 194, 215, 221, 296
Brownlee, T.P. 30, 35
Brunell, Frank H. 15, 73–74, 80, 87, 89, 101, 104, 113–114
Brush, John T. 93, 190, 191, 202, 209, 217; Brush Rule 212
Bryan, Will C. 39, 40, 42, 231, 239
Bryan, William Jennings 10
Bryan, Ohio 259
Buchtel College (team) 158
Buckenberger, Al 85, 135, 155, 238, 239, 242
Bucyrus (teams) 26, 181
Buelow, Charley 230
Buelow, Fritz 281
Buffalo Bill Wild West Show 200
Buffalo Bisons 51, 54, 240, 242, 243, 244, 245, 246
Buridan's ass 100
Burke, Eddie 193
Burke, Jimmy 216
Burkett, Jesse 5, 10, 33–34, 59, 61, 63, 64, 66, 68, 69, 85, 114, 115, 117, 120, 126, 131, 135, 137, 138, 140, 142, 143, 147, 148, 149, 153–154, 155, 156, 157, 160, 162, 163, 169, 173, 175, 176, 177, 182, 183, 185, 187, 188, 196, 202, 203, 205, 206, 207, 212–213, 218, 220, 222, 236, 243, 275, 287, 293
Burnett, W.R. 274
Burnham, Watch 92

Burns, Farmer 181
Burns, Joseph 229
Burns, Oyster 45, 77–78
Burns, Thomas F. 249, 251
Burns, Tom 109
Bush, Donie 260, 261–262, 263, 272–273, 286
Businessmen's Athletic Club, Cleveland 229
Butler University 253
Butternut Ridge Cemetery, North Eaton, Ohio 29
Byrne, Charles H. 62, 190, 191

Calhoun, W.A. 230
California 50, 102, 105, 132
Callahan, Nixey 214
Callahan, William T. 238–239
Calvary Cemetery, Cleveland 290, 291
Cambridge, Massachusetts 280
Campau, Count 238–239
Canada 23, 34, 50, 216, 281
Canton, Ohio 90, 108–109, 229, 248
Canton (Ohio) (team) 209
Canton (Ohio) Athletic Club (team) 248
Canton (Ohio) Cantons 74
Canton (Ohio) Deubers 248
Canton (Ohio) Marines (team) 248, 249, 251
Canton (Ohio) Nadjys 248
Canton (Ohio) Red Stockings 253
Canton Bulldogs 240, 248
Canton Chinamen 266, 272
Cantonsville (Maryland) (team) 197
Carbondale Anthracites 158
Carey, Scoops 58, 114, 115, 168, 293
Carlyle, Thomas 11, 12
Carney, Jack 92
Carney, Pat 255
Carpenter, William 208
Carroll, Lewis (Through the Looking-Glass) 7, 9, 56, 111, 166, 197, 232, 278, 293
Carroll, Scrappy 76
Carrollton Hotel, Baltimore 194, 195, 234, 236
Carsey, Kid 164, 177, 223
Carson, Anne 279
Carson, Dr. Frank C. 259, 265, 267, 268–269, 270, 271, 276, 278
Cartwright, Ed 29, 30, 35, 42–43, 90, 173, 218
Caruthers, Bob 77
Caskin, Ed 46
Casway, Jerrold 100, 113
Catholics 18, 21–22, 25, 38, 44, 67, 68, 182, 204, 258
Caylor, O. P. 7, 73
Cedar Avenue Race Track, Cleveland 83
Cedarville, Ohio 151
Central League 252, 253, 254, 258, 259, 260, 263–264, 265, 266, 267, 269, 270, 271, 272, 273, 275, 276, 278, 279
Chadwick, Henry 73, 159, 183, 191–192, 202

Chamberlain, Ice Box 36, 77, 78, 152
Chambers, Boyd 274
Champion farm machinery 253, 270
Chapman, Jack 166
Charleston Seagulls 42
Chase, Hal 247
Chattanooga Lookouts 41
Chesapeake Bay 224
Chester County, Pennsylvania 23
Chesterfield (Philip Stanhope) 212
Chicago, Illinois 61, 96, 213, 253, 259, 270
Chicago Black Sox scandal 115
Chicago Colts (Orphans, Cubs) (National League) 36, 40, 41, 56, 59, 69, 91, 96, 105, 106, 109, 127, 129, 132, 135, 145, 148, 152, 162, 168, 177, 188, 189–190, 193, 203, 208, 210, 214, 224, 228, 258, 266, 281
Chicago White Sox 259, 271, 276
Childs, Cupid 7–9, 10, 16, 17, 56, 114, 117, 118, 119, 122, 123, 124, 125, 126, 128–129, 131, 134, 135, 137, 140, 142, 148, 149, 153–154, 157, 158, 160, 163, 169, 173, 174, 175, 176, 177, 193, 196, 202, 203, 206, 208, 209, 212, 213, 215, 217, 220, 221, 222, 224–225, 226, 230, 236, 244, 271, 286, 290, 295, 296
Chippewas 43
Chute Lake, St. Louis 206
Cicotte, Eddie 276
Cincinnati, Ohio 61, 76, 90, 128, 147, 174, 258
Cincinnati Kelly's Killers 40
Cincinnati Red Stockings of 1869 26
Cincinnati Reds (American Association) 27, 40, 73, 76, 78–79, 81, 98, 112
Cincinnati Reds (National League) 27, 40, 47, 56, 97, 98, 109, 121, 122–124, 125, 128–129, 132, 149, 151–152, 164, 174–175, 179, 193, 196, 212–213, 214–215, 221, 223, 253; Reds Field Day 271
Civil War 19, 23, 26, 38, 47
Claflin, Waldo M. 119
Clark, Leroy 274
Clarke, Boileryard 63, 64, 114, 154–155, 170, 235
Clarke, Dad 164, 177, 186
Clarke, Fred 183, 189
Clarke, Henry 214
Clarkson, Dad 41, 58, 66, 115, 152, 280, 281
Clarkson, John 41, 46, 58, 93, 97, 124, 125, 135, 138, 139, 140, 141, 142, 144, 146, 148, 149, 150, 152, 155, 157, 280, 281; John Clarkson Park, Bay City 280
Clements, _____ 282
Clements, Jack 92, 123, 217
Cleveland, Ohio 1, 3, 5, 7–18, 20, 22, 24, 41, 46, 56, 65, 69–70, 72–73, 85, 87, 88, 95–96, 97, 100, 101, 102–103, 106, 118, 119, 121, 126, 127, 128, 130, 131, 138, 142, 144, 151, 156, 157, 160, 161, 163, 167, 170–171, 172, 175, 180–181, 182, 183–184, 188–189,

192, 198–199, 204, 205, 206, 209, 210, 211, 214–215, 216, 217, 218, 219, 221, 222–223, 226, 227, 228, 229, 230, 241–242, 247, 255, 259, 266, 272, 276, 278, 279, 280, 286, 288, 289, 296
Cleveland, S.D.W. 72–74
Cleveland (proposed American Association) (team) 229, 230
Cleveland (proposed Columbia League) (team) 289
Cleveland (teams) 43
Cleveland Amateur Base Ball Association 26
Cleveland & Toledo Rail Road 19
Cleveland Athletic Club 11, 64, 142, 157, 160, 172, 181, 205
Cleveland Athletic Club (team) 130
Cleveland Blues (American Association) 13, 14, 29, 32, 33, 47, 49, 54, 55, 69, 72–87, 88, 94, 101, 106, 112, 117, 123, 137, 158, 162, 183, 285
Cleveland Blues (National League) 30, 32, 43, 46, 55, 59, 80, 88, 93, 100, 119, 214
Cleveland brothel 207
Cleveland Cardinals 40, 41, 51, 76, 84
Cleveland City Hall 182
Cleveland-Columbus-Cincinnati Railroad 25
Cleveland Electrics 74
Cleveland Elks Club, Superior Avenue 7–18, 197, 235, 273, 274
Cleveland Forest Citys (independent) 27
Cleveland Forest Citys (National Association) 45, 276
Cleveland Heights, Ohio 3
Cleveland In-Door League 157
Cleveland Indians (American League) 1, 17–18, 66, 172, 201, 218, 255, 290
Cleveland Infants (Players' League) 14, 35, 47, 69, 94, 98–103, 106, 110, 119, 121, 126, 148, 150
Cleveland Lakeshores (American League minors) 230, 247
Cleveland Lyceum 111
Cleveland Malleables 74
Cleveland Music Hall 293
Cleveland Naps (Blues/Bronchos) (American League) 34, 97, 166, 173, 198, 201, 228, 230, 231, 243, 248, 250, 255, 257, 266, 269, 283, 286–287, 288; Cleveland-Pittsburgh annual series 97
Cleveland Old Leaguers 130
Cleveland Public Library 14
Cleveland Pythians (in-door) 157
Cleveland Red Cross Rink 157
Cleveland Shamrocks 74
Cleveland Spiders (Indians/Wanderers/Misfits) (National League) 4, 5, 7–18, 27, 33–34, 40, 41, 45, 50, 56–70, 72, 78, 88–219, 220, 221, 222–224, 225, 226, 228, 230, 232–237, 238, 240, 243, 248, 250, 253, 255, 266, 267, 270, 281, 282, 286–287, 288, 293–297; barnstorming and exhibition games 97, 105–106, 162, 164, 194, 208, 209; in 1892 World's Series 45, 126, 135, 136, 131, 137, 138–143, 144, 176, 222, 238, 243, 280; in 1895 Temple Cup 103, 111–118, 119, 131, 166–171, 172, 173, 176, 181, 182, 192, 194, 195, 197, 201, 232–237, 240, 245, 273, 274, 286, 287, 290, 293–297; in 1896 Temple Cup 119, 182, 183, 193–197, 238, 242, 245; nicknamed 89, 104; old-timers' game 1909 287–288; spring training 90, 102–103, 104–106, 107, 122, 131–132, 147–148, 157–158, 172, 174, 205, 209, 211, 218, 219, 255; Sunday baseball in Cleveland 61, 65, 83, 86–87, 174, 176, 178, 204–205, 207–208, 210, 219
Cleveland YMCA 95
Cobb, Ty 286
Cole, Leonard 281
Coleman, John 147
Colliflower, Harry 222
Collins, Hub 78, 79
Collins, Joe 271, 274
Collins, Officer _____ 185
Collinwood, Ohio 210
Colorado 250
Colorado Gold Rush 249
Colorado Springs, Colorado 248, 249, 250
Colorado Springs Millionaires 248, 249–252, 253, 254, 258, 269
Columbus (Georgia) Stars 41–42
Columbus, Ohio 40, 90, 147, 148
Columbus (Ohio) Buckeyes 146
Columbus (Ohio) Senators 205
Columbus (Ohio) Solons 97, 98–99, 148, 186
Comiskey, Charlie 77, 91, 136, 159
Confederate states 38
Congalton, Bunk 250
Congress Street Grounds, Boston 163
Connecticut 269
Connecticut Western Reserve in Ohio 19, 27, 248
Connolly, Eddie 229
Connor, Roger 234
Constableville, New York 49
Coogan, Dan 66
Coogan, James J. 93
Coogan's Bluff 93
Cooley, Bill 252, 254
Cooley, Duff 208
Corbett, Gentleman Jim 195
Corbett, Joe 59, 195, 196
Corcoran, Larry 36
Corcoran, Tommy 45, 66, 269
Cork, Ireland 27
Corkhill, Pop 134
Corn Belt 20
Corns, Harry 271, 273, 274
Corrigan, Bill 44, 45
County Cork, Ireland 23
Cox, James M. 263
Crane, Stephen 12

Index

Cranley, John 130
Crawford, George H. 280–281
Crawford, Lacy 227
Crawford, Lorina N. 280–281, 284
Creighton, Charles M. 217, 227
Creoles 50
Criger, Elmer 282
Criger, Lou 201, 206–207, 211, 222, 225, 282
Cripple Creek, Colorado 249
Crisham, Pat 247
Crooks, Jack 227
Cross, Amos 259
Cross, Frank 259, 267
Cross, Lave 87, 226, 259
Cross, Monte 161
Crothers, Douglass 55
Crowell, Billy 76, 84, 87, 90
Cuba 47, 130
Cuban All-Stars 248
Culver Field, Rochester 49, 51, 52, 53, 54, 55, 210, 216, 239–240, 242, 243, 244, 246, 247
Cummings, _____ 282
Cunningham, Bert 206
Cuppy, Nig (George Koppe) 9, 56–57, 64, 111, 114, 117, 119–120, 126, 131, 132, 135, 137, 141, 145, 148, 149, 150, 155, 158, 160, 163, 164, 167, 168–170, 174, 175–176, 178, 179, 181, 184, 186, 188, 189, 195–197, 202, 205, 206, 215, 222, 233
Curtis, Gene 253
Cushman, Charley 212
Cuthbert, Ned 78, 79
Cuyahoga County, Ohio 9, 148

Dahlen, Bill 72, 113, 148, 213
Dailey, Vince 104, 105–106
Daily, Con 193
Daily, One Arm 74, 81–82, 209
Daly, George 281
Dargan, H.H. 210
Darrah, _____ 36
Darrow, Clarence 26
Daub, Dan 189
Dauvray, Helen 13
Dauvray Cup 13, 56
Davies, George 126, 147–148
Davis, George 3, 4, 106, 110, 113, 120–121, 122, 124, 125, 127, 128–129, 131, 133, 134, 137, 138, 140, 144, 149, 156–157, 203, 220, 225
Dayton, Ohio 158, 248, 259–260, 263, 267, 268
Dayton Old Soldiers 205
Dayton Veterans 259–269, 270, 272, 274, 286
Deadrick, _____ 39
Decker, Albert 261–262
De Haven Comedy Company 181
Delahanty, Ed 3, 11, 18, 72, 85, 92, 99–100, 101, 106, 113, 119, 130, 164, 176, 180, 203, 290, 291
Delahanty, Joe 243

Delahanty, Tom 190, 250, 251
Delaney, William L. 248
Democrats 10, 67, 217, 263
Demontreville, Gene 240
Demontreville, Lee 240
Denver, Colorado 173, 252
Denver Grizzlies 249, 250
Denver Mountaineers 89, 105–106
Des Moines Midgets 238
Des Moines Prohibitionists 105, 158
Des Moines Underwriters 250
designated hitter 144
Detroit, Michigan 60, 107, 121–122, 140, 219, 286
Detroit Tigers 248, 253
Detroit Wolverines (International Association) 121
Detroit Wolverines (International League) 239
Detroit Wolverines (National League) 40–41, 46, 51, 59, 88, 121, 258
Dever, Ireland 182
Devonian Springs water 107–108
DeWolf Hopper, William 195
Dickey, Guy 270, 273, 274
Dillon, John 244, 246
Donahue, Frank 253, 271, 274
Donahue, Jigs 271
Donahue, Red 34, 190, 206, 214
Donlin, Mike 227
Donnelly, Jim 207
Donneybrook fairs of Ireland 69
Donovan, _____ 276
Donovan, Patsy 69, 202
Douglass, Frederick 50
Douglass, Klondike 255, 256
Dowagiac, Michigan 268
Dowse, Tom 105
Doyle, Conny 42
Doyle, Dirty Jack 126, 131, 196, 197
Doyle, John 44, 45, 46
Drohan, John J. 139
Duffy, Hugh 45, 138, 139, 141, 142, 143, 154
Dugan, Sam 148
Duluth White Sox 289
Dunham Avenue, Cleveland 181
Dunlap, Fred 88
Durkee Road, Eaton, Ohio 24
Durocher, Leo 137
Duryea, Jesse 123–124, 150
Dwyer, Fred 151

Eakins, Thomas 200
Earle, Howard 109
Easlie, Bob 57
East, Walter R. 255
East Liberty Stars 30, 33, 37
East Liverpool Potters 269, 275
Eastern League 30, 43, 44, 45, 58, 85, 238, 239, 240, 242, 243, 244, 245, 246, 247, 248, 249

Eastern Park, Brooklyn 188, 193
Eaton, Ohio 20, 22, 23, 24, 25
Eclipse Park, Louisville 182, 183–186
Economic panic of 1893 144, 146
Edwards, Henry P. 288
Egan, James M., Jr. 32, 126–127, 160, 170, 183–184
Ehman, Buck 248
Ehret, Red 163, 175, 179, 255
Elkhart, Indiana 61, 211
Ely, Fred 112
Elyria, Ohio 19, 28, 29
Elyria Elks Club (team) 247
Elyria Elyrias 26, 27
Elyria Southern Rocks 26
Emslie, Robert 160, 166, 195, 208
England 23, 67, 146
English, Captain _____ 204
Enigma Tornado of 1884 30
Erdman, Charles 259
Erskine College 253
Esper, Duke 150, 164, 177, 189, 195, 206, 233, 234, 242, 246
Euclid Beach Amusement Park, Collinwood, Ohio 210
Euclid Beach Park (team) 209
Euclid Opera House (Euclid Theatre), Cleveland 57, 64
Evans, Billy 29, 33
Evans, Steve 266, 267, 269
Evansville, Indiana 258, 259
Evansville Black Birds 174
Evansville Hoosiers 105
Evansville River Rats 148, 252, 254, 258–259, 260, 263–264, 267, 272, 273
Ewing, Buck 67, 92, 104, 116, 120–121, 144–145, 146, 148, 149, 152, 153, 154, 155, 156, 157, 160, 162, 174–175, 183
Eyler, Elwood 251

Faatz, Jay 55, 85, 90, 91, 92, 95
Fairview Park, Dayton 260, 263
Falkenberg, Cy 243
Farmer, J.S. 65
Farrell, Duke 150, 153
Federal League 281
Fennelly, Frank 3, 112
Fessenden, Wallace 92
Fielder, Judge _____ 204
Finlay, Ohio 60
Fisher, Chauncey 160
Fitzgerald, F. Scott 238, 239
Fleitz, David 59, 66
Flint Vehicles 282
Florida 122
floriography 16
Fogarty, Jim 97
Fordham University 44
Ford's Theater, DC 149, 197
Foreman, Brownie 179
Forest City House, Cleveland 189

Fort Wayne, Indiana 93, 201, 276, 277, 278, 279, 280
Fort Wayne Billikens 275–279, 285
Fort Wayne Farmers 174, 190, 201
Fort Wayne Indians 205
Fort Wayne Kekiongas 276
Fort Wayne Municipal Court 278
Fort Wayne Railroaders 252
Foster, John B. 14–15, 123, 159, 175, 190
Foutz, Dave 77, 280
France 253
Francis, Ike 242
Frank, Fred 216
Franklin (team) 30, 37
Fraser, Chick 189
Freedman, Andrew 132, 209
Freeman, Jim 259
Fremer, Anthony 274
French, Charlie 259
Friel, Bill 253
Frommer, Harvey 61
Fuller, Shorty 156

Gaffney, John H. 135
Gainesville, Florida 132
Gainesville (team) 122
Galion, Ohio 147
Galion (team) 181
Gallagher, Thomas 25
Ganzel, Charlie 138, 141
Ganzel, Joe 260
Ganzel, John 260
Gatins, Frank 249
Geauga Lake Park, Ohio 87
German-Americans 23, 33, 66
Getzein, Pretzels 91, 127
Gibbons, James Cardinal 18
Gibert, Jack 255
"Gibson girls" 9
Gilks, Bobby 50, 82, 90, 91, 95, 96, 100, 104, 105, 109, 255
Gilman, Jim 151
Gilman, Jonathan H. 28
Gilman, Marie 29
Gilman, Miranda (Pitkin) 28
Gilman, Nicholas 28
Gilman, Pit 3, 28–29, 33
Gish, Lillian 253–254
Glasscock, Jack 3, 4, 32, 44, 55, 71, 74, 85, 88, 91, 93, 96, 113, 155, 161, 183
Gleason, Kid 56, 58, 66, 115, 116, 117, 118, 127, 169
Goodman, Chief 285
Goodwin 26
Gough, Irwin 283
Grafton, Ohio 11, 19–22, 23–25, 26, 27, 28, 29, 30, 38, 41, 55, 72, 73, 87, 102, 107–108, 130, 147, 157, 158, 181–182, 206, 213, 253, 286, 288, 291
Grafton (teams) 27
Grafton High School 24

Index

Grafton Stone Company 19
Grand Rapids (team) 158
Grand Rapids Bobolinks 205
Grand Rapids Boers 230
Grand Rapids Furnituremakers 230
Grand Rapids Orphans 252, 262, 263
Grand Rapids Rippers 122
Grand Rapids Wolverines 260, 263, 275, 276, 278
Granger Movement 100
Grant, Angus 261
Great Lakes 52
Green, Roy 283
Grey, Zane 240
Griffin, Mike 83
Griffith, Clark 59, 102, 117, 189
Griffith Stadium, DC 212
Grimm, Jack 267
Grogan, Bob 266, 267
Gruber, Henry 88, 90, 91, 101, 127, 129
Gumbert, Ad 178

Hackett, Walter 46, 51
Hale, Ray 268
Halifax, Nova Scotia 44
Hall, Mayor _____ 210
Halligan, Joko 132
Hallman, Bill 92
Hallman, Del 274
Halpin, Jim 54
Hamilton, Billy 109, 123, 164
Hamilton, Ohio 241
Hamilton Clippers 51, 51–52, 54
Hamilton Field (The Grand Duchess), Fort Wayne 276
Hammond, Harry 274
Hankinson, Frank 88
Hanlon, Ned 51, 56–59, 63, 66, 67, 88, 100, 103, 115, 117, 168, 191, 194, 195, 197, 201, 217, 219, 220, 234, 262, 268, 296
Hanna, Mark 14, 210
Harding, Warren G. 16, 289
Harkins, John 79–80
Harley, Dick (Henry R.) 253
Harrington, _____ 49–50
Harris, Bill 283
Hart, Billy 209
Hart, James 188, 191
Hartford Dark Blues 44
Havel, Ed 289
Hawaii 47
Hawke, Bill 153
Hawkins, Tom 263
Hawley, Davis 12–13, 14, 74, 79, 81, 93, 98, 100, 101, 103, 108, 109, 119, 121, 122, 169, 176, 209
Hawley House, Cleveland 100, 158
Hayden, Jack 104, 240–241, 243, 245, 246, 247
Healy, Egyptian 134
Hector 128

Heidrick, Emmet 216, 222
Hemming, George 195
Henderson (Kentucky) Blue Birds 281
Hendricks, Jack 252, 253, 261, 265, 269–270, 271, 273–274, 275, 276, 277–278, 279
Henley, W.E. 65
Henry, Frank 181
Hickey, Ed 255
Hilltop Park, Springfield, Ohio 253, 272, 276
Hinkel, M.J. 29, 108, 286, 289
Hinkel's Base Ball Club 286
Hoagland, Willard 161–162
Hodson, George 163
Hofer, _____ 35
Hoffer, Bill 57, 58, 114, 115, 166, 168–169, 194–195, 196, 230, 293–294
Hogan, G. 108
Hogan, Timothy 283
Hollenden House, Cleveland 196–197, 204
Holliday, Bug 129
Hollison, John 145–146
Holy Cross College 182, 201, 202, 258
Homer (Odyssey) 12, 192
Hopke, Bill 289
Hopkins, Ralph 277
Horatio Alger 146
Horner, Jack 50
horse racing 73, 210
Horton, Elmer 241, 244, 246
Hot Springs, Arkansas 90, 102–103, 104–105, 106, 107, 108, 132, 211, 218, 220, 230, 256
Hot Springs Picked Nine 90
Hotaling, Pete 76, 79, 87, 88, 90, 285
Hotel and Restaurant Employees and Bar Tenders International Union 286
Hotel Rennert, Baltimore 191, 201
Householder, Charlie 49–50
Houston Babies 91
Howe, _____ 74
Howe, George W. 137
Hoy, Dummy 149–150
Hudson, Nat 86
Hughey, Jim 189 223–224
Huntington Avenue, Baltimore 236
Hurst, Tim 67–68, 153–154, 163, 166, 186–187, 204, 235, 293–295
Hutchinson, Bill 96, 109, 127, 146, 177
Hyndman, Jim 36

Illinois Cycling Club (team) 270
Immaculate Conception Church, Grafton 21–22, 25
Imperial Hotel, St. Louis 217–218
Indiana 174, 252, 278
Indianapolis, Indiana 205, 259
Indianapolis Hoosiers (minor league) 40, 174
Indianapolis Hoosiers (National League) 44, 91, 93
Ingersoll, Frederick 289
Inks, Bert 177

International Association 47, 121
International Harvester 253
International League 11, 38, 46, 47, 49, 50, 51, 52, 55, 72, 73, 76, 77, 78, 82, 90, 239, 239–240
Inter-State league 33, 158, 201, 248
Ireland 21, 22–23, 25, 26, 34, 182, 199
Irish-Americans 5, 11, 12, 13, 16–17, 20, 22, 25, 26, 34, 38, 50–51, 59, 66–67, 70, 75, 95, 97, 100, 105, 129, 130, 132, 143, 154, 155, 158, 168, 173, 182, 191, 192, 200, 207, 208, 233, 234–235, 253, 271, 276, 288, 289
Irish Family Memorial, Cleveland, Ohio 22
Irish Famine 22–23
Irwin, Arthur 71

Jackson, Joe S. 284
Jackson, Shoeless Joe 200, 271
Jackson, Michigan 284
Jackson (Michigan) Convicts 282
Jacoby, Harry 50
Jaeger, Joseph 278
James, Bill (author) 3, 4
Jay Street, Ohio City 216, 288, 289–290
Jenkins, Tom 181, 229
Jennings, Hughie 4, 17, 18, 59, 60, 66, 71, 72, 102, 111, 112, 114, 115, 116, 117, 154, 156, 166, 169, 170, 194, 217, 224, 233–234, 253, 286, 295
Jersey City Skeeters 45, 244, 247
John Clarkson Park, Bay City, Michigan 285
Johns, Pete 289
Johnson, _____ 244
Johnson, Al 98, 99, 100, 101, 102–103, 119, 139
Johnson, Ban 17, 33, 74, 122, 231
Johnson, Ralph 120, 125, 128
Johnson, Tom 103
Johnson Street Bridge, Saginaw 283
Johnstown (New York) Jags 241
Johnstown, Pennsylvania 249
Johnstown (Pennsylvania) (team) 30, 37
Jonah 121, 202
Jones, Bumpus 151
Jones, Cowboy 222
Joss, Addie 69, 158, 257, 286
Joyce, Bill 173, 227
Just So 10

Kalamazoo White Sox 280, 283
Kansas City, Missouri 90
Kansas City Blues 251
Kansas City Cowboys 42–43, 87, 105
Kappel, Heinie 33
Karger, Ed 256
Katz, _____ 52
Kearns, Tim 229
Keas, Ed 84
Keefe, Tim 43, 94, 116, 118, 188, 193, 235
Keeler, Willie 59, 66, 114, 116, 169, 294, 295
Keenan, Owen 35–37, 217

Kelley, Joe 59, 63, 64, 66, 68, 114, 116, 153, 168, 169, 170, 194, 196, 217, 234, 235, 295–296
Kelley, Thomas B. 242
Kellogg, Nate 40, 41, 52, 54–55
Kelly, Bill 271, 274, 275
Kelly, John O. 209
Kelly, King 12, 97, 125, 136, 138–139
Kennard House, Cleveland 127, 130, 198
Kennard Street Grounds, Cleveland 41, 84
Kennedy, Brickyard 261–262, 263, 266, 267, 268–269, 275
Kennedy, Doc 51, 55
Kent (Ohio) (team) 28
Kerr, W.W. 161
Kilbane, Johnny 288
Kilfoyl, John 230
Killen, Frank 148, 155, 163, 207, 255, 266
King, Silver 68, 77, 87, 203
Kinney, Billy 32
Kirby, John 81
Kittridge, Malachi 109, 146, 266
Klobedanz, Fred 214
Knabe, Otto 250, 251
Knauss, Frank 147
Knell, Phil 161, 173, 176
Knight, Lon 46, 47, 52, 53, 54
Knoll, Punch 267
Knox, Ivan 23

Lajoie, Larry 121, 173, 201
Lake Erie 19, 278
Lake Huron 41
Lakeside Apartments, Cleveland 182
Lally, Bud 187
Landis, Doc 45
Lange, Bill 148
Lansche, Jerry 235
Lansing, Tom 185
Lansing Senators 282–283
LaPorte, Ohio 27, 28, 29
Lardner, Ring 11, 281
Larkin, Ted (Henry) 69, 150
Las Vegas, Nevada 275
Latham, Arlie 56, 123, 128–129, 152, 270
Lavigne, Kid 280
Lawrence, _____ 51
Lawrence, Tom 83–84
Lazarus 115
Leadley, Bob 69, 107, 109, 110, 121–122, 124, 125, 126–128
League Park, Cincinnati 128–129, 132, 210
League Park, Cleveland I (American Association/National League) 14, 77, 78, 79, 80, 83–84, 85, 89, 91, 94, 96, 97, 98, 106, 109, 110, 146
League Park, Cleveland II (National League) 1, 7, 17, 57, 61, 64–65, 67, 110, 111, 114, 115, 118, 121, 122–123, 124, 127, 130, 132, 135, 138, 139, 142, 144, 145, 146, 148, 150
League park ii 152, 153, 160, 162, 164,

166–168, 170, 175, 178, 179, 189, 190, 196, 198, 200, 202, 204, 205, 206, 208–209, 210, 213, 214, 216, 221, 223, 227, 228, 230, 234, 236, 285
League Park, Cleveland III (American League) 17, 286–287
League Park, Fort Wayne 276, 277
Leber, Emil 289
Leever, Sam 222
Lejeune, Sheldon 271, 274
Letcher, Tom 259
Lewis, Franklin 65–66
Lewis, Ted 214
Liberality Park, Wheeling 262
Liebhardt, Glenn 257
Lima Lushers 94
Lincoln, Abraham 38
Lindell Hotel, St. Louis 219
Little Rock, Arkansas 248, 256
Little Rock Indians 118, 255–258
Little Rock Travelers 255, 271
Livingston, Paddy 254
Lochhead, Harry 217
Lodi, Ohio 19
Loftus, Tom 86, 88, 89, 90, 91, 92, 95, 97, 98, 107, 109, 121, 122, 230
Logansport, Indiana 155, 186
Lohbeck, Joseph 91
Long, Herman 3, 60, 71, 113, 138, 139–140, 141, 142, 149, 153, 156, 157, 213, 225
Long, Loren 4
Lorain Avenue, Ohio City 289
Lorain County, Ohio 3, 19, 22, 28, 29, 72, 288
Louisville, Kentucky 61, 90, 185, 186, 187, 197–198, 258, 259
Louisville Colonels (American Association) 40, 77, 78, 81, 82, 87, 113
Louisville Colonels (minor league) 241, 243
Louisville Colonels (National League) 56, 61, 132, 145, 151, 152, 163, 175, 177, 178, 179–180, 182, 183–187, 188, 189, 190, 191, 193, 205, 206–207, 213, 216, 221, 241
Louisville Eclipse 27, 39
Lovett, Tom 283
Lowe, Bobby 36, 124, 140, 149
Luna Park, Cleveland 289
Lynch, Tom 152, 193
Lynn-Newburyport Clamdiggers 46

Maag, Henry 248
Mack, Connie 92
Mack, Ed 240
Mackey, Biz 288
MacLane, Mary 239
Macon, Georgia 224
Macon (team) 39
Macon Central Citys 224
Madden, Kid 95
Madison, Ohio 15–16
Magee, Bill 216

Mahaffey, Lou 213
Mahaffey Park, Canton (Ohio) 248
Mahoning Valley 29
Malloy, Herm 267
Maloney, Mrs. _____ 118
Maloney, William 272
Mann, Fred 79
Mansfield, Ohio 90
Mansfield Mansfields 74
Mantle, Mickey 211
Marion Senators 289
Marquard, Rube 266–267
Marr, Lefty 40, 52
Mason, Harry C. 204
Massillon, Ohio 27, 229
Mauch, Gene 200
Maul, Al 153, 216
Maumee River 278
McAleer, Ann Keenan 34, 37
McAleer, Annie Durbin 34
McAleer, Jimmy 5, 11, 14, 28, 29, 30, 33–34, 36–37, 42, 59, 66, 73, 74, 89, 91, 97, 100, 102, 104, 106, 112, 114, 116, 117, 119, 120, 122, 124, 126, 127, 128, 129, 132, 135–136, 140, 141, 144, 145, 147, 151–152, 154, 155, 163, 164, 169, 172, 174, 176, 177, 181, 183–188, 198, 202, 206, 217, 218, 228, 230
McAleer, Owen 34
McAllister, Sport 3, 209, 212
McCafferty, Charles 254
McCarthy, Tommy 45, 138, 140, 141, 143
McCloskey, Bill 49–50
McCloskey, John 256
McCormick, Jim 119
McDermott, Sandy 205
McDonald, James F. 61–62, 116
McFarlan, Dan 242, 246
McFarland, Eddie 151, 155
McGarr, Chippy 66, 78, 90, 114, 115, 151, 154, 155, 160, 162, 172, 174, 176, 182, 190, 202
McGill, Willie 148–149
McGinnis, Jumbo 76
McGinnity, Joe 270
McGinty, Owney 68
McGlone, John T. 105–106
McGraw, John 5, 17, 18, 58, 63, 64, 66, 114, 116, 120, 123, 132, 153–154, 166–168, 169, 194, 195, 196, 197, 217, 218, 224, 228, 233, 234, 235, 295–296
McGraw, Ted 271
McGuire, Deacon 11, 29, 40, 84, 173
McGuire, Jimmy 153
McGunnigle, Bill 185
McJames, Doc 227
McKean, _____ Clark (grandmother) 22
McKean, Belle Moran (wife) 21, 182, 216, 217, 249, 275, 278, 279, 290
McKean, Ed (Edward John): appearance 2, 10–11; barkeeping 1, 3, 5, 29, 218, 227, 229,

275, 286, 289; batting stance 1, 2, 125, 190; birth 24–25, 28, 287, 288; boxing 5, 22, 147, 229, 280, 286, 287, 288; Capel Road farm 24, 29, 38, 168; charity game 1907 288; contract disputes 55, 72–74, 98, 99–104, 144–145, 156–158, 240, 284; death 113, 289–290, 291; education 21, 22, 25; final appearance at League Park 285, 287–288; final major league game 227; final professional game 283; first major league game 76; first professional game; ghostwriting 5, 22, 158; hitting streaks 72, 76, 79, 176–180, 272, 275; malaria 200, 217–218, 225, 227, 228, 239, 261; managing in minors 238–247, 249–252, 260–269, 270, 275, 289; marriage 21, 182; politics 5, 10, 217, 254, 255, 256, 262, 263; sacrifice hits, strategy of 86, 91, 98–99, 107, 273, 285; shooting accident 4, 60, 133, 134, 137, 142, 146, 154, 209; throwing manner 112, 209, 221; weight 5, 11, 130–131, 147, 172, 213, 217, 240, 250, 265, 283–284; wrestling 5, 146–147, 157, 158, 164–165, 181

McKean, Edward J., Jr. (son) 182, 216, 217, 278, 290
McKean, Margaret Moran (mother) 19–20, 24, 181–182
McKean, Marie M. (daughter) 182, 290
McKean, Martin (father) 19–20, 22, 23, 26, 29, 34, 38, 52, 206, 253, 275, 280, 286, 288
McKean, Martin B. (brother) 19, 22, 24, 25, 26, 158
McKean, Martin J. (son) 182, 278, 290
McKean, Mary E. (sister) 24, 25
McKean, Matt (brother) 158
McKean, Robert D. (son) 3, 182, 278, 288, 290
McKean, Thomas (grandfather) 22, 23
McKean, Gov. Thomas 23, 28
McKeans 133
McKeesport Tubers 267
McKenzie Candy Company 29
McKinley, Tom 260, 262, 263
McKinley, William 10, 210
McKisson, Robert 13, 189, 204
McMahon, John 181
McMahon, Sadie 56, 57, 58, 66, 115, 116, 117, 166, 170, 189, 195
McNutt, Clyde 280–281, 284
McPhee, Bid 27, 129
McQuaid, Jack 81, 126, 151, 164
Meadville (team) 37, 119–120
Meaney, Pat 255
Mears, Charles W. 14, 22, 90–91, 94–95, 99, 107–108, 128, 132, 133, 134, 136, 147, 150, 152, 159–160, 162, 175, 177, 179, 202, 208, 209, 289, 297
Medina, Ohio 19
Meekin, Jouett 216
Memphis, Tennessee 250
Memphis Egyptians 257
Memphis Reds 76

Mercer, Win 177, 178, 179, 189
Meriden Maroons 44–45
Merritt, Bill 164
Merryman, Sidney 254
Merwin, Henry Childs 67
Messitt, Tom 250
Mexico 122
Michigan 280
Miller, Doggie 185
Milwaukee, Wisconsin 90, 255
Minneapolis, Minnesota 218
Minneapolis (team) 42
Minneapolis Millers 35
Minnesota 43
Minnesota-Wisconsin League 289
Montgomery (team) 41
Montgomery Senators 255, 258, 268
Montreal Royals 242, 244, 245
Moore, Eugene 278
Moran, Bridget Ruddy (mother in law) 182
Moran, John 24
Moran, Mabel (teacher) 21, 25
Moran, Margaret (grandmother) 21
Moran, Margaret (neighbor) 20
Moran, Michael (father in law) 182
Moran, Sam 180
Moran, Thomas (grandfather) 21
Morans 25, 182
Morrill, John 126
Morrison, Mike 54, 78–79, 84
Morton, Charlie 27, 41, 79
Moses Cleveland Up to Date (skit) 64, 160
Mott, Albert 64, 197, 235
Mound City Peach Pies 68
Mounds Casino, Cleveland 68
Mount St. Mary's of the West Seminary, Cedar Point, Ohio 22
Mueller, Dutch 283
Muldowney, Matthew 271, 274
Mullane, Tony 27, 36, 75, 76, 78, 153, 163
Murphy, Ed 69
Murphy, Thomas 66, 195
Murray, Justice _____ 236
Musial, Stan 9, 125

Narragansett Hotel, Providence 43
NASCAR 63
Nash, Billy 125, 159
Nash, Ogden ("Line-Up for Yesterday") 294
Nashville, Tennessee 38
Nashville Americans 24, 36, 38–43, 45, 47, 49, 52, 54–55, 76, 109, 228, 231, 239, 255
Nashville Seraphs 174
Nashville Volunteers 255
National Agreement 30, 72, 119
National Association 76, 276
National Association of Independent Ball Clubs 248
National Baseball Hall of Fame 3, 4, 5, 13, 27, 29, 45, 57, 60, 93, 113, 116, 121, 133, 135, 138, 140, 154, 208

Index

National League 5, 7, 11, 13, 14, 15, 17, 27, 30, 32, 33, 41, 43, 44, 47, 51, 56, 58, 59, 61–62, 63, 64–65, 67, 72, 74, 84, 88, 89, 91, 93, 96, 98, 99, 100, 101, 102, 103, 104, 105, 106, 109, 110, 113, 114, 115, 116, 119, 120, 121, 125, 128, 129–130, 131, 133, 134, 135, 137, 139, 140, 142, 146, 148, 149, 151, 152, 154, 155, 156, 157, 160, 162, 163, 164, 169, 173, 174, 182, 183, 186, 188, 190, 191, 192, 198, 200, 201, 202, 203, 205, 210, 211, 212, 214, 215, 216, 217, 218, 219, 220, 225, 226, 227, 229, 230, 234, 238, 240, 249, 255, 257, 258, 260, 261, 269, 279, 280, 287; barnstorming team to Cuba 130; board of directors 190–192, 194
National Military Home, Dayton 267
Native Americans 77, 182, 200, 257, 281
Neale, Joe 26–27, 78, 79
Nebraska Indians 248
Negro Leagues 289
Nemec, David 3, 15, 74, 78
New Aveline Hotel Fire 277–278
New Bedford, Massachusetts 55
New Bedford Whalers 269
New Brighton (team) 30, 37, 76
New Castle (teams) 140
New Castle Neshannocks 30, 32, 34–37, 141
New Castle Quakers 260
New England 19
New England Association 178
New England League 43, 275
New Hampshire 28
New Orleans, Louisiana 50, 103
New Orleans Pelicans 255, 256
New York, New York 65, 156, 159, 162–163, 219, 251, 254
New York Giants 7, 8, 46, 58, 59, 62, 92, 93, 94, 95, 110, 120–121, 132, 133, 151, 156, 163, 164, 176–177, 179, 180, 183, 203, 210, 216, 225, 230, 239, 241
New York Gothams 46
New York Knickerbockers 71
New York Metropolitans 43, 82, 83
New York State League 42, 239, 241, 250, 289
New York Stock Exchange 148
New York Yankees 290
Newark (team) 197
Newark Little Giants 45
Newark Sailors 243, 246, 249
Newcombe, Patrick 281
Newton, Rev. B.G 204
Niagara University 253
Nichols, Kid 59, 138, 141, 142, 162, 163, 177, 178, 189
Niles, Ohio 146
Nipple, C.A. 283
Noble, Judge _____ 192
Nolan, The Only 79
Northwestern League 30, 280
Northwestern University 14, 253

Norwalk, Ohio 15
Notre Dame College 200

Oberlin, Ohio 19
Oberlin (team) 27
Oberlin College (team) 26
O'Brien, Darby (William D.) 83
O'Brien, John (Chewing Gum) 184
O'Brien, John (Cinders, Darby) 84, 87, 90, 91, 92, 93–94, 95, 96, 101, 132
O'Brien, Judge _____ 101
O'Brien, Tom 232, 289
O'Connor, Jack 5, 63, 66, 68–69, 116, 126, 131, 135, 139, 142, 143, 144 O'Connor 152, 154, 155, 158, 161–162, 164, 176, 178, 184–188, 192, 198, 202, 203, 205, 206, 211, 212, 218, 222, 234, 287
O'Day, Hank 75, 79, 177, 179, 180, 205, 212, 280
Odysseus 286
O'Hagan, Hal 238, 247
Ohio 21, 24, 26, 38, 75, 94, 100, 108, 147, 148, 159, 175, 189, 222, 223, 247, 252, 253, 263, 278, 281, 286
Ohio City (West Cleveland), Ohio 21, 32–33, 216–217, 229, 288
Ohio Court of Common Pleas 204–205
Ohio Fifth Regiment 209–210
Ohio-Michigan League 248
Ohio-Pennsylvania League 255
Ohio State League 30, 241–242
Ohio Supreme Court 204, 210
Ohio Valley 30
Ohio Valley Base Ball Association 30
Oil and Iron League 30, 36, 37, 39, 42
Oil City Exchange 30, 37
Old J.H. Cutter Kentucky Whiskies 286
Old Judge 1, 2, 46–47
O'Loughlin, Silk 183
Olympic Stadium, Buffalo 246
Omaha, Nebraska 250
Omaha Lambs 105
Omaha Rourkes 250
O'Meara, Eddie (Tom) 176
O'Neill, Tip 250, 252
O'Neill, Tip (James) 77
Ong, Judge Walter C. 204–205
Oregon Street (Rockwell Avenue), Cleveland 216
O'Rourke, Orator 46, 137, 149–150
Orth, Al 189
Osborne, Fred W. 107
Osteen, Champ 253, 270–271, 274, 276
Oswego Starchboxes 50, 51, 52, 53, 77
O'Toole, _____ 283
Owens, _____ 285

Painesville, Ohio 181
Pappalau, John 206
Parnell, Charles Stewart 97
Parrott, Jiggs 152

342   Index

Parrott, Tom 148, 174
Parsons, Charlie 49, 52, 54, 104
Pasco, Elmer E. 183, 193, 198
Paskert, Dode 260–261
Pawtucket Phenoms 208
Payne, Harley 206
Pearce, Dickey 71
Pearson, Alex 269
Pearson, Bill 267
Pechiney, George 76, 77, 79, 81
Pennsylvania-Ohio-Maryland League 267, 269, 275
Penobscots 212
Pfeffer, Fred 193
Phelan, Dick 158
Phelps, Judge _____ 119
Philadelphia, Pennsylvania 56, 81, 119, 201, 215
Philadelphia Athletics (American League) 240
Philadelphia Athletics (American Association) 8, 32, 45, 55, 78, 80, 81, 86, 150
Philadelphia Phillies (Athletics/Quakers) (National League) 46, 56, 82, 85, 92, 96–97, 110, 118, 123, 127, 149, 152, 154, 164, 176, 177, 189, 190–191, 201, 203, 208, 213, 214, 216, 220–221, 255
Philadelphia Quakers (Players' League) 110
Phillips, Bill 46, 88
Phillips, John 3, 125, 138, 228, 296
Piatt, Wiley 216
Piggott, J.J. 43
Pinkerton Detective Agency 42
Pinnance, Ed 281
Pittsburgh, Pennsylvania 13, 37, 65, 71, 101–102, 165, 186, 190, 192, 194, 203
Pittsburgh Alleghenys (American Association) 39, 72
Pittsburgh Burghers (Players' League) 122
Pittsburgh Pirates (Alleghenys) (National League) 13, 56, 68–69, 88, 97, 107, 132, 133–134, 135, 148, 150, 155, 157, 160–162, 163, 179, 180, 189, 190–191, 202, 207, 209, 210, 213, 222, 248, 256, 271
Plateau Hotel, Hot Springs, Arkansas 90
Players' League (Brotherhood) 3, 10, 14, 15, 47, 69, 73, 97–98, 99, 100, 103–104, 110, 118, 119, 120, 121, 122, 144, 192, 257
Polo Grounds, New York 93, 97, 111, 128, 149, 159, 164, 176, 179, 210
Pond, Arlie 195, 208
Pope, the 67
Pope Leo XIII 18
Portland, Maine (team) 178
Portsmouth, Ohio 116
Potawotomis 268
Powell, Boog 218
Powell, Jack 34, 201, 205, 207–208, 211, 213, 221, 222
Powers, John 289
Powers, P.T. 242

Powers, Phil 124–125, 128–129
Pretz, Florence 277
Pritchard, Joe 102
Prohibition Era 286
Protective Association of Professional Baseball Players 102, 117, 257
Protestant Ministers' Association 204
Proudfit, Alexander 39–40
Providence, Rhode Island 44, 46, 55, 208
Providence Grays (minor league) 42, 43–45, 239, 242, 245, 246–247
Providence Grays (National League) 43, 46, 47, 49, 54, 71
Pueblo (Colorado) Indians 251, 252
Pulliam, Henry M. 186, 191

Queen Elizabeth 244
Quinn, Joe 138, 141, 221, 226, 238

Radbourn, Hoss 43, 47, 49, 54, 183
Radford, Paul 153
Ramsay, Toad 77, 78, 87
Reach, A.J. 191
Recreation Park, Saginaw 282
Reilly, Charlie 66, 202
Reisling, Doc 209
Reitz, Heinie 58, 197
Republicans (GOP) 10, 16, 217, 263, 289
Rettger, George 126, 135
Revolutionary War 28
Rhue, George 39, 40, 42
Richardson, Bill 261–262, 266, 269, 272
Richardson, Hardy 51
Richmond, Lee 46, 140
Richmond, Ohio 181
Richmond Virginias 30
Rickey, Branch 253
Rigler, _____ 253
riots in baseball 5, 61, 63, 66, 69, 70, 128–129, 160–162, 166–168, 182–189, 190–191, 193, 197–198, 205, 234–236, 241, 253, 293
Ripken, Cal, Jr. 216
Robinson, Jackie 201
Robinson, Mary O. 66
Robinson, Wilbert 17, 18, 58, 114, 115, 116–117, 153–154, 168, 170, 194, 234
Robison, Frank 13, 14, 60, 69, 78, 80–81, 83–84, 86–87, 93, 98, 99, 100, 101, 103, 110, 113, 119, 120, 121, 122, 127, 130, 133, 135, 144–145, 147, 152, 156–158, 160, 163, 167, 174, 175, 176, 178, 180, 188–189, 190, 191, 192, 193, 194, 198, 201–202, 204, 207, 210, 214, 216, 219–220, 221, 228, 229, 238, 288
Robison, Howard 13, 14, 144, 157
Robison, Stanley 13, 14, 15, 144, 191, 204, 221, 223, 228, 229, 288
Robison, Wilbert 13
Robison brothers 13, 14, 17, 74, 83, 85, 98, 103, 122, 127, 144–145, 151, 158, 196, 204, 210, 214, 217, 219, 221, 226, 228

Index

Robison Field, St. Louis 210
Rochester, New York 11, 50–51, 55, 238, 239, 241, 242, 243, 246, 247
Rochester (Weidman) (team) 241
Rochester (teams) 239
Rochester Bronchos 85, 104, 116, 238–247, 239, 249, 270
Rochester Brownies 241
Rochester Hop Bitters 183
Rochester Maroons 14, 39, 42, 43–44, 45–55, 72–74, 83, 84, 100, 117, 216, 239–240
Rocky Mountains 253
Rocky Point Park, Providence 242
Rogers, Hiram 249
Rogers, John I. 191
Ropke, Jack 185
Rose, Pete 275
rowdy baseball 5, 17, 35, 57, 59, 63–70, 85–86, 92, 105–106, 116, 120, 126, 127, 135, 137, 138–139, 143, 151–154, 158–160, 161–162, 164, 166, 173, 183, 187–188, 190–193, 202, 205, 207, 208, 212, 232–233, 243–244, 256, 259, 261, 267, 271, 272, 278, 293–294, 295, 296; see riots, baseball
Rowe, Dave 106
Ruddy, Mary 182
Ruddy, Pat 182
Rusie, Amos 59, 111, 162, 175, 176–177, 255
Ryan, Jimmy 148, 250, 252, 254, 258, 259, 270
Ryan, Paddy 170

SABR (Society for American Baseball Research) 4, 113
Sage, George 283
Saginaw, Michigan 283
Saginaw Old Golds 280
Saginaw Wa-Was 281, 282, 283
St. Augustine 122
St. Clair Street and Seneca Street, Cleveland 227
St. Joseph, Missouri 250
St. Joseph Clay Eaters 90
St. Joseph Reds 158
St. Joseph Saints 250
St. Louis, Missouri 56, 61, 68–69, 90, 136, 162, 164, 204, 210, 217, 220, 223, 224–226, 227, 290
St. Louis Base Ball Company 219
St. Louis Browns (American Association) 35, 37, 44, 74, 77, 82, 86, 87, 90, 123, 239
St. Louis Browns (American League) 33
St. Louis Browns (National League) 56, 58, 115, 117, 119, 152, 155, 163, 175, 176, 179, 187, 190, 206, 208–209, 213, 214, 217, 218, 219, 228, 238
St. Louis Court House 219–220
St. Louis Maroons (Union Association) 50
St. Louis Perfectos (Maroons, Cardinals) 14, 46, 65, 69, 77, 182–183, 201, 214, 217–227, 228, 229–230, 240, 253, 256, 275, 279, 288

St. Mary's Cemetery, Grafton 25
St. Mary's Theological Seminary, Cleveland, Ohio 22
St. Patrick's Catholic Church, Ohio City 290
St. Paul Saints 269
Salisbury, Luke 4
San Francisco 49, 59
Sandusky, Ohio 22, 162, 289
Sandusky (team) 43
Sandusky Elks Club (team) 247
Savannah Dixies 147
Savannah Electrics 151
Savannah Savannahs 27, 79
Scenic Park, Rocky River, Ohio 229
Scheible, Jack 152–153
Schellerman, Bill 147
Schenectady Dorphians 241, 245
Scherzo, Dr. Ralph A. 289–290
Schmelz, Gus 35, 98–99, 102, 104–105, 106, 108, 109, 122, 125
Schmit, Crazy 222, 224
Schomberg, Otto 44, 45, 49
Schreckengost, Ossee 211, 216, 222, 230
Schriver, Pop 250, 268, 269
Scotland 281
Scott, O.B. 258
Scranton (team) 197
Selee, Frank 138, 155
Serad, Billy 51, 55
Settler, Percy 275
Seward, Ed 45, 142
Shannan, Owen 253
Sharon (Ohio) Steels 271
Shaw, Dan 42
Shea, Mike 76
Shearon, John 126, 190
Sheher, _____ 242
Sheriff Street, Cleveland 130
Shindle, Billy 153
Shoch, George 92
Short Stop Inn, Cleveland 3, 218
Shreveport, Louisiana 250
Shreveport Pirates 255
Sinin, Lee 4
Sioux City, Iowa 250
Sioux City Huskers 105
Sioux City Packers 250
Smalley, Will 105, 106, 123
Smith, Billy 247
Smith, Edgar 45
Smith, Elmer 81
Smith, George 114
Smith, Germany 74
Smith, Harry 248
Smith, Jerry 229
Smith, Phenomenal 45, 87
Smith, Samuel 248
Smith, Tom E. 176
Smith, Tommy 286
Snyder, _____ 245
Snyder, Pop 81, 84, 85, 91, 101, 138

Snyder Field, Springfield, Ohio 270
Social Darwinists 67
Sockalexis, Chief 116, 182, 200–201, 202–203, 205–206, 207, 208, 209, 211, 212, 213
Soden, Arthur 49
Solders, Judge George B. 204
Solomon 98
Somers, Charles 230
Souders, Holly 242
South Bend, Indiana 261
South Bend Greens 252, 254, 261, 263, 269, 272, 273, 278
South Carolina textile leagues 271
South End Grounds, Boston 141, 142–143, 149, 180, 188
Southern Hotel, St. Louis 204
Southern League (Southern Association) 27, 38–40, 76, 79, 224, 250, 255, 256, 257, 268
Southern Michigan League 280, 282, 283, 284–285
Sowders, Leonard 39
Spalding, J.W. 191
Spalding ball 30
Spanish-American War 210
Speaker, Tris 121, 255, 271
Spink, Alfred H. 219, 220
Sportsman's Park, St. Louis 206, 218, 219, 220, 221, 222, 226, 228
Sprague, Charlie 91
Springfield, Ohio 93, 253–254, 270, 272, 273, 275, 279
Springfield (Ohio) Babes 252–254, 261, 262, 265–269, 275, 287
Stackhouse, George E. 159
Stage, Billy 160
Staley, Harry 139–140, 163
Stallings, George 240, 243
Stanley Cup 13
Stanton Field, Chattanooga 148
Staples Studio, South Bend, Indiana 275
Stemmeyer, Bill 31, 32–33, 34
Stenzel, Jake 222
Steubenville Stubs 275
Stevens, Harry 146, 160
Stevens Park, Niles, Ohio 146
Stimmel, Archie 250
Stivetts, Jack 138, 140, 141, 149, 162, 175, 176, 179, 203, 222–223
Stockdale, Otis 178
Stovey, Harry 124
Stricker, Cub 7, 10, 46, 77, 79, 80, 82, 84, 85, 86, 89, 90, 91, 92, 101, 104, 130, 131, 150
Strife, George 285
Stucky, Dr. Thomas H. 186, 191, 197–198
Sudhoff, Willie 213
Sugden, Joe 269
Sulfur Dell (Spring Bottom) field, Nashville 38, 39
Sullivan, Jim 177
Sullivan, Joe 66, 153
Sullivan, John L. 12, 170
Sullivan, Mike 163, 164, 174, 180
Sullivan, Ted 42
Sullivan's Tower, Boston 141
Summers, Ed 253
Summit Street, Cleveland 182
Sunset Country Club, Sheffield Lake, Ohio 290
Sutcliffe, Sy 79, 88, 90, 95, 101
Svengali 128
Swaim, Cy 201
Swartwood, Ed 27, 67
Sweeney, _____ 246
Sweeney, Charlie 49, 74, 77, 80–81
Sweeney, George W. 242
Syracuse Stars (American Association) 9, 119
Syracuse Stars (minor leagues) 49, 52, 55

Taft, William Howard 34, 212
Tannehill, Jesse 207
Tanner, Jack 249, 252
Taylor, Brewery Jack 164, 189, 214
Taylor, Frederick 4
Taylor, M.E. 280
Tebeau, George (White Wings) 76, 156, 172–173, 176, 178, 190, 201, 230, 250, 251
Tebeau, Patsy (Oliver) 5, 11, 13, 15, 16, 17, 47, 51, 57, 60, 61, 63, 64–65, 66, 67–68, 69–70, 76, 89, 90, 91, 92–93, 97, 99, 101, 104, 106, 113, 114, 115, 116, 117, 118, 119, 120, 121, 122, 123, 126–128, 129, 131, 132, 134, 135, 136–137, 140, 141, 143, 144, 145, 147, 148, 149, 150, 151, 152, 153–159, 161–162, 163, 164, 166, 169, 172, 173, 176–177, 178, 181, 182–185, 187–189, 190–194, 195, 196, 197–199, 201, 202–203, 205, 206, 207, 208, 210, 211–212, 213, 215, 218, 219, 220, 221, 222, 225, 226, 227, 228, 229–230, 235, 237, 243, 253, 261, 271, 279, 286, 290, 291, 293–294, 295, 296
Tebeau, Pussy (Charles) 178
Temple, William C. 13, 60, 62, 149, 196, 236
Temple Cup 1, 4, 7–18, 41, 56–70, 166, 169, 171, 179, 181, 196, 234, 235, 236, 245, 294–295
Terre Haute Hottentots 266–267
Terry, Adonis 81, 135, 189
Thompson, Magistrate _____ 186–187
Thompson, Sam 40–41, 164
Tiant, Luis 94
Tiffany & Company 13
Tiffin, Ohio 204
Toledo, Ohio 286
Toledo Blue Stockings 30, 74
Toledo Mud Hens 27, 50, 205, 276, 286
Tolles, _____ 192
Toronto Canucks 49, 52, 55, 76
Toronto Maple Leafs 240, 242, 243, 244, 245, 246, 248
Toy, Tim 76–77
Travelers Field, Little Rock 256
Trilby 128

Trinker's Oyster and Chop House, Cleveland 8
Tri-State League 85, 94, 158, 195, 248
Troy, Turkey 128
Troy Trojans 46, 94
Tucker, Tommy 64, 124, 138, 140, 143
Turner, Tuck 164
Twitchell, Larry 88–89, 101, 285
Tyholland, Ireland 34

Uhl, Charley 147
Underground Railroad 50
Union Association 30, 46, 47
Union Park, Baltimore 56–57, 66, 155, 194–196, 202, 232–233, 234, 235, 236, 296
Uniontown Coal Barons 269
University of Delaware 14
University of Pennsylvania 240
University of Rochester 183, 244
University of Rochester (team) 241
Utica, New York 52–53
Utica Pent Ups 49, 50, 51, 52, 53, 54, 55, 77, 241, 244

Van Haltren, George 177
Varnell, Claude H. 270, 274, 275, 276, 277–278
Vaughan, Farmer 255
Veach, Peekaboo 78, 104–105, 106
Vermont 181
Viau, Leon 124–125, 127, 128
Vila, Joe 158–159
Villa Hedges, Bratenhal, Ohio 144
Virtue, Jake 60, 106, 120, 123, 126, 129, 133, 135, 138, 139, 142, 145, 150, 151, 152, 156, 160, 163
Visner, Joe 42–43, 51, 52
Vizquel, Omar 3
von der Ahe, Chris 119, 152, 191, 201, 204, 210, 217, 219–220, 228, 238
Von der Horst, Henry R. 191, 196, 235
Voorhees, Cy 27

Wabash College 253
Waddell, Rube 224
Wadsworth, Jack 163
Wadsworth, Ohio 27, 78
Wagner, Earl 202, 204
Wagner, Honus 1, 4, 71, 216, 256
Wagner, J. Earle 191
Wales 214
Walker, Fleetwood 26, 30, 41, 45
Walker, John 259
Walker, Scott 266
Walker, Weldy 26, 41
Wallace, Bobby 3, 34, 60, 156, 164, 173, 174, 176, 195, 196, 201, 208, 209, 212, 213, 219, 220, 221, 222, 226, 286
Ward, John Montgomery 4, 13, 62, 92, 98, 101, 113, 121, 136, 156, 159, 183, 236, 257
Warner, Ed 51

Washington, DC 179, 279
Washington (proposed American Association) (team) 39, 231
Washington Avenue, St. Louis 232
Washington Monument 269
Washington Nationals 35, 56, 92, 96, 149–150, 152–153, 173, 177, 178, 179, 180, 189, 204, 206, 208, 225, 227
Washington Senators (American League) 34
Waterbury Brassmen 45
Watkins farm in Eaton, Ohio 24
Webster, Cliff 281
Weddell House, Cleveland 107
Weeder, George 282
Weidman, Stump 183–186, 189, 241
Welch, Mickey 93
Wellington, Ohio 163
West, George J. 43
West, Milton 40
West Federal Street Grounds, Youngstown 32
West New York Field Club Grounds, Weehawken 210
West Point Military Academy 181
West Side (Cleveland) Reds 26
West Side Grounds, Chicago 189, 210, 258
West Side Grounds, Youngstown 97
West Side Market, Ohio City 288
West Side Park, Jersey City 247
West Troy, New York 132
West Virginia University 253
Western Association 90, 158
Western League 40, 74, 122, 173, 174, 230, 250, 251, 251–252
Western Reserve College 27, 96
Weyhing, Gus 82, 164
Wheeling, West Virginia 85, 270
Wheeling Nailers 85
Wheeling Stogies 254, 258, 260, 271, 272, 276–277, 278
Whiskey Island (Cleveland) Shamrocks 26
White, Bill 113
White, Deacon 51
White, Howard 122–123
Whitman, Walt 5
Wild West 249
Wilkes-Barre (team) 197
Williams, Jimmy 32, 73, 74, 79–80, 81, 82, 83, 84, 85, 86, 122
Williams, Tom 126
Williamson, Ned 72
Willis, Vic 227
Wilmington Quicksteps 30
Wilmot, Walt 92–93, 258
Wilson, Zeke 179, 189–190, 204, 208, 222
Wing, Francis J. 192
Winne, _____ 52
Winnie, F.R. 74
Wisconsin 23, 24, 26, 52, 286
Wisconsin State League 255
Wise, Sam 4, 27, 28, 92, 139, 150, 153, 285, 288

Wister, Owen 12
Wittenberg College 253, 260
Wolf, George A. 267–268
Wolf, Jimmy (Chicken) 78, 207
Wood, Monte 261
Woods, Al 147
Woods, Walt 214
Wood's gymnasium, Cleveland 130
Worcester, Massachusetts 243
Worcester Busters 243, 275
Worcester Grays 46
Worcester Hustlers 243, 246
World Series (world's series) 1, 14, 18, 41, 43, 45, 65, 68, 98, 115, 126, 131, 135, 137, 138–143, 144, 150, 176, 222, 238, 243, 256, 268, 280
World War I 253
World War II 288
World's Columbian Exposition, Chicago 144
Worth, Richard 32
Wright, George 71–72
Wright, Harry 11, 26, 27, 127
Wright, R.W. 102, 103
Wright brothers 259–260

Yale University 88, 127, 148
Yost, Eddie 258
Young, Cy 9, 13, 14, 56, 57, 59, 60, 108–109, 110, 111, 114, 115, 116, 117, 119, 120, 121, 123–124, 125, 126, 127, 129, 131, 132, 135, 136, 138–139, 140, 142, 148, 149, 150, 152, 153–154, 155, 157, 160, 164, 170, 174, 175, 176–180, 183, 188, 189, 193, 194, 195, 201, 202, 203, 205, 206, 207, 208, 209, 215, 221, 222–223, 227, 237, 266, 268, 282, 286, 293, 295–296
Young, Nick 56, 60, 61–62, 72, 74, 128, 131, 134, 138–139, 152, 156, 183, 191, 192, 193, 209
Youngstown, Ohio 26, 29, 30, 34, 35, 40, 73, 87, 152, 206, 250, 279
Youngstown Little Giants 260
Youngstown Mahonings 29–30
Youngstown Youngstowns 26–37, 42, 43, 76, 90, 97, 112, 117, 140–141, 218, 227

Zimmer, Chief 11, 14, 67, 69, 74, 80, 83, 84, 89, 92–93, 96–97, 100, 102, 104, 105, 106, 107, 109, 114, 115, 116, 117–118, 128, 130, 131–132, 135, 138–139, 140, 141, 142, 146, 147, 149, 157–158, 160, 162, 173, 176, 177, 180, 181, 186–187, 195, 196, 202, 203, 206, 211, 217, 218, 221, 222, 230, 255, 256, 257, 258, 285, 286, 288; board game 158; cigars 257
Zwilling, Dutch 281

www.ingramcontent.com/pod-product-compliance
Ingram Content Group UK Ltd.
Pitfield, Milton Keynes, MK11 3LW, UK
UKHW041922140426
5217IPUK00014B/271